Shojo Beat

Millennium Snow

Vol. 4   Story & Art by **Bisco Hatori**

Table of Contents

Millennium Snow™

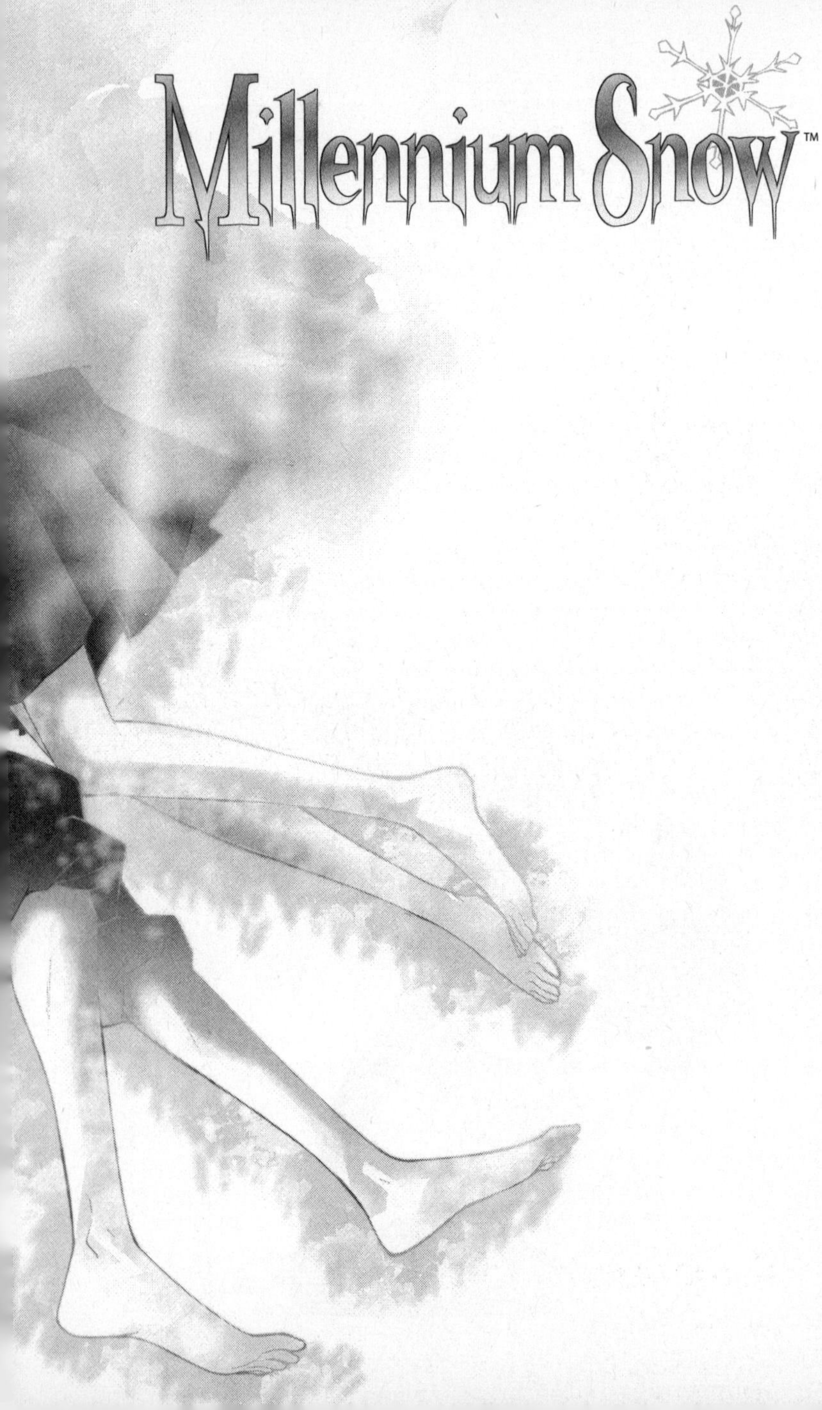

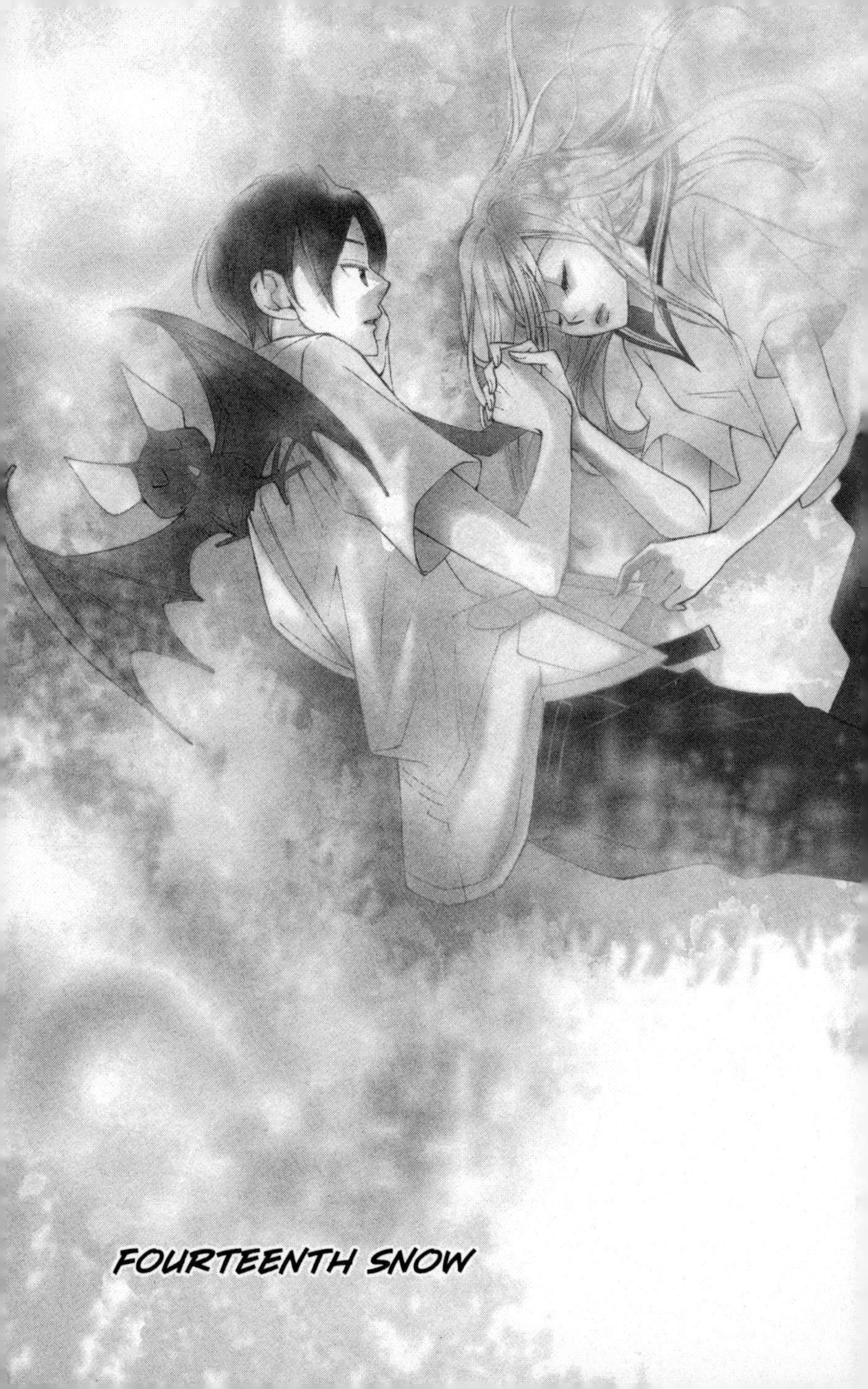
FOURTEENTH SNOW

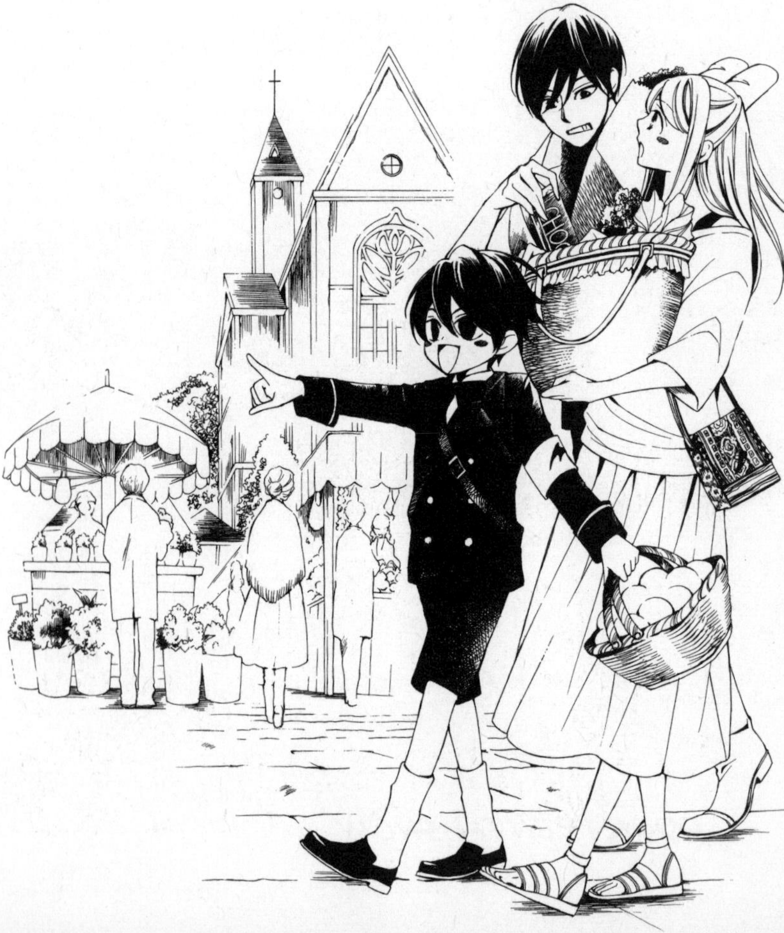

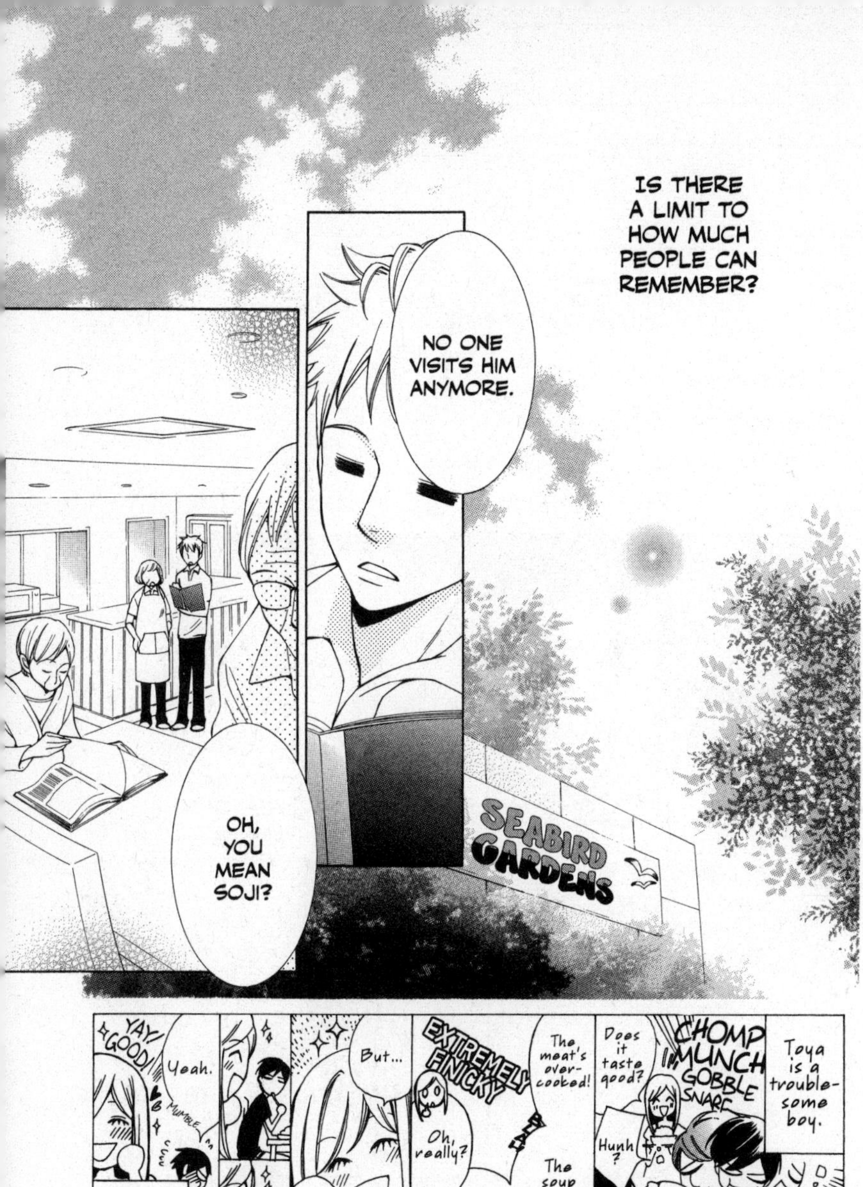
IS THERE A LIMIT TO HOW MUCH PEOPLE CAN REMEMBER?
NO ONE VISITS HIM ANYMORE.
SEABIRD GARDENS
OH, YOU MEAN SOJI?

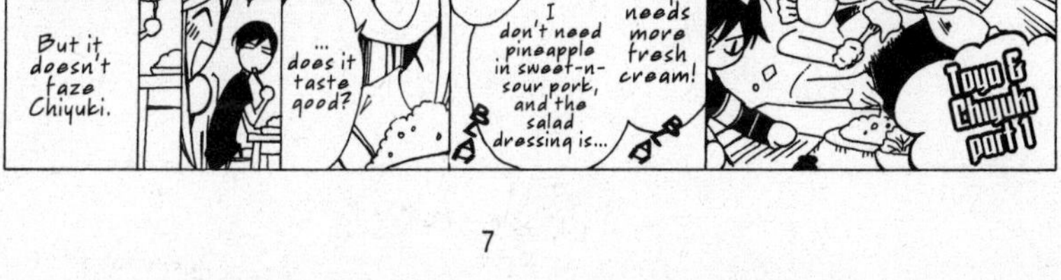
Toya is a trouble-some boy.
Toya & Chiyuki part 1
CHOMP MUNCH GOBBLE SNARF
Does it taste good?
Hunh?
EXTREMELY FINICKY
The meat's over-cooked!
Oh, really?
The soup needs more fresh cream!
I don't need pineapple in sweet-n-sour pork, and the salad dressing is...
But...
...does it taste good?
YAY! GOOD!
Yeah.
MUMBLE
But it doesn't faze Chiyuki.

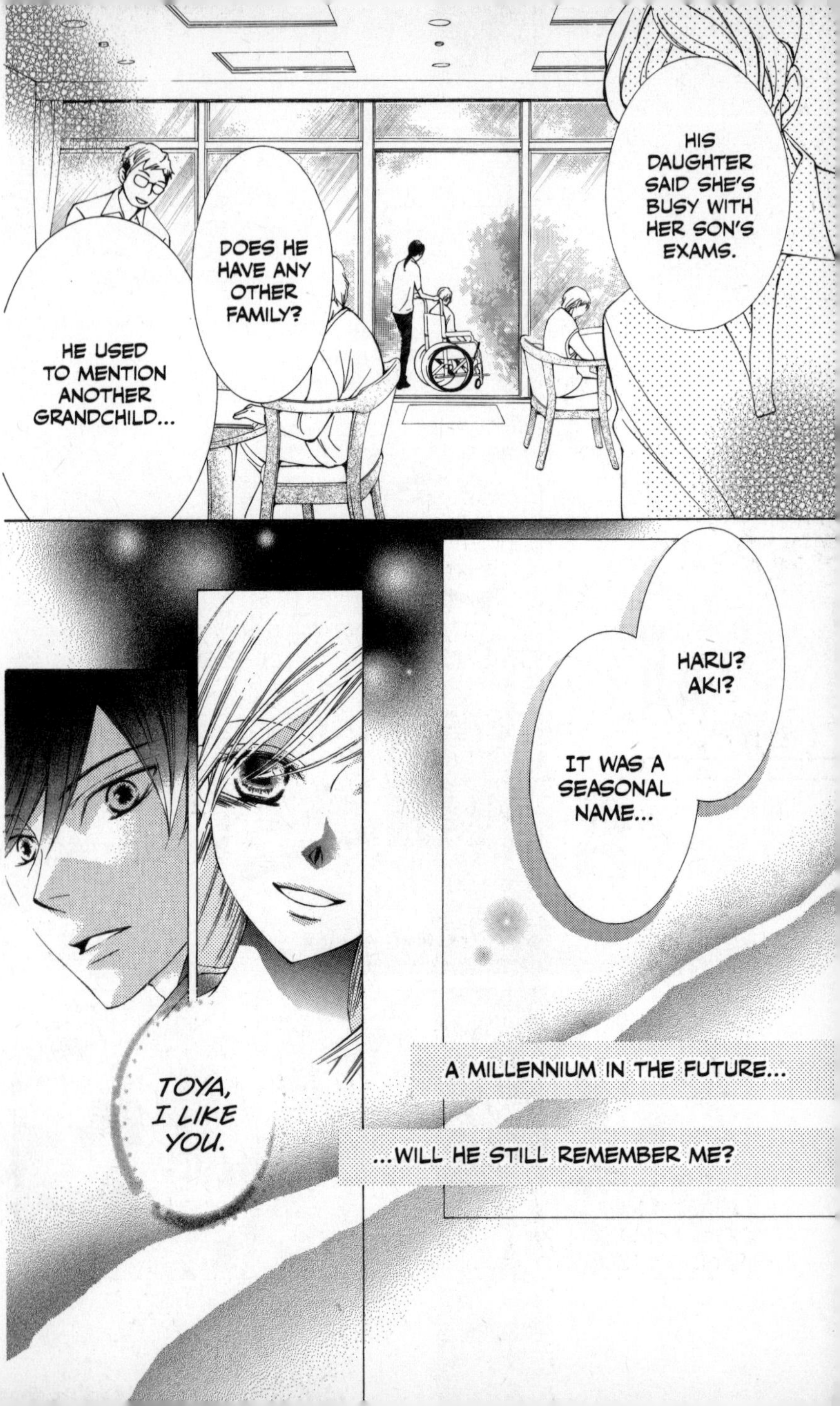
HIS DAUGHTER SAID SHE'S BUSY WITH HER SON'S EXAMS.
DOES HE HAVE ANY OTHER FAMILY?
HE USED TO MENTION ANOTHER GRANDCHILD...
HARU? AKI?
IT WAS A SEASONAL NAME...
A MILLENNIUM IN THE FUTURE...
...WILL HE STILL REMEMBER ME?
TOYA, I LIKE YOU.

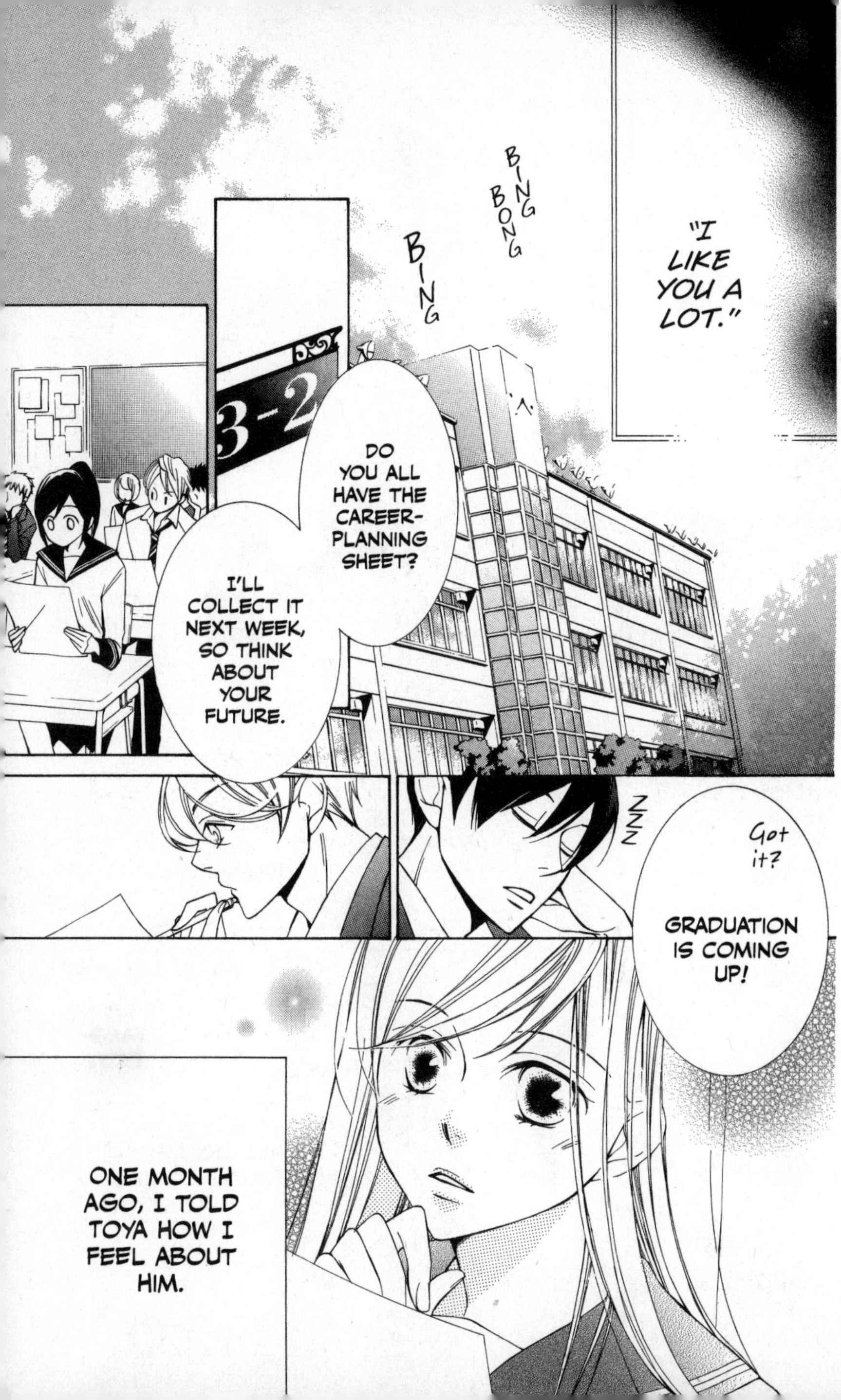
"I LIKE YOU A LOT."
BING BONG
BING
DO YOU ALL HAVE THE CAREER-PLANNING SHEET?
I'LL COLLECT IT NEXT WEEK, SO THINK ABOUT YOUR FUTURE.
ZZZ
Got it?
GRADUATION IS COMING UP!
ONE MONTH AGO, I TOLD TOYA HOW I FEEL ABOUT HIM.

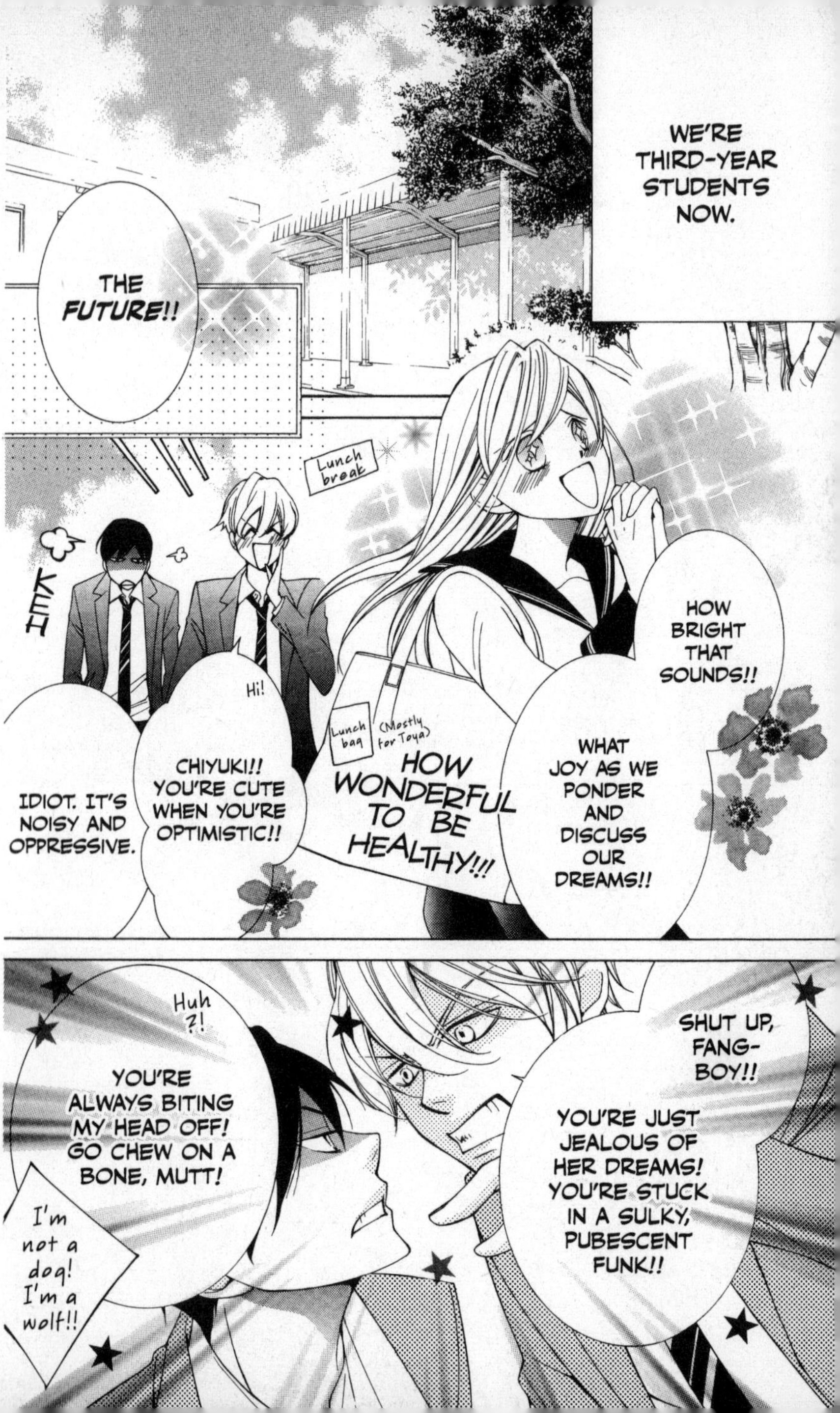
WE'RE THIRD-YEAR STUDENTS NOW.
THE FUTURE!!
HOW BRIGHT THAT SOUNDS!!
WHAT JOY AS WE PONDER AND DISCUSS OUR DREAMS!!
HOW WONDERFUL TO BE HEALTHY!!!
Lunch break
Lunch bag
(Mostly for Toya)
Hi!
CHIYUKI!! YOU'RE CUTE WHEN YOU'RE OPTIMISTIC!!
KEH
IDIOT. IT'S NOISY AND OPPRESSIVE.
SHUT UP, FANG-BOY!!
YOU'RE JUST JEALOUS OF HER DREAMS! YOU'RE STUCK IN A SULKY, PUBESCENT FUNK!!
Huh?!
YOU'RE ALWAYS BITING MY HEAD OFF! GO CHEW ON A BONE, MUTT!
I'm not a dog! I'm a wolf!!

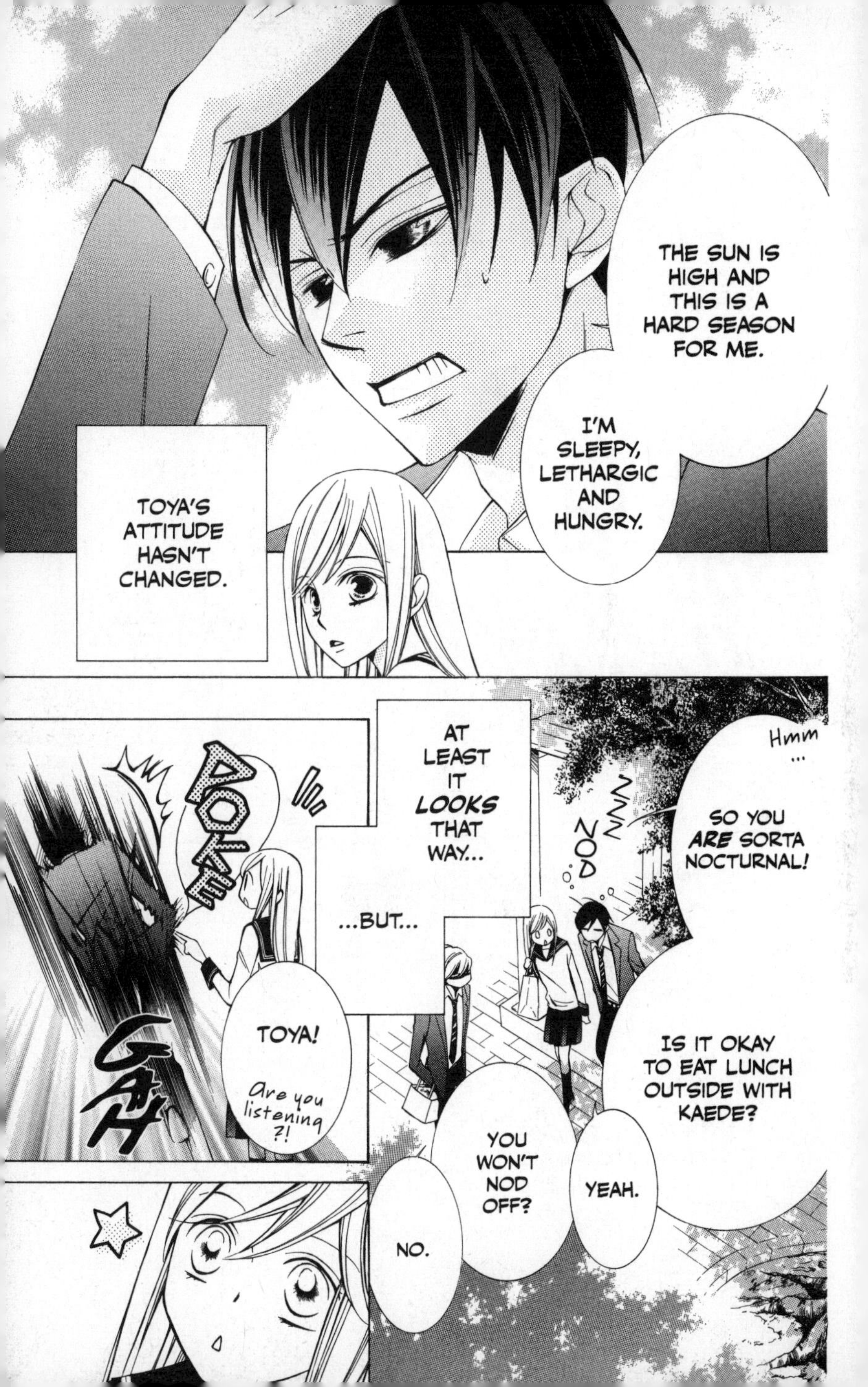
THE SUN IS HIGH AND THIS IS A HARD SEASON FOR ME.
I'M SLEEPY, LETHARGIC AND HUNGRY.
TOYA'S ATTITUDE HASN'T CHANGED.
Hmm...
SO YOU *ARE* SORTA NOCTURNAL!
NOD NOD
IS IT OKAY TO EAT LUNCH OUTSIDE WITH KAEDE?
YEAH.
YOU WON'T NOD OFF?
NO.
AT LEAST IT *LOOKS* THAT WAY...
...BUT...
POKE
TOYA!
Are you listening?!
GAH

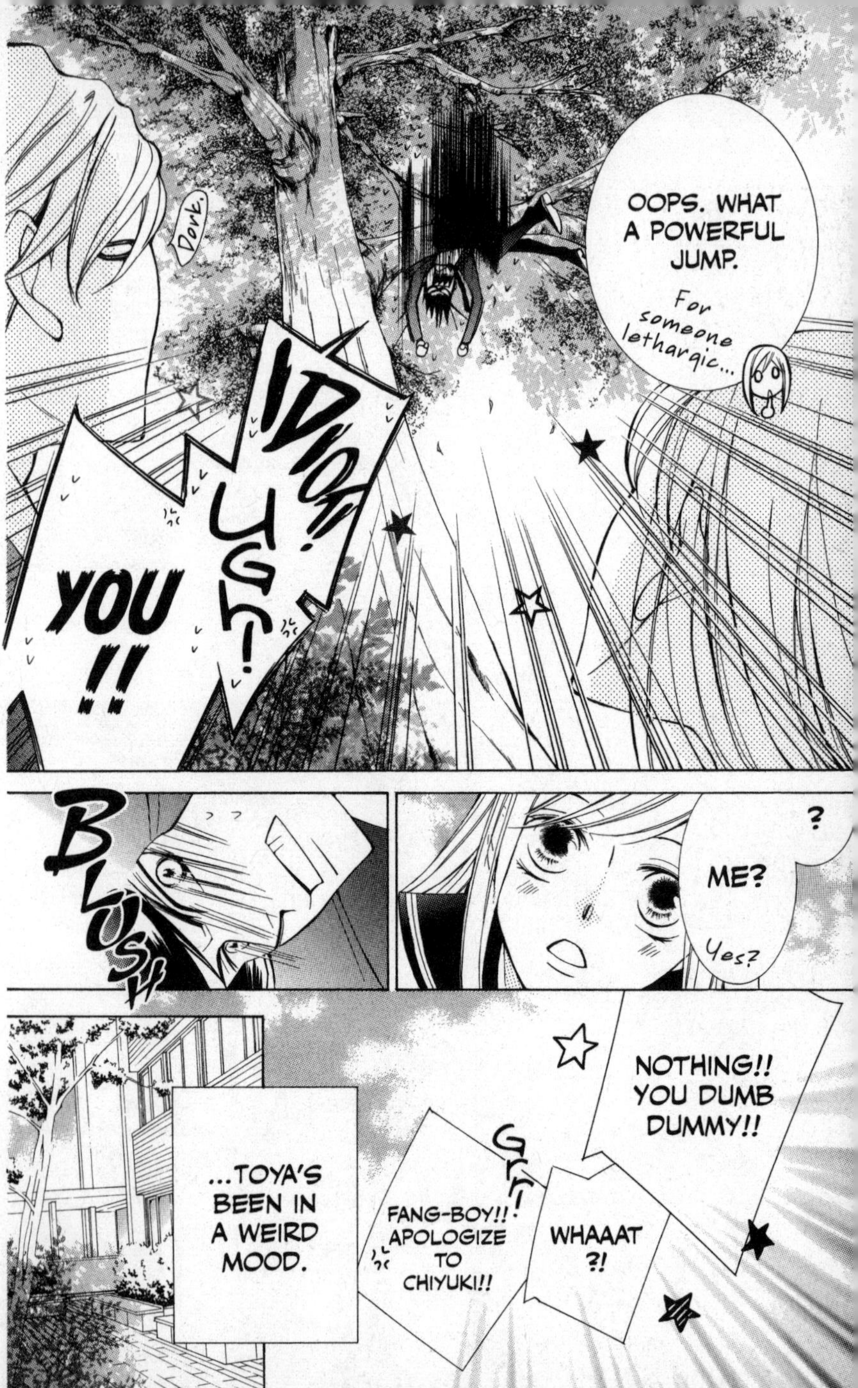
OOPS. WHAT A POWERFUL JUMP.
For someone lethargic...
Dork.
IDIOT!! UGH!
YOU!!
?
ME?
Yes?
BLUSH
NOTHING!! YOU DUMB DUMMY!!
WHAAAT?!
GRR!
FANG-BOY!! APOLOGIZE TO CHIYUKI!!
...TOYA'S BEEN IN A WEIRD MOOD.

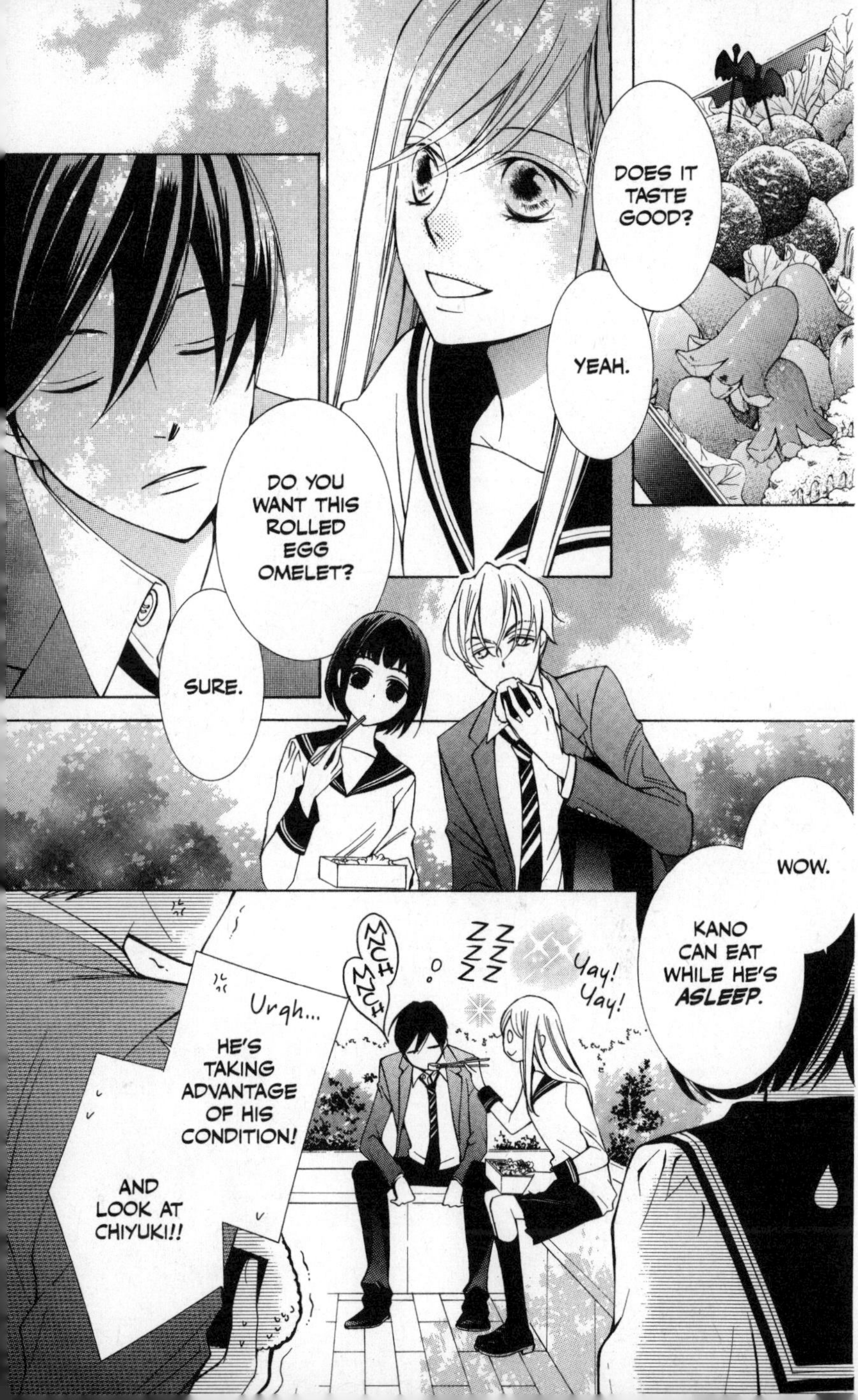
DOES IT TASTE GOOD?
YEAH.
DO YOU WANT THIS ROLLED EGG OMELET?
SURE.
WOW.
KANO CAN EAT WHILE HE'S *ASLEEP*.
Yay! Yay!
ZZZ ZZZ
MNCH MNCH
Urgh...
HE'S TAKING ADVANTAGE OF HIS CONDITION!
AND LOOK AT CHIYUKI!!

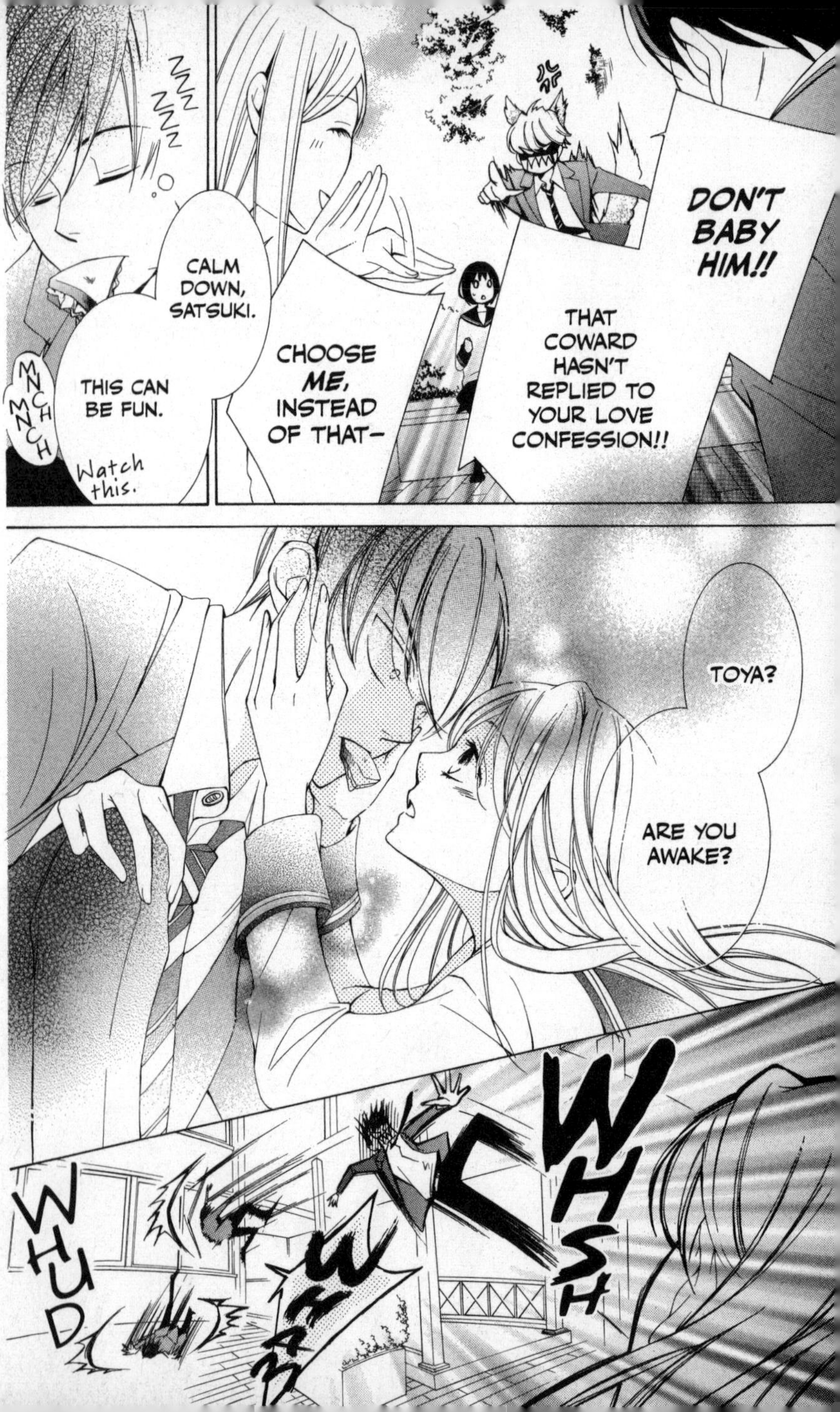
DON'T BABY HIM!!
THAT COWARD HASN'T REPLIED TO YOUR LOVE CONFESSION!!
CHOOSE *ME,* INSTEAD OF THAT–
CALM DOWN, SATSUKI.
THIS CAN BE FUN.
Watch this.
ZZZ ZZZ
MNCH MNCH
TOYA?
ARE YOU AWAKE?
WHSH
WHAM
WHUD

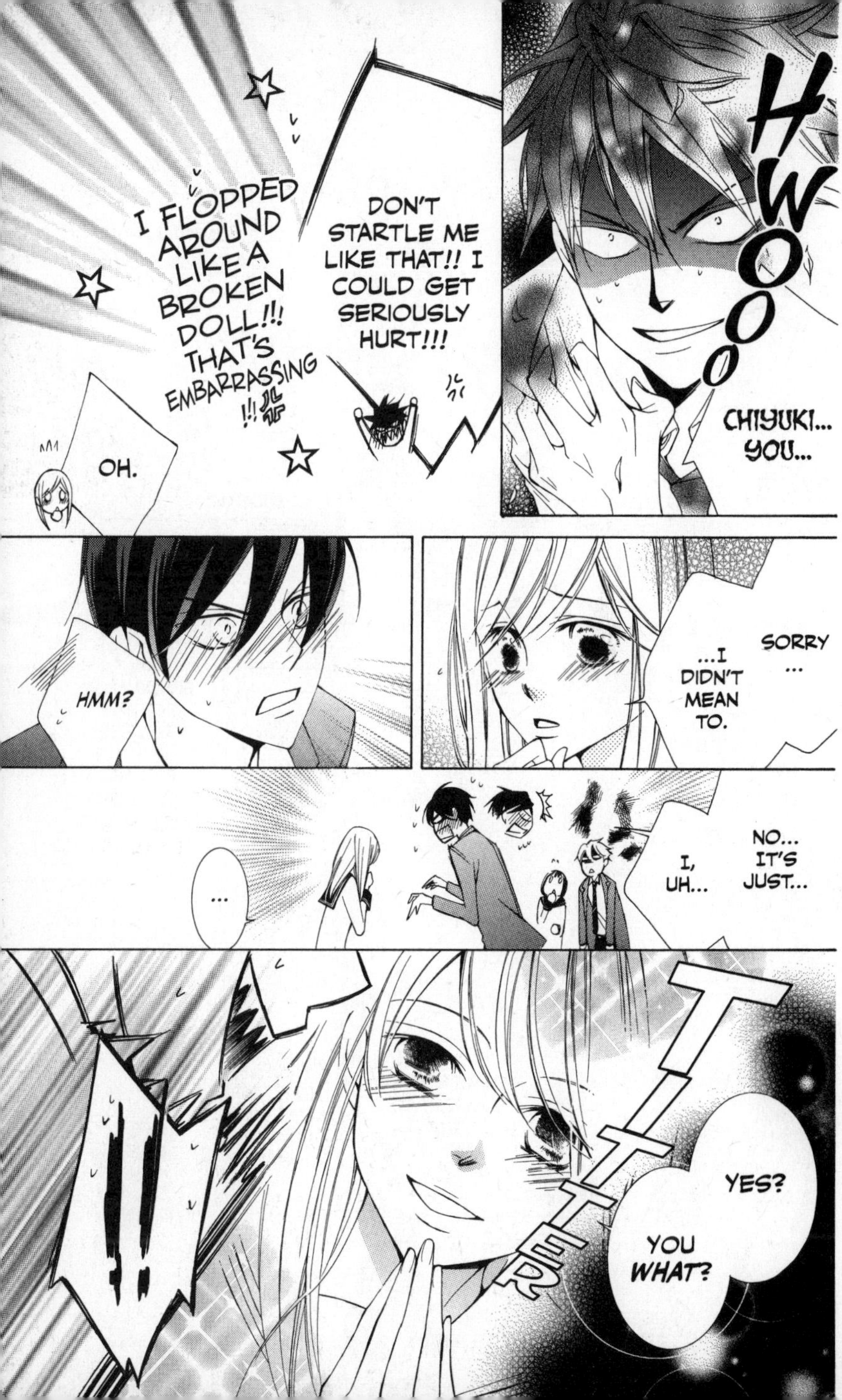
HWOOOO
CHIYUKI... YOU...
DON'T STARTLE ME LIKE THAT!! I COULD GET SERIOUSLY HURT!!!
I FLOPPED AROUND LIKE A BROKEN DOLL!!! THAT'S EMBARRASSING!!!
OH.
SORRY...
...I DIDN'T MEAN TO.
HMM?
NO... IT'S JUST...
I, UH...
...
TITTER
YES?
YOU WHAT?
!!

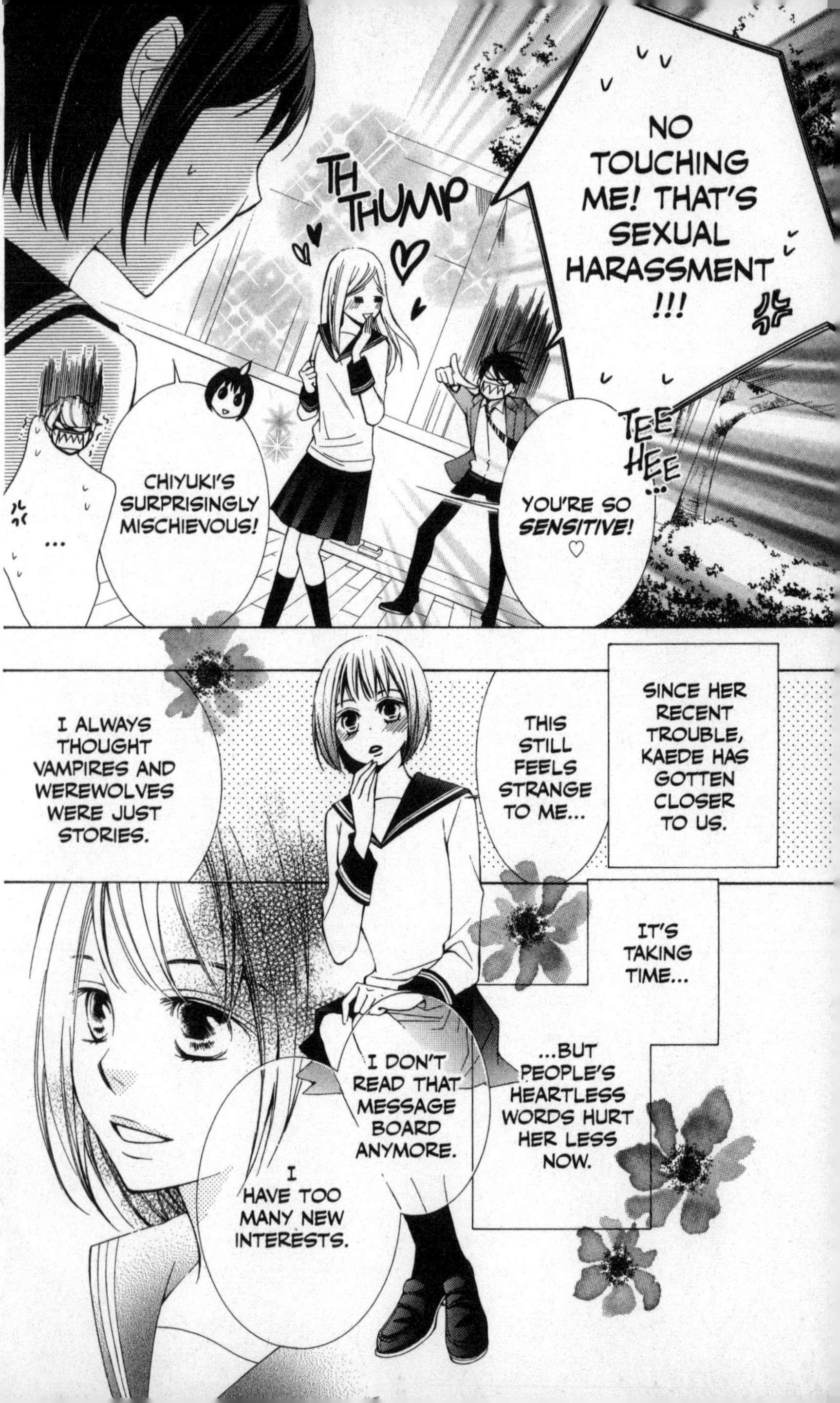
NO TOUCHING ME! THAT'S SEXUAL HARASSMENT!!!
TH THUMP
TEE HEE...
YOU'RE SO SENSITIVE! ♡
CHIYUKI'S SURPRISINGLY MISCHIEVOUS!
...
SINCE HER RECENT TROUBLE, KAEDE HAS GOTTEN CLOSER TO US.
THIS STILL FEELS STRANGE TO ME...
I ALWAYS THOUGHT VAMPIRES AND WEREWOLVES WERE JUST STORIES.
IT'S TAKING TIME...
...BUT PEOPLE'S HEARTLESS WORDS HURT HER LESS NOW.
I DON'T READ THAT MESSAGE BOARD ANYMORE.
I HAVE TOO MANY NEW INTERESTS.

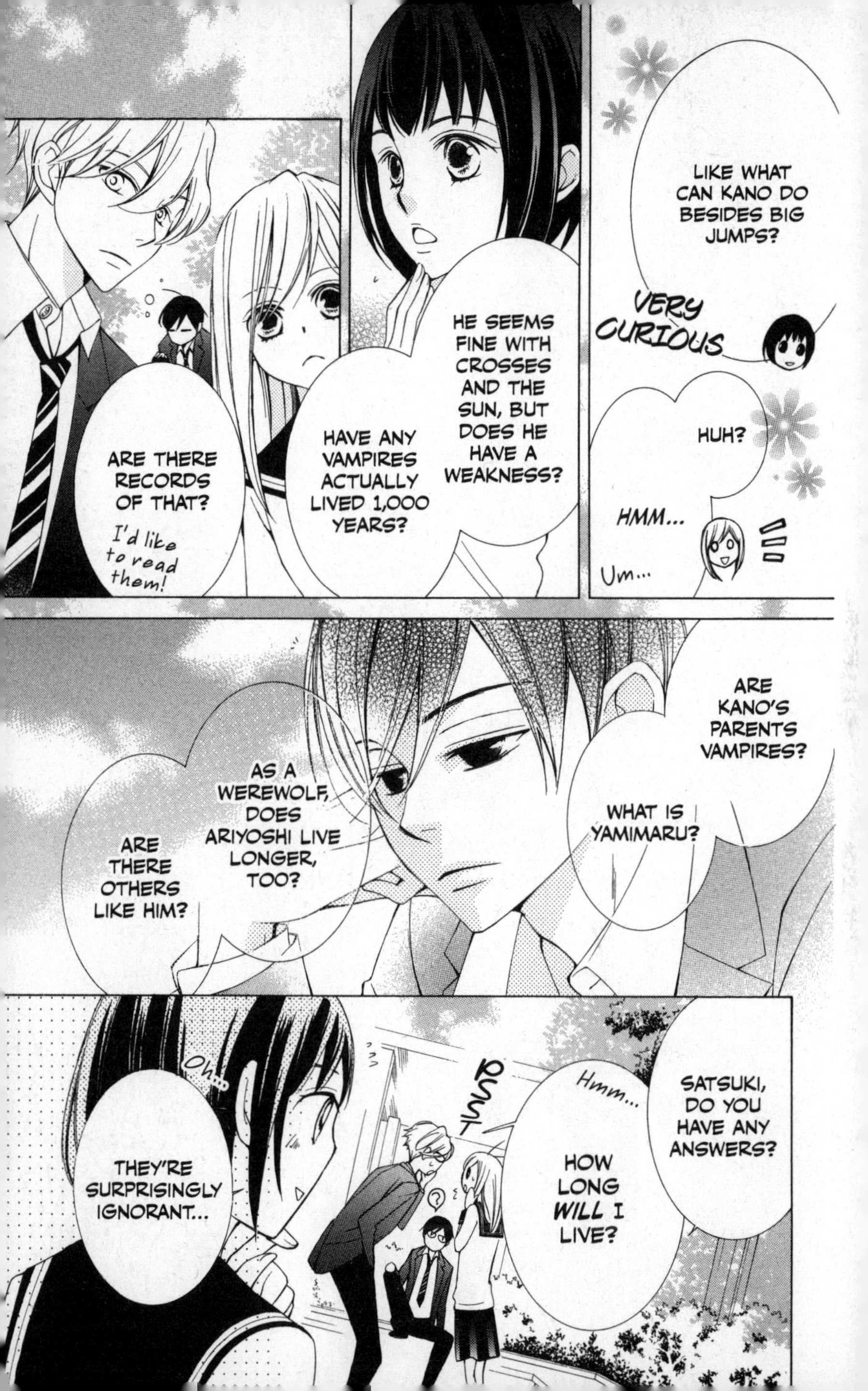
LIKE WHAT CAN KANO DO BESIDES BIG JUMPS?
VERY CURIOUS
HUH?
HMM...
Um...
HE SEEMS FINE WITH CROSSES AND THE SUN, BUT DOES HE HAVE A WEAKNESS?
HAVE ANY VAMPIRES ACTUALLY LIVED 1,000 YEARS?
ARE THERE RECORDS OF THAT?
I'd like to read them!
ARE KANO'S PARENTS VAMPIRES?
WHAT IS YAMIMARU?
AS A WEREWOLF, DOES ARIYOSHI LIVE LONGER, TOO?
ARE THERE OTHERS LIKE HIM?
SATSUKI, DO YOU HAVE ANY ANSWERS?
Hmm...
HOW LONG *WILL* I LIVE?
Oh...
THEY'RE SURPRISINGLY IGNORANT...

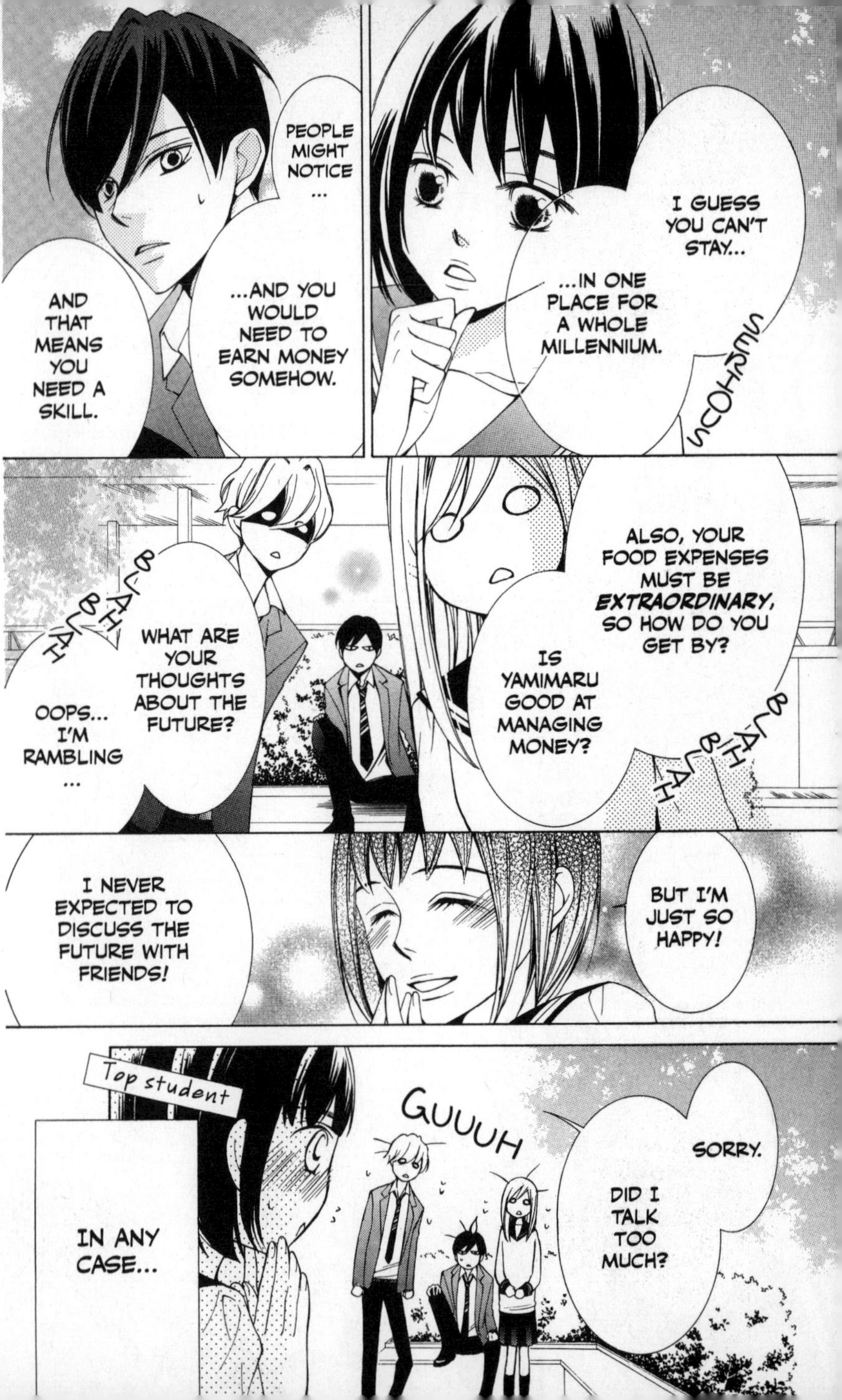
I GUESS YOU CAN'T STAY...
...IN ONE PLACE FOR A WHOLE MILLENNIUM.
PEOPLE MIGHT NOTICE...
...AND YOU WOULD NEED TO EARN MONEY SOMEHOW.
AND THAT MEANS YOU NEED A SKILL.
ALSO, YOUR FOOD EXPENSES MUST BE ***EXTRAORDINARY,*** SO HOW DO YOU GET BY?
IS YAMIMARU GOOD AT MANAGING MONEY?
BLAH BLAH
WHAT ARE YOUR THOUGHTS ABOUT THE FUTURE?
BLAH BLAH
OOPS... I'M RAMBLING...
BUT I'M JUST SO HAPPY!
I NEVER EXPECTED TO DISCUSS THE FUTURE WITH FRIENDS!
SORRY.
DID I TALK TOO MUCH?
GUUUH
Top student
IN ANY CASE...

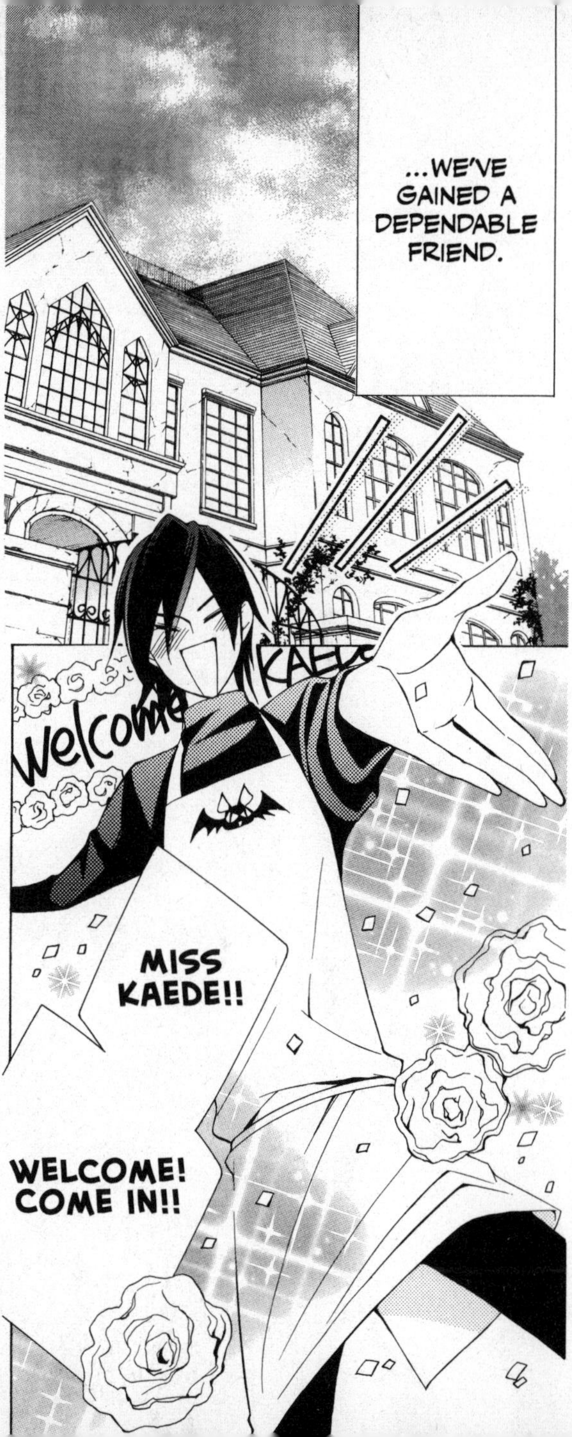
...WE'VE GAINED A DEPENDABLE FRIEND.
Welcome
MISS KAEDE!!
WELCOME! COME IN!!

Greetings

How do you do? Thanks for picking up the final volume of Millennium Snow!!

Thank you... ...so much!!!

This may be the last volume, but there's no new material at the back (I used as many pages as possible for the main story), so I'll try to talk about stuff in the sidebars without any spoilers.

Having said that...it might be better to read the sidebars after finishing the volume!

Now on to the end!

★

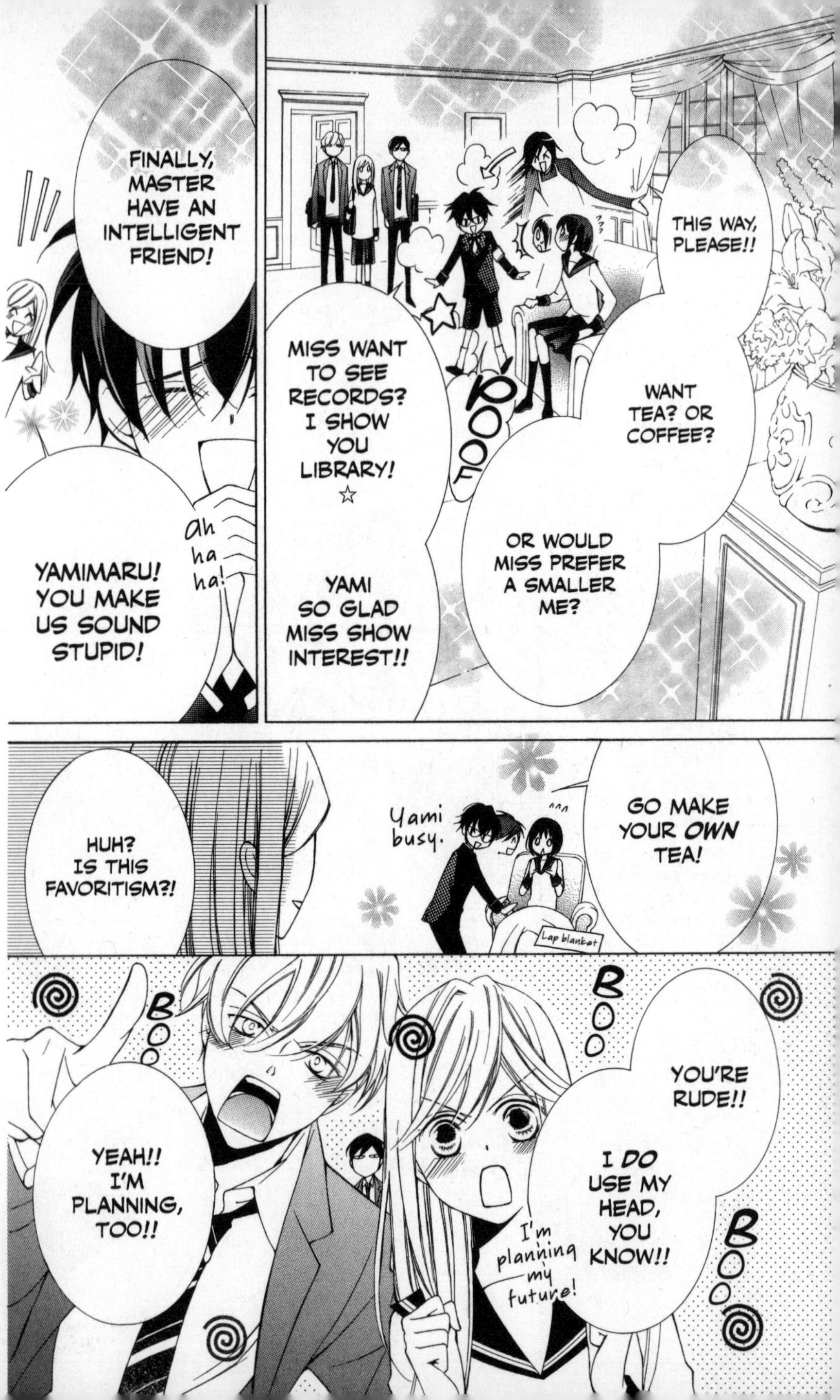
THIS WAY, PLEASE!!
WANT TEA? OR COFFEE?
OR WOULD MISS PREFER A SMALLER ME?
POOF
MISS WANT TO SEE RECORDS? I SHOW YOU LIBRARY! ☆
YAMI SO GLAD MISS SHOW INTEREST!!
FINALLY, MASTER HAVE AN INTELLIGENT FRIEND!
Ah ha ha!
YAMIMARU! YOU MAKE US SOUND STUPID!
GO MAKE YOUR *OWN* TEA!
Yami busy.
Lap blanket
HUH? IS THIS FAVORITISM?!
BOOO
YOU'RE RUDE!!
I *DO* USE MY HEAD, YOU KNOW!!
BOOO
I'm planning my future!
BOOO
YEAH!! I'M PLANNING, TOO!!

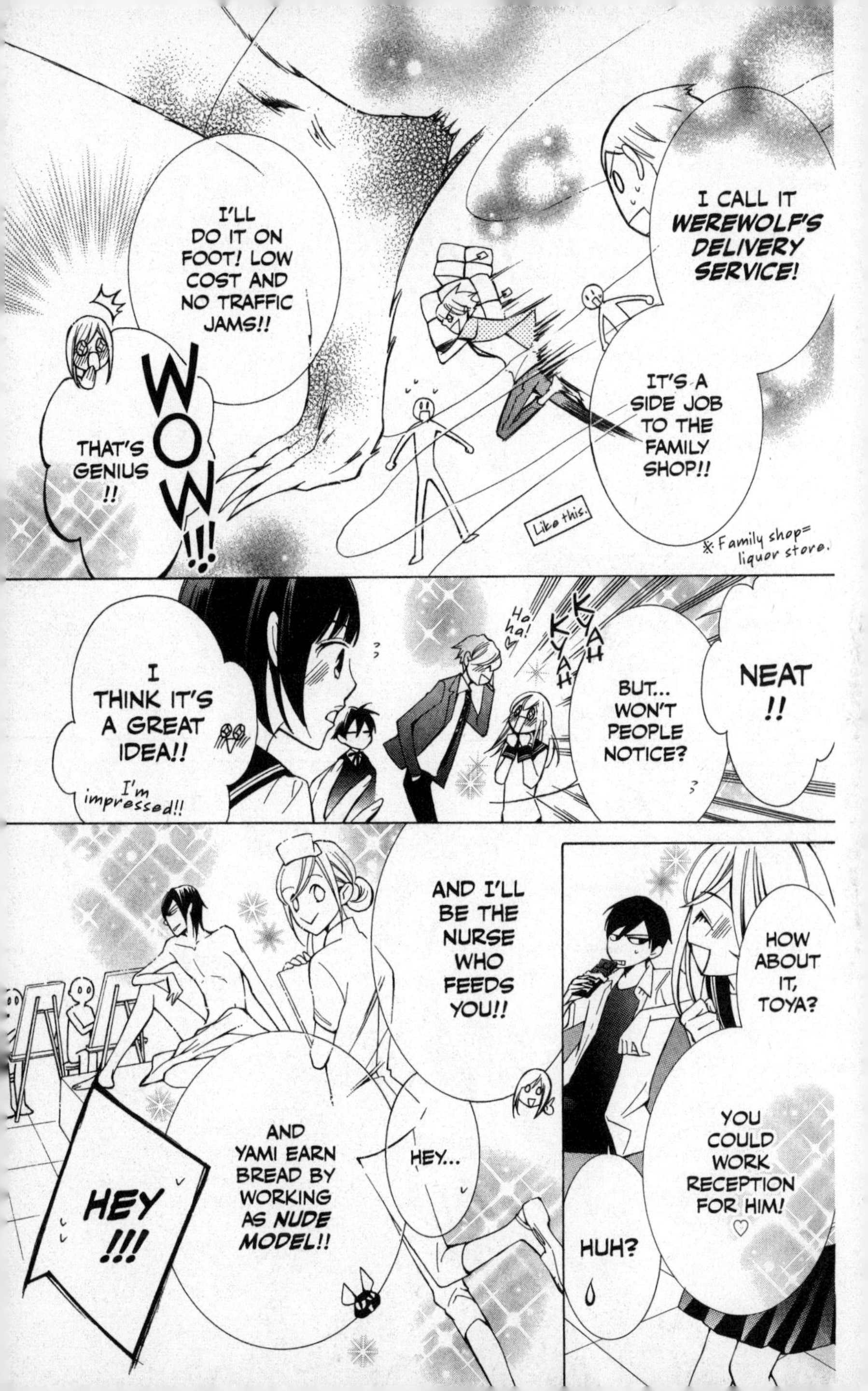

I CALL IT WEREWOLF'S DELIVERY SERVICE!
IT'S A SIDE JOB TO THE FAMILY SHOP!!
Like this.
※Family shop= liquor store.
I'LL DO IT ON FOOT! LOW COST AND NO TRAFFIC JAMS!!
WOW!!!
THAT'S GENIUS!!
NEAT!!
BUT... WON'T PEOPLE NOTICE?
KYAH KYAH
Ho ha!
I THINK IT'S A GREAT IDEA!!
I'm impressed!!
HOW ABOUT IT, TOYA?
YOU COULD WORK RECEPTION FOR HIM! ♡
HUH?
AND I'LL BE THE NURSE WHO FEEDS YOU!!
HEY...
AND YAMI EARN BREAD BY WORKING AS NUDE MODEL!!
HEY!!!

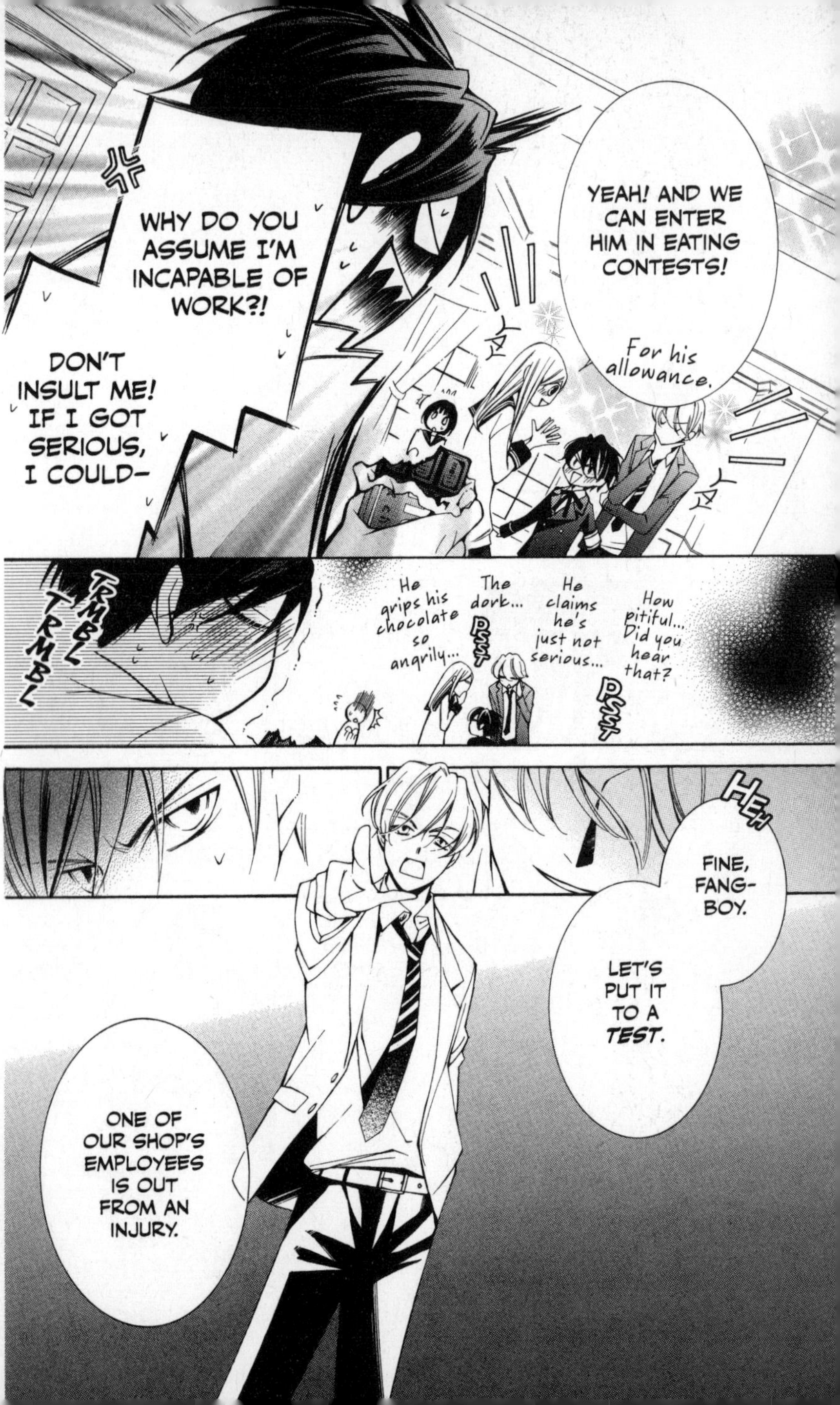
YEAH! AND WE CAN ENTER HIM IN EATING CONTESTS!
For his allowance.
WHY DO YOU ASSUME I'M INCAPABLE OF WORK?!
DON'T INSULT ME! IF I GOT SERIOUS, I COULD–
How pitiful... Did you hear that?
PSST
He claims he's just not serious...
The dork...
PSST
He grips his chocolate so angrily...
TRMBL TRMBL
HEH
FINE, FANG-BOY.
LET'S PUT IT TO A TEST.
ONE OF OUR SHOP'S EMPLOYEES IS OUT FROM AN INJURY.

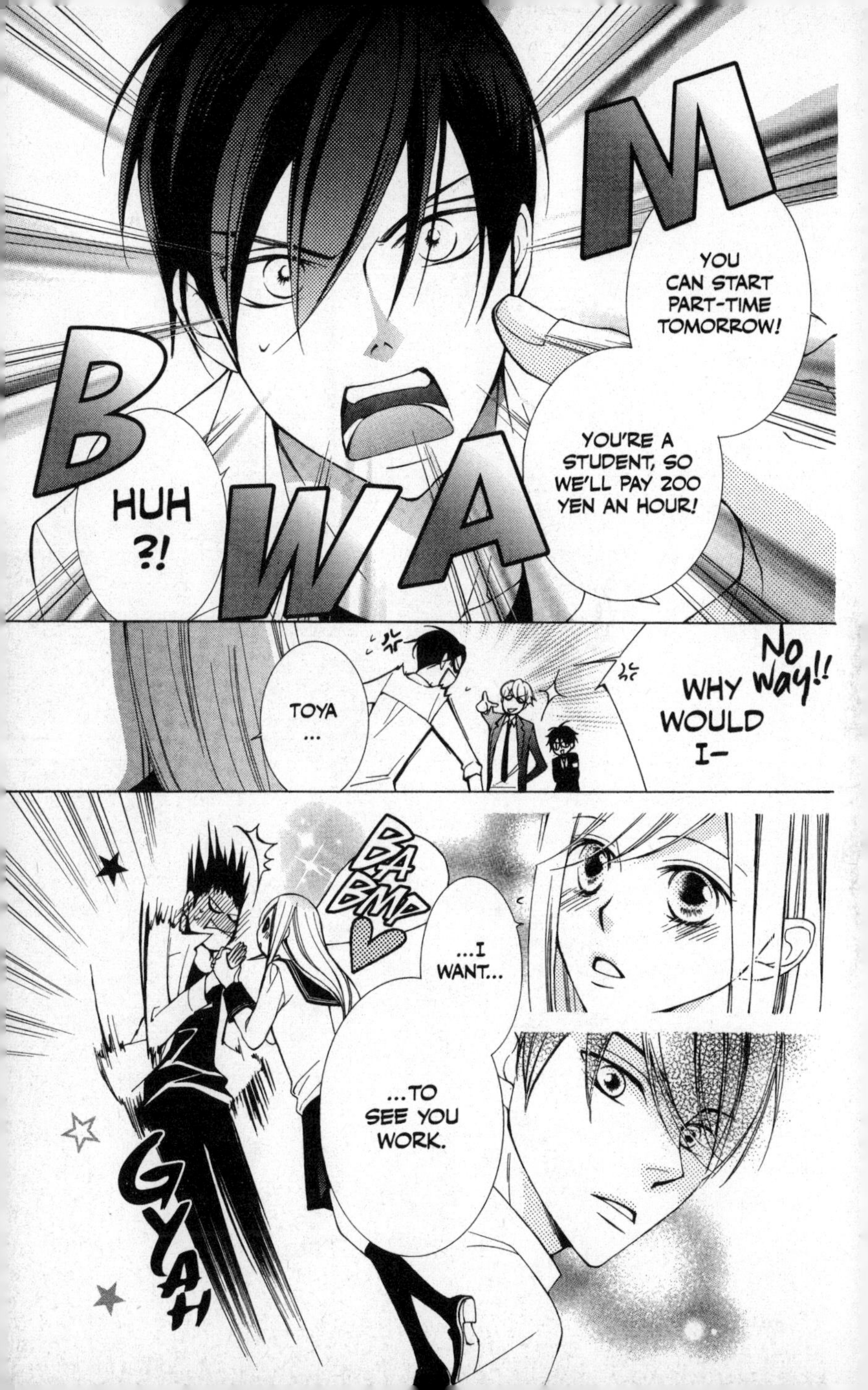
YOU CAN START PART-TIME TOMORROW!
YOU'RE A STUDENT, SO WE'LL PAY 200 YEN AN HOUR!
BWAM
HUH ?!
No way!!
WHY WOULD I—
TOYA ...
BA-BMP
...I WANT...
...TO SEE YOU WORK.
GYAH

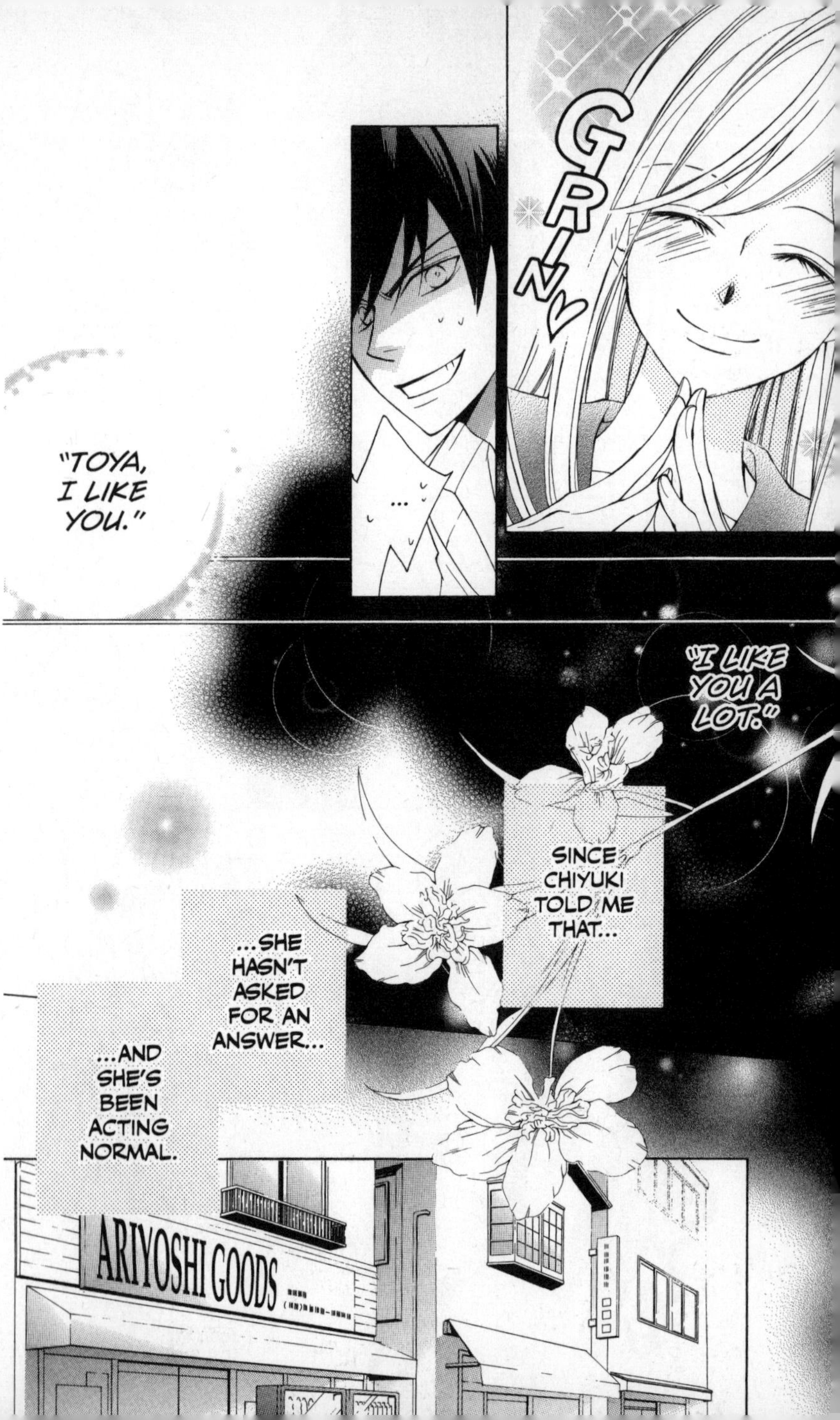
GRIN♥
...
"TOYA, I LIKE YOU."
"I LIKE YOU A LOT."
SINCE CHIYUKI TOLD ME THAT...
...SHE HASN'T ASKED FOR AN ANSWER...
...AND SHE'S BEEN ACTING NORMAL.
ARIYOSHI GOODS

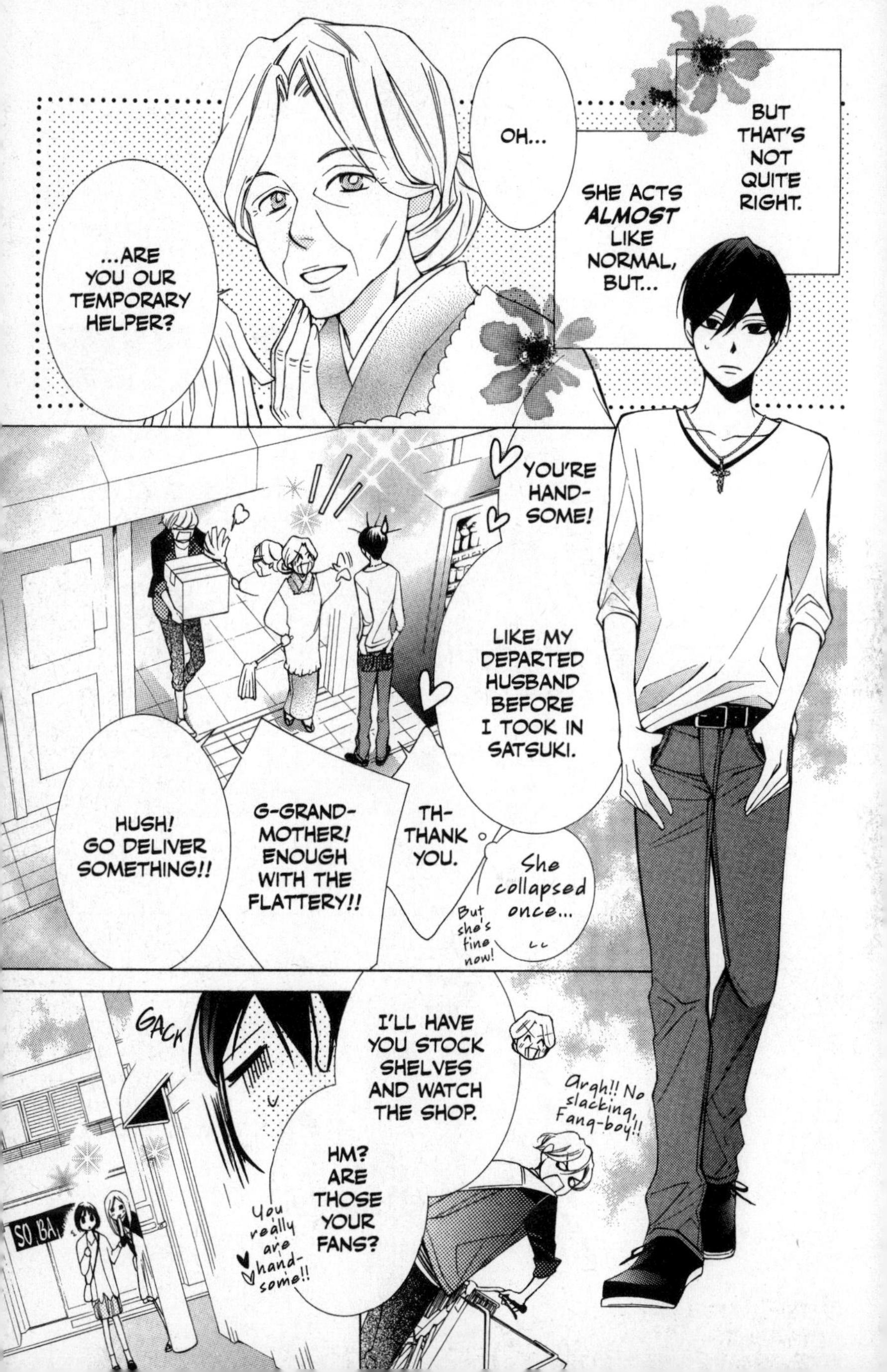

OH...
...ARE YOU OUR TEMPORARY HELPER?
SHE ACTS *ALMOST* LIKE NORMAL, BUT...
BUT THAT'S NOT QUITE RIGHT.
YOU'RE HANDSOME!
LIKE MY DEPARTED HUSBAND BEFORE I TOOK IN SATSUKI.
TH-THANK YOU.
She collapsed once...
But she's fine now!
G-GRANDMOTHER! ENOUGH WITH THE FLATTERY!!
HUSH! GO DELIVER SOMETHING!!
I'LL HAVE YOU STOCK SHELVES AND WATCH THE SHOP.
Argh!! No slacking, Fang-boy!!
GACK
HM? ARE THOSE YOUR FANS?
You really are hand-some!!
SO BA

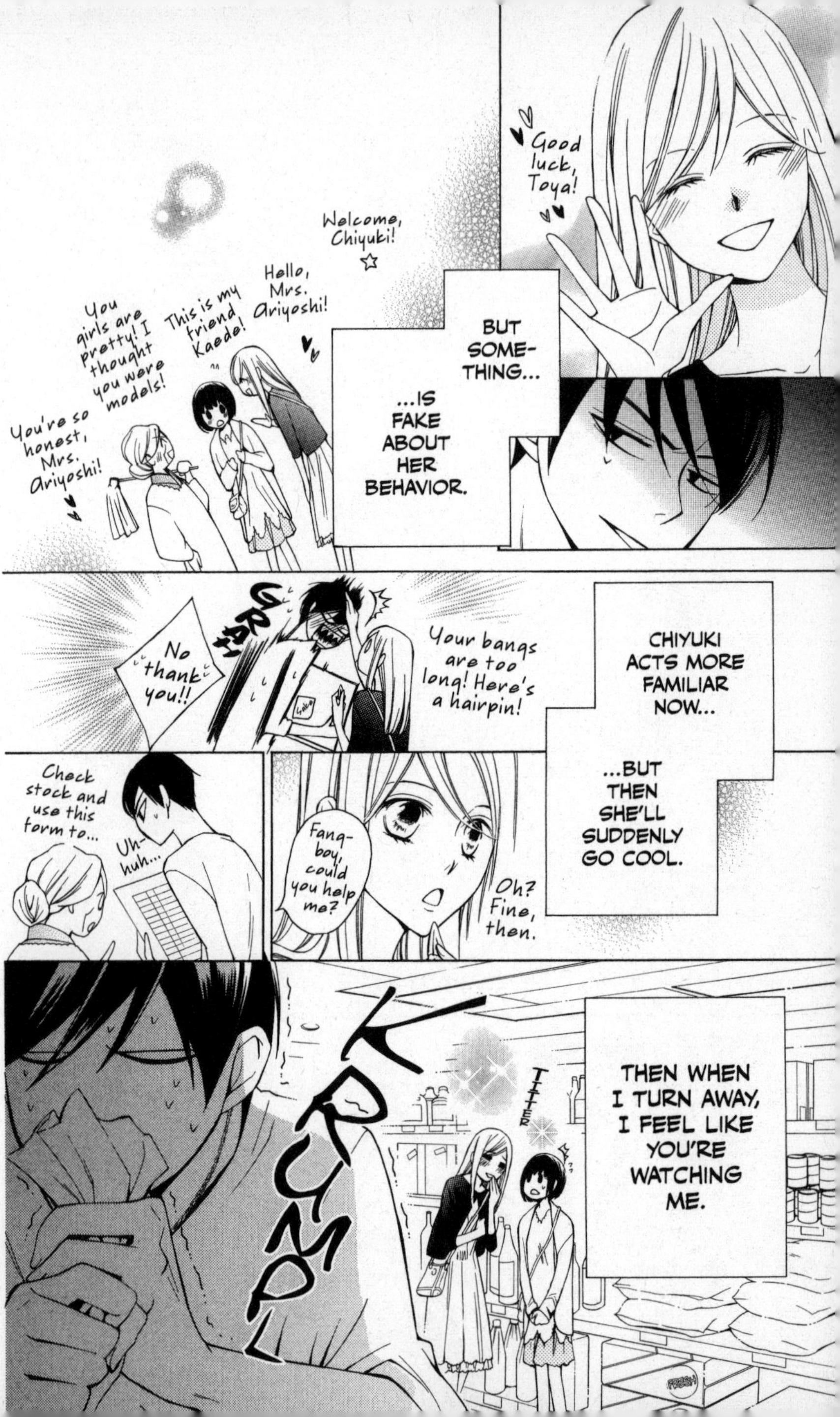
Good luck, Toya!
BUT SOMETHING...
...IS FAKE ABOUT HER BEHAVIOR.
Welcome, Chiyuki!
Hello, Mrs. Ariyoshi!
This is my friend Kaede!
You girls are pretty! I thought you were models!
You're so honest, Mrs. Ariyoshi!
CHIYUKI ACTS MORE FAMILIAR NOW...
Your bangs are too long! Here's a hairpin!
GRAB
No thank you!!
...BUT THEN SHE'LL SUDDENLY GO COOL.
Fang-boy, could you help me?
Oh? Fine, then.
Check stock and use this form to...
Uh-huh...
THEN WHEN I TURN AWAY, I FEEL LIKE YOU'RE WATCHING ME.
TITTER
KRUMPL

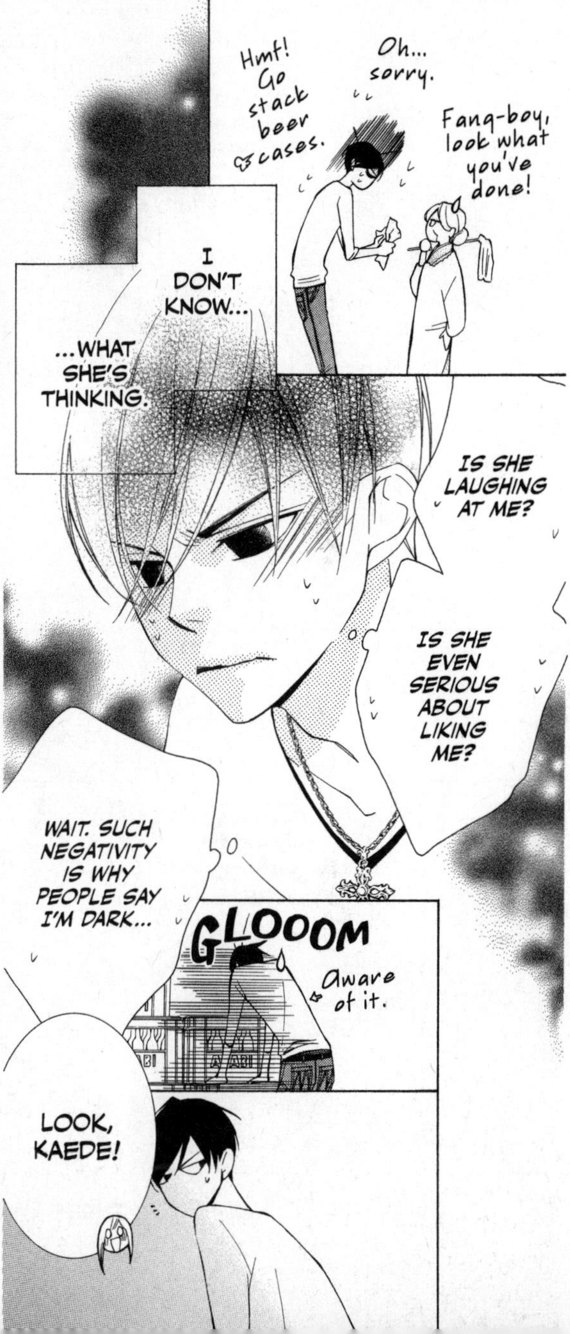
Fang-boy, look what you've done!
Oh... sorry.
Hmf! Go stack beer cases.
I DON'T KNOW...
...WHAT SHE'S THINKING.
IS SHE LAUGHING AT ME?
IS SHE EVEN SERIOUS ABOUT LIKING ME?
WAIT. SUCH NEGATIVITY IS WHY PEOPLE SAY I'M DARK...
GLOOOM
Aware of it.
LOOK, KAEDE!

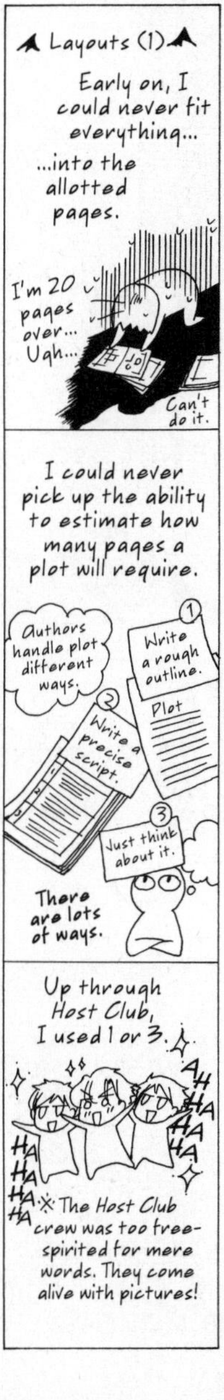
Layouts (1)
Early on, I could never fit everything...
...into the allotted pages.
I'm 20 pages over... Ugh...
Can't do it.
I could never pick up the ability to estimate how many pages a plot will require.
Authors handle plot different ways.
1 Write a rough outline.
Plot
2 Write a precise script.
3 Just think about it.
There are lots of ways.
Up through Host Club, I used 1 or 3.
AH HA HA HA HA
HA HA HA HA HA
※ The Host Club crew was too free-spirited for mere words. They come alive with pictures!

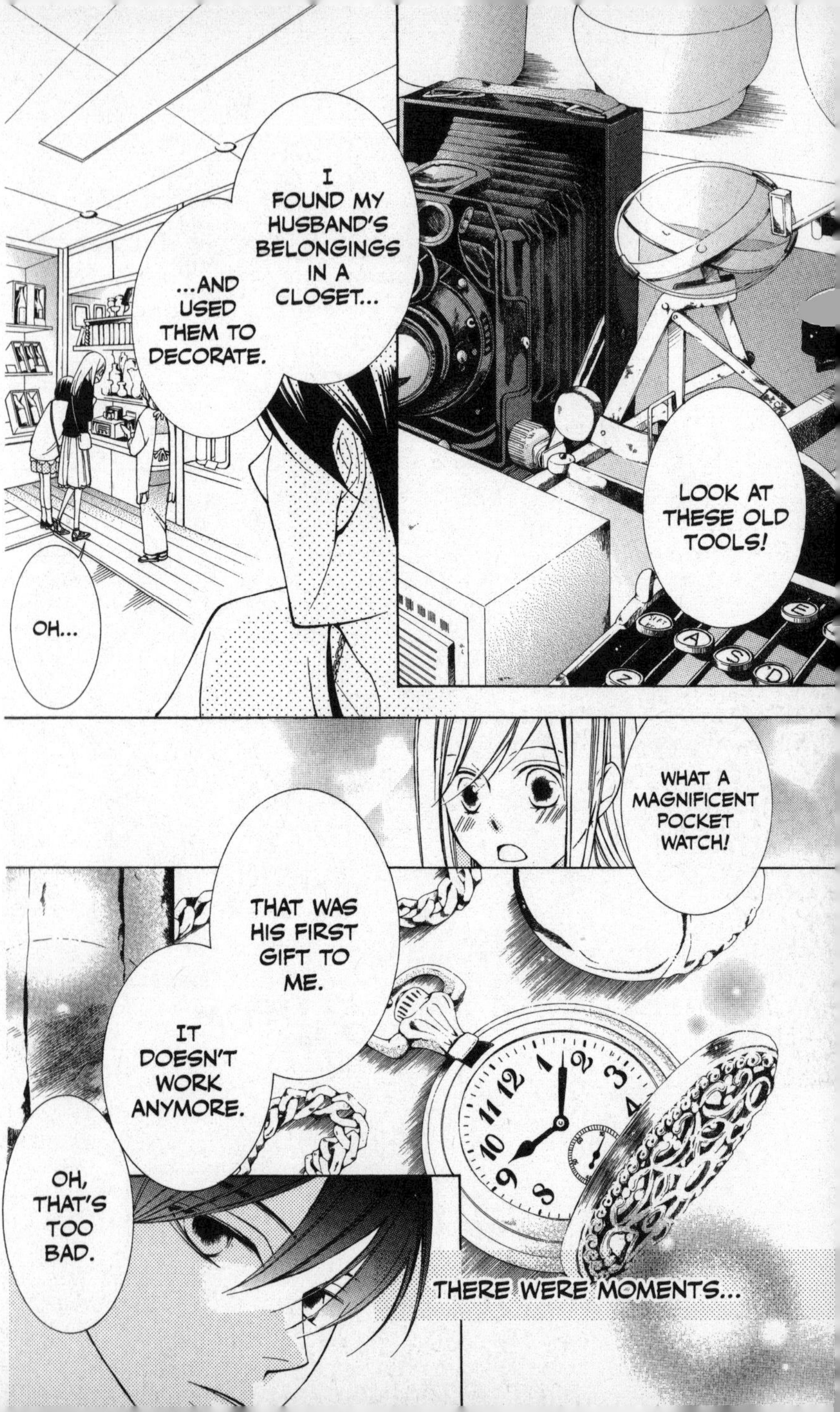
LOOK AT THESE OLD TOOLS!
I FOUND MY HUSBAND'S BELONGINGS IN A CLOSET...
...AND USED THEM TO DECORATE.
OH...
WHAT A MAGNIFICENT POCKET WATCH!
THAT WAS HIS FIRST GIFT TO ME.
IT DOESN'T WORK ANYMORE.
OH, THAT'S TOO BAD.
THERE WERE MOMENTS...

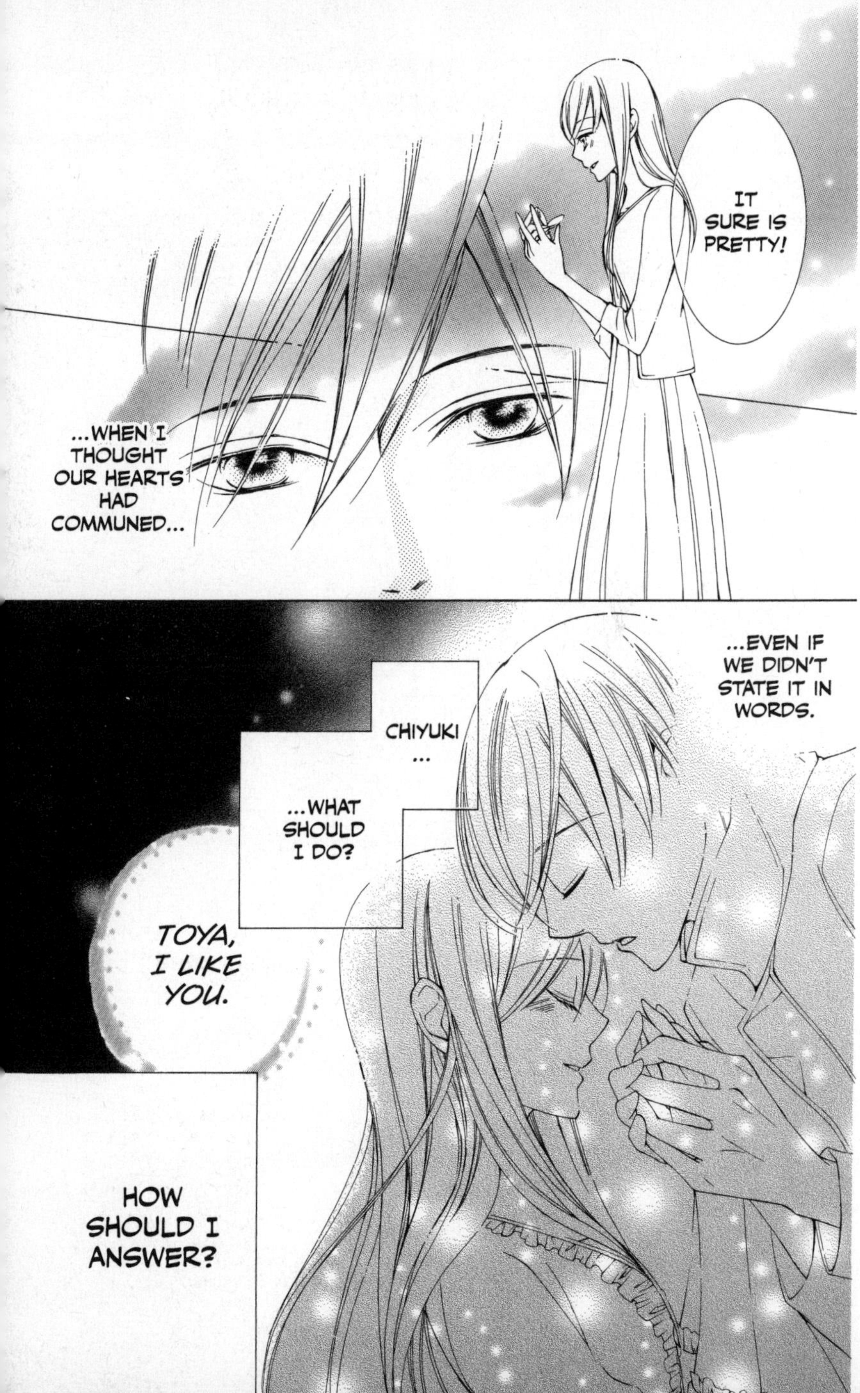
IT SURE IS PRETTY!
...WHEN I THOUGHT OUR HEARTS HAD COMMUNED...
...EVEN IF WE DIDN'T STATE IT IN WORDS.
CHIYUKI ...
...WHAT SHOULD I DO?
TOYA, I LIKE YOU.
HOW SHOULD I ANSWER?

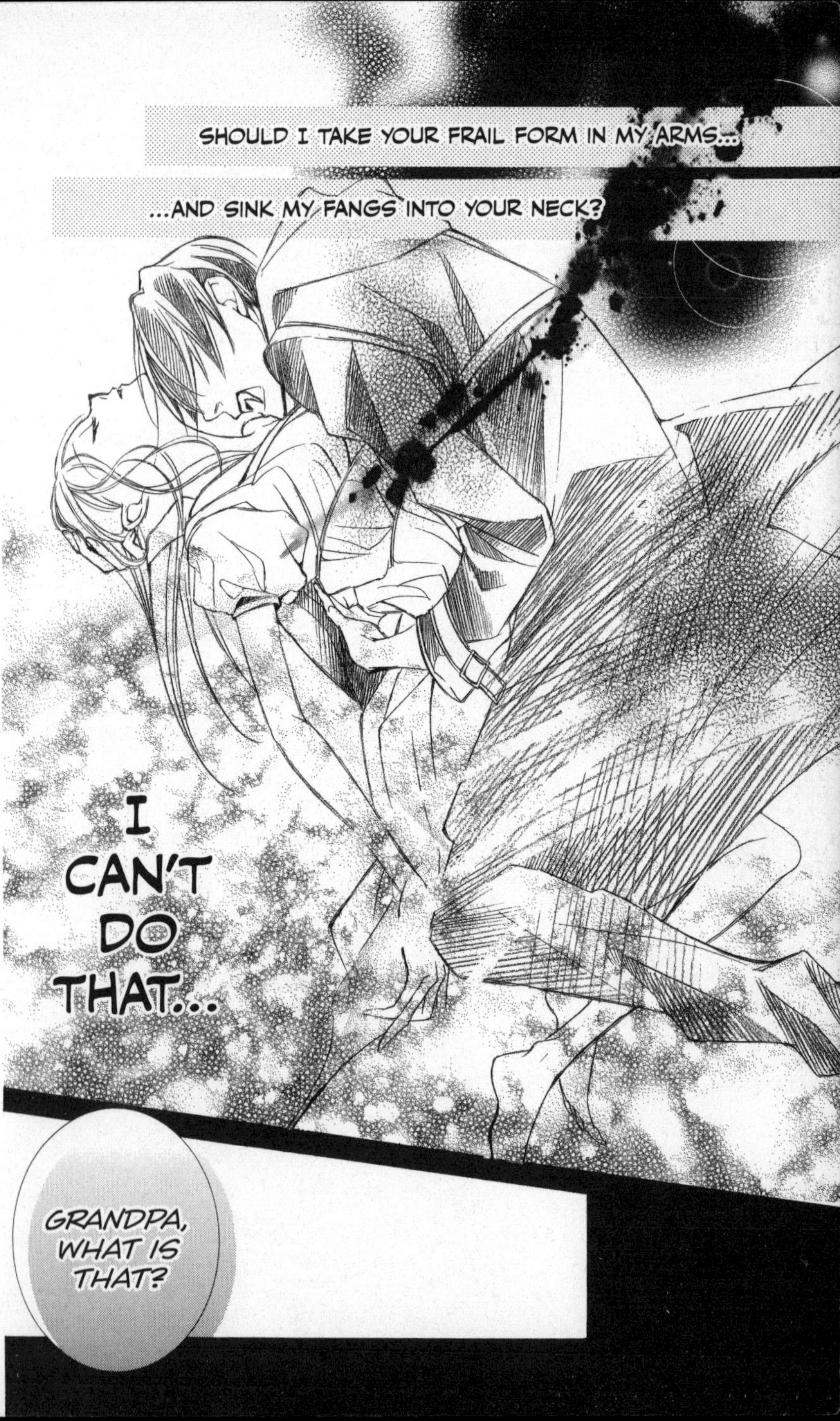
SHOULD I TAKE YOUR FRAIL FORM IN MY ARMS...
...AND SINK MY FANGS INTO YOUR NECK?
I CAN'T DO THAT...
GRANDPA, WHAT IS THAT?

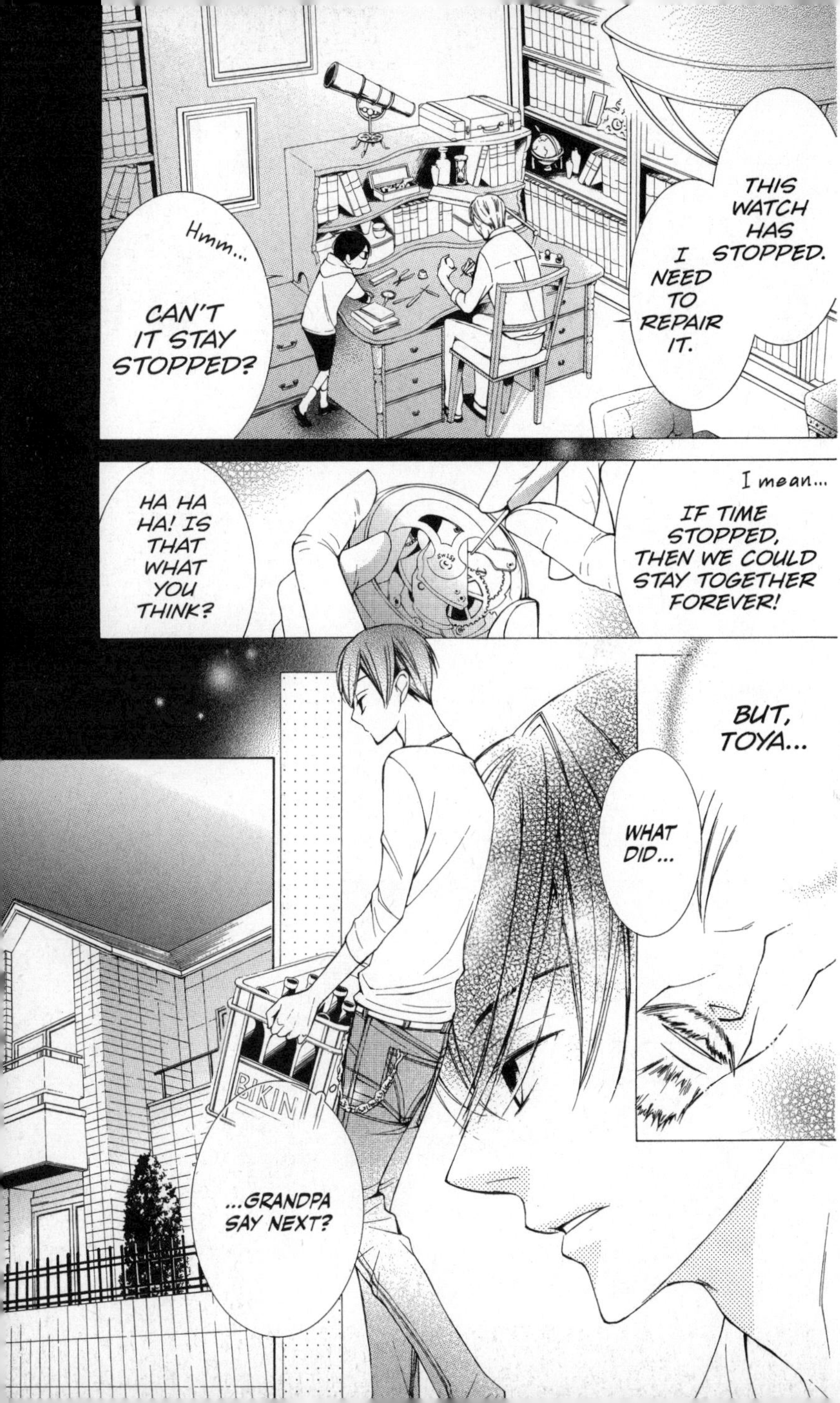
THIS WATCH HAS STOPPED.
I NEED TO REPAIR IT.
Hmm...
CAN'T IT STAY STOPPED?
I mean...
IF TIME STOPPED, THEN WE COULD STAY TOGETHER FOREVER!
HA HA HA! IS THAT WHAT YOU THINK?
BUT, TOYA...
WHAT DID...
BIKIN
...GRANDPA SAY NEXT?

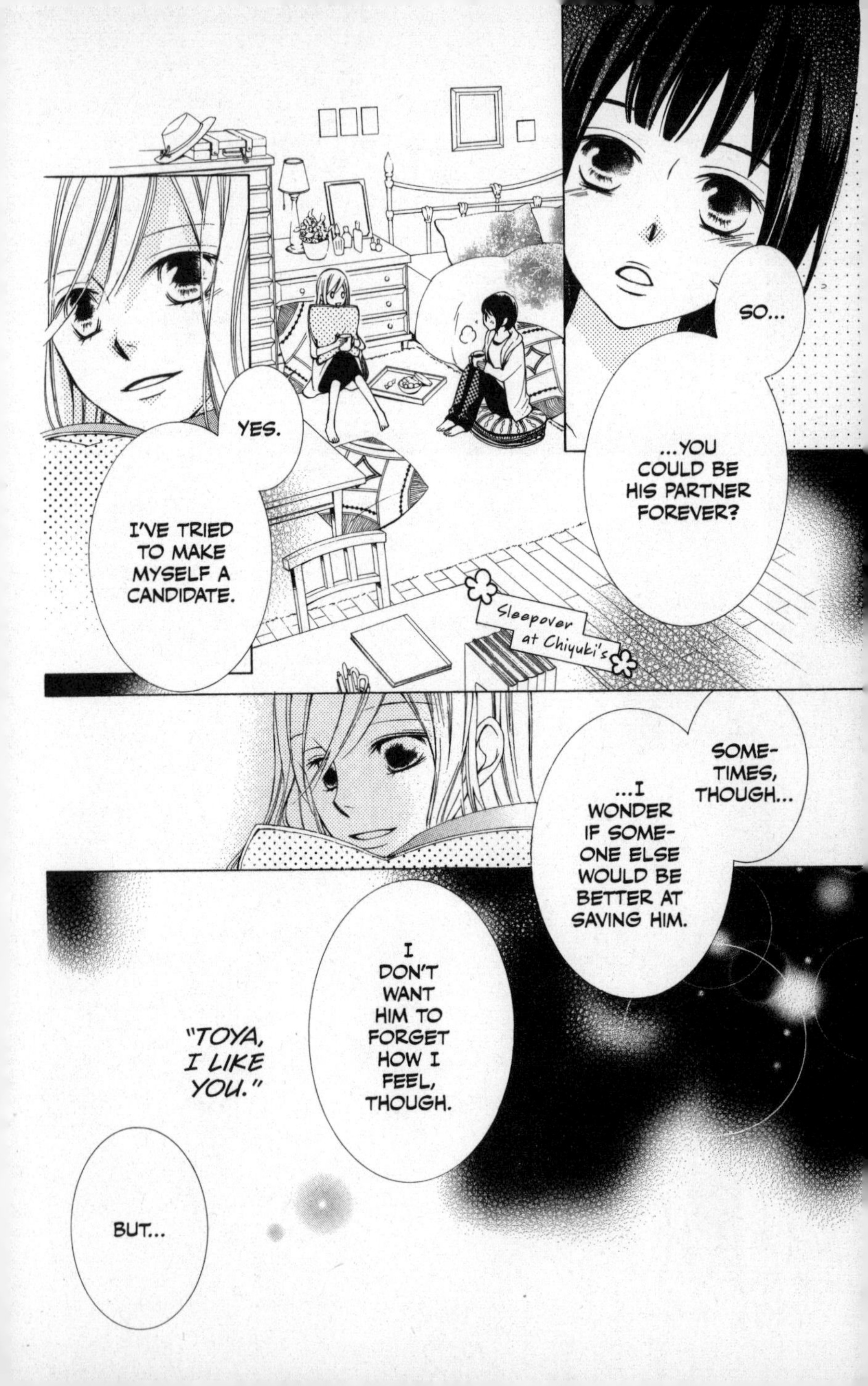
SO...
...YOU COULD BE HIS PARTNER FOREVER?
Sleepover at Chiyuki's
YES.
I'VE TRIED TO MAKE MYSELF A CANDIDATE.
SOME-TIMES, THOUGH...
...I WONDER IF SOME-ONE ELSE WOULD BE BETTER AT SAVING HIM.
I DON'T WANT HIM TO FORGET HOW I FEEL, THOUGH.
"TOYA, I LIKE YOU."
BUT...

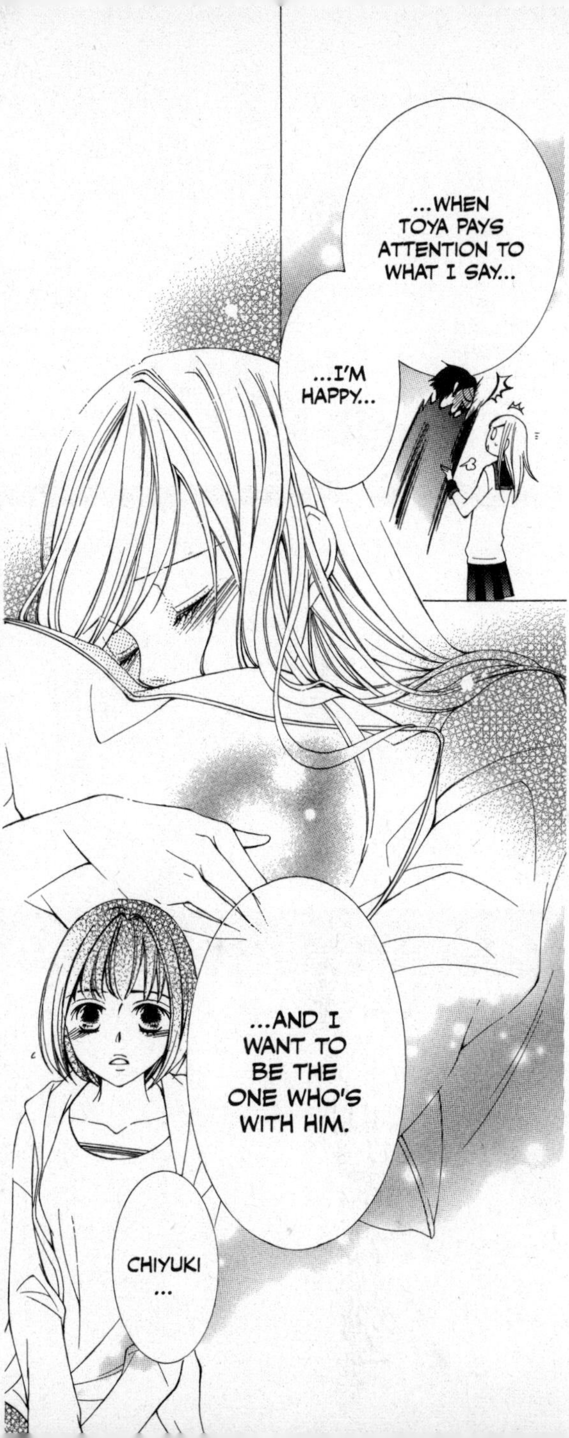
...WHEN TOYA PAYS ATTENTION TO WHAT I SAY...
...I'M HAPPY...
...AND I WANT TO BE THE ONE WHO'S WITH HIM.
CHIYUKI ...

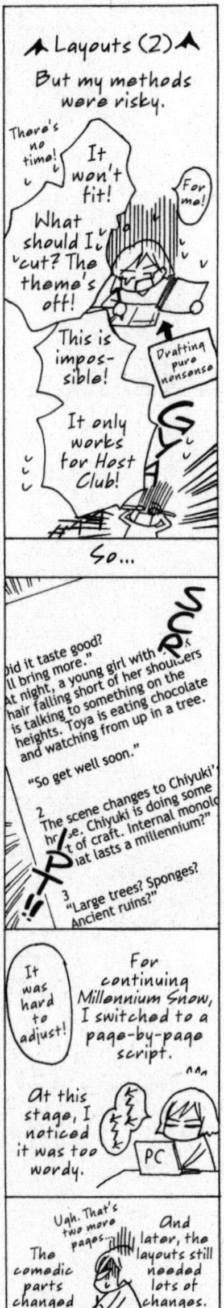
Layouts (2)
But my methods were risky.
There's no time!
It won't fit!
For me!
What should I cut? The theme's off!
This is impossible!
Drafting pure nonsense
It only works for Host Club!
GYU
So...
SCRUNCH
Did it taste good?
ll bring more."
At night, a young girl with
hair falling short of her shoulders
is talking to something on the
heights. Toya is eating chocolate
and watching from up in a tree.
"So get well soon."
2
The scene changes to Chiyuki's
house. Chiyuki is doing some
of craft. Internal monolo
that lasts a millennium?"
3
"Large trees? Sponges?
Ancient ruins?"
RIP!!
It was hard to adjust!
For continuing Millennium Snow, I switched to a page-by-page script.
At this stage, I noticed it was too wordy.
PC
Ugh. That's two more pages...
The comedic parts changed the most.
And later, the layouts still needed lots of changes.

I'll keep experimenting.

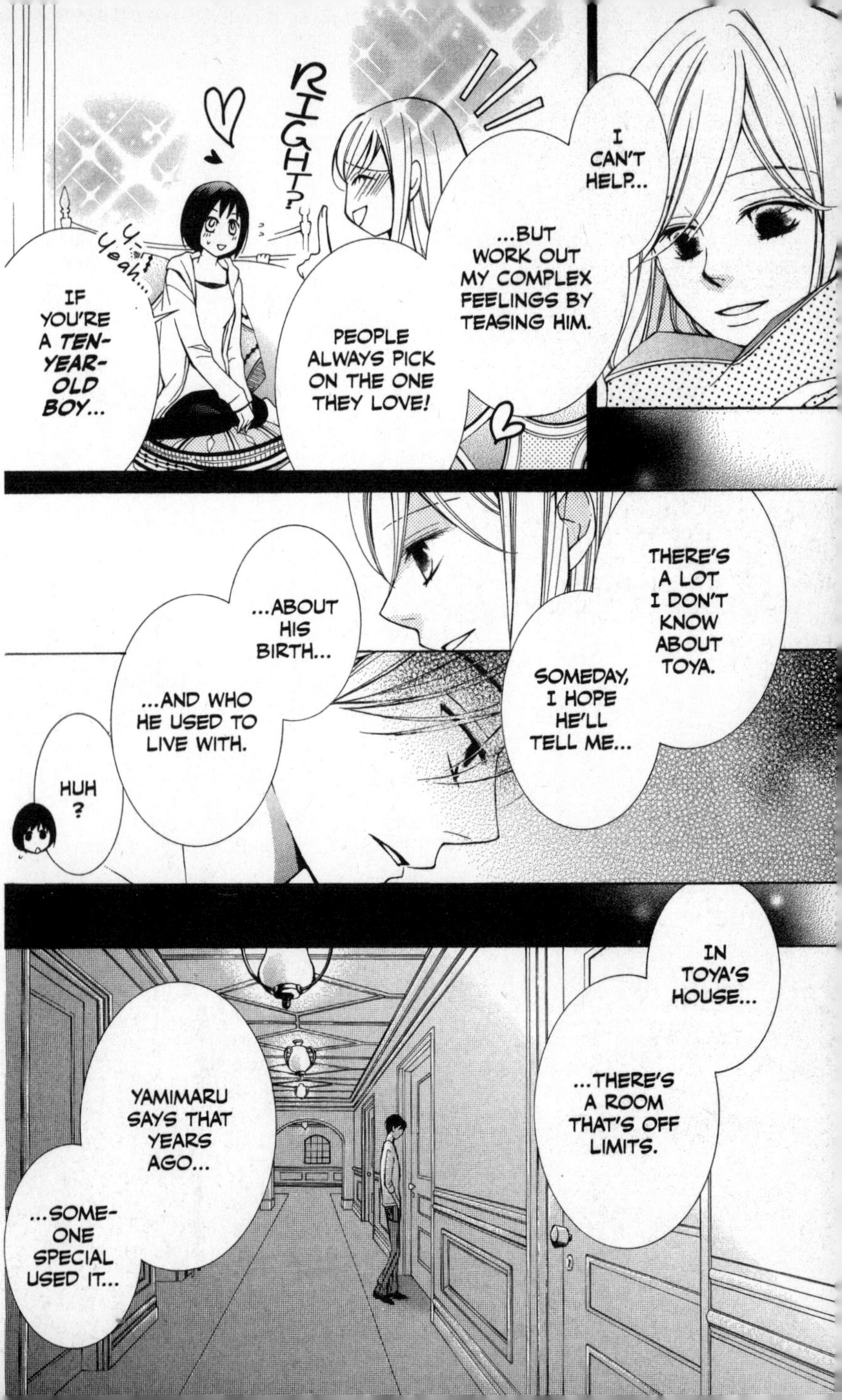
I CAN'T HELP...
...BUT WORK OUT MY COMPLEX FEELINGS BY TEASING HIM.
RIGHT?
PEOPLE ALWAYS PICK ON THE ONE THEY LOVE!
Y-Yeah...
IF YOU'RE A TEN-YEAR-OLD BOY...
THERE'S A LOT I DON'T KNOW ABOUT TOYA.
SOMEDAY, I HOPE HE'LL TELL ME...
...ABOUT HIS BIRTH...
...AND WHO HE USED TO LIVE WITH.
HUH?
IN TOYA'S HOUSE...
...THERE'S A ROOM THAT'S OFF LIMITS.
YAMIMARU SAYS THAT YEARS AGO...
...SOME-ONE SPECIAL USED IT...

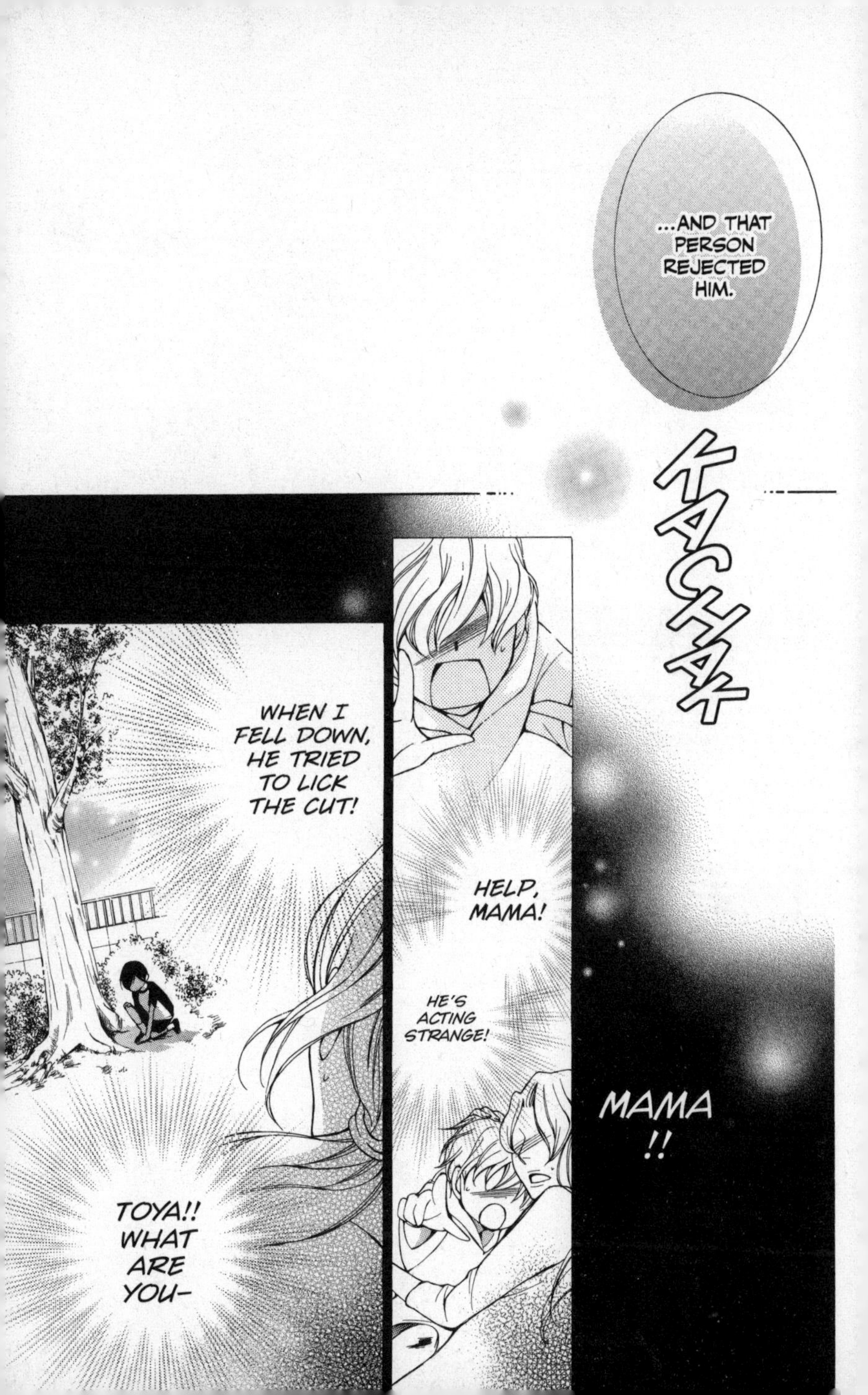
...AND THAT PERSON REJECTED HIM.
KACHAK
HELP, MAMA!
HE'S ACTING STRANGE!
MAMA!!
WHEN I FELL DOWN, HE TRIED TO LICK THE CUT!
TOYA!! WHAT ARE YOU-

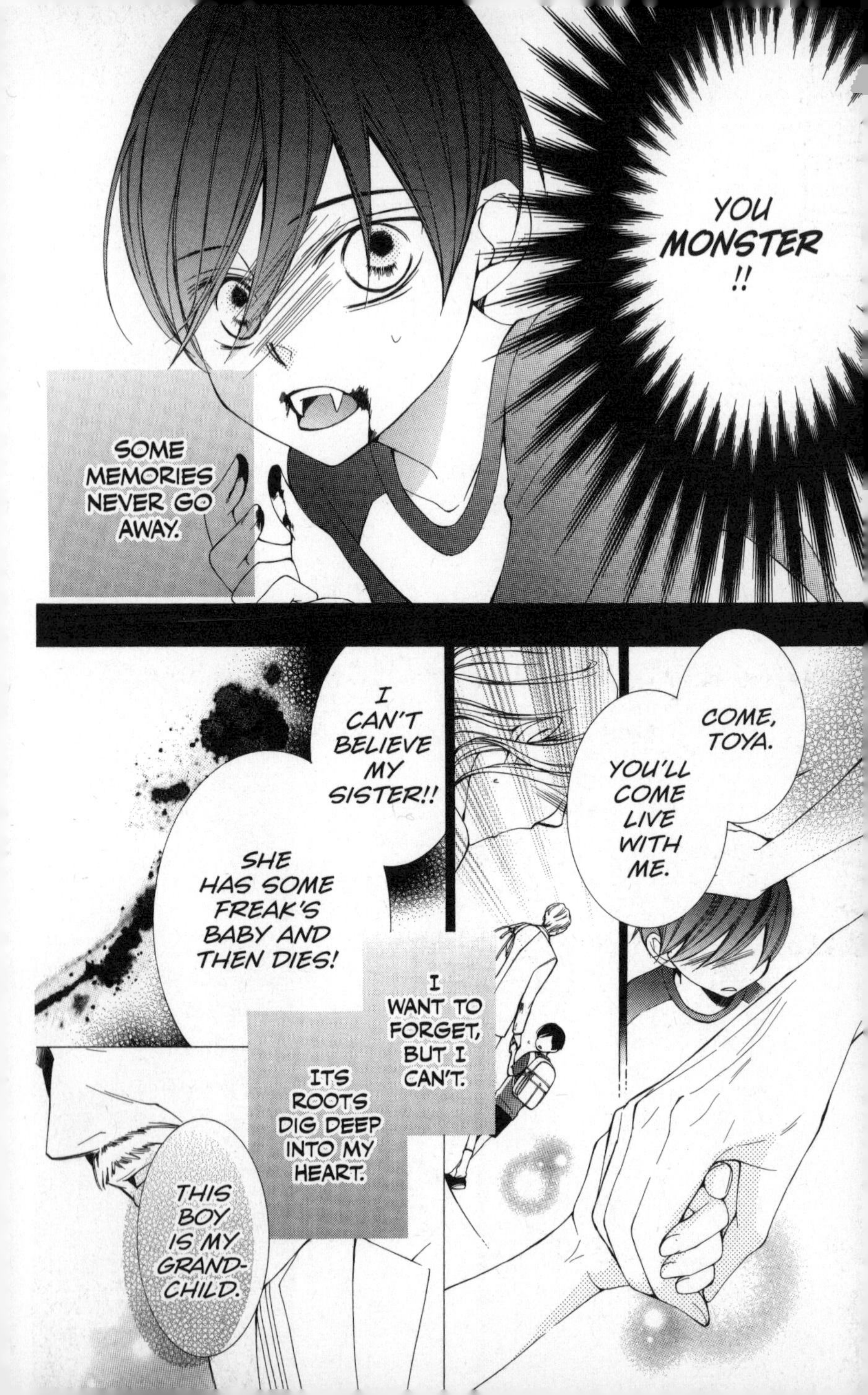
YOU MONSTER!!
SOME MEMORIES NEVER GO AWAY.
COME, TOYA.
YOU'LL COME LIVE WITH ME.
I CAN'T BELIEVE MY SISTER!!
SHE HAS SOME FREAK'S BABY AND THEN DIES!
I WANT TO FORGET, BUT I CAN'T.
ITS ROOTS DIG DEEP INTO MY HEART.
THIS BOY IS MY GRAND-CHILD.

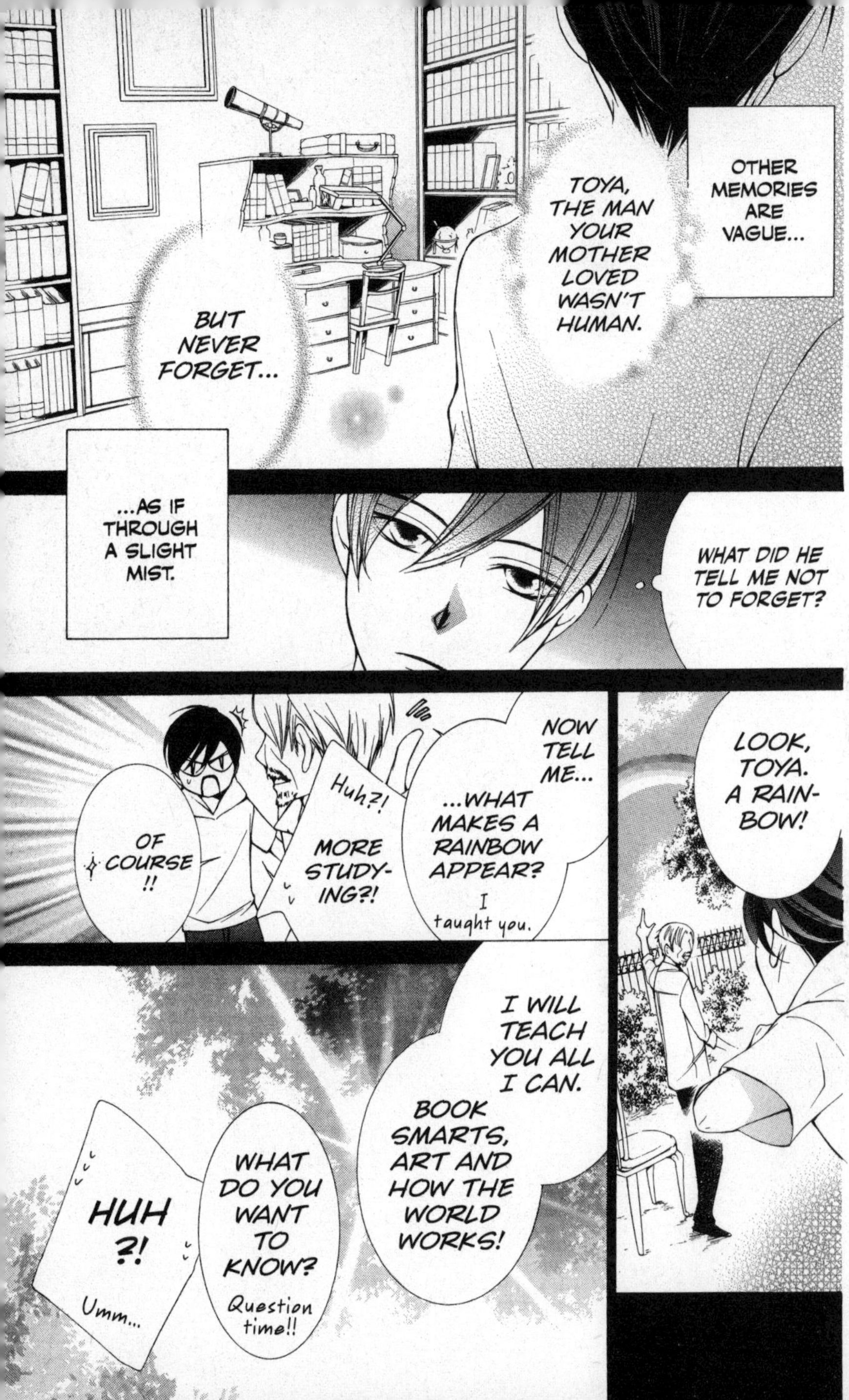
OTHER MEMORIES ARE VAGUE...
TOYA, THE MAN YOUR MOTHER LOVED WASN'T HUMAN.
BUT NEVER FORGET...
WHAT DID HE TELL ME NOT TO FORGET?
...AS IF THROUGH A SLIGHT MIST.
LOOK, TOYA. A RAINBOW!
NOW TELL ME...
...WHAT MAKES A RAINBOW APPEAR?
I taught you.
Huh?!
MORE STUDYING?!
OF COURSE!!
I WILL TEACH YOU ALL I CAN.
BOOK SMARTS, ART AND HOW THE WORLD WORKS!
WHAT DO YOU WANT TO KNOW?
Question time!!
HUH?!
Umm...

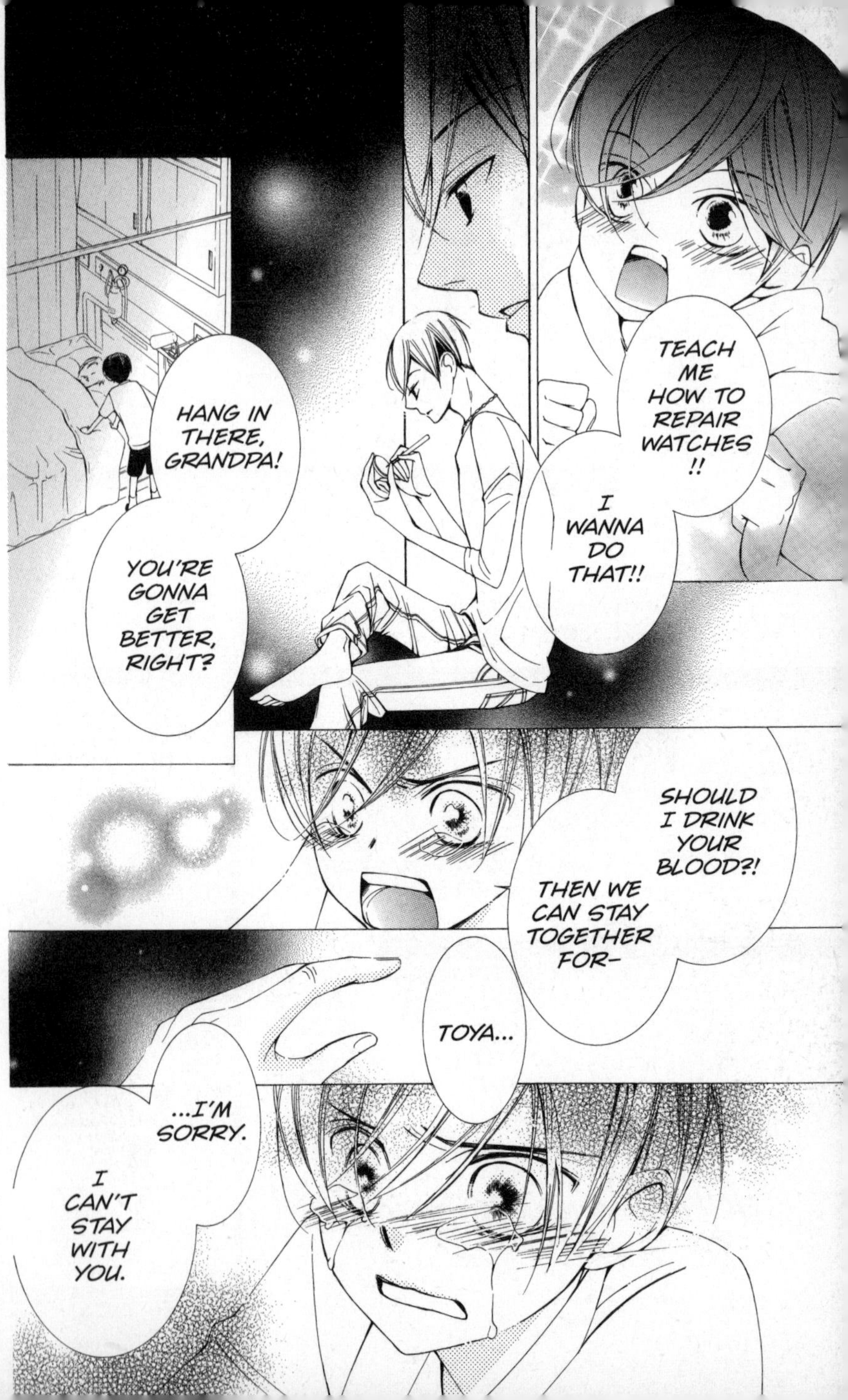
TEACH ME HOW TO REPAIR WATCHES!!
I WANNA DO THAT!!
HANG IN THERE, GRANDPA!
YOU'RE GONNA GET BETTER, RIGHT?
SHOULD I DRINK YOUR BLOOD?!
THEN WE CAN STAY TOGETHER FOR-
TOYA...
...I'M SORRY.
I CAN'T STAY WITH YOU.

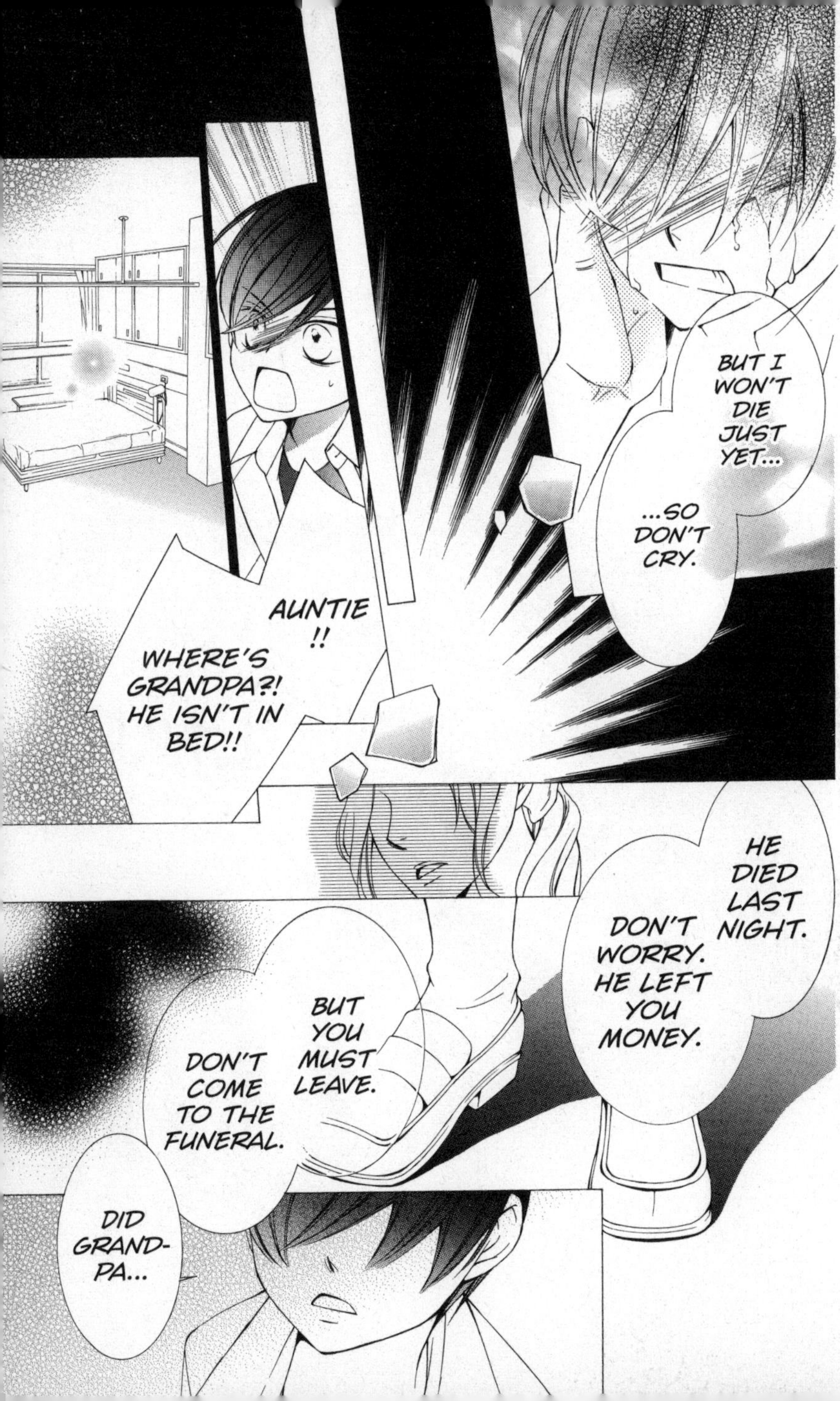
BUT I WON'T DIE JUST YET...
...SO DON'T CRY.
AUNTIE!!
WHERE'S GRANDPA?! HE ISN'T IN BED!!
HE DIED LAST NIGHT.
DON'T WORRY. HE LEFT YOU MONEY.
BUT YOU MUST LEAVE.
DON'T COME TO THE FUNERAL.
DID GRAND-PA...

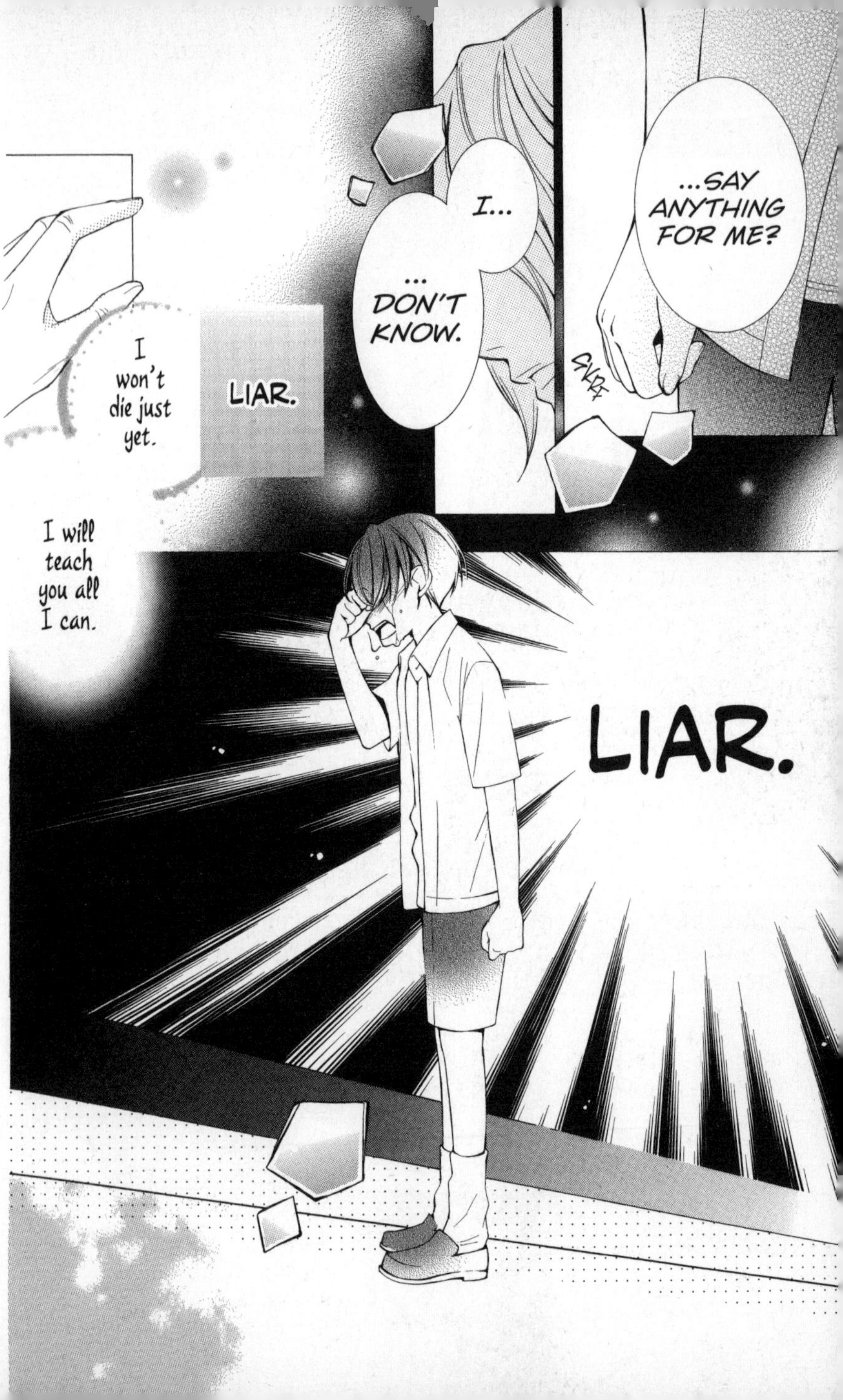
...SAY ANYTHING FOR ME?
I...
...DON'T KNOW.
LIAR.
I won't die just yet.
I will teach you all I can.
LIAR.

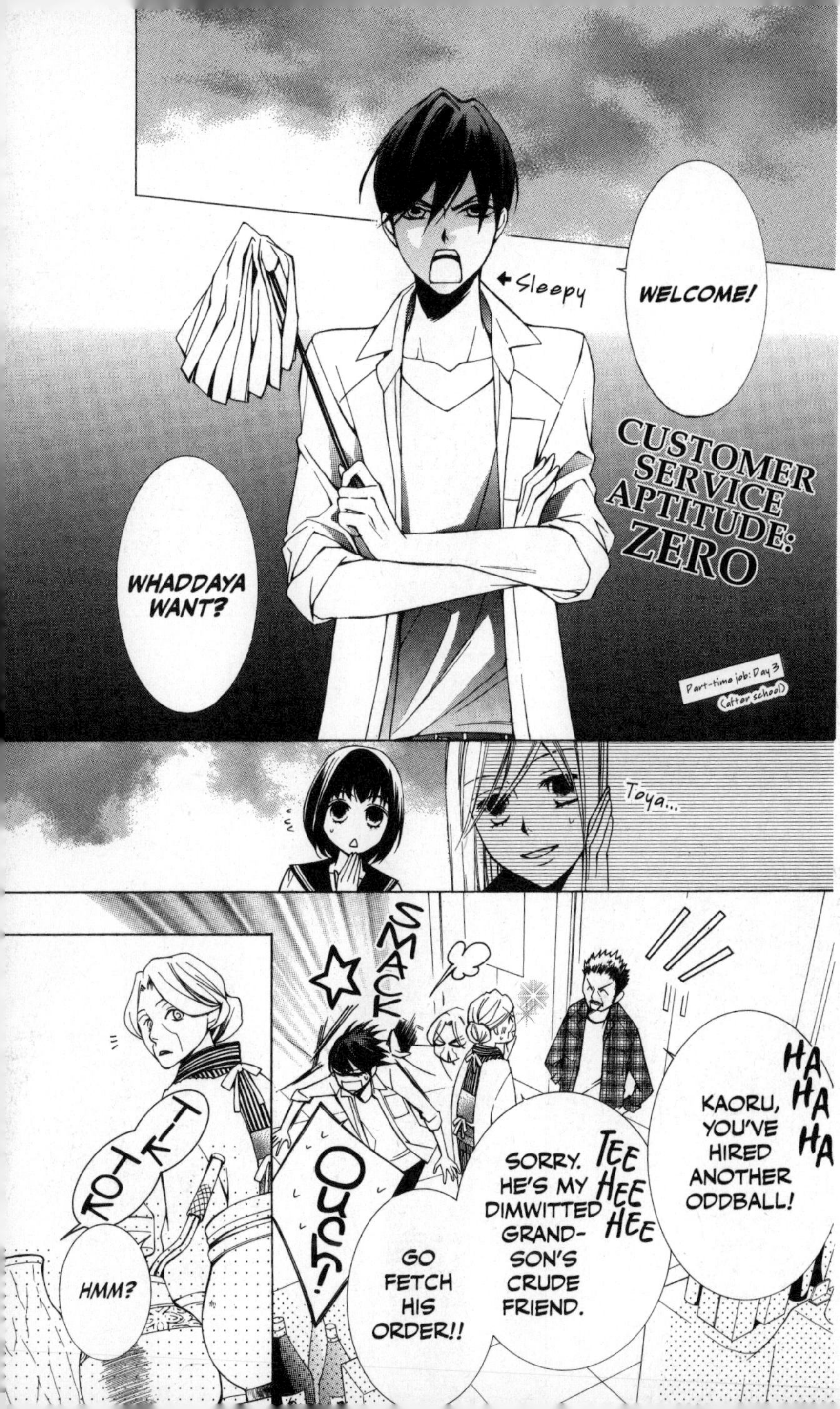
WELCOME!
← Sleepy
CUSTOMER SERVICE APTITUDE: ZERO
Part-time job: Day 3 (after school)
WHADDAYA WANT?
Toya...
HA HA HA HA
KAORU, YOU'VE HIRED ANOTHER ODDBALL!
TEE HEE HEE
SORRY. HE'S MY DIMWITTED GRAND-SON'S CRUDE FRIEND.
SMACK
OUCH!
GO FETCH HIS ORDER!!
TIK TOK
HMM?

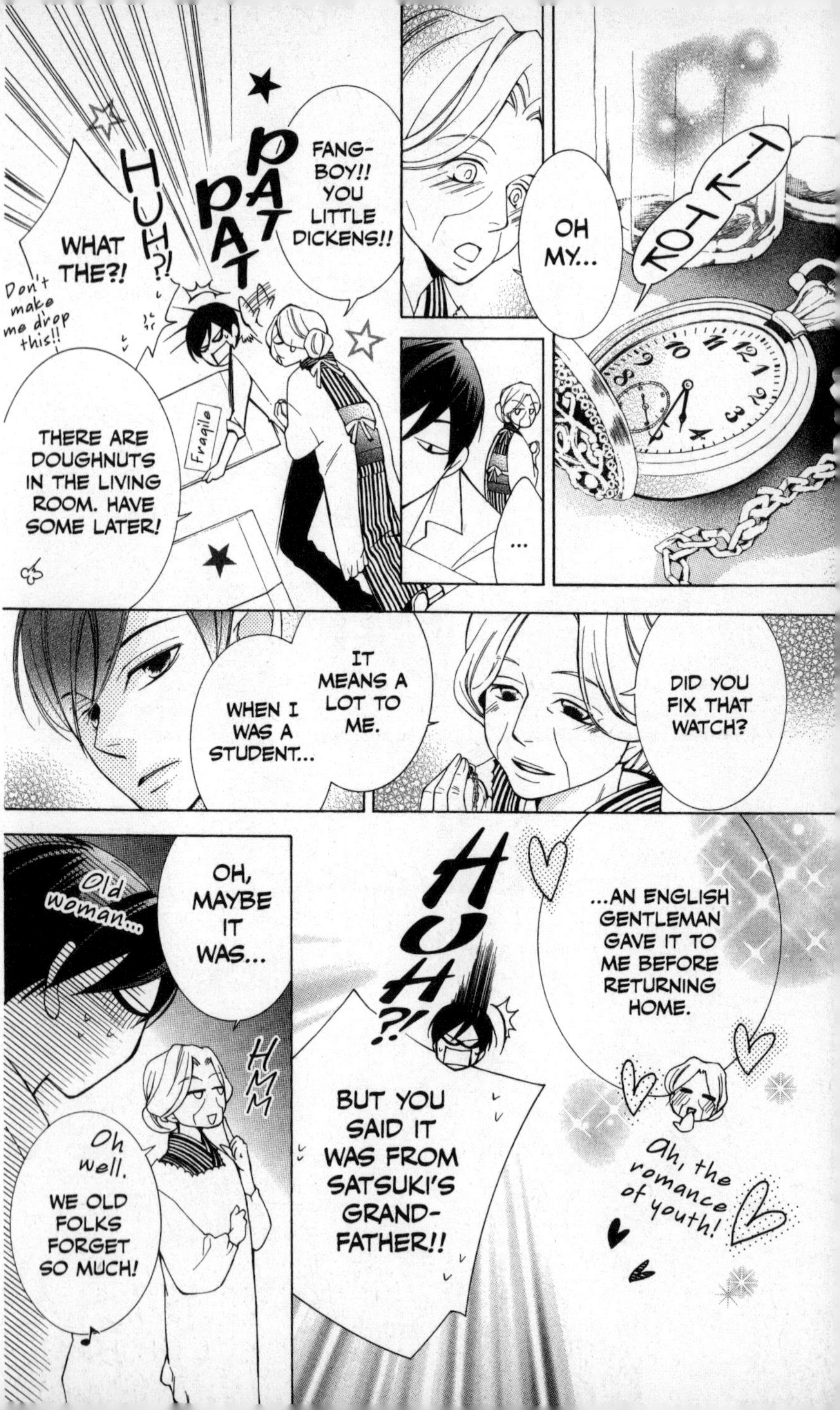
TIK TOK
OH MY...
...
FANG-BOY!! YOU LITTLE DICKENS!!
PAT PAT
HUH?!
WHAT THE?!
Don't make me drop this!!
Fragile
THERE ARE DOUGHNUTS IN THE LIVING ROOM. HAVE SOME LATER!
DID YOU FIX THAT WATCH?
IT MEANS A LOT TO ME.
WHEN I WAS A STUDENT...
...AN ENGLISH GENTLEMAN GAVE IT TO ME BEFORE RETURNING HOME.
Ah, the romance of youth!
HUH?!
BUT YOU SAID IT WAS FROM SATSUKI'S GRANDFATHER!!
OH, MAYBE IT WAS...
Old woman...
HMM
Oh well.
WE OLD FOLKS FORGET SO MUCH!

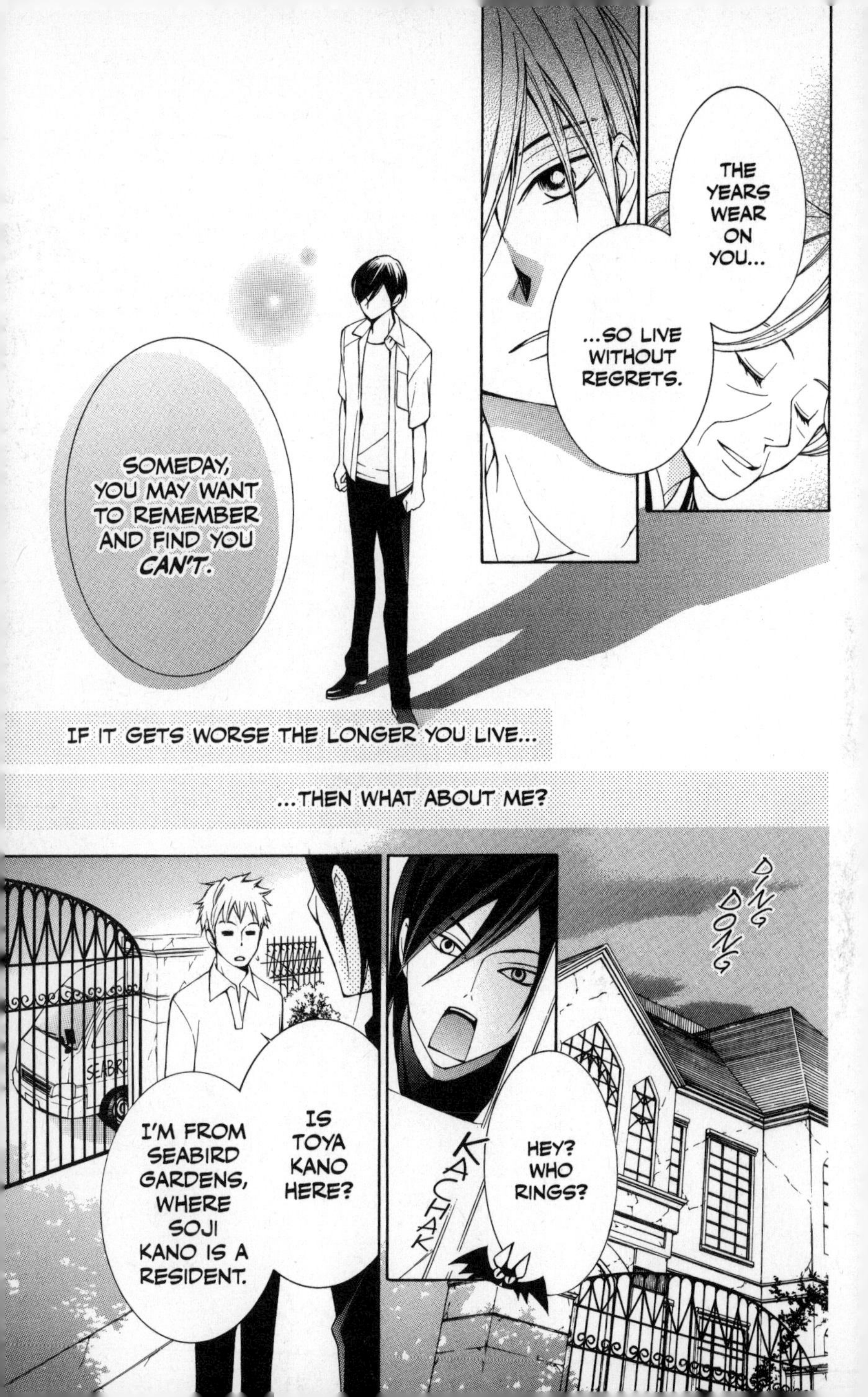
THE YEARS WEAR ON YOU...
...SO LIVE WITHOUT REGRETS.
SOMEDAY, YOU MAY WANT TO REMEMBER AND FIND YOU *CAN'T*.
IF IT GETS WORSE THE LONGER YOU LIVE...
...THEN WHAT ABOUT ME?
DING DONG
KACHAK
HEY? WHO RINGS?
IS TOYA KANO HERE?
I'M FROM SEABIRD GARDENS, WHERE SOJI KANO IS A RESIDENT.

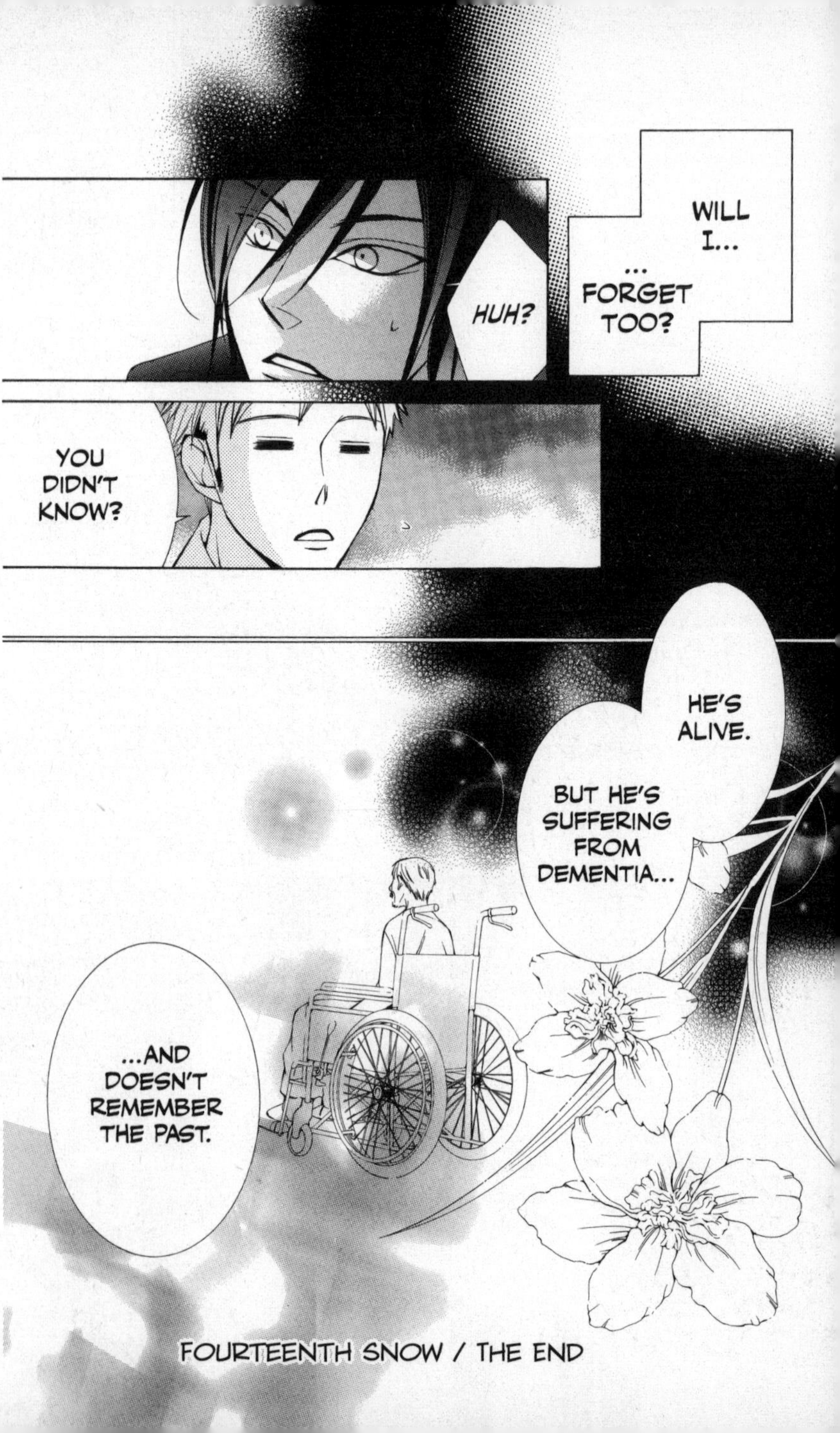
WILL I...
...FORGET TOO?
HUH?
YOU DIDN'T KNOW?
HE'S ALIVE.
BUT HE'S SUFFERING FROM DEMENTIA...
...AND DOESN'T REMEMBER THE PAST.
FOURTEENTH SNOW / THE END

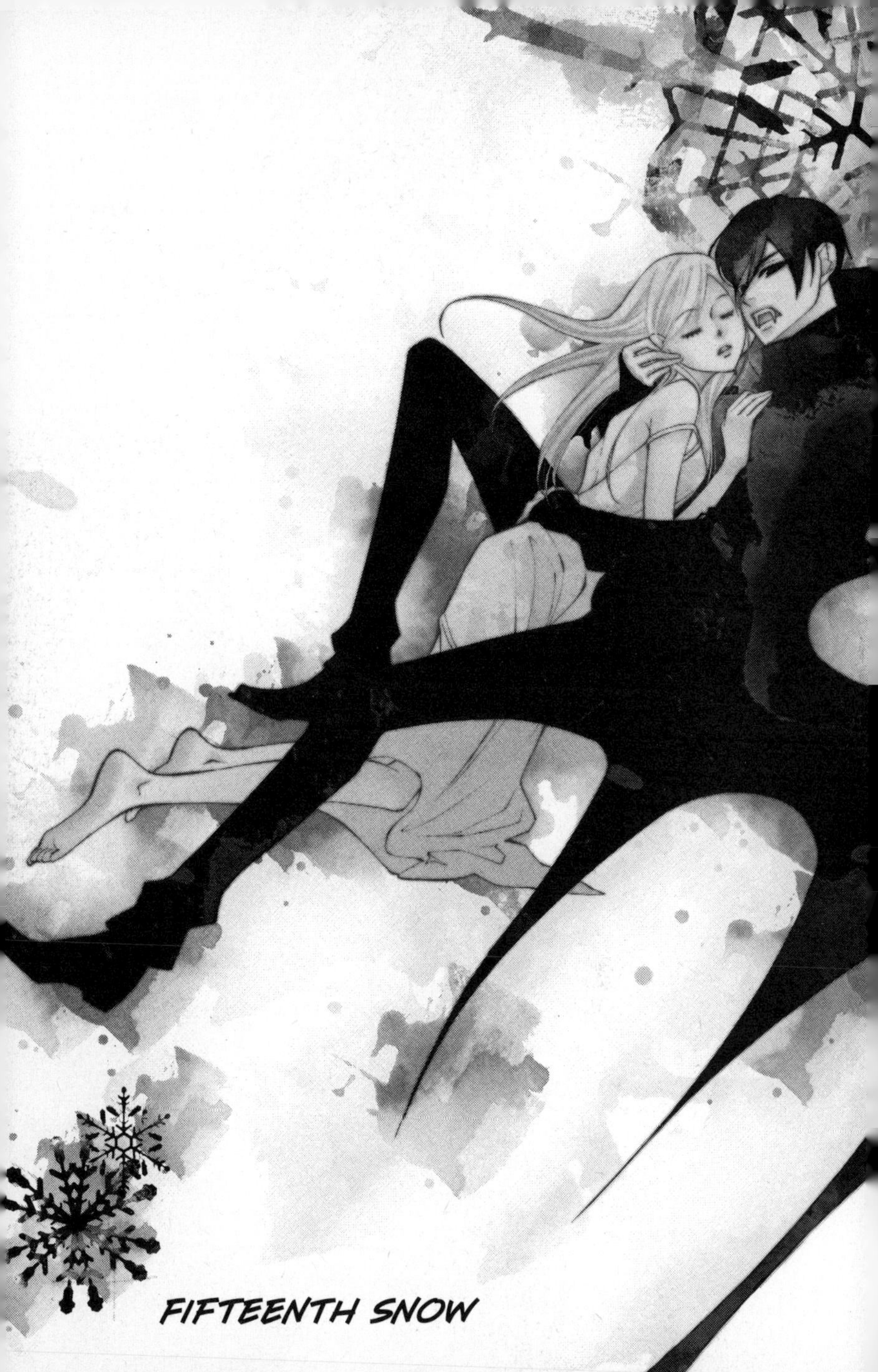

FIFTEENTH SNOW

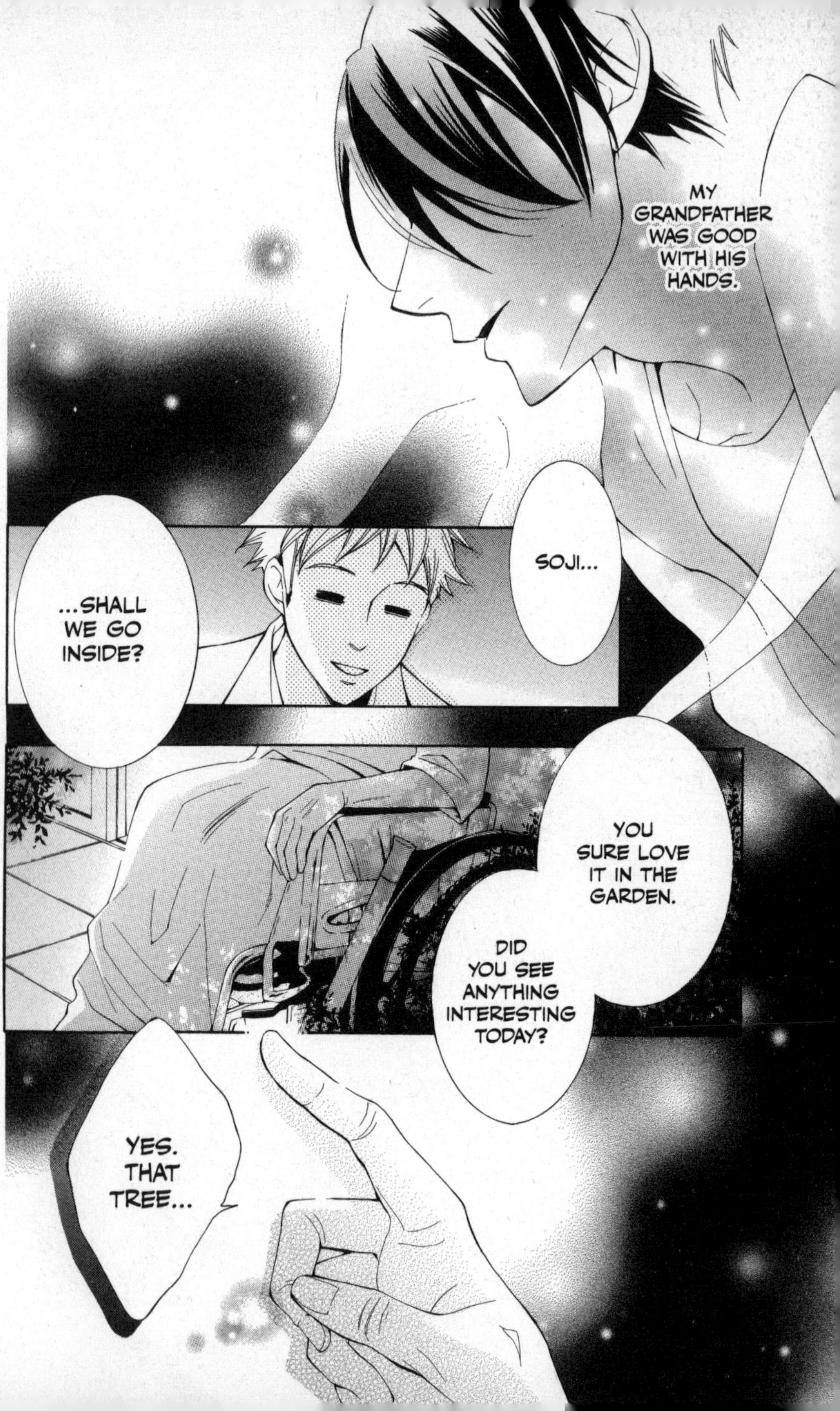
MY GRANDFATHER WAS GOOD WITH HIS HANDS.
SOJI...
...SHALL WE GO INSIDE?
YOU SURE LOVE IT IN THE GARDEN.
DID YOU SEE ANYTHING INTERESTING TODAY?
YES. THAT TREE...

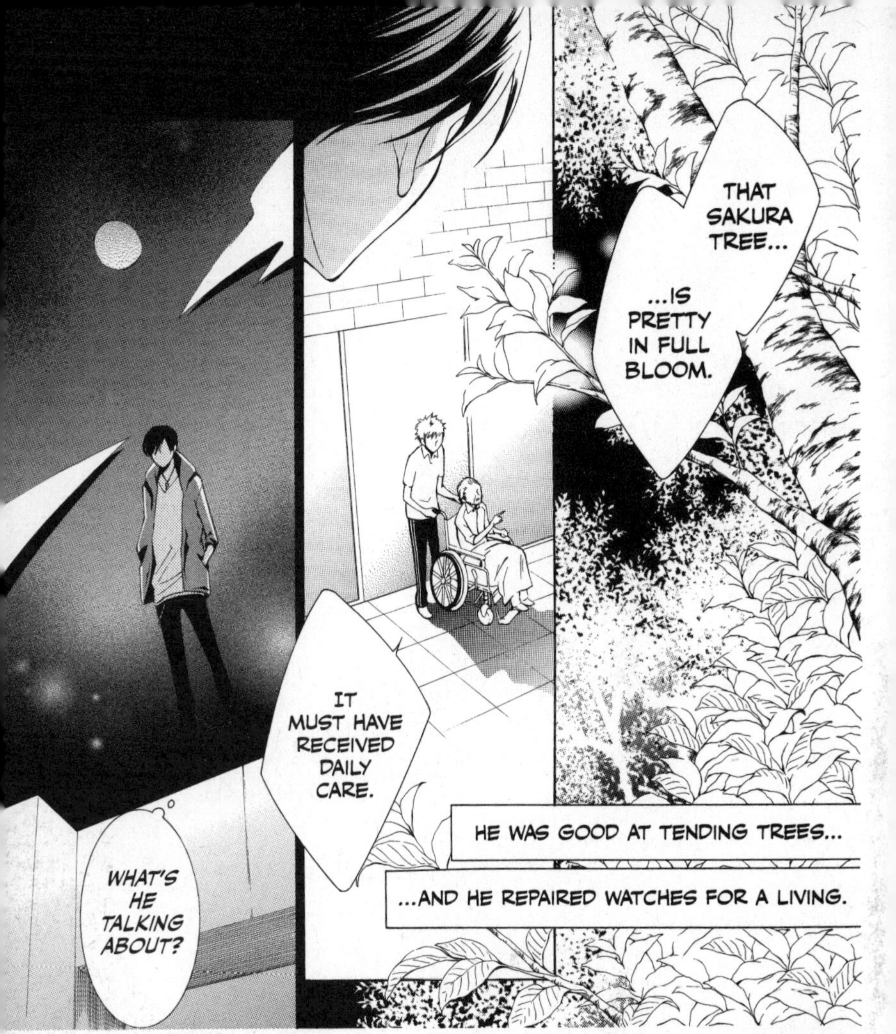
THAT SAKURA TREE...
...IS PRETTY IN FULL BLOOM.
IT MUST HAVE RECEIVED DAILY CARE.
HE WAS GOOD AT TENDING TREES...
...AND HE REPAIRED WATCHES FOR A LIVING.
WHAT'S HE TALKING ABOUT?

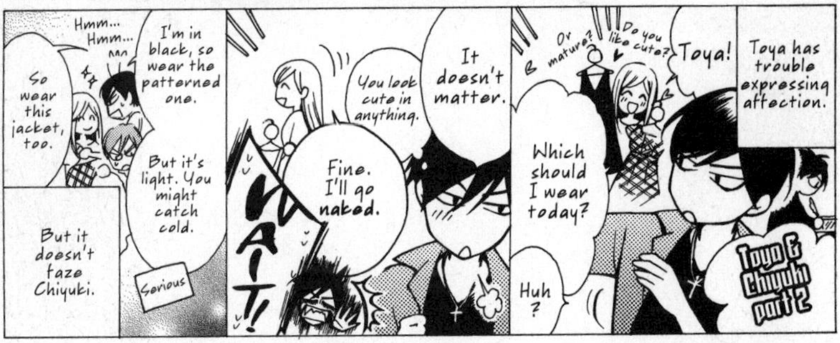
Toya has trouble expressing affection.
Toya & Chiyuki part 2
Toya!
Do you like cute?
Or mature?
Which should I wear today?
Huh?
It doesn't matter.
You look cute in anything.
Fine. I'll go naked.
WAIT!!
I'm in black, so wear the patterned one.
Hmm... Hmm...
So wear this jacket, too.
But it's light. You might catch cold.
Serious
But it doesn't faze Chiyuki.

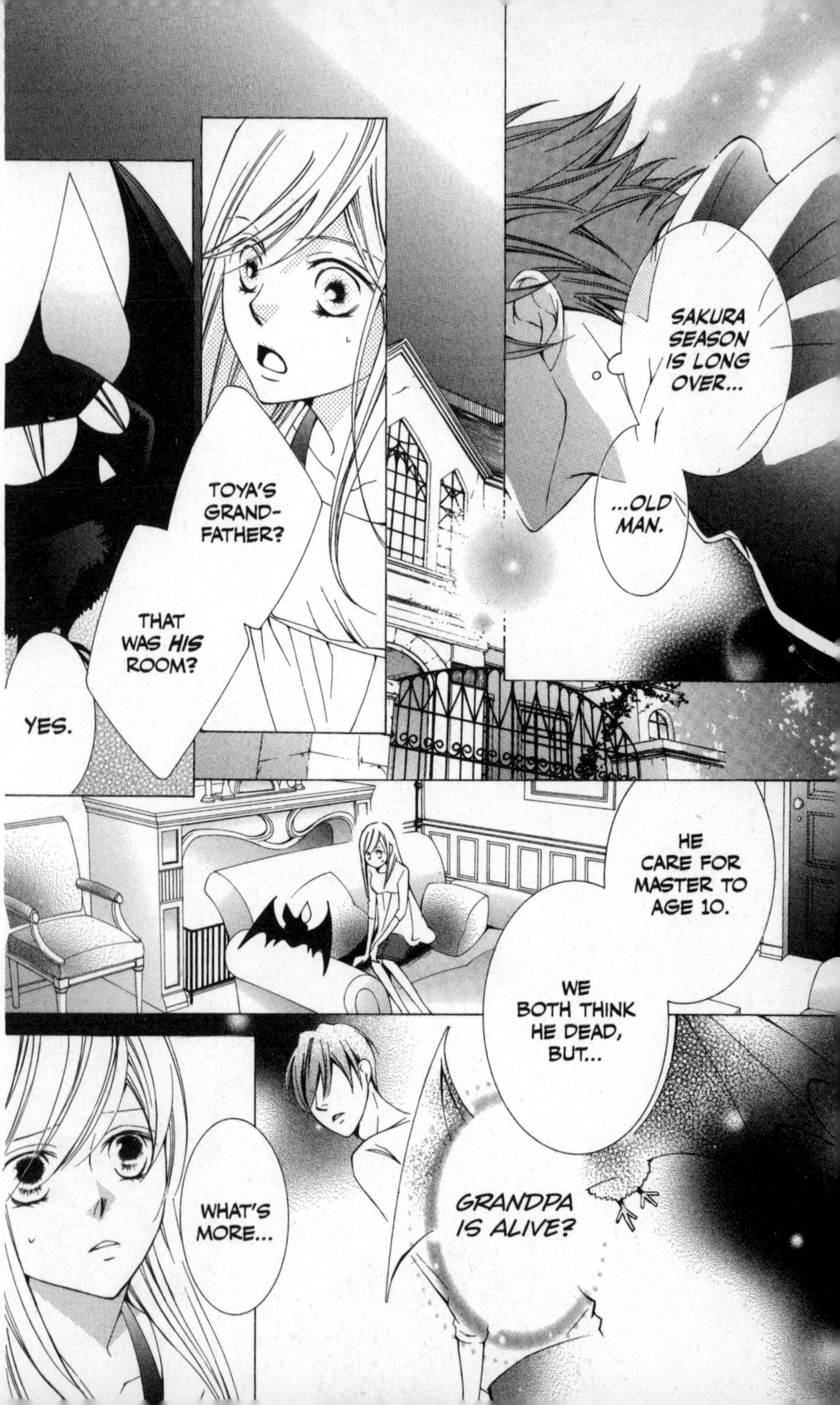
SAKURA SEASON IS LONG OVER...
...OLD MAN.
TOYA'S GRAND-FATHER?
THAT WAS *HIS* ROOM?
YES.
HE CARE FOR MASTER TO AGE 10.
WE BOTH THINK HE DEAD, BUT...
GRANDPA IS ALIVE?
WHAT'S MORE...

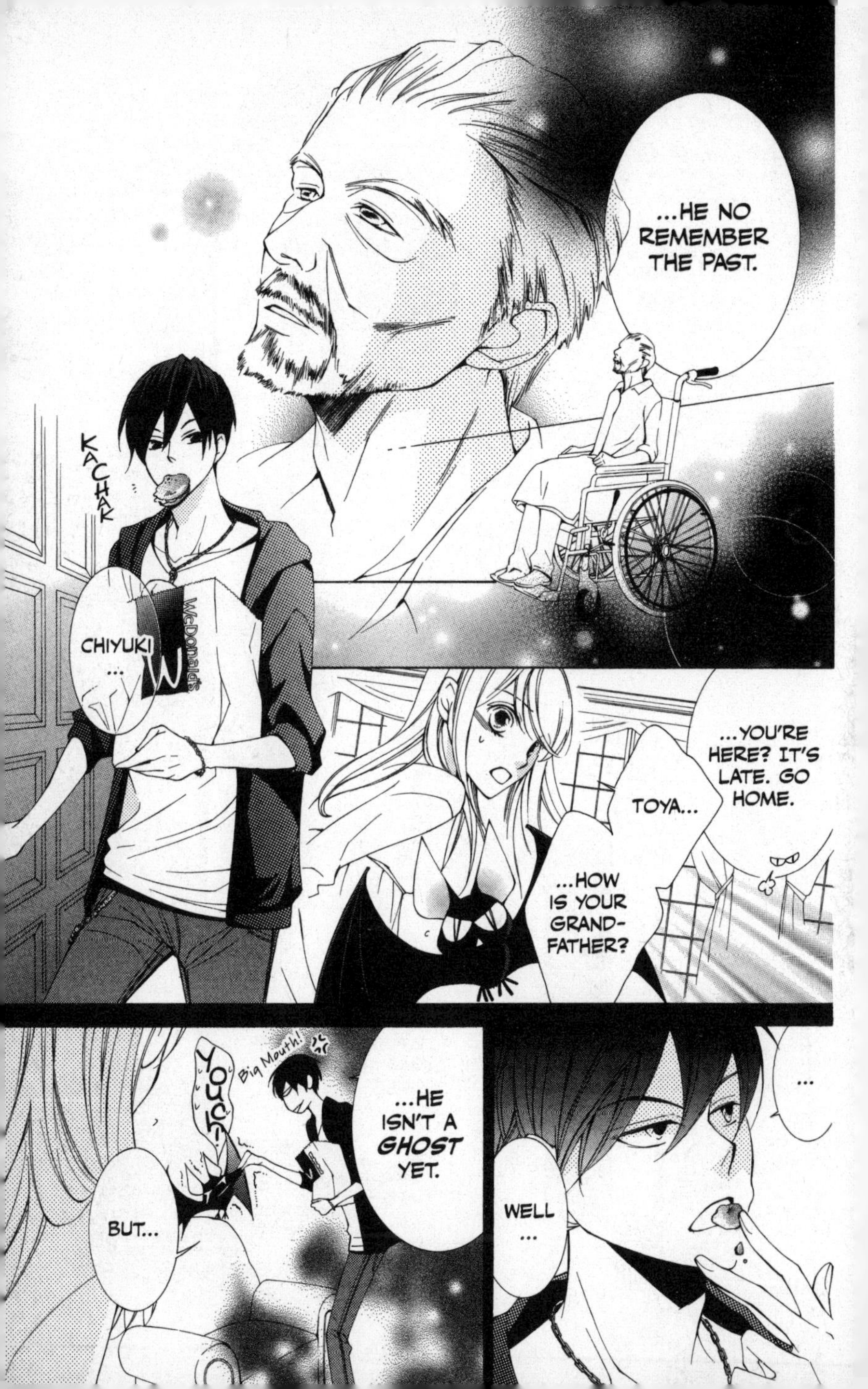
...HE NO REMEMBER THE PAST.
...YOU'RE HERE? IT'S LATE. GO HOME.
TOYA...
...HOW IS YOUR GRAND-FATHER?
KACHAK
CHIYUKI ...
...
WELL ...
...HE ISN'T A GHOST YET.
Big Mouth!
YOUCH!
BUT...

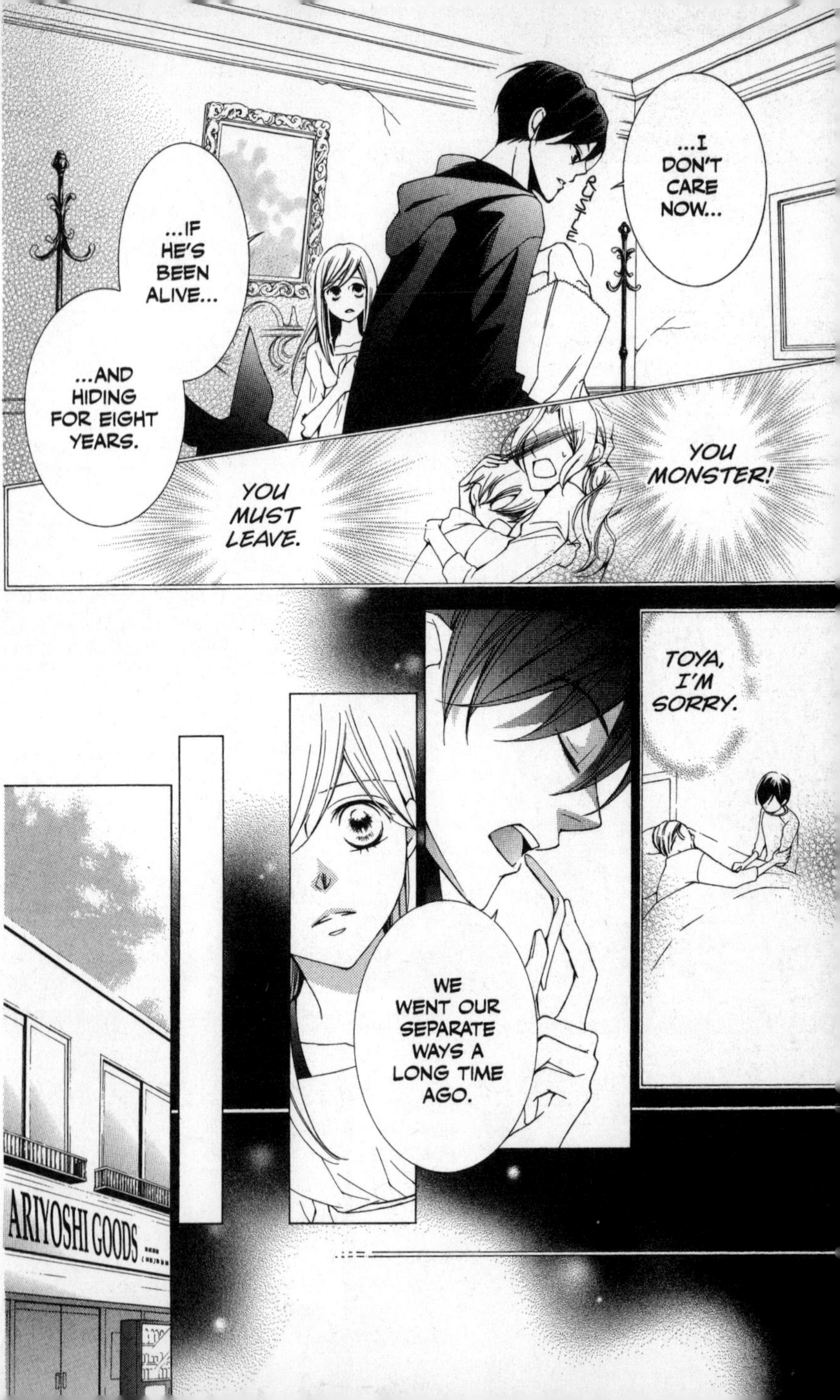
...I DON'T CARE NOW...
RUSTLE
...IF HE'S BEEN ALIVE...
...AND HIDING FOR EIGHT YEARS.
YOU MONSTER!
YOU MUST LEAVE.
TOYA, I'M SORRY.
WE WENT OUR SEPARATE WAYS A LONG TIME AGO.
ARIYOSHI GOODS

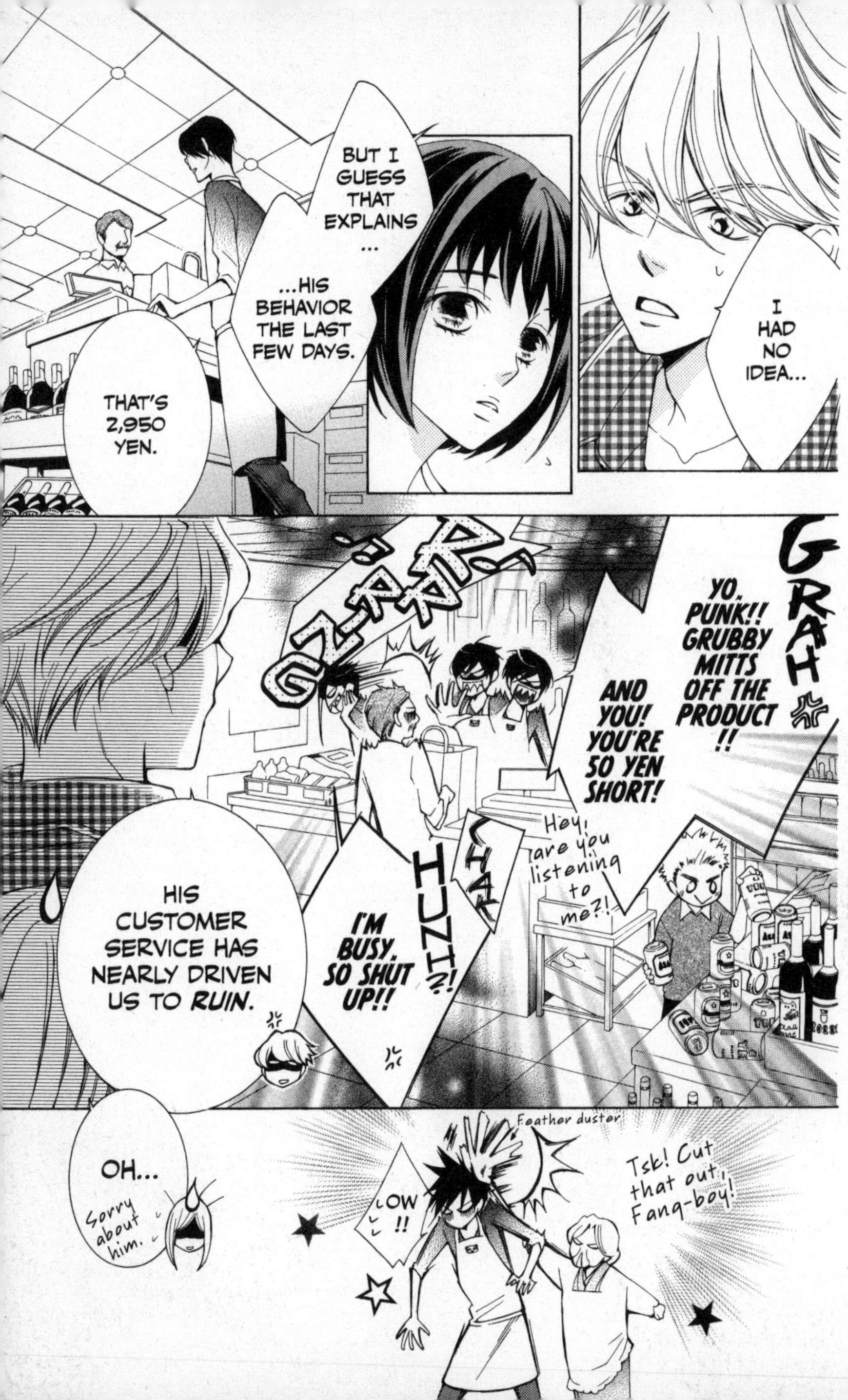
I HAD NO IDEA...
BUT I GUESS THAT EXPLAINS...
...HIS BEHAVIOR THE LAST FEW DAYS.
THAT'S 2,950 YEN.
GRAH
YO, PUNK!! GRUBBY MITTS OFF THE PRODUCT!!
AND YOU! YOU'RE SO YEN SHORT!
GZ-RRR
Hey, are you listening to me?!
CHA
HUNH?!
I'M BUSY, SO SHUT UP!!
HIS CUSTOMER SERVICE HAS NEARLY DRIVEN US TO RUIN.
Tsk! Cut that out, Fang-boy!
Feather duster
LOW!!
OH...
Sorry about him.

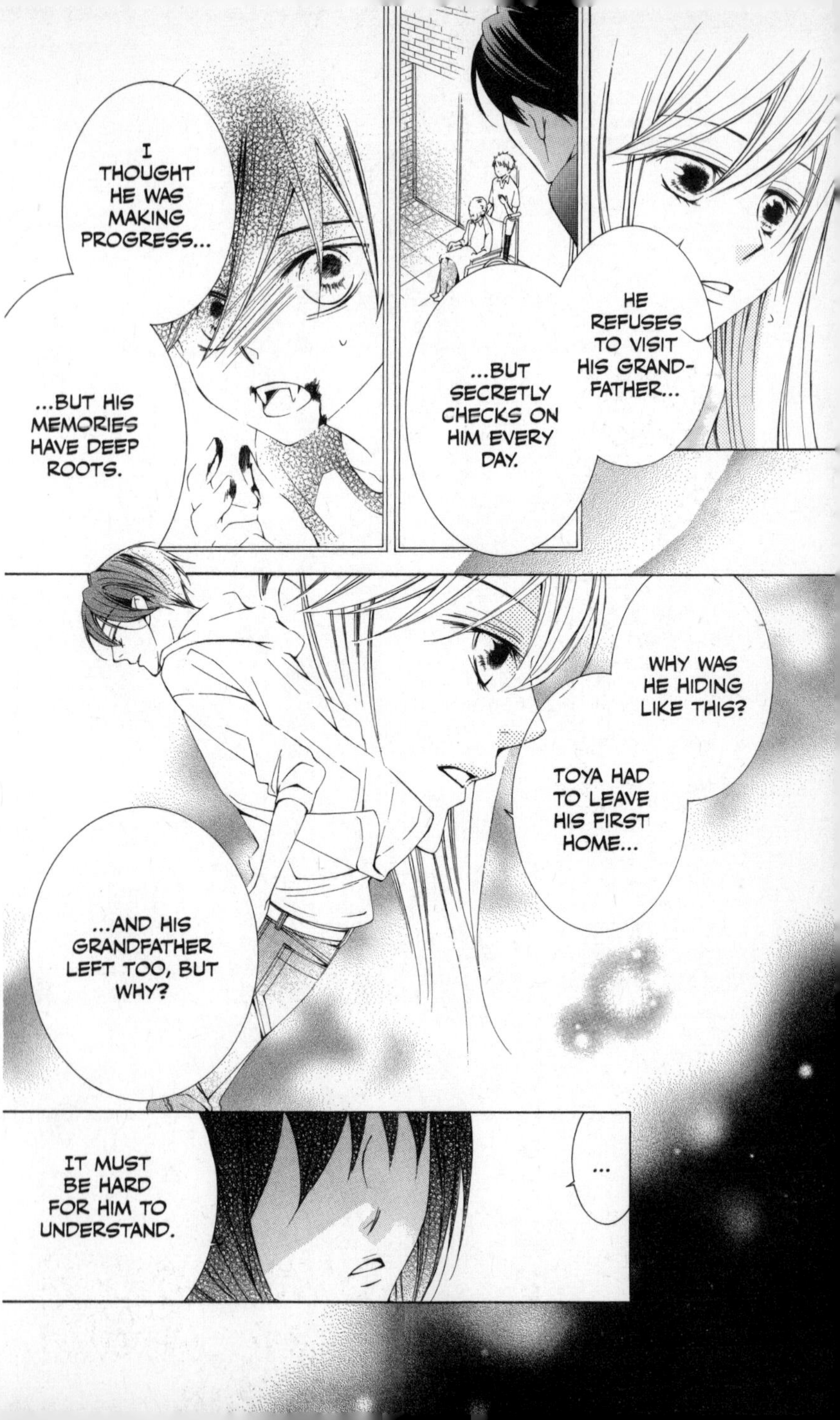
HE REFUSES TO VISIT HIS GRAND-FATHER...
...BUT SECRETLY CHECKS ON HIM EVERY DAY.
I THOUGHT HE WAS MAKING PROGRESS...
...BUT HIS MEMORIES HAVE DEEP ROOTS.
WHY WAS HE HIDING LIKE THIS?
TOYA HAD TO LEAVE HIS FIRST HOME...
...AND HIS GRANDFATHER LEFT TOO, BUT WHY?
...
IT MUST BE HARD FOR HIM TO UNDERSTAND.

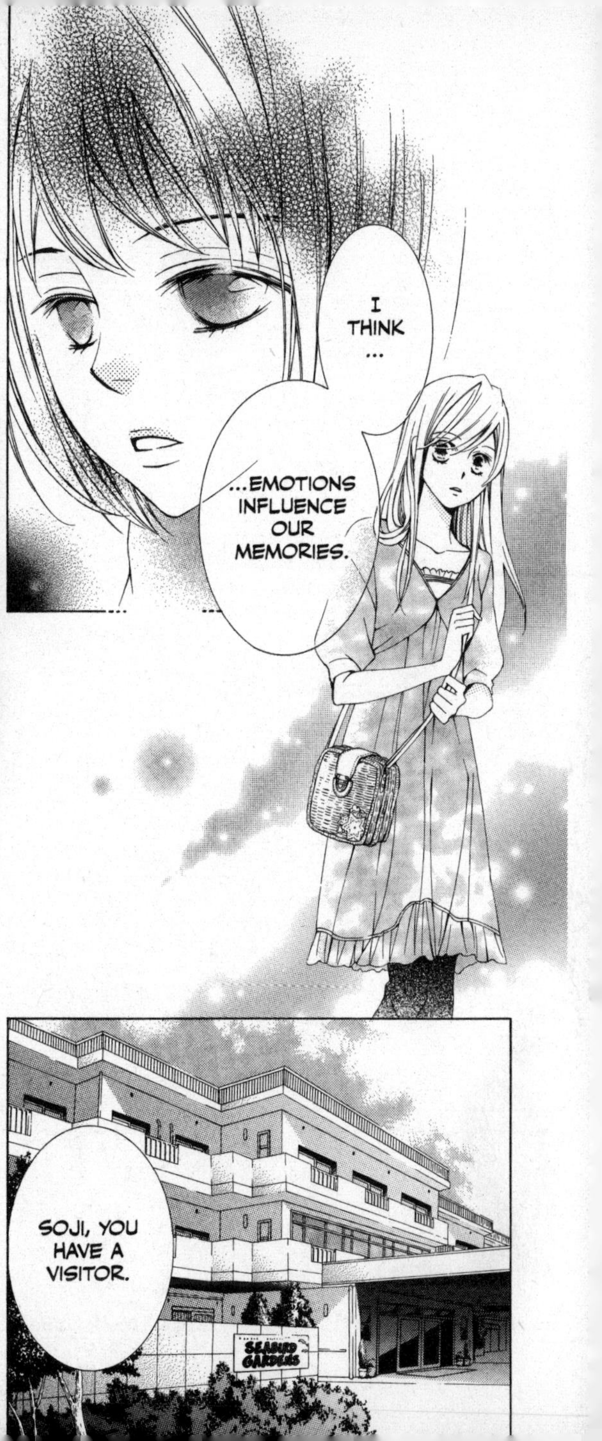
I THINK ...
...EMOTIONS INFLUENCE OUR MEMORIES.
SOJI, YOU HAVE A VISITOR.
SEABIRD GARDENS

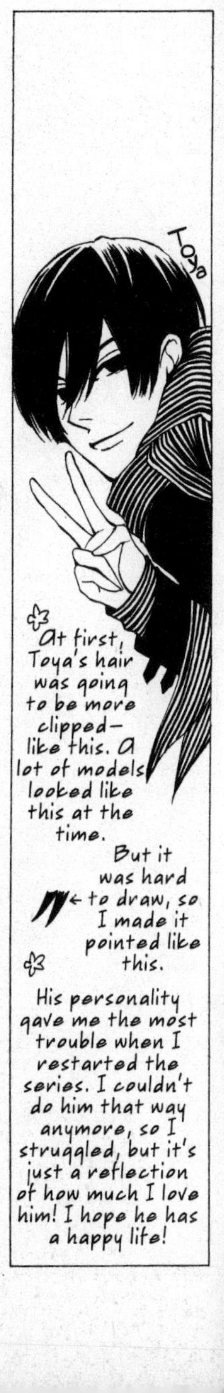
Toya

At first, Toya's hair was going to be more clipped—like this. A lot of models looked like this at the time.

But it was hard ← to draw, so I made it pointed like this.

His personality gave me the most trouble when I restarted the series. I couldn't do him that way anymore, so I struggled, but it's just a reflection of how much I love him! I hope he has a happy life!

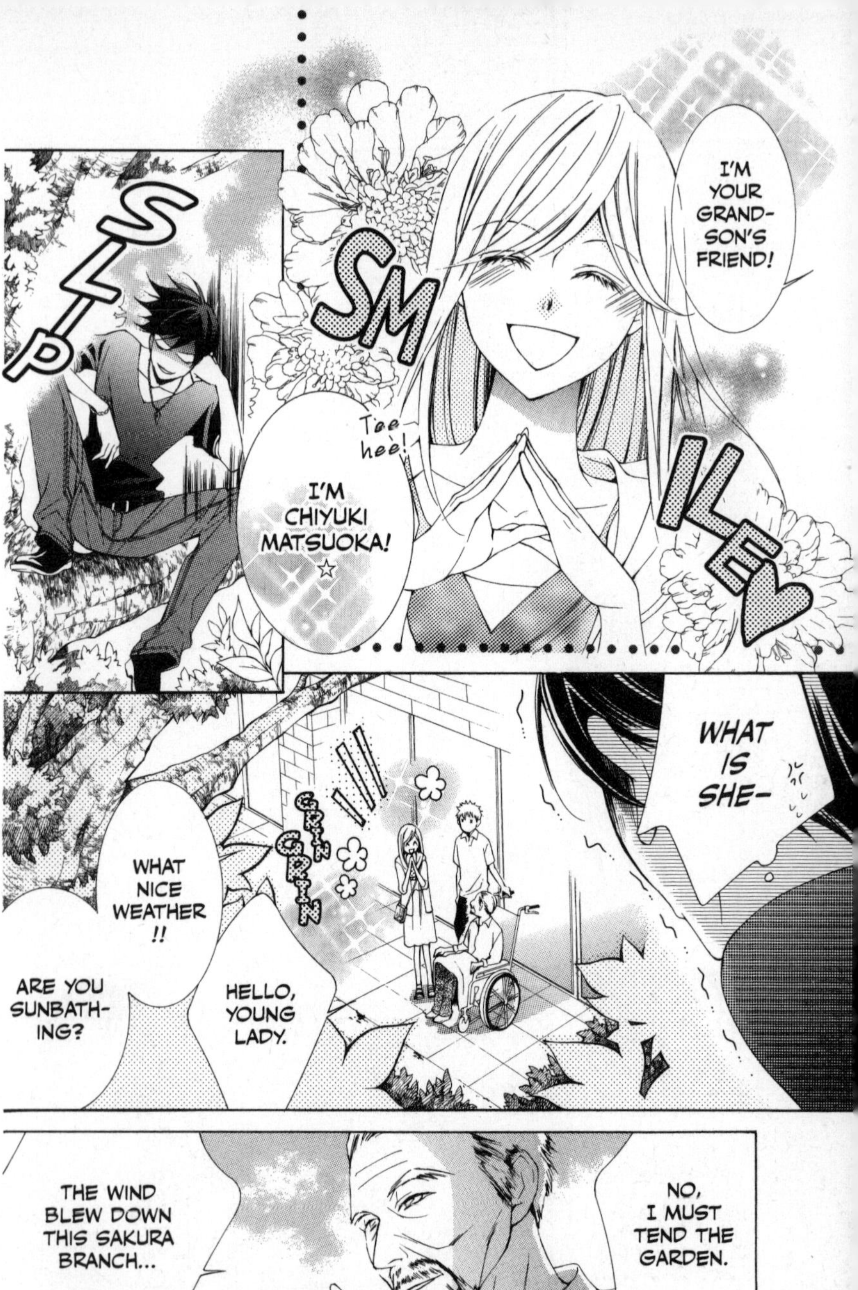
I'M YOUR GRAND-SON'S FRIEND!
SMILE♥
Tee hee!
I'M CHIYUKI MATSUOKA! ☆
SLIP
WHAT IS SHE-
GRIN GRIN
WHAT NICE WEATHER !!
HELLO, YOUNG LADY.
ARE YOU SUNBATH-ING?
NO, I MUST TEND THE GARDEN.
THE WIND BLEW DOWN THIS SAKURA BRANCH...

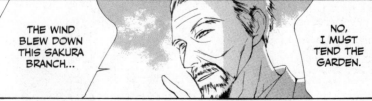

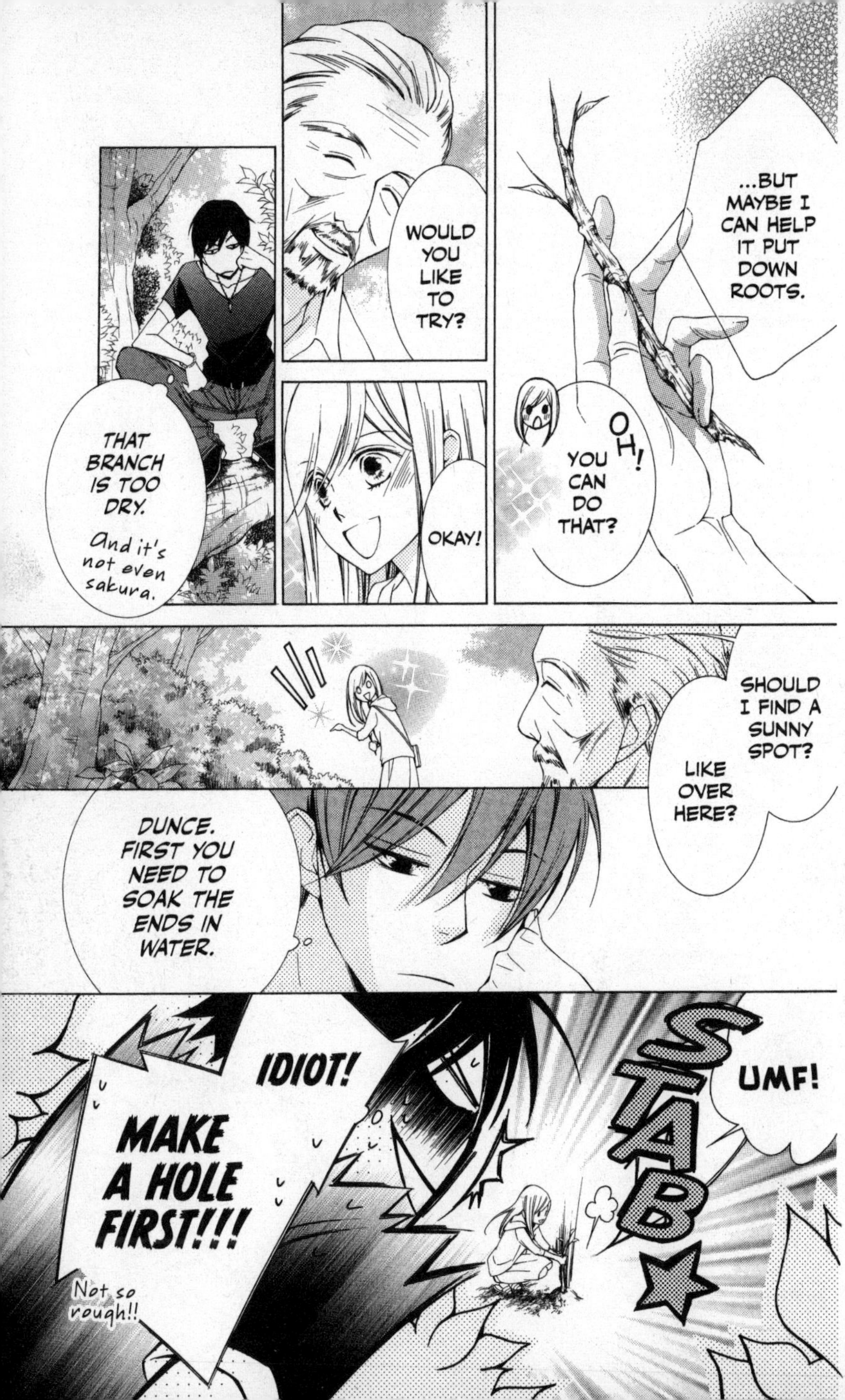
...BUT MAYBE I CAN HELP IT PUT DOWN ROOTS.
OH!
YOU CAN DO THAT?
WOULD YOU LIKE TO TRY?
OKAY!
THAT BRANCH IS TOO DRY.
And it's not even sakura.
SHOULD I FIND A SUNNY SPOT?
LIKE OVER HERE?
DUNCE. FIRST YOU NEED TO SOAK THE ENDS IN WATER.
UMF!
STAB
IDIOT!
MAKE A HOLE FIRST!!!
Not so rough!!

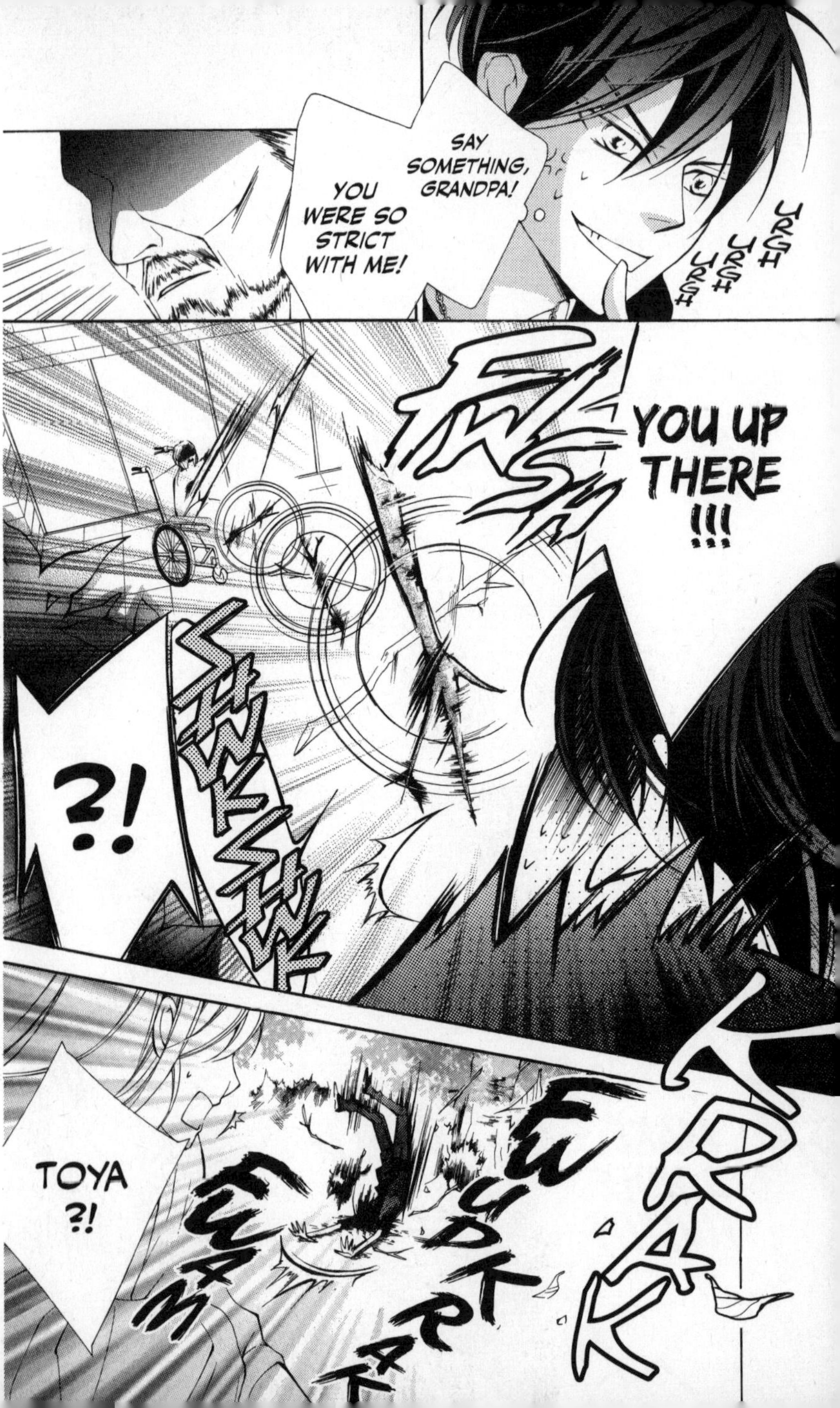
URGH URGH URGH
SAY SOMETHING, GRANDPA!
YOU WERE SO STRICT WITH ME!
FWSH
YOU UP THERE!!!
SHWSHWK
?!
KRAK
FWUDK
FWAM
TOYA?!

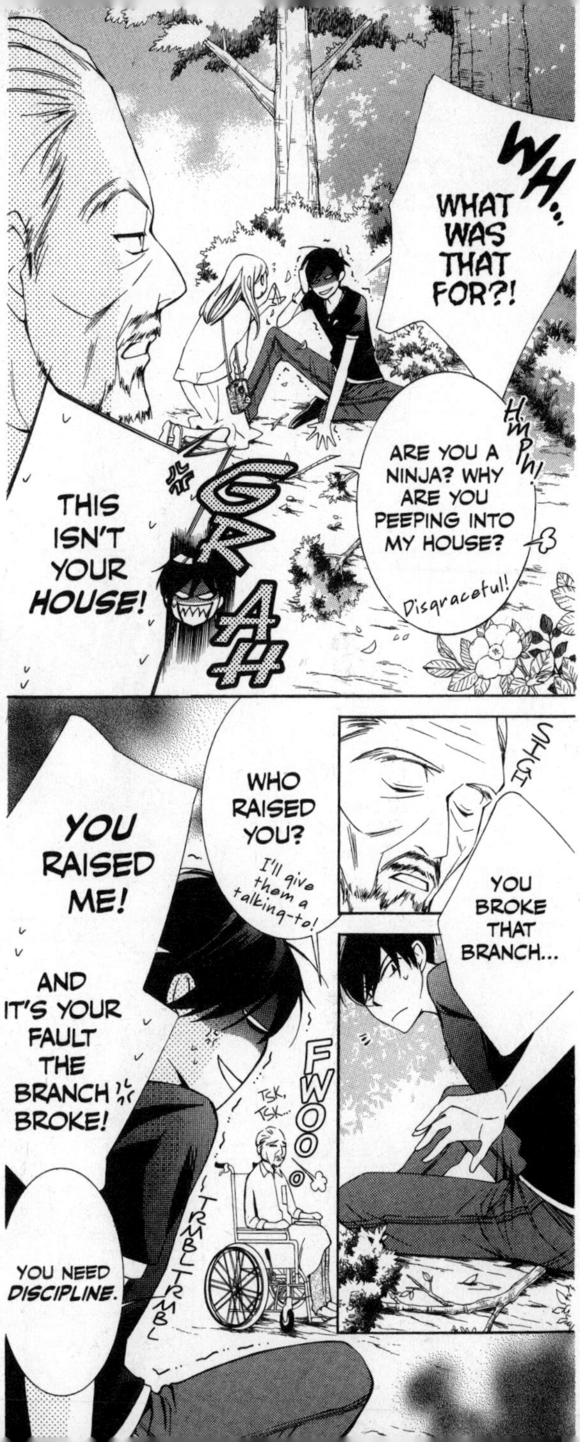
WH...
WHAT WAS THAT FOR?!
HMPH!
ARE YOU A NINJA? WHY ARE YOU PEEPING INTO MY HOUSE?
Disgraceful!
THIS ISN'T YOUR HOUSE!
GRAAH
SIGH
YOU BROKE THAT BRANCH...
WHO RAISED YOU?
I'll give them a talking-to!
YOU RAISED ME!
AND IT'S YOUR FAULT THE BRANCH BROKE!
FWOOO
TSK, TSK...
TRMBL TRMBL
YOU NEED DISCIPLINE.

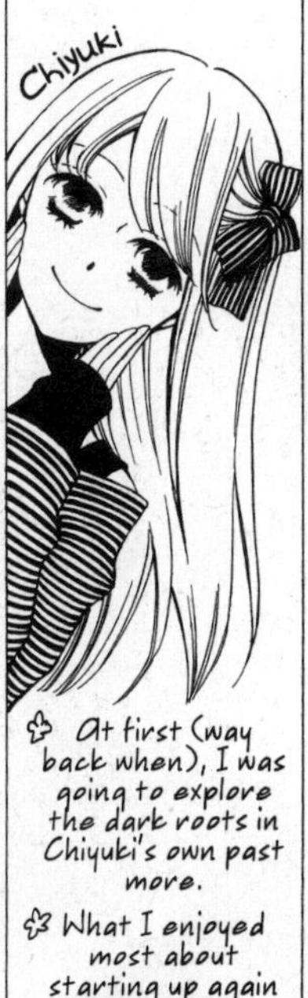
Chiyuki

- At first (way back when), I was going to explore the dark roots in Chiyuki's own past more.
- What I enjoyed most about starting up again after ten years was thinking about what Chiyuki should be like.

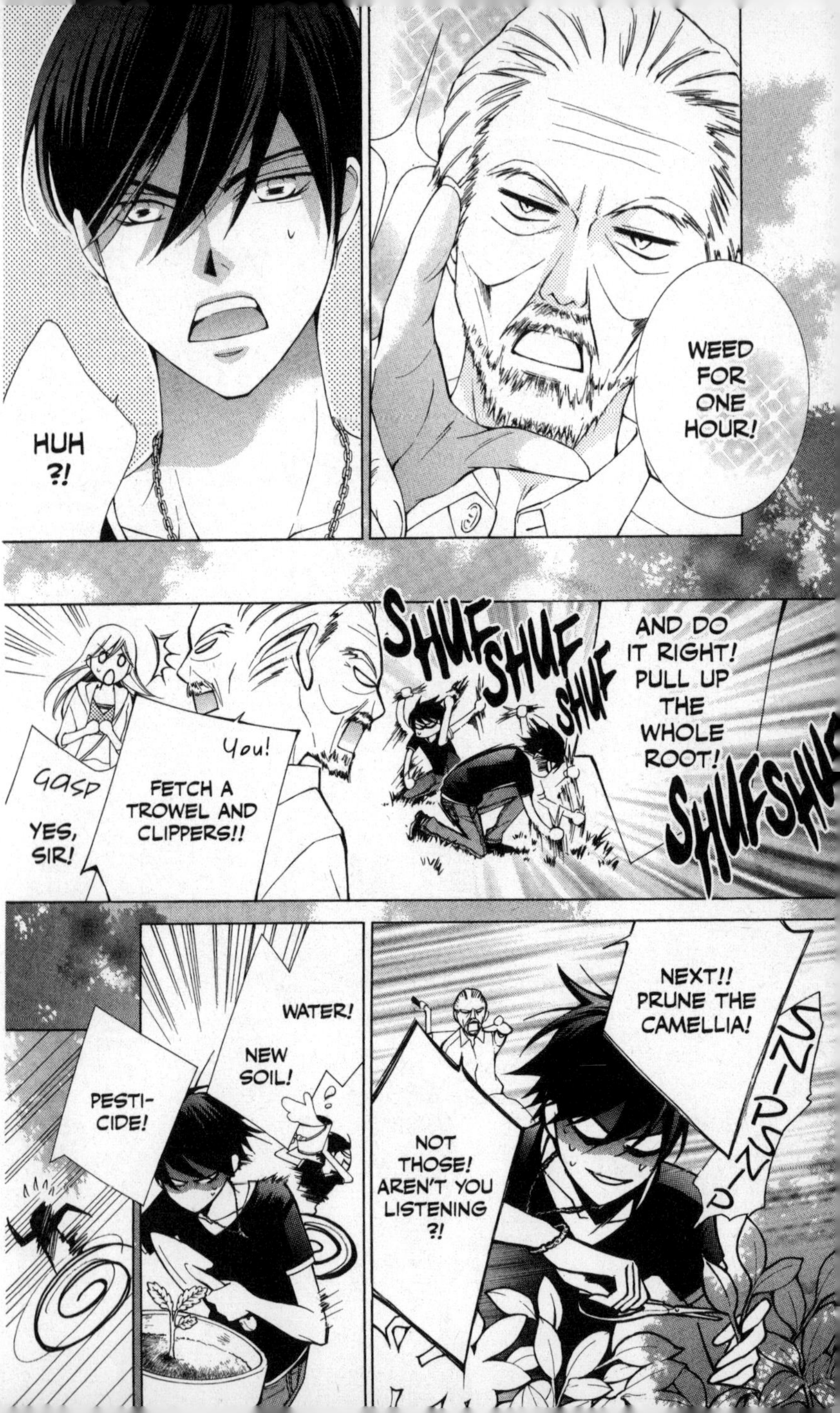
WEED FOR ONE HOUR!
HUH ?!
AND DO IT RIGHT! PULL UP THE WHOLE ROOT!
SHUF SHUF SHUF
SHUFSHU
You!
FETCH A TROWEL AND CLIPPERS!!
Gasp
YES, SIR!
NEXT!! PRUNE THE CAMELLIA!
SNIPSNIP
NOT THOSE! AREN'T YOU LISTENING ?!
WATER!
NEW SOIL!
PESTI-CIDE!

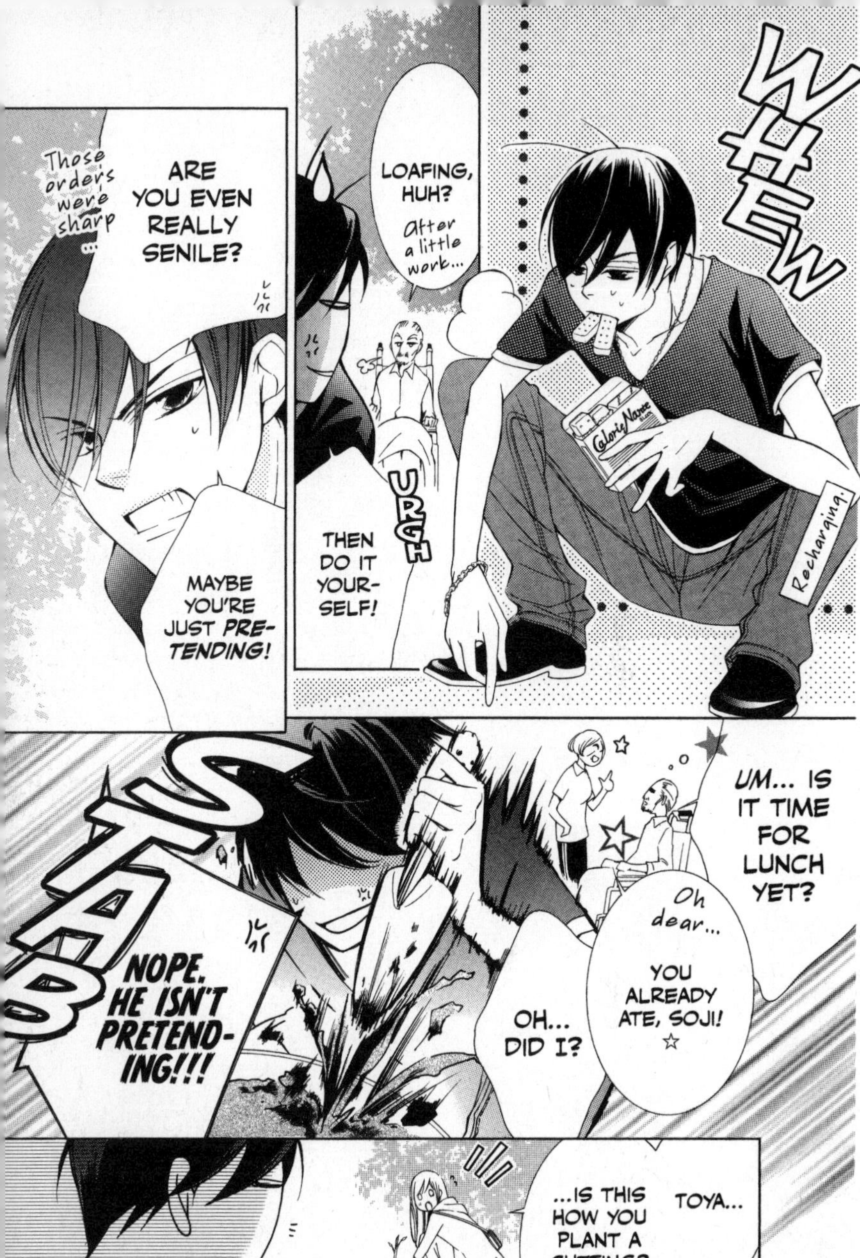
WHEW
Recharging.
LOAFING, HUH?
After a little work...
URGH
THEN DO IT YOURSELF!
ARE YOU EVEN REALLY SENILE?
Those orders were sharp...
MAYBE YOU'RE JUST PRETENDING!
UM... IS IT TIME FOR LUNCH YET?
Oh dear...
YOU ALREADY ATE, SOJI!
OH... DID I?
STAB
NOPE. HE ISN'T PRETENDING!!!
TOYA...
...IS THIS HOW YOU PLANT A CUTTING?

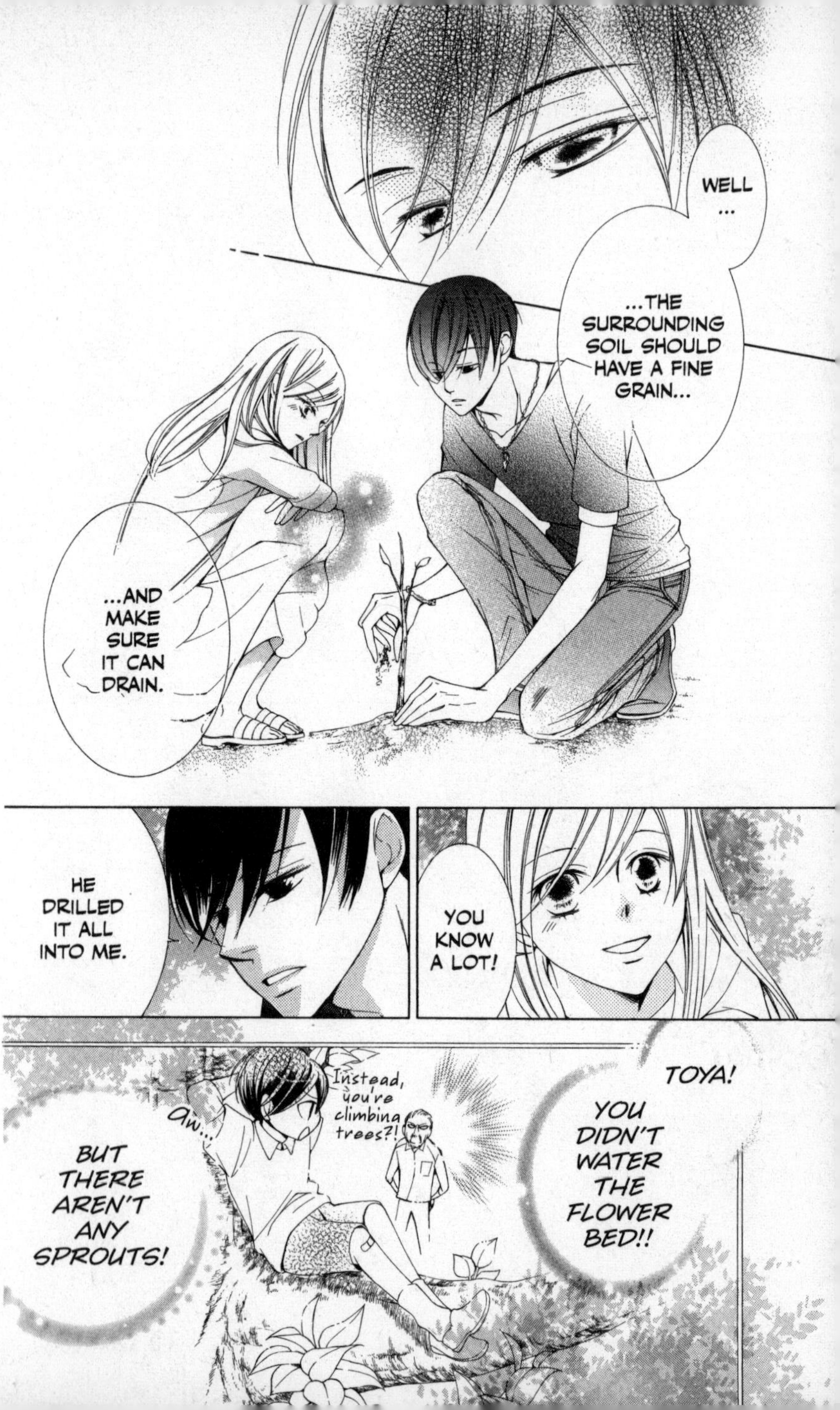
WELL...
...THE SURROUNDING SOIL SHOULD HAVE A FINE GRAIN...
...AND MAKE SURE IT CAN DRAIN.
YOU KNOW A LOT!
HE DRILLED IT ALL INTO ME.
TOYA!
YOU DIDN'T WATER THE FLOWER BED!!
Instead, you're climbing trees?!
aw...
BUT THERE AREN'T ANY SPROUTS!

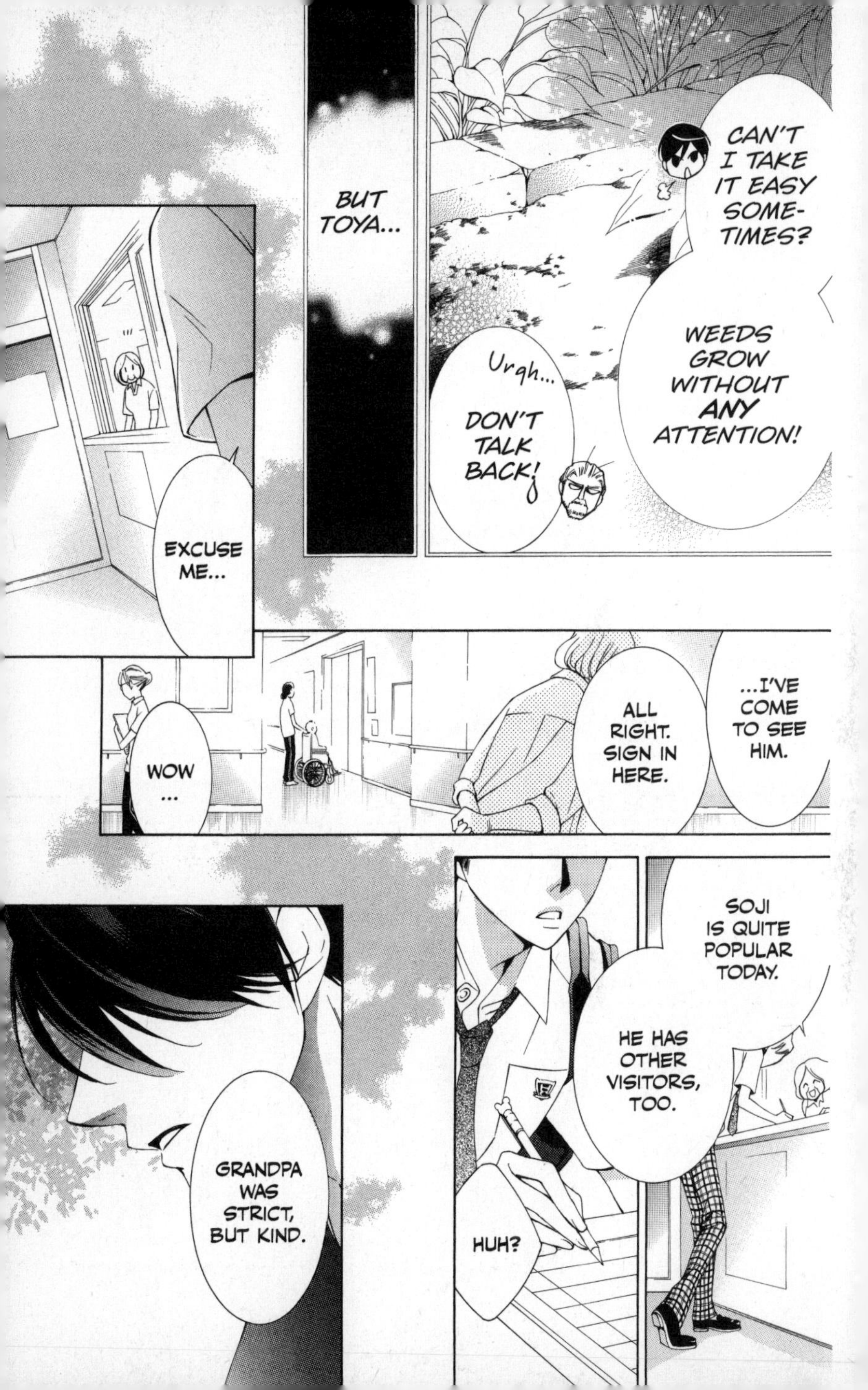
CAN'T I TAKE IT EASY SOME-TIMES?
WEEDS GROW WITHOUT ANY ATTENTION!
Urgh...
DON'T TALK BACK!
BUT TOYA...
EXCUSE ME...
...I'VE COME TO SEE HIM.
ALL RIGHT. SIGN IN HERE.
WOW ...
SOJI IS QUITE POPULAR TODAY.
HE HAS OTHER VISITORS, TOO.
HUH?
GRANDPA WAS STRICT, BUT KIND.

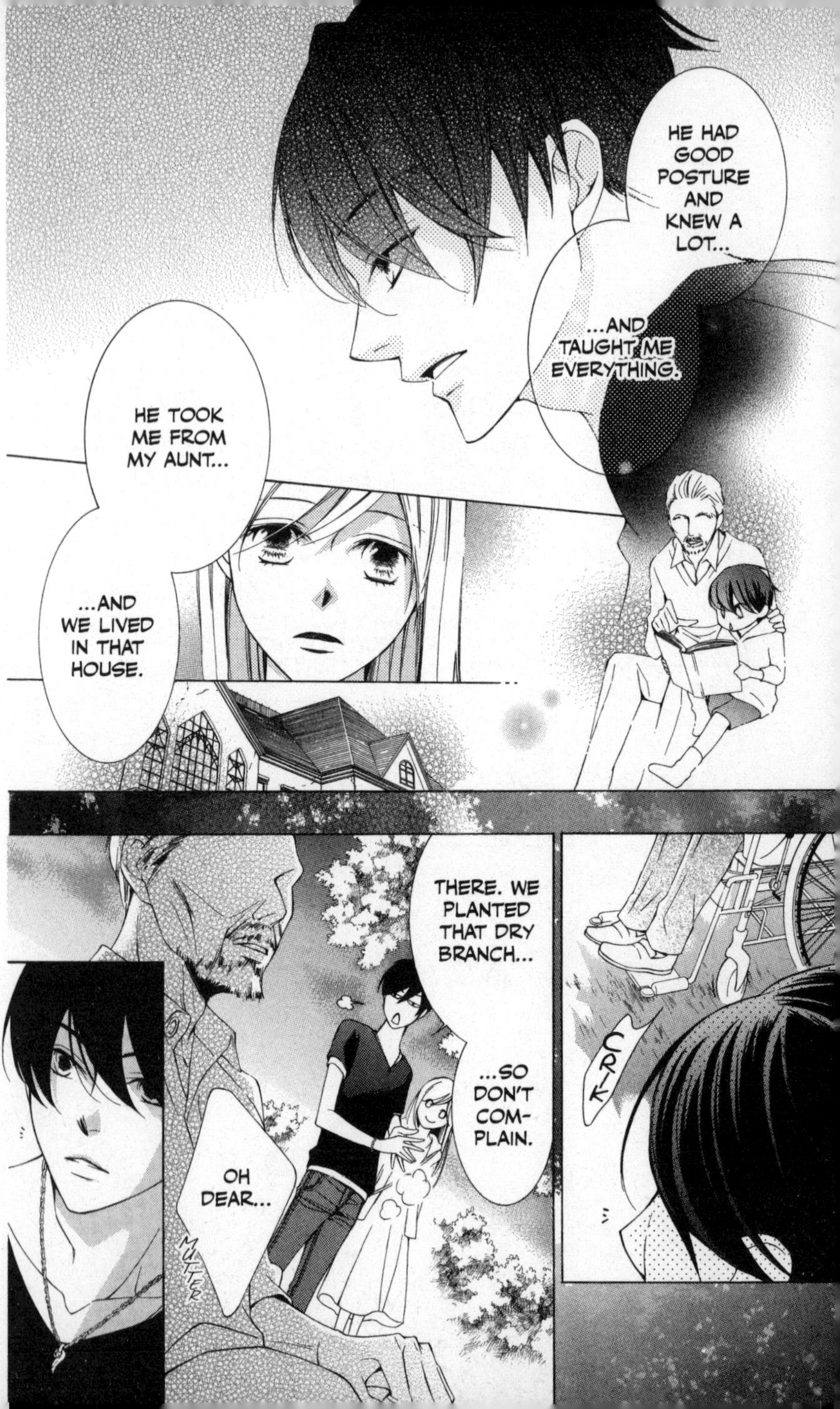
HE HAD GOOD POSTURE AND KNEW A LOT...
...AND TAUGHT ME EVERYTHING.
HE TOOK ME FROM MY AUNT...
...AND WE LIVED IN THAT HOUSE.
CRIK
THERE. WE PLANTED THAT DRY BRANCH...
...SO DON'T COM-PLAIN.
OH DEAR...
MUTTER

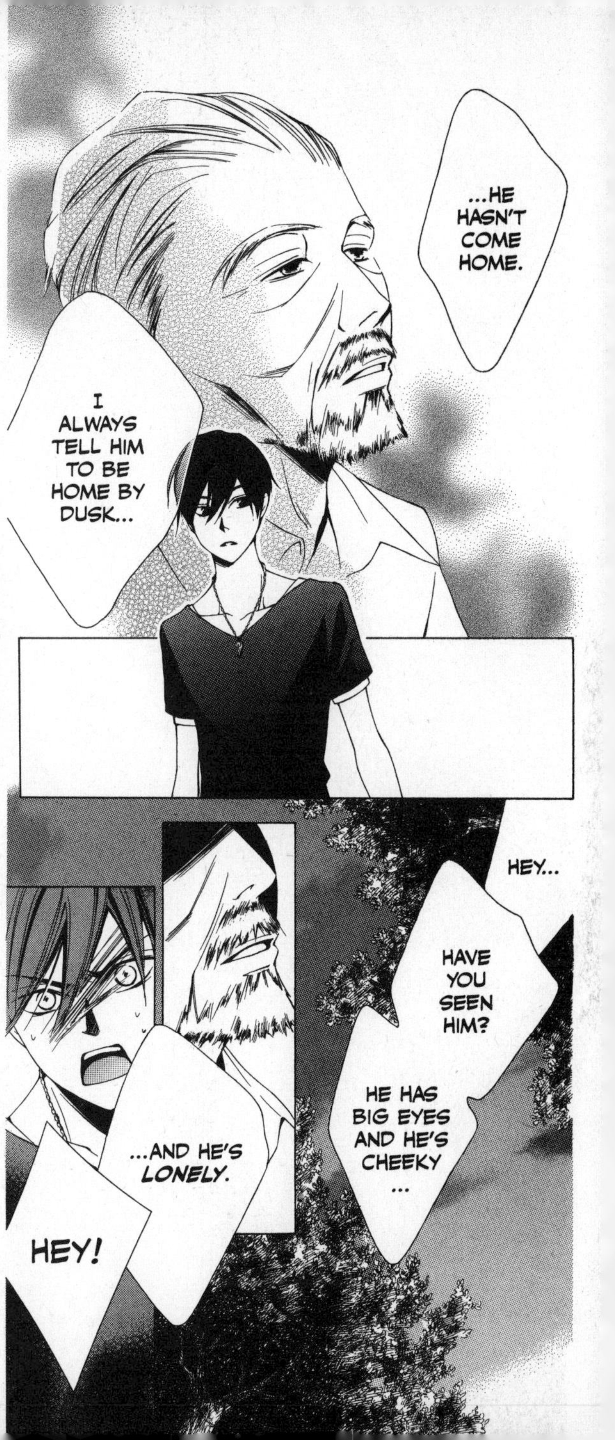
...HE HASN'T COME HOME.
I ALWAYS TELL HIM TO BE HOME BY DUSK...
HEY...
HAVE YOU SEEN HIM?
HE HAS BIG EYES AND HE'S CHEEKY ...
...AND HE'S *LONELY.*
HEY!

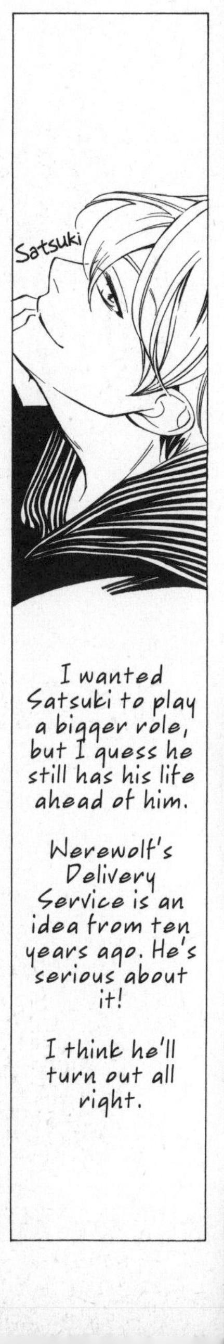
Satsuki

I wanted Satsuki to play a bigger role, but I guess he still has his life ahead of him.

Werewolf's Delivery Service is an idea from ten years ago. He's serious about it!

I think he'll turn out all right.

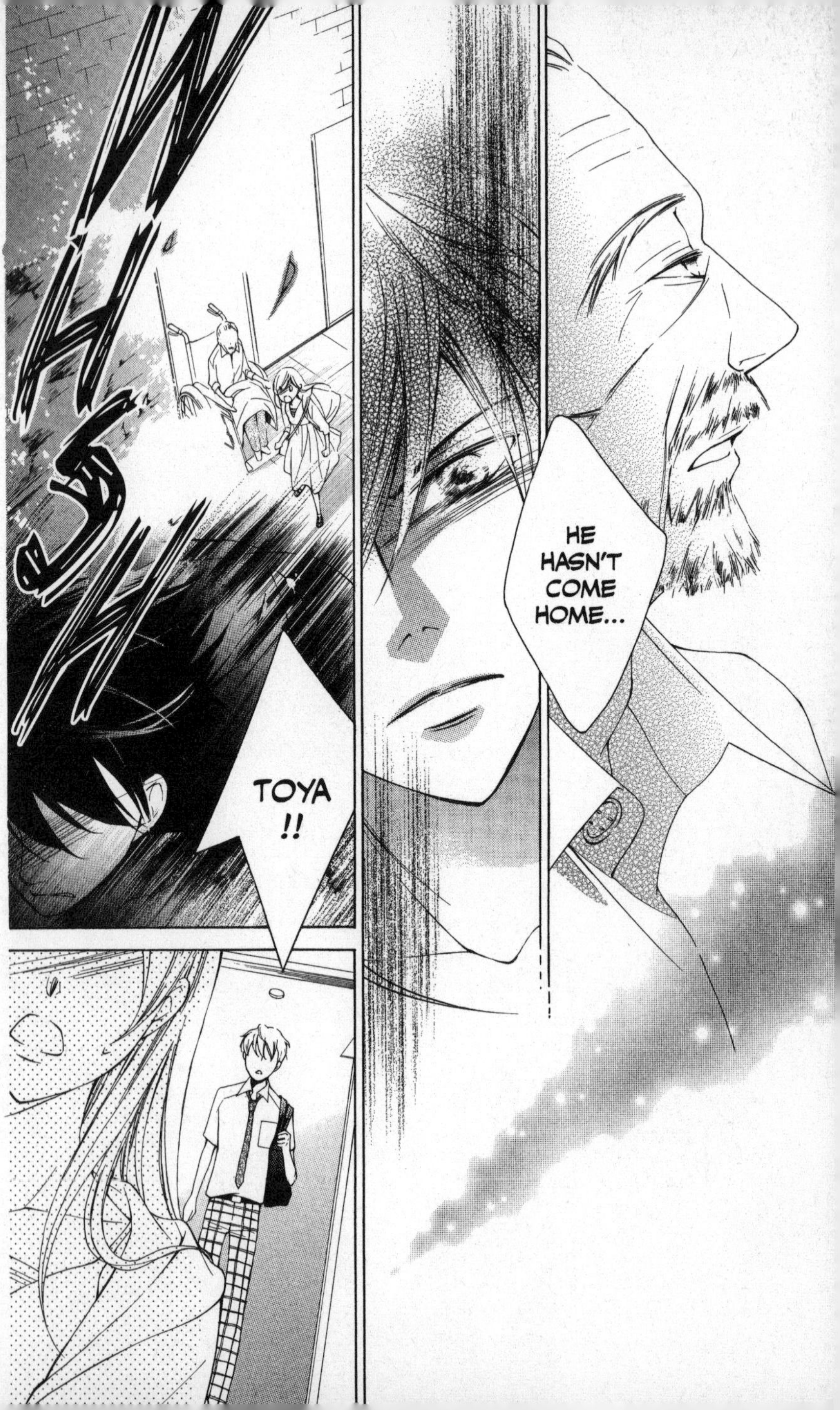

HE HASN'T COME HOME...
TOYA !!

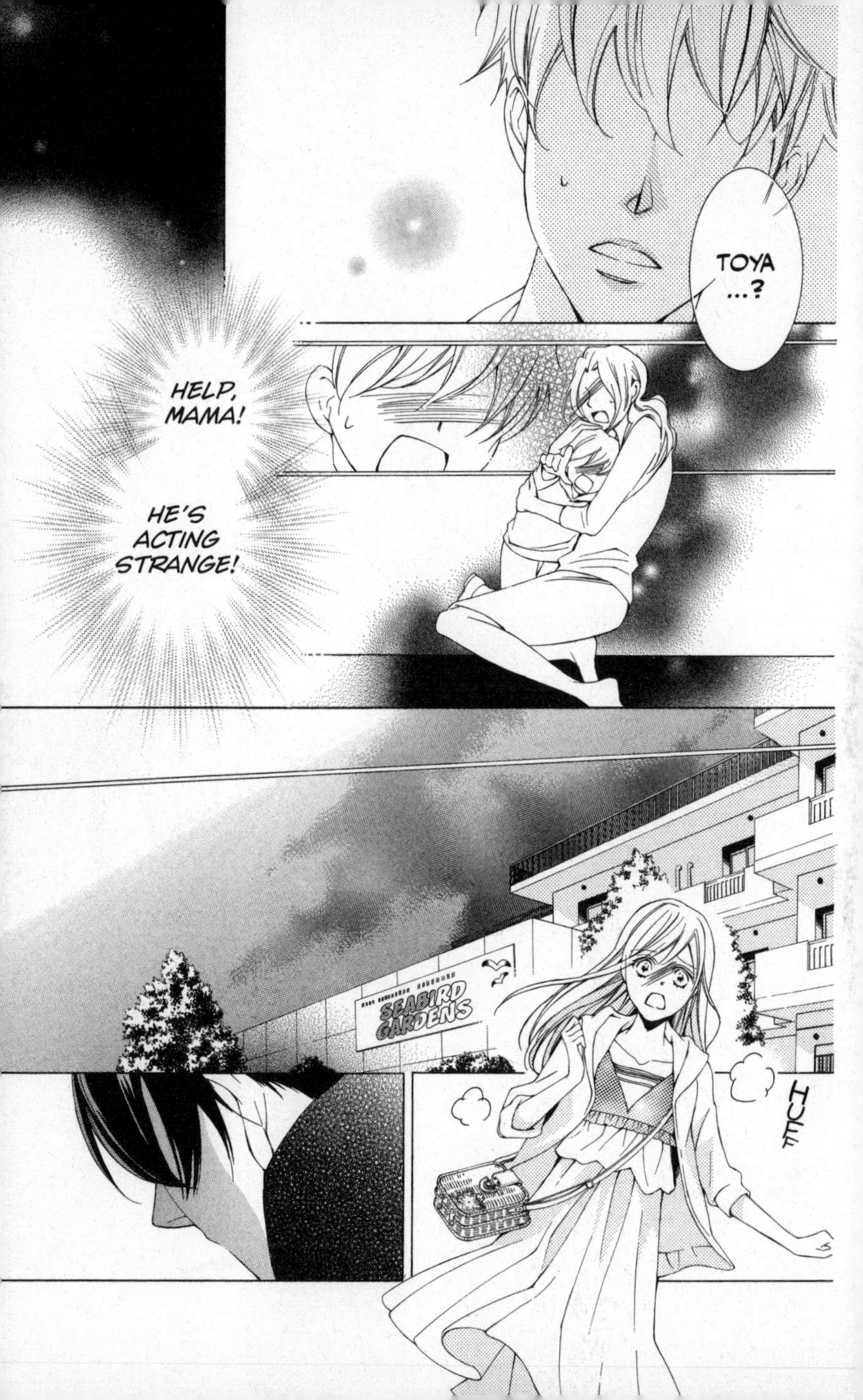
TOYA ...?
HELP, MAMA!
HE'S ACTING STRANGE!
SEABIRD GARDENS
HUFF

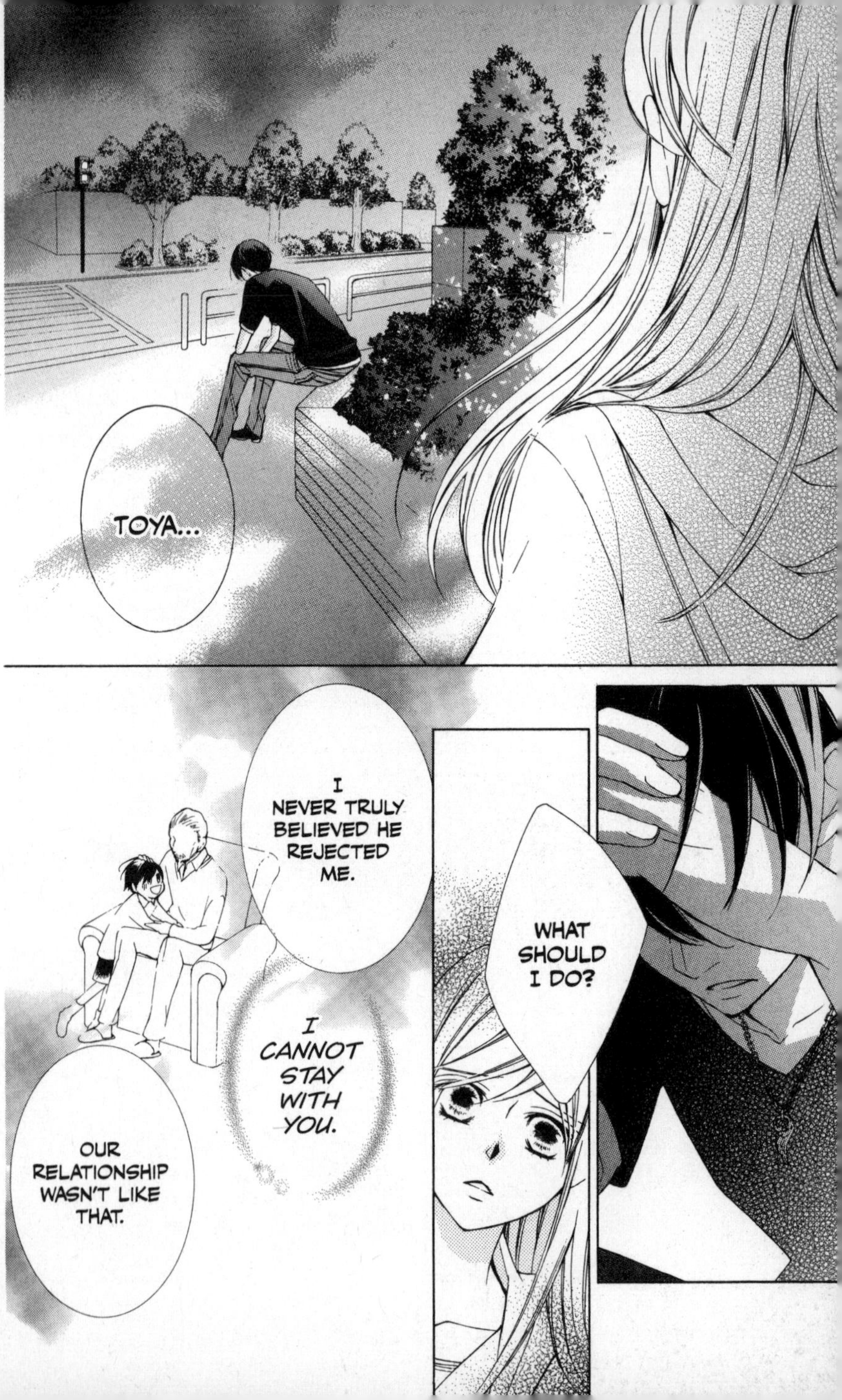
TOYA...
WHAT SHOULD I DO?
I NEVER TRULY BELIEVED HE REJECTED ME.
I CANNOT STAY WITH YOU.
OUR RELATIONSHIP WASN'T LIKE THAT.

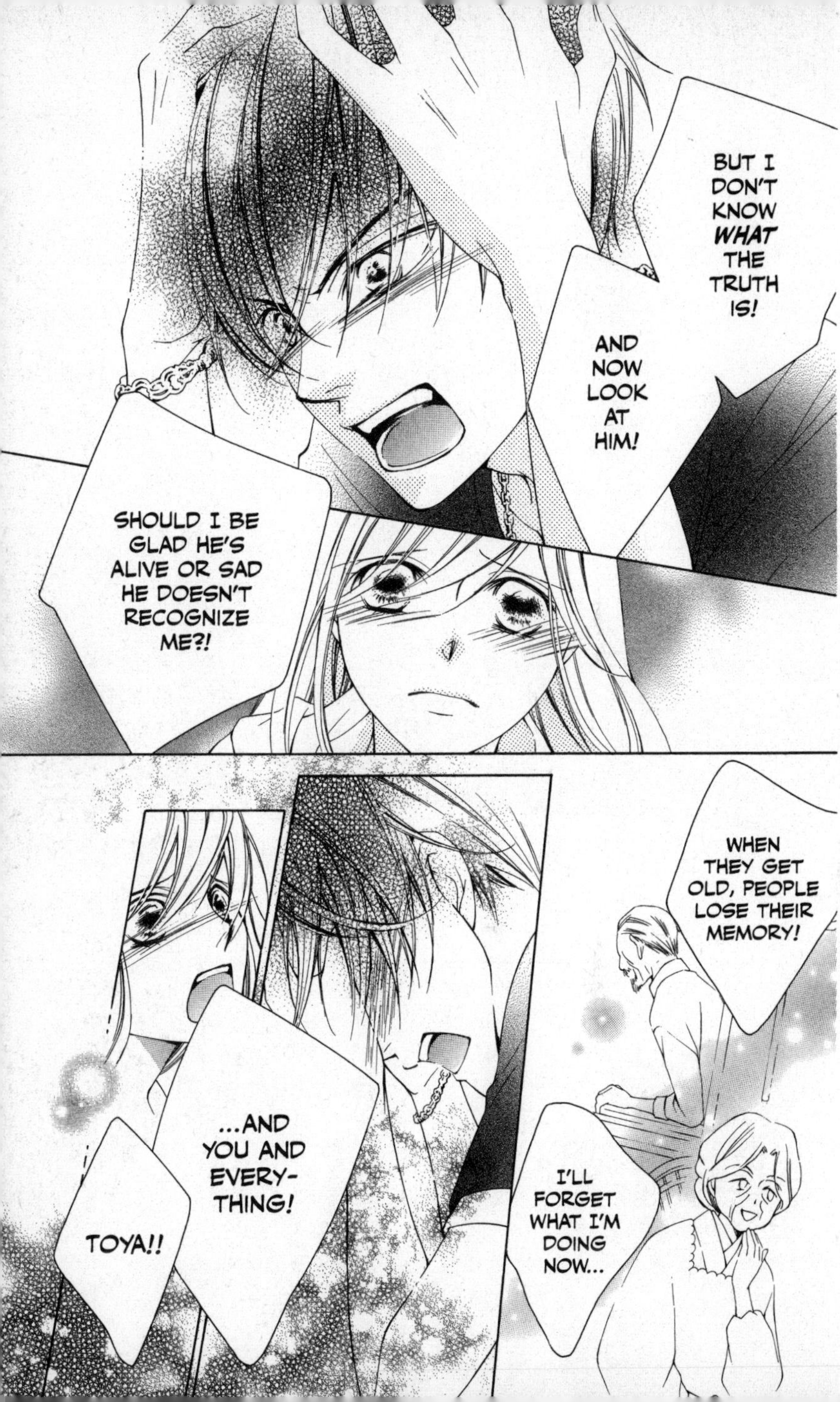
BUT I DON'T KNOW *WHAT* THE TRUTH IS!
AND NOW LOOK AT HIM!
SHOULD I BE GLAD HE'S ALIVE OR SAD HE DOESN'T RECOGNIZE ME?!
WHEN THEY GET OLD, PEOPLE LOSE THEIR MEMORY!
I'LL FORGET WHAT I'M DOING NOW...
...AND YOU AND EVERY-THING!
TOYA!!

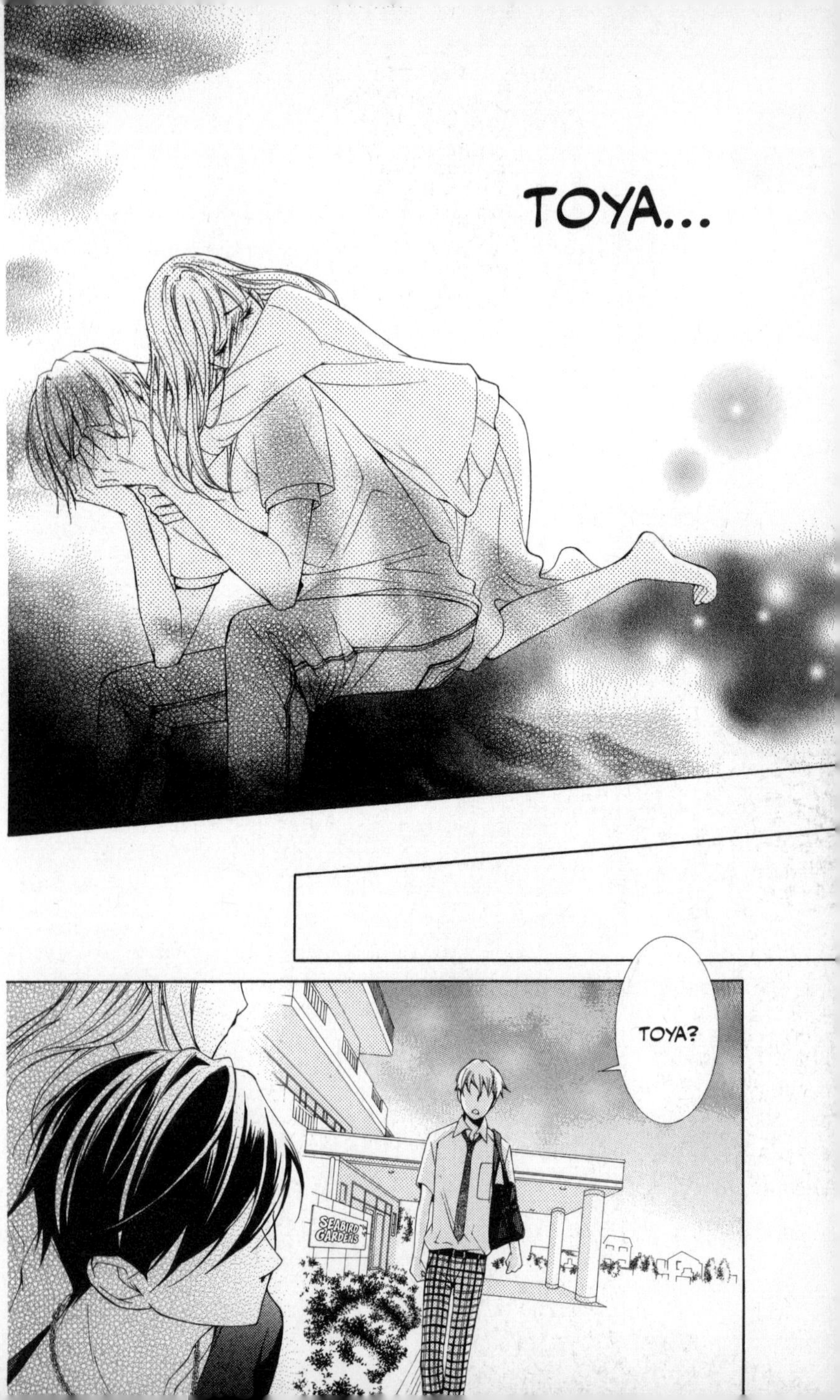
TOYA...
TOYA?
SEABIRD GARDENS

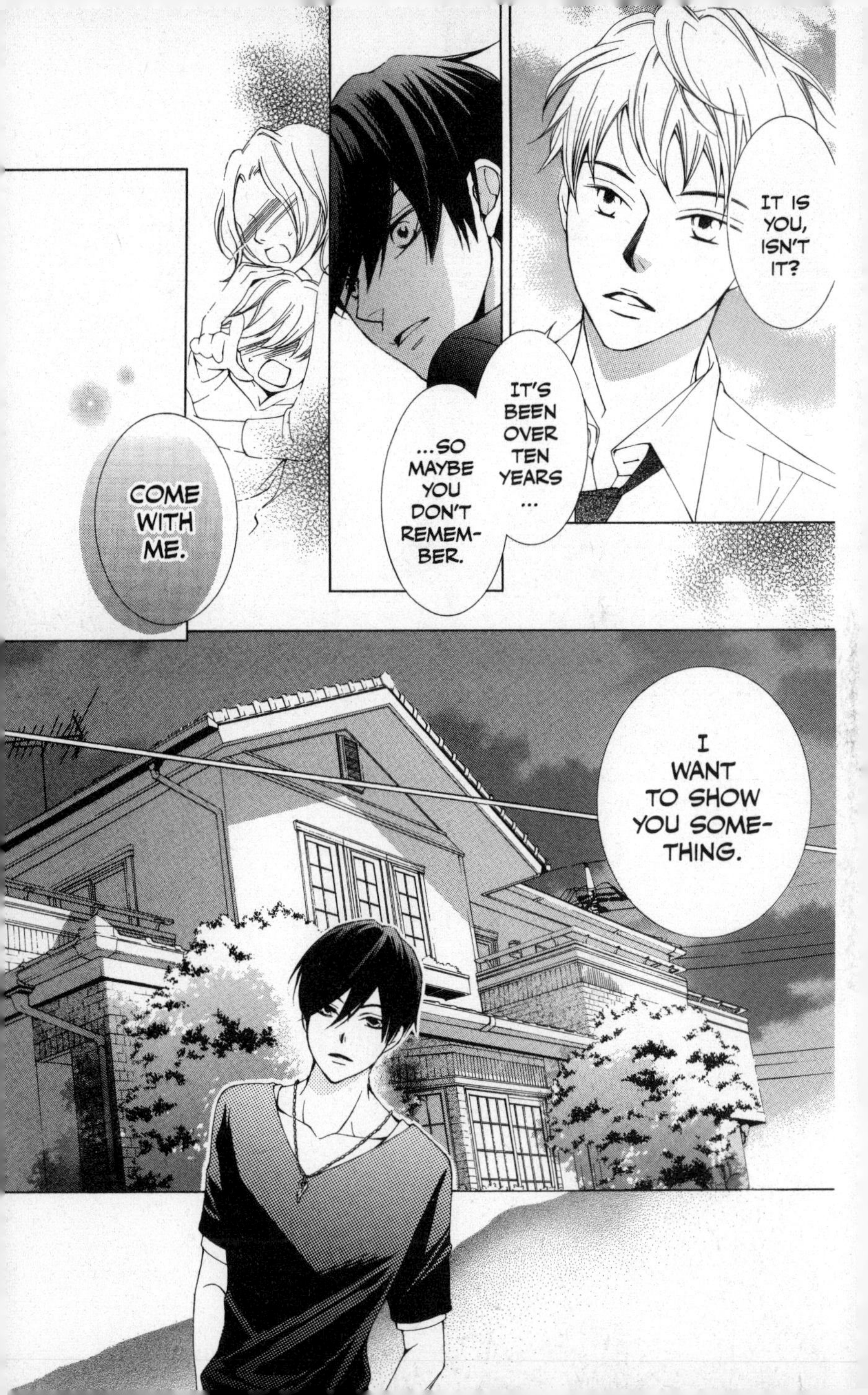
IT IS YOU, ISN'T IT?
IT'S BEEN OVER TEN YEARS ...
...SO MAYBE YOU DON'T REMEMBER.
COME WITH ME.
I WANT TO SHOW YOU SOMETHING.

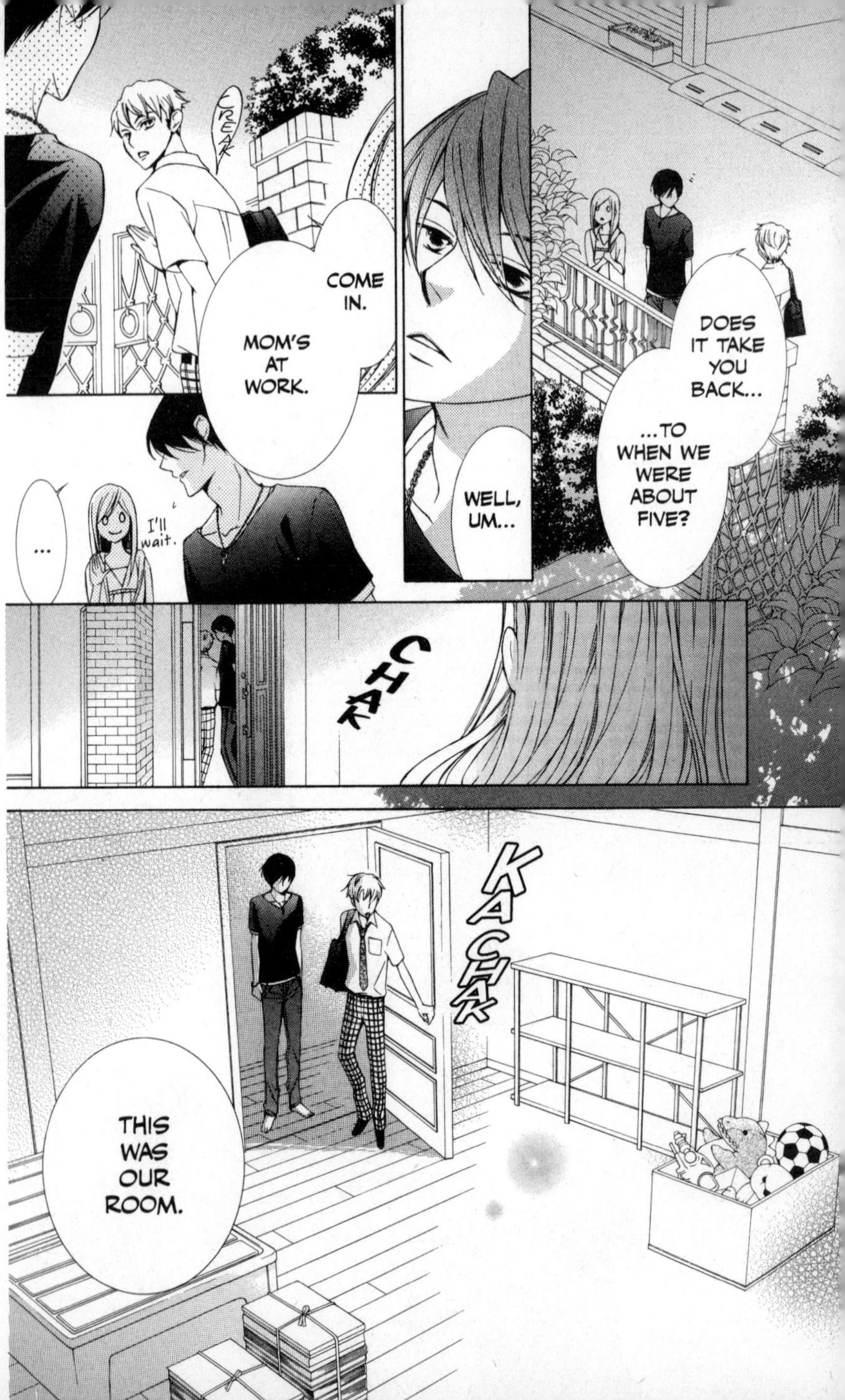
DOES IT TAKE YOU BACK...
...TO WHEN WE WERE ABOUT FIVE?
WELL, UM...
CREAK
COME IN.
MOM'S AT WORK.
I'll wait.
...
CHAK
KACHAK
THIS WAS OUR ROOM.

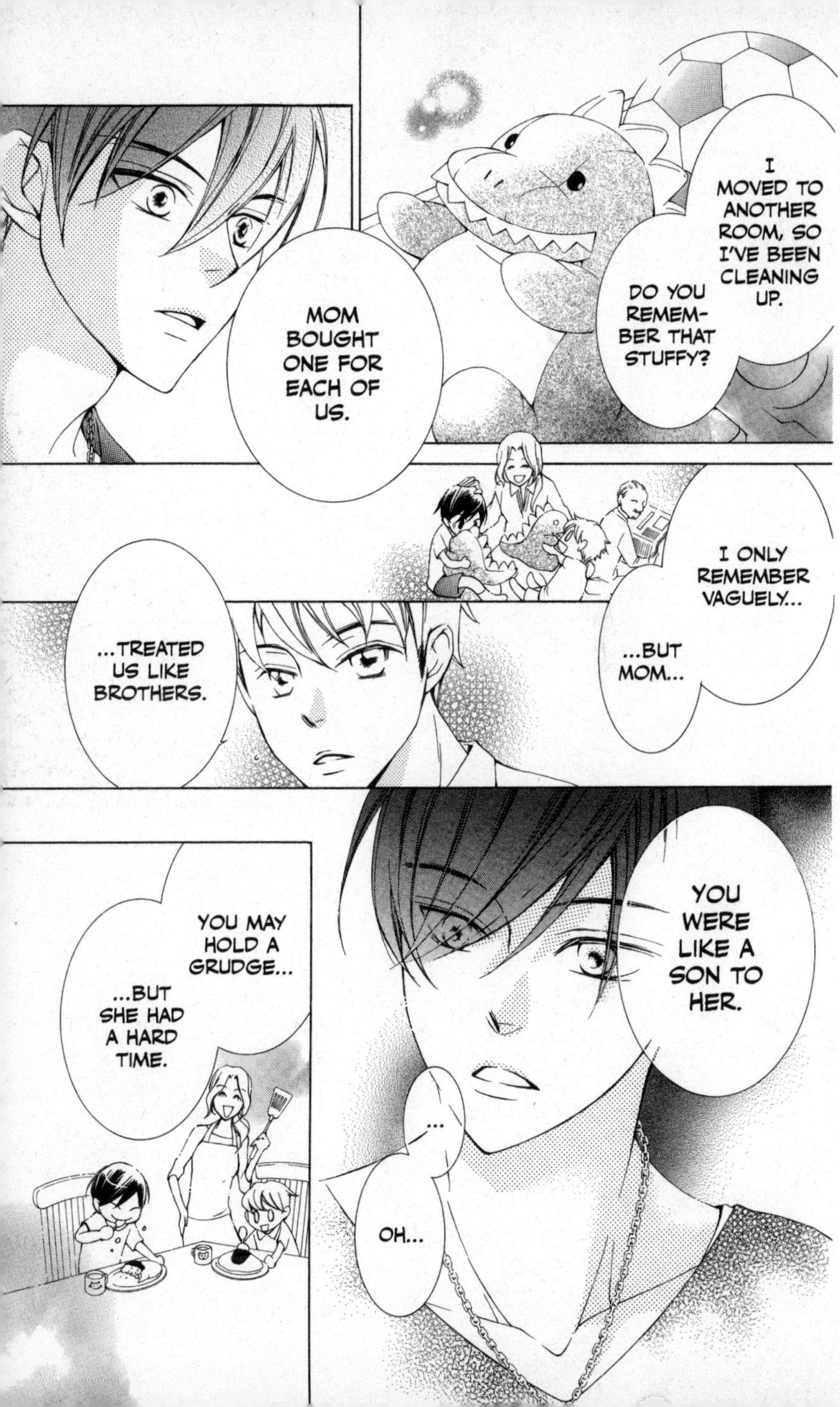
I MOVED TO ANOTHER ROOM, SO I'VE BEEN CLEANING UP.
DO YOU REMEMBER THAT STUFFY?
MOM BOUGHT ONE FOR EACH OF US.
I ONLY REMEMBER VAGUELY...
...BUT MOM...
...TREATED US LIKE BROTHERS.
YOU WERE LIKE A SON TO HER.
...
OH...
YOU MAY HOLD A GRUDGE...
...BUT SHE HAD A HARD TIME.

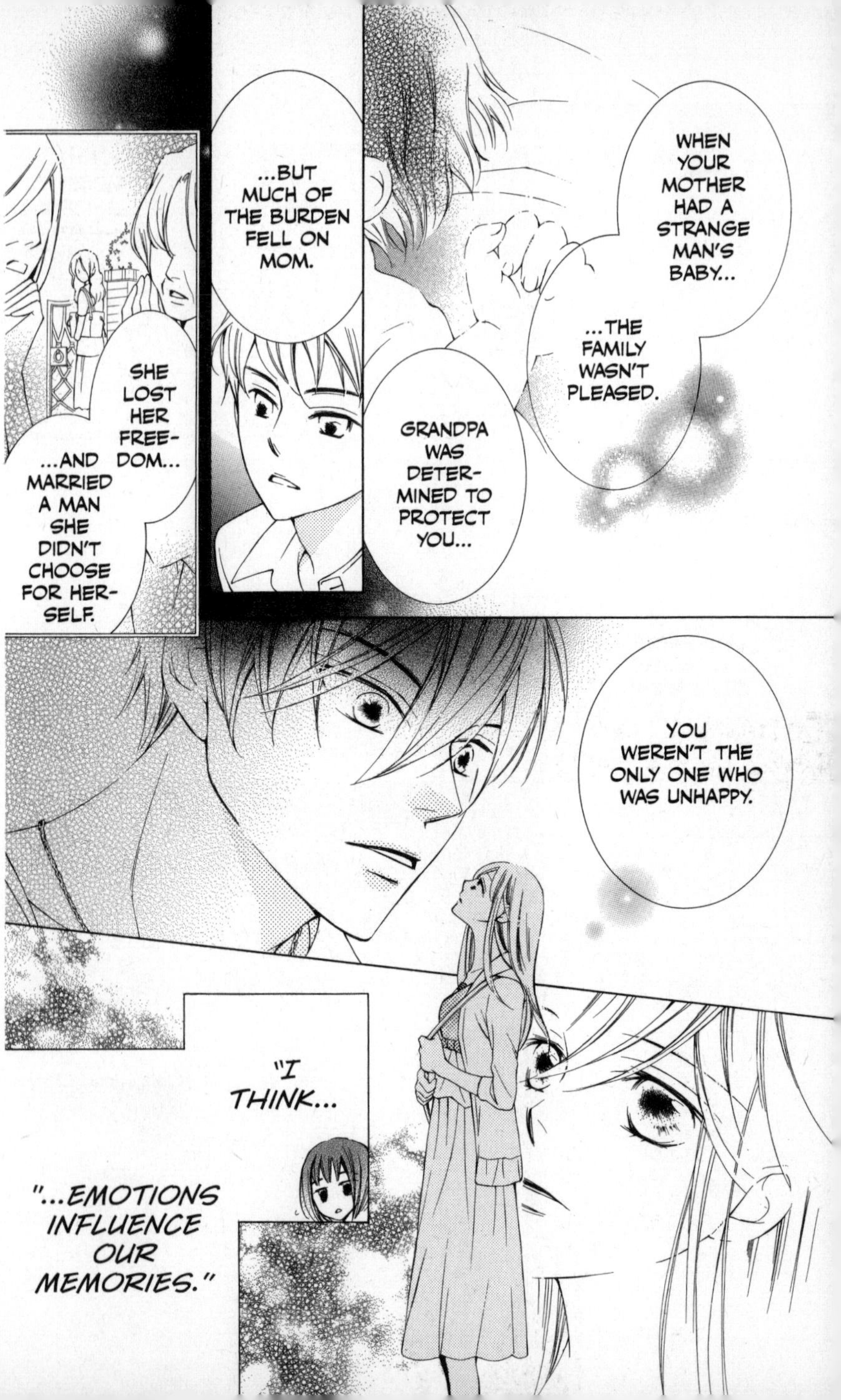
WHEN YOUR MOTHER HAD A STRANGE MAN'S BABY...
...THE FAMILY WASN'T PLEASED.
GRANDPA WAS DETER-MINED TO PROTECT YOU...
...BUT MUCH OF THE BURDEN FELL ON MOM.
SHE LOST HER FREE-DOM...
...AND MARRIED A MAN SHE DIDN'T CHOOSE FOR HER-SELF.
YOU WEREN'T THE ONLY ONE WHO WAS UNHAPPY.
"I THINK...
"...EMOTIONS INFLUENCE OUR MEMORIES."

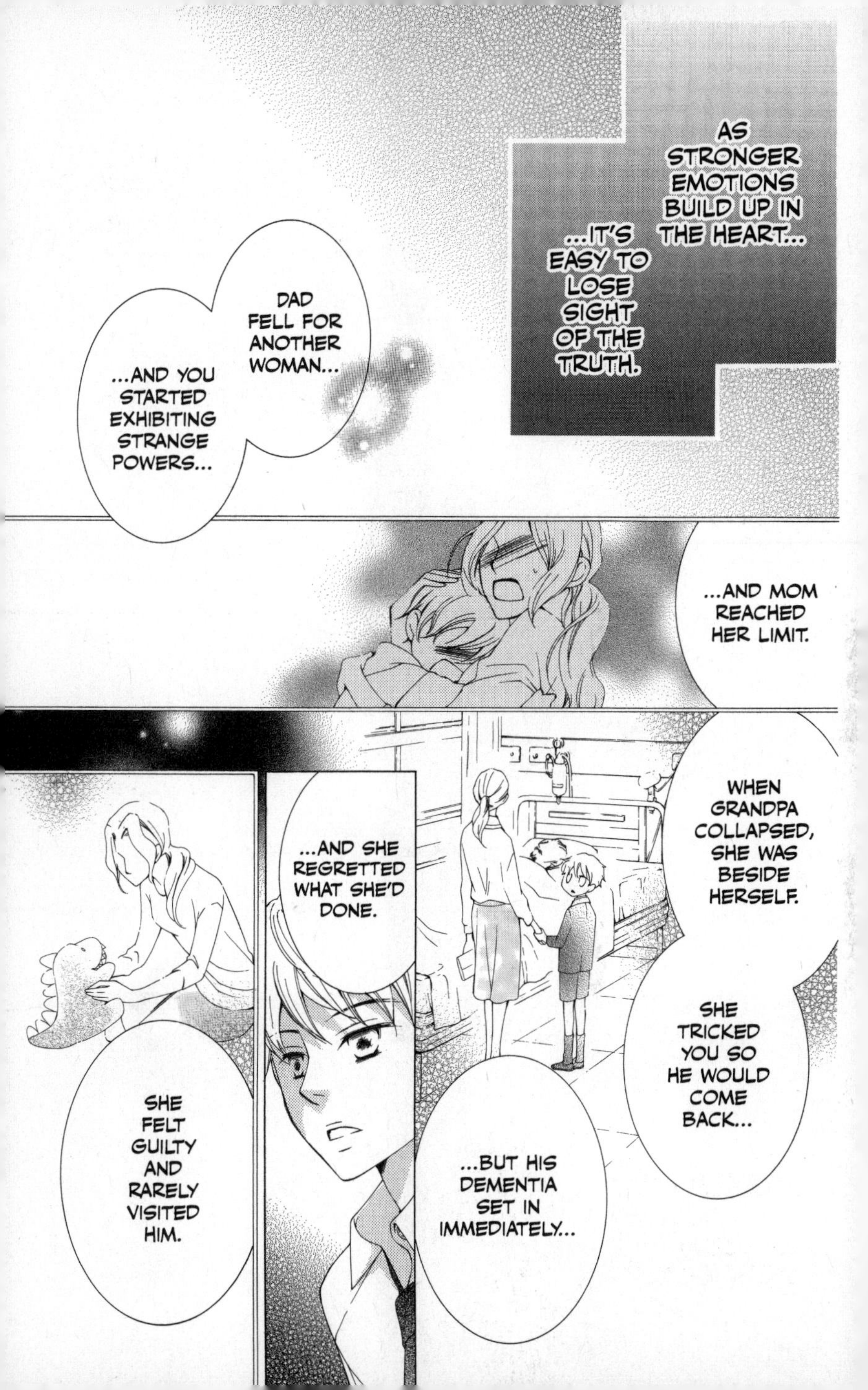
AS STRONGER EMOTIONS BUILD UP IN THE HEART...
...IT'S EASY TO LOSE SIGHT OF THE TRUTH.
DAD FELL FOR ANOTHER WOMAN...
...AND YOU STARTED EXHIBITING STRANGE POWERS...
...AND MOM REACHED HER LIMIT.
WHEN GRANDPA COLLAPSED, SHE WAS BESIDE HERSELF.
SHE TRICKED YOU SO HE WOULD COME BACK...
...BUT HIS DEMENTIA SET IN IMMEDIATELY...
...AND SHE REGRETTED WHAT SHE'D DONE.
SHE FELT GUILTY AND RARELY VISITED HIM.

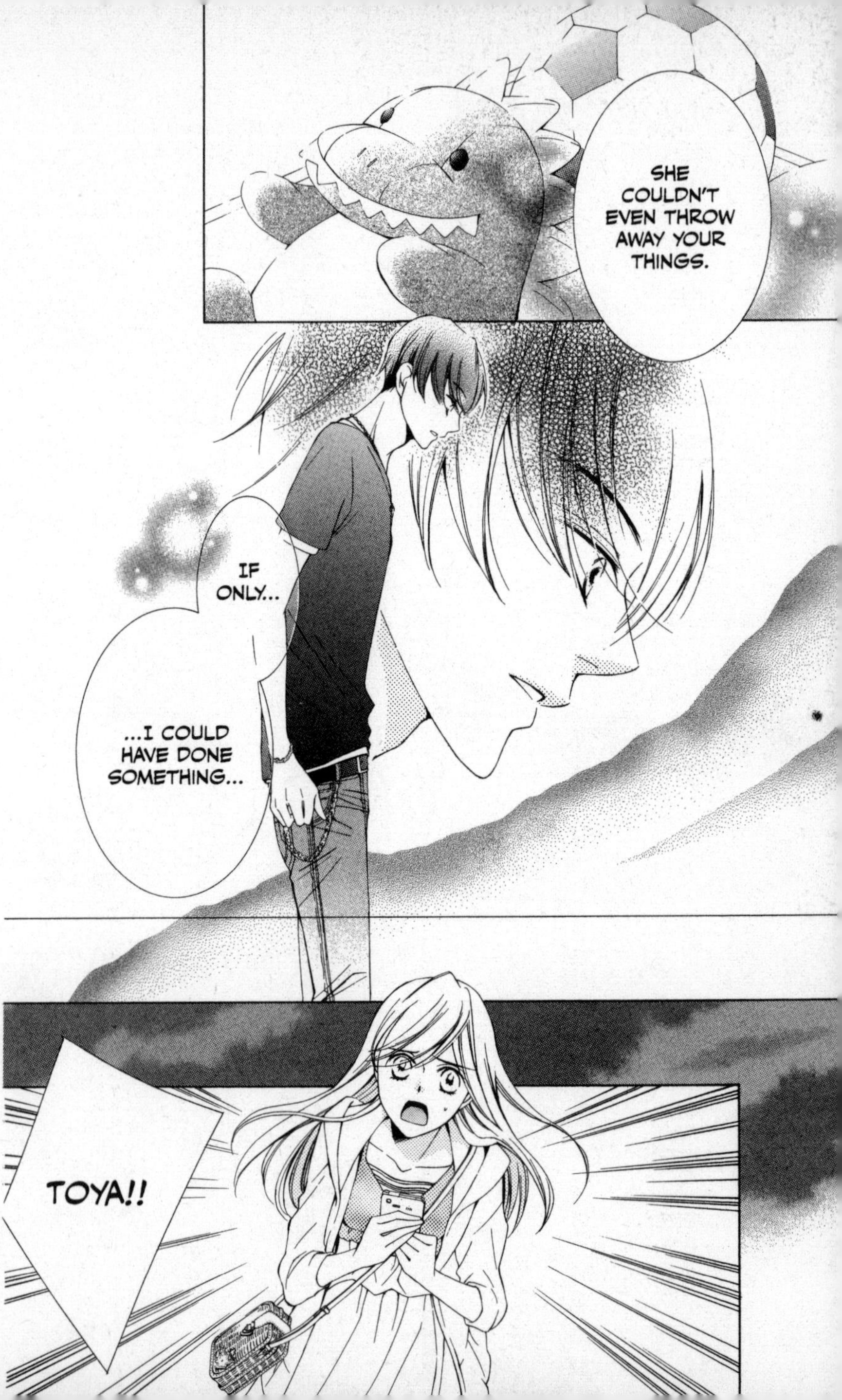
SHE COULDN'T EVEN THROW AWAY YOUR THINGS.
IF ONLY...
...I COULD HAVE DONE SOMETHING...
TOYA!!

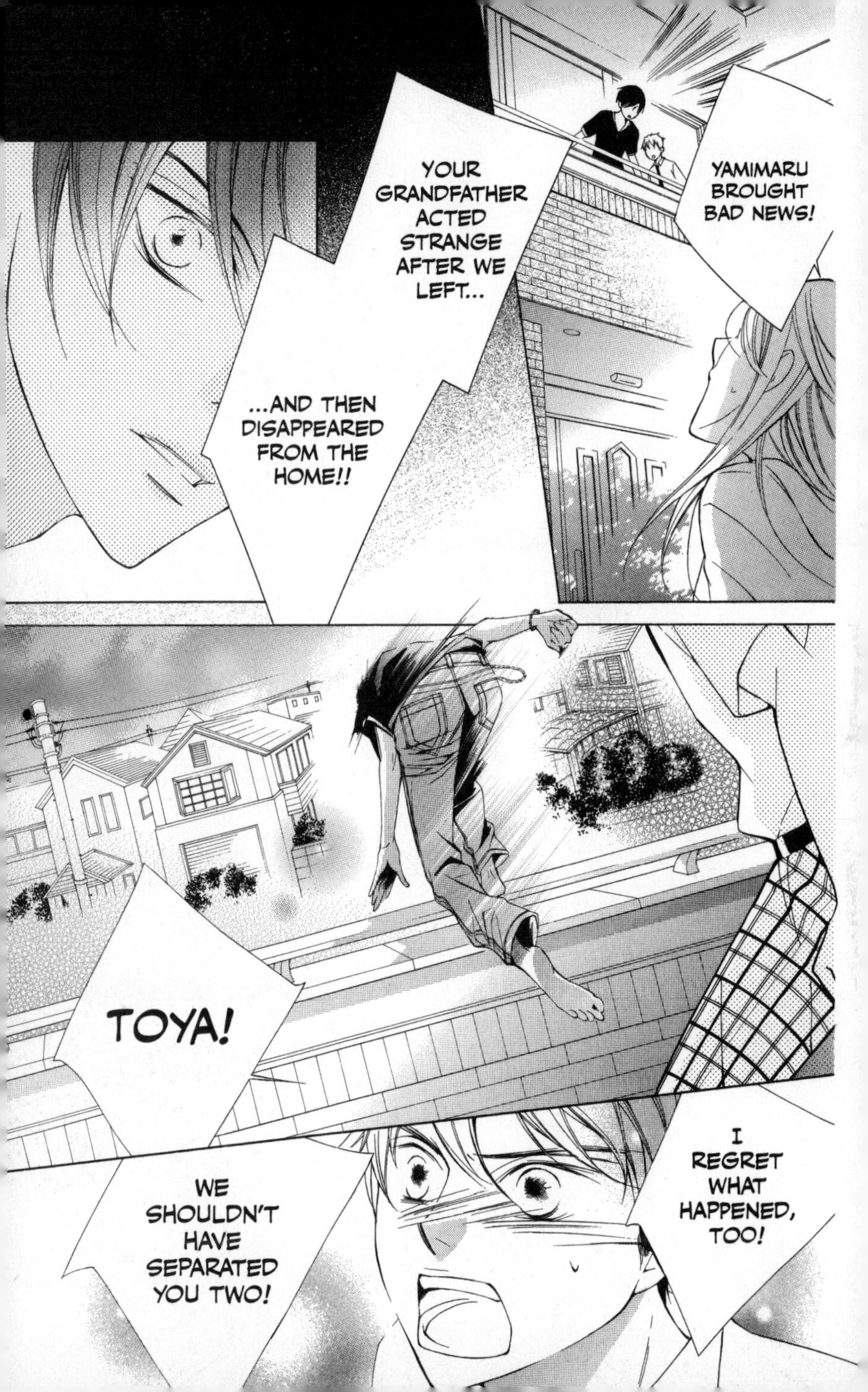

YAMIMARU BROUGHT BAD NEWS!
YOUR GRANDFATHER ACTED STRANGE AFTER WE LEFT...
...AND THEN DISAPPEARED FROM THE HOME!!
TOYA!
I REGRET WHAT HAPPENED, TOO!
WE SHOULDN'T HAVE SEPARATED YOU TWO!

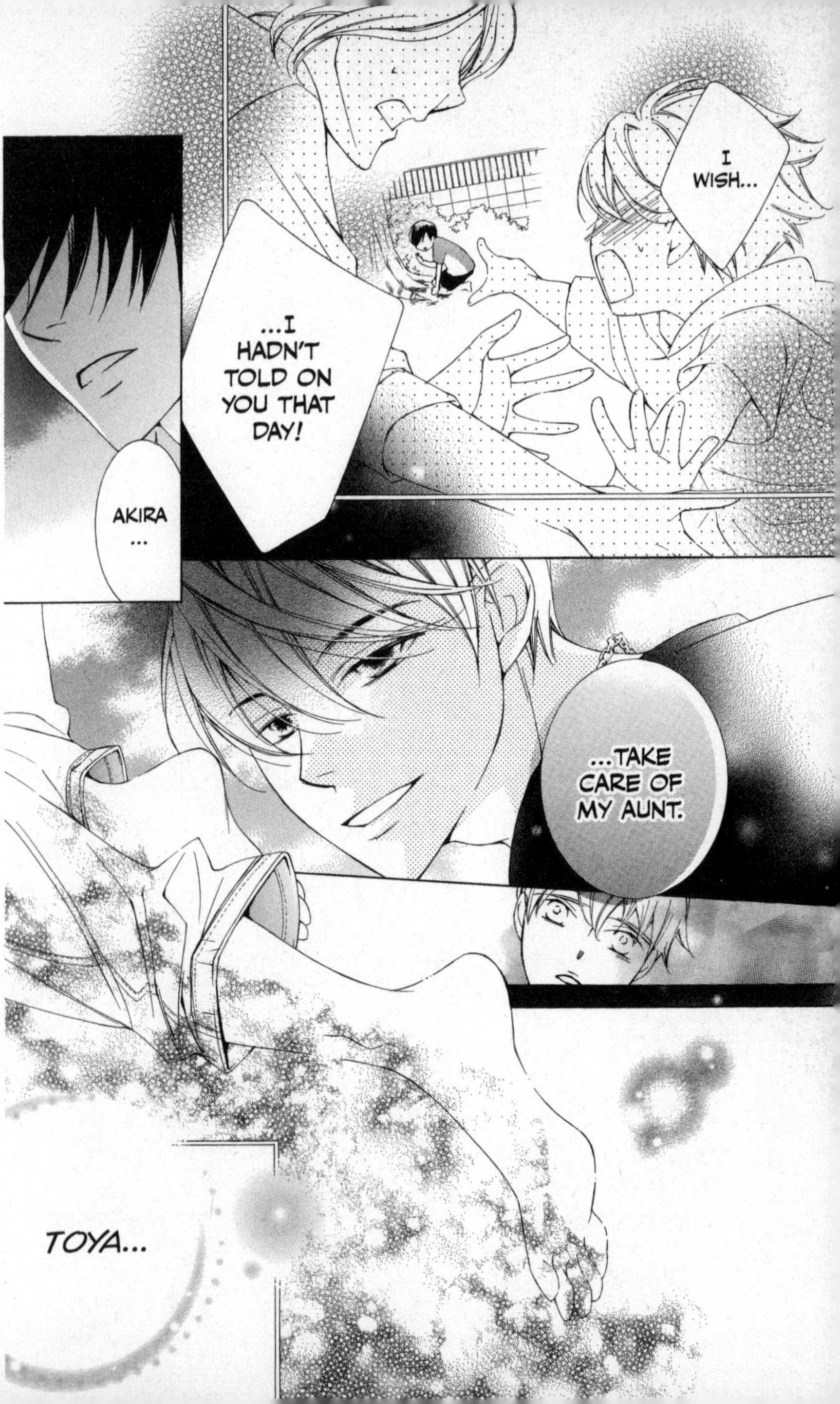
I WISH...
...I HADN'T TOLD ON YOU THAT DAY!
AKIRA ...
...TAKE CARE OF MY AUNT.
TOYA...

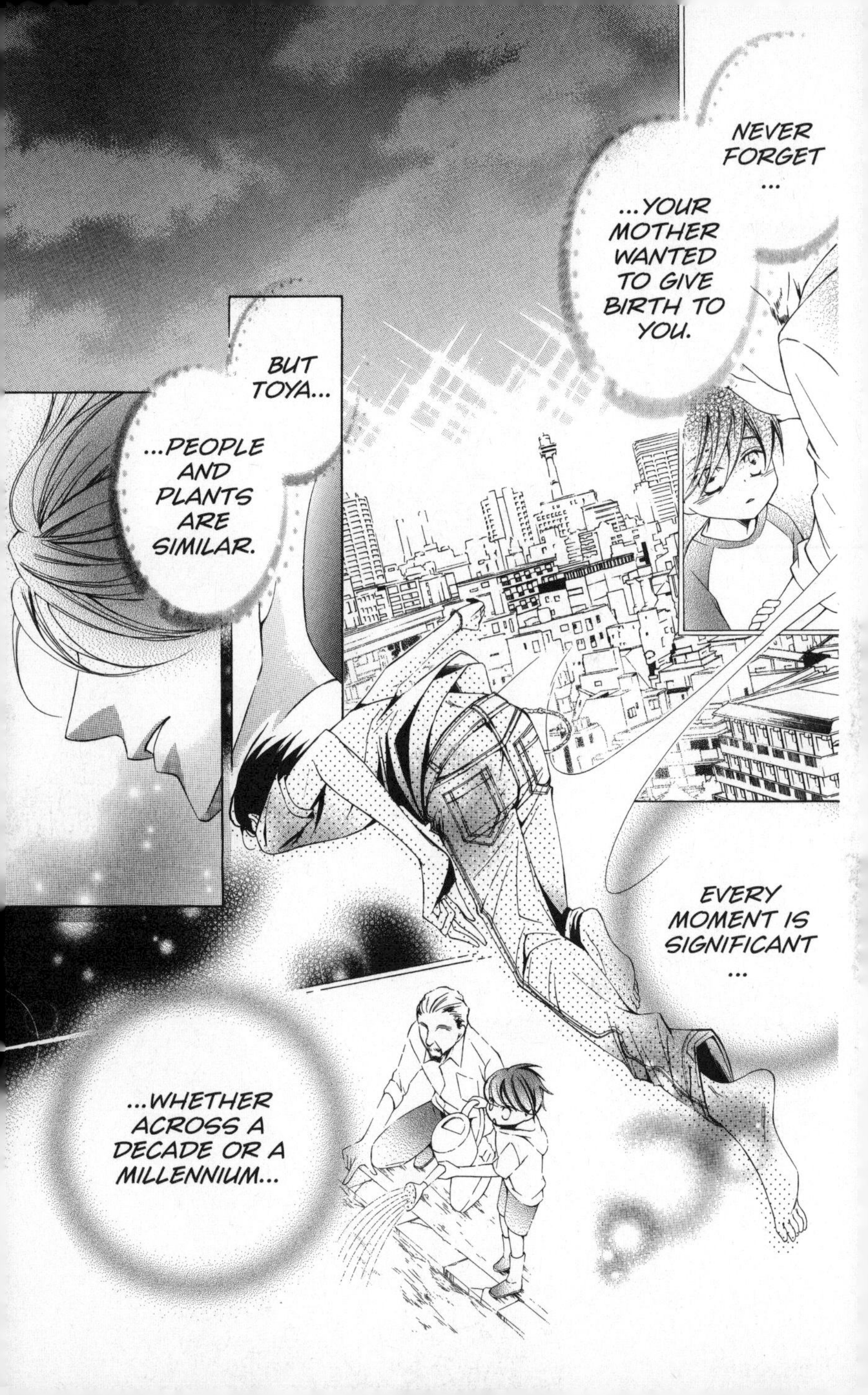
NEVER FORGET ...
...YOUR MOTHER WANTED TO GIVE BIRTH TO YOU.
BUT TOYA...
...PEOPLE AND PLANTS ARE SIMILAR.
EVERY MOMENT IS SIGNIFICANT ...
...WHETHER ACROSS A DECADE OR A MILLENNIUM...

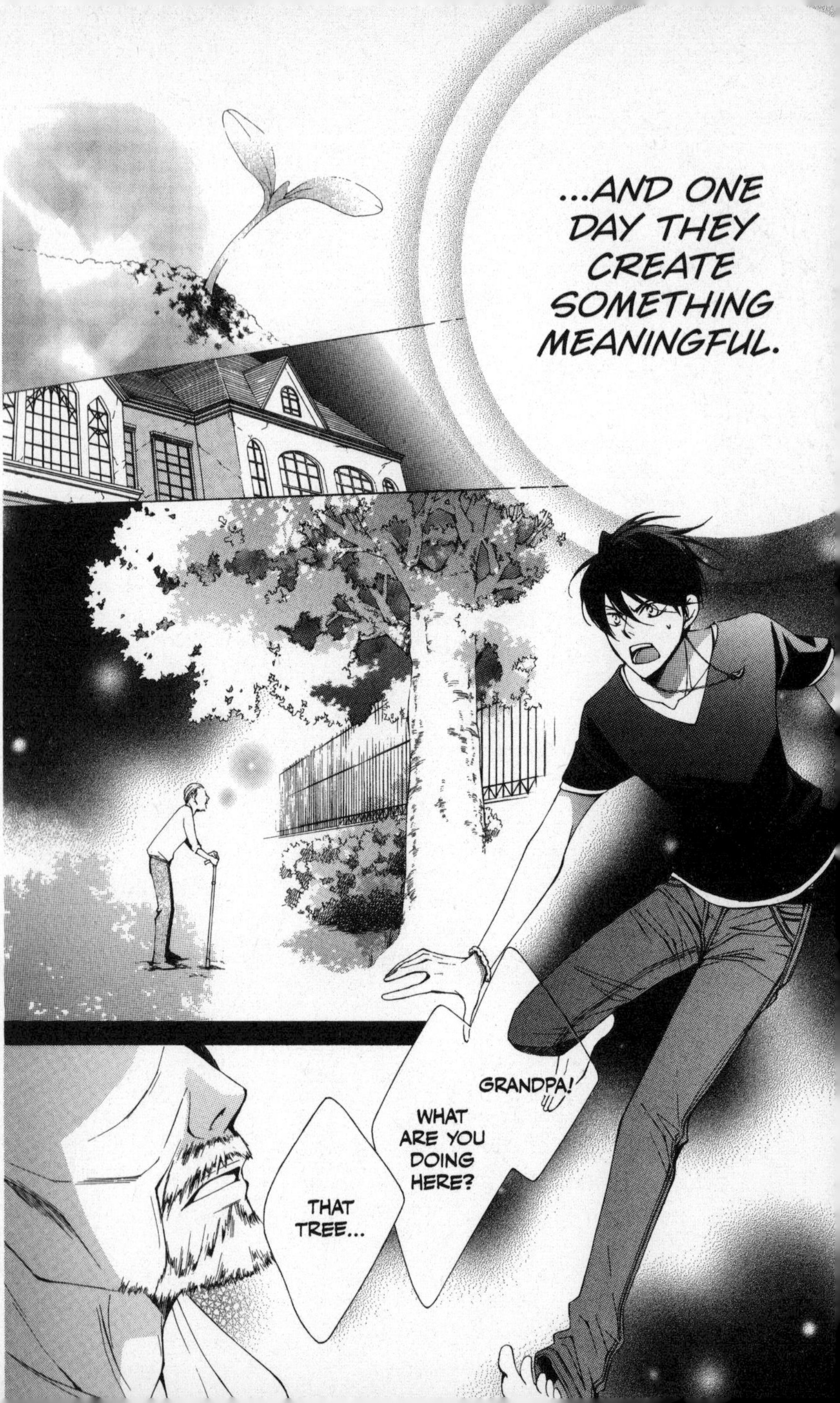
...AND ONE DAY THEY CREATE SOMETHING MEANINGFUL.
GRANDPA!
WHAT ARE YOU DOING HERE?
THAT TREE...

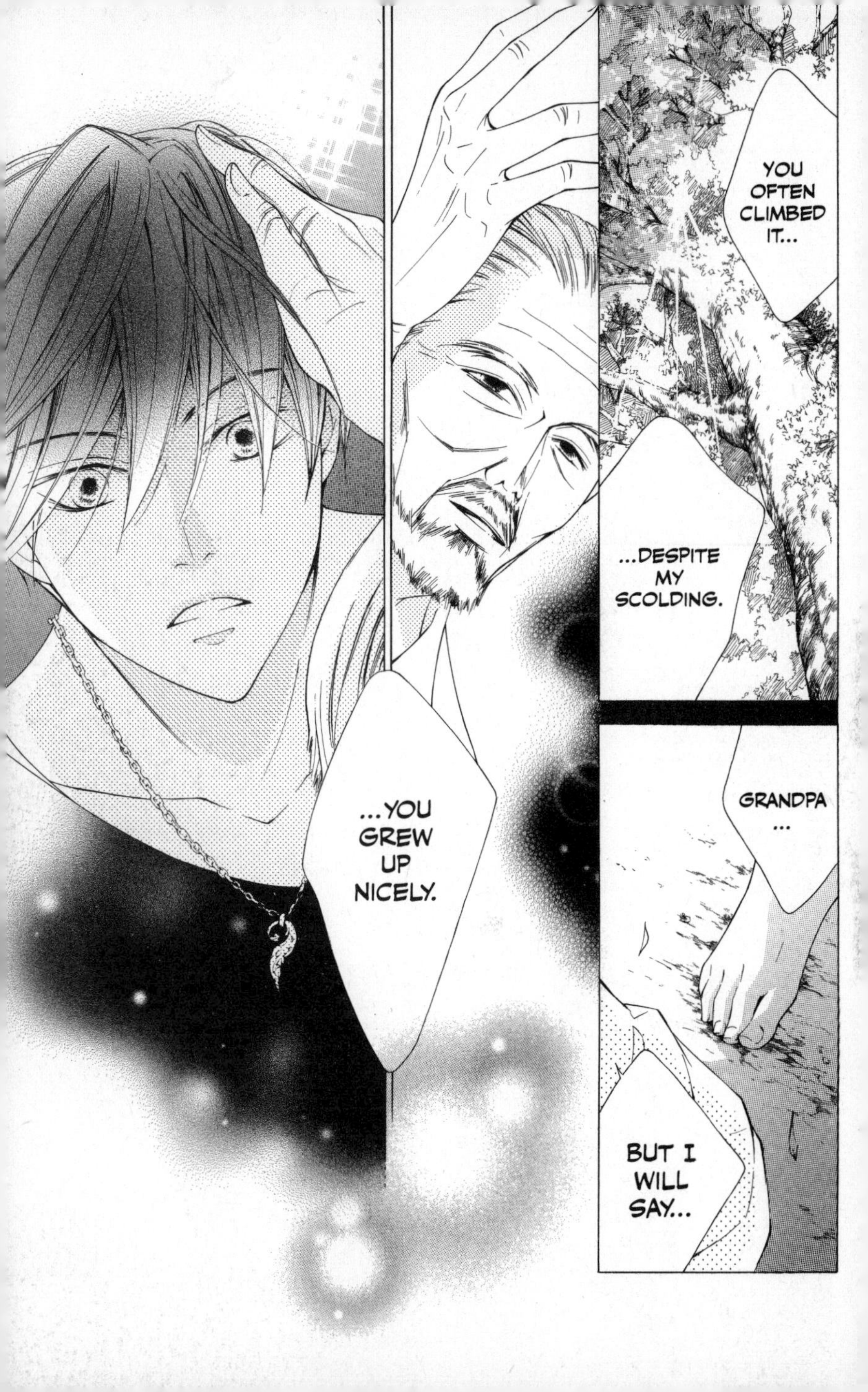
YOU OFTEN CLIMBED IT...
...DESPITE MY SCOLDING.
GRANDPA ...
BUT I WILL SAY...
...YOU GREW UP NICELY.

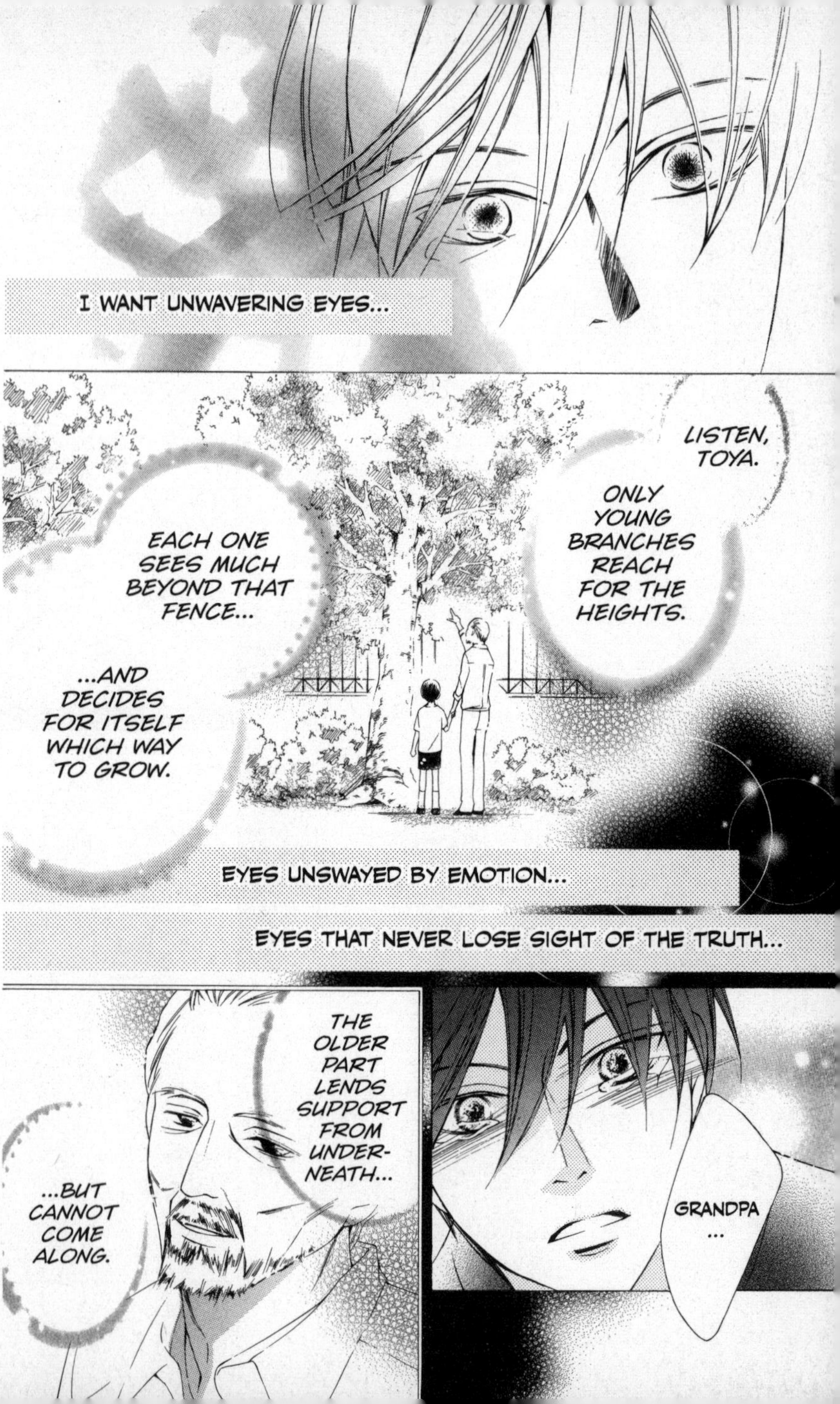
I WANT UNWAVERING EYES...
LISTEN, TOYA.
ONLY YOUNG BRANCHES REACH FOR THE HEIGHTS.
EACH ONE SEES MUCH BEYOND THAT FENCE...
...AND DECIDES FOR ITSELF WHICH WAY TO GROW.
EYES UNSWAYED BY EMOTION...
EYES THAT NEVER LOSE SIGHT OF THE TRUTH...
GRANDPA...
THE OLDER PART LENDS SUPPORT FROM UNDER-NEATH...
...BUT CANNOT COME ALONG.

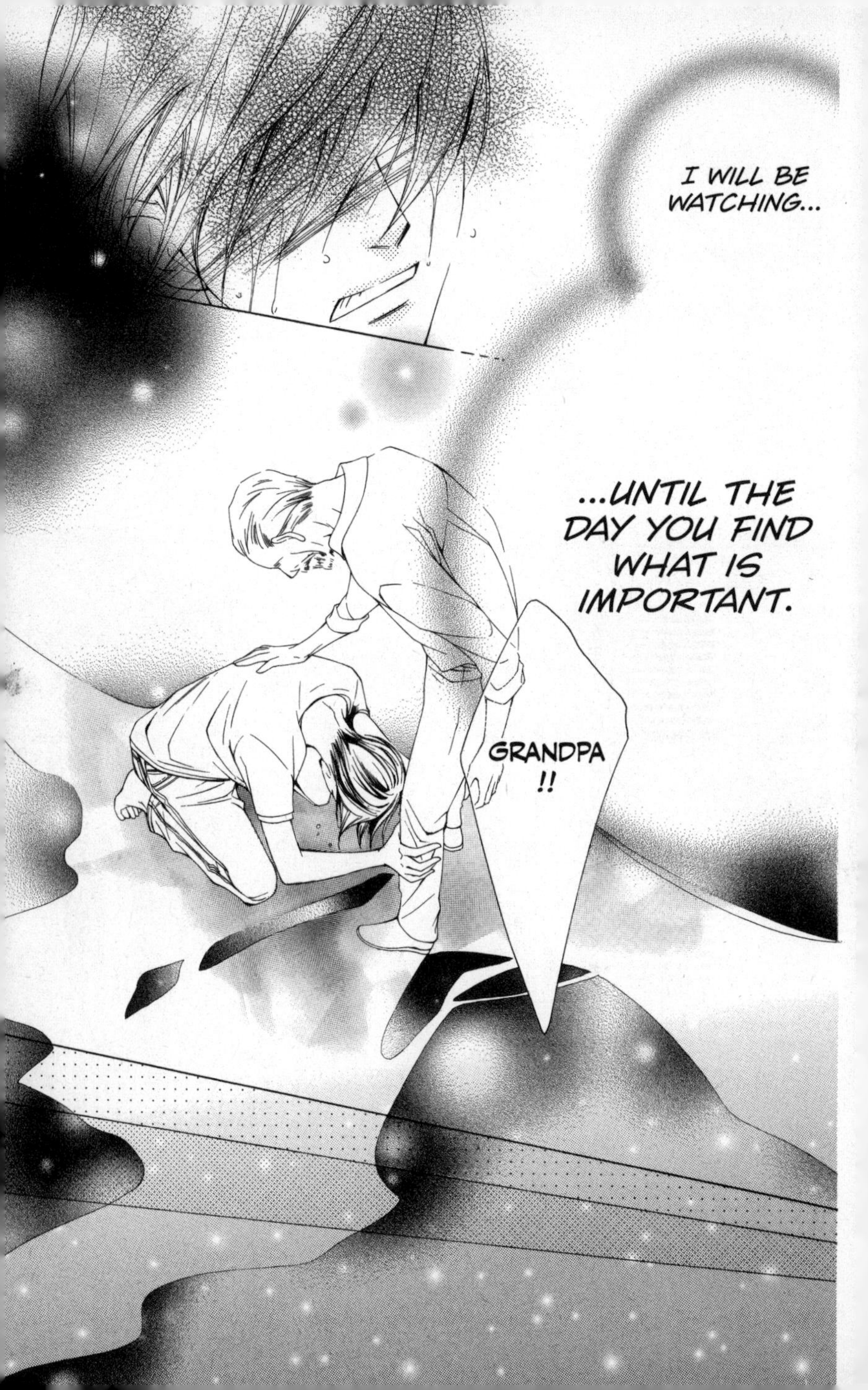
I WILL BE WATCHING...
...UNTIL THE DAY YOU FIND WHAT IS IMPORTANT.
GRANDPA !!

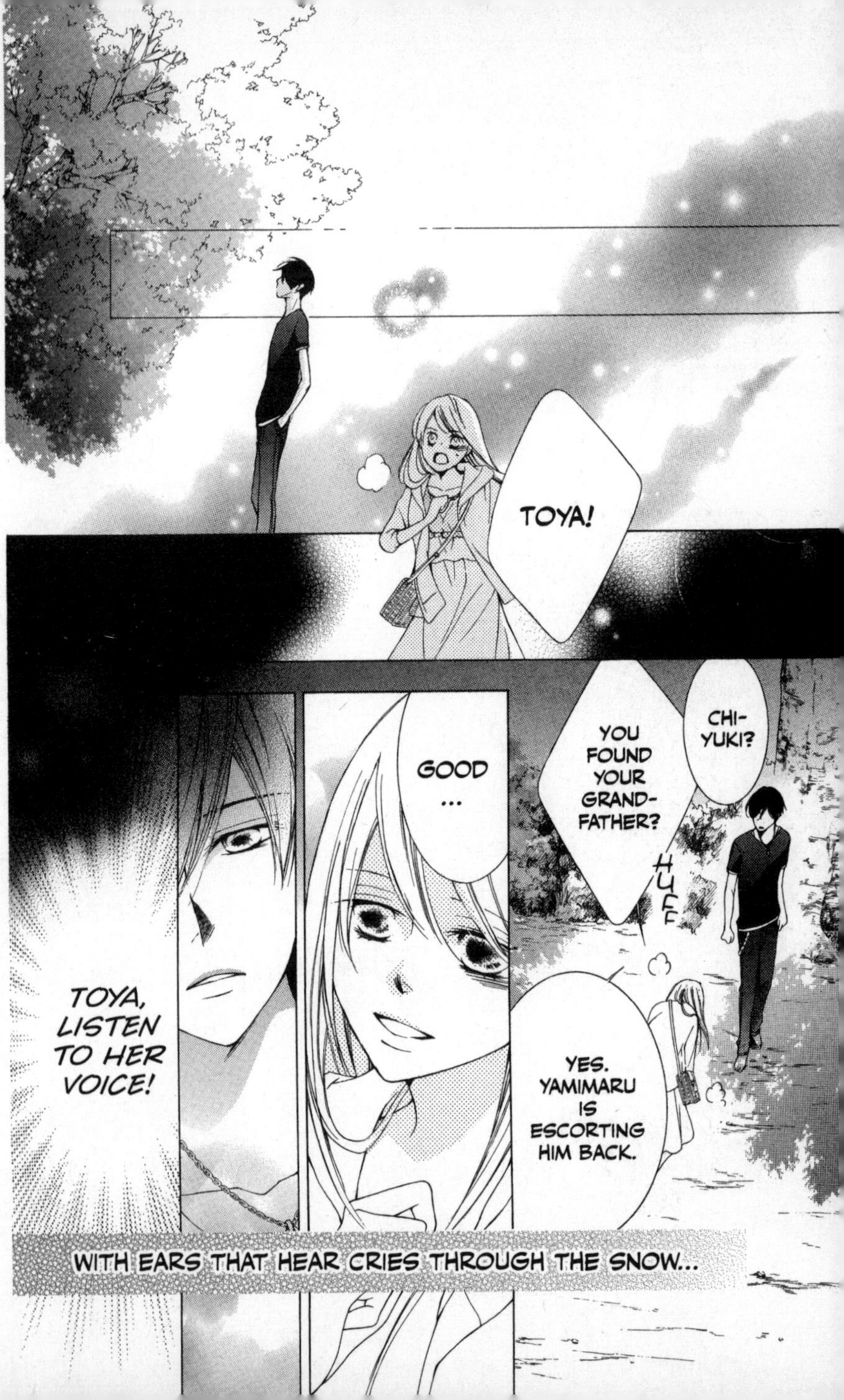
TOYA!
CHI-YUKI?
YOU FOUND YOUR GRAND-FATHER?
HUFF
YES. YAMIMARU IS ESCORTING HIM BACK.
GOOD ...
TOYA, LISTEN TO HER VOICE!
WITH EARS THAT HEAR CRIES THROUGH THE SNOW...

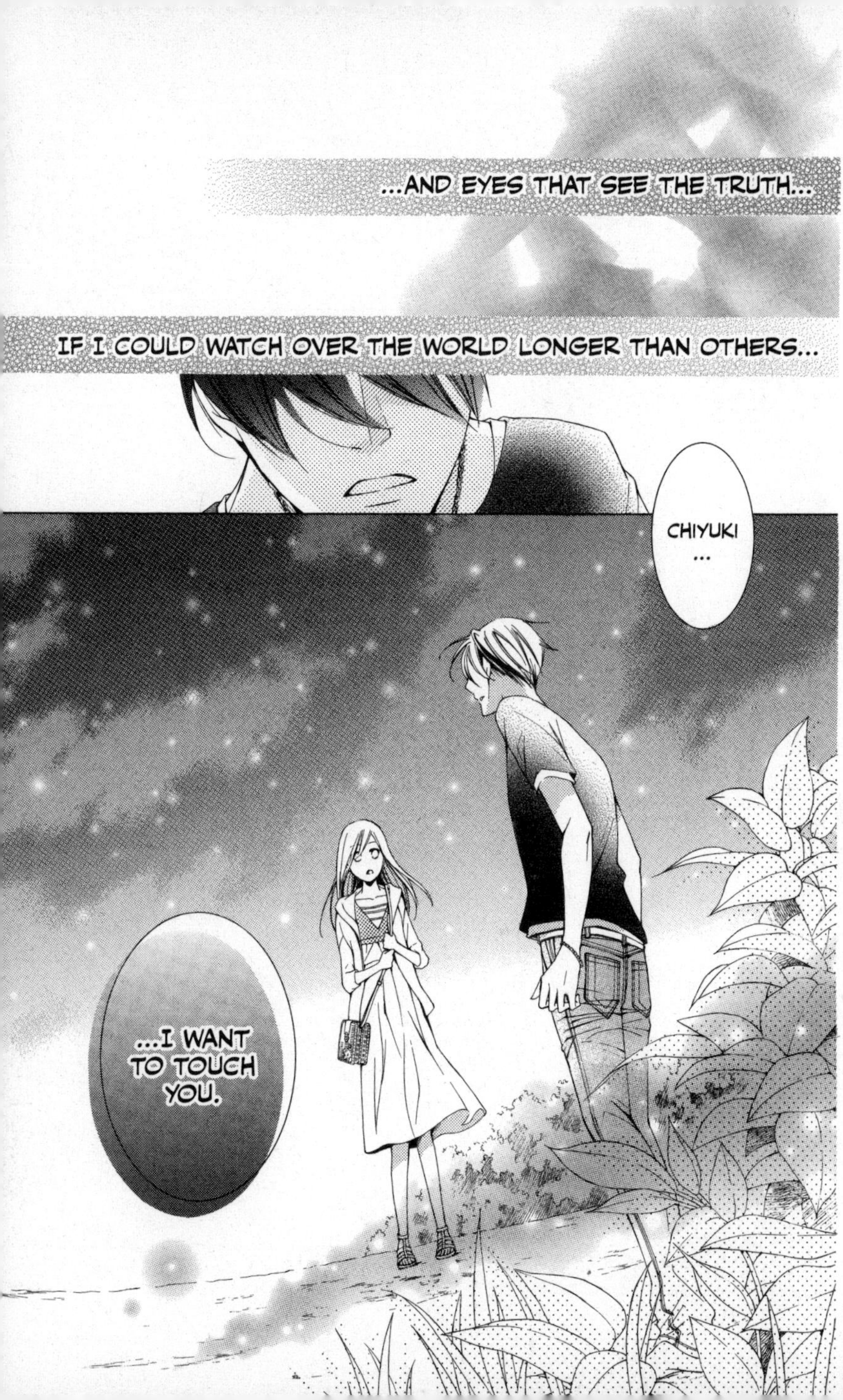
...AND EYES THAT SEE THE TRUTH...
IF I COULD WATCH OVER THE WORLD LONGER THAN OTHERS...
CHIYUKI ...
...I WANT TO TOUCH YOU.

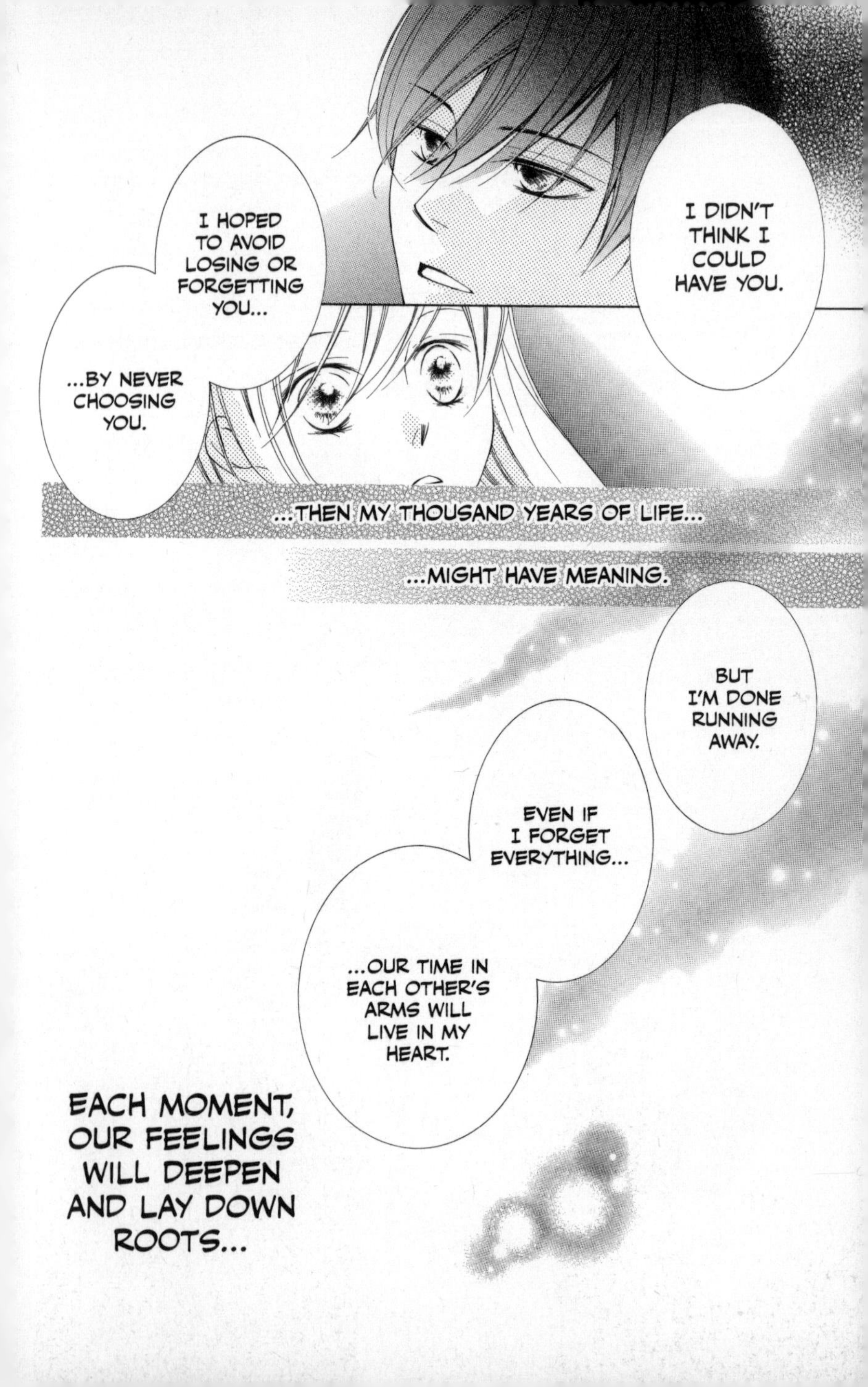
I DIDN'T THINK I COULD HAVE YOU.
I HOPED TO AVOID LOSING OR FORGETTING YOU...
...BY NEVER CHOOSING YOU.
...THEN MY THOUSAND YEARS OF LIFE...
...MIGHT HAVE MEANING.
BUT I'M DONE RUNNING AWAY.
EVEN IF I FORGET EVERYTHING...
...OUR TIME IN EACH OTHER'S ARMS WILL LIVE IN MY HEART.
EACH MOMENT, OUR FEELINGS WILL DEEPEN AND LAY DOWN ROOTS...

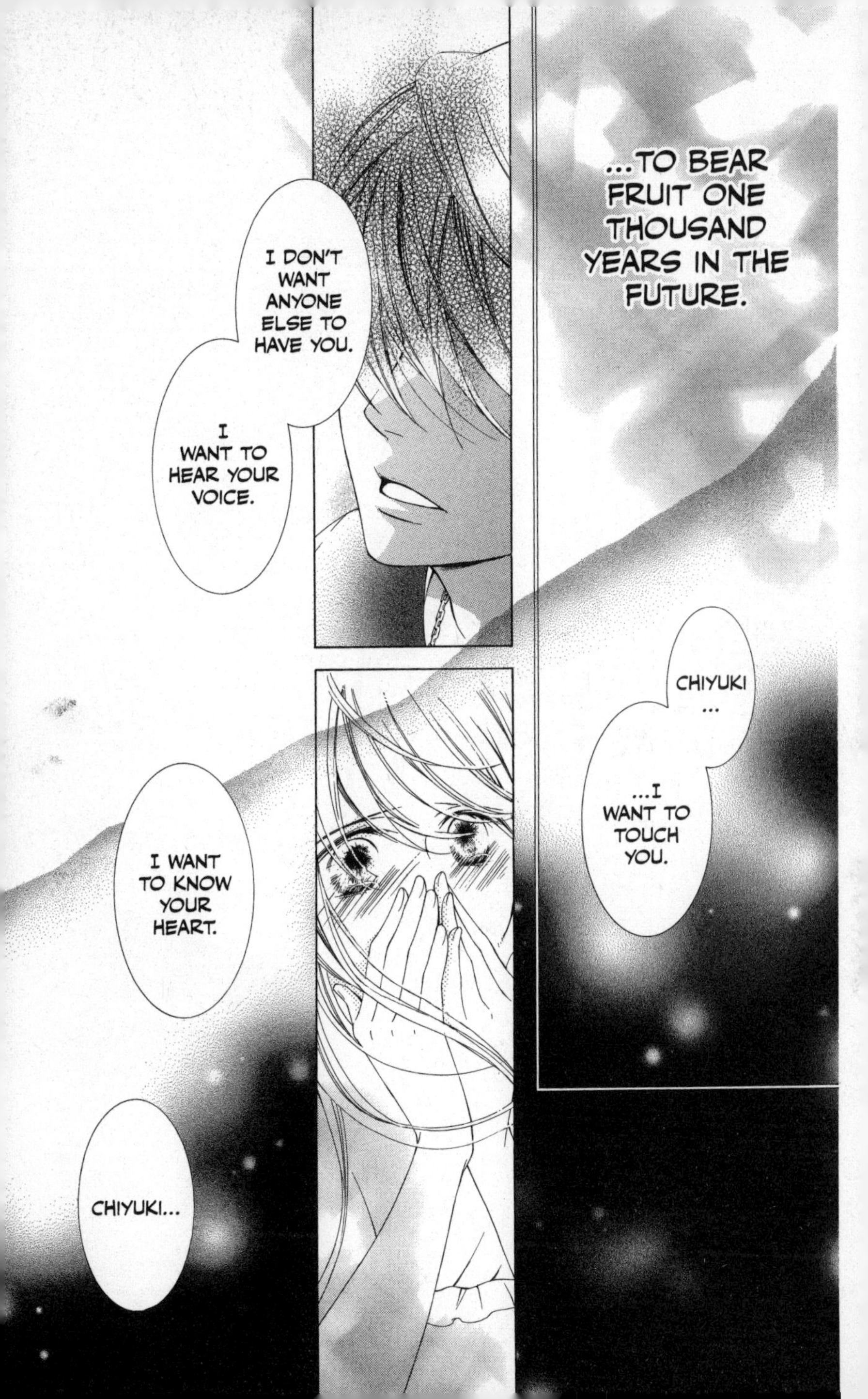

...TO BEAR FRUIT ONE THOUSAND YEARS IN THE FUTURE.
CHIYUKI...
...I WANT TO TOUCH YOU.
I DON'T WANT ANYONE ELSE TO HAVE YOU.
I WANT TO HEAR YOUR VOICE.
I WANT TO KNOW YOUR HEART.
CHIYUKI...

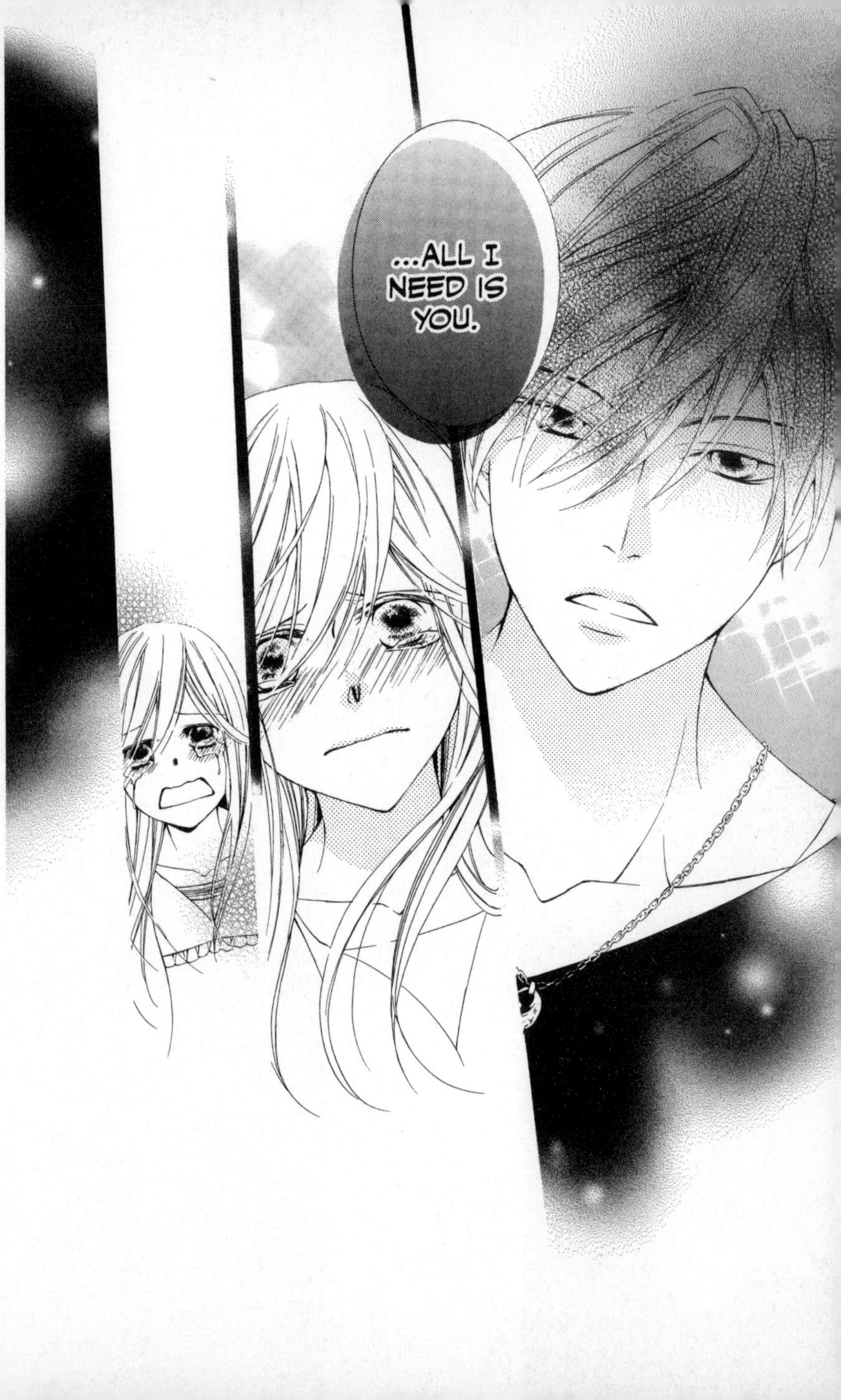
...ALL I NEED IS YOU.

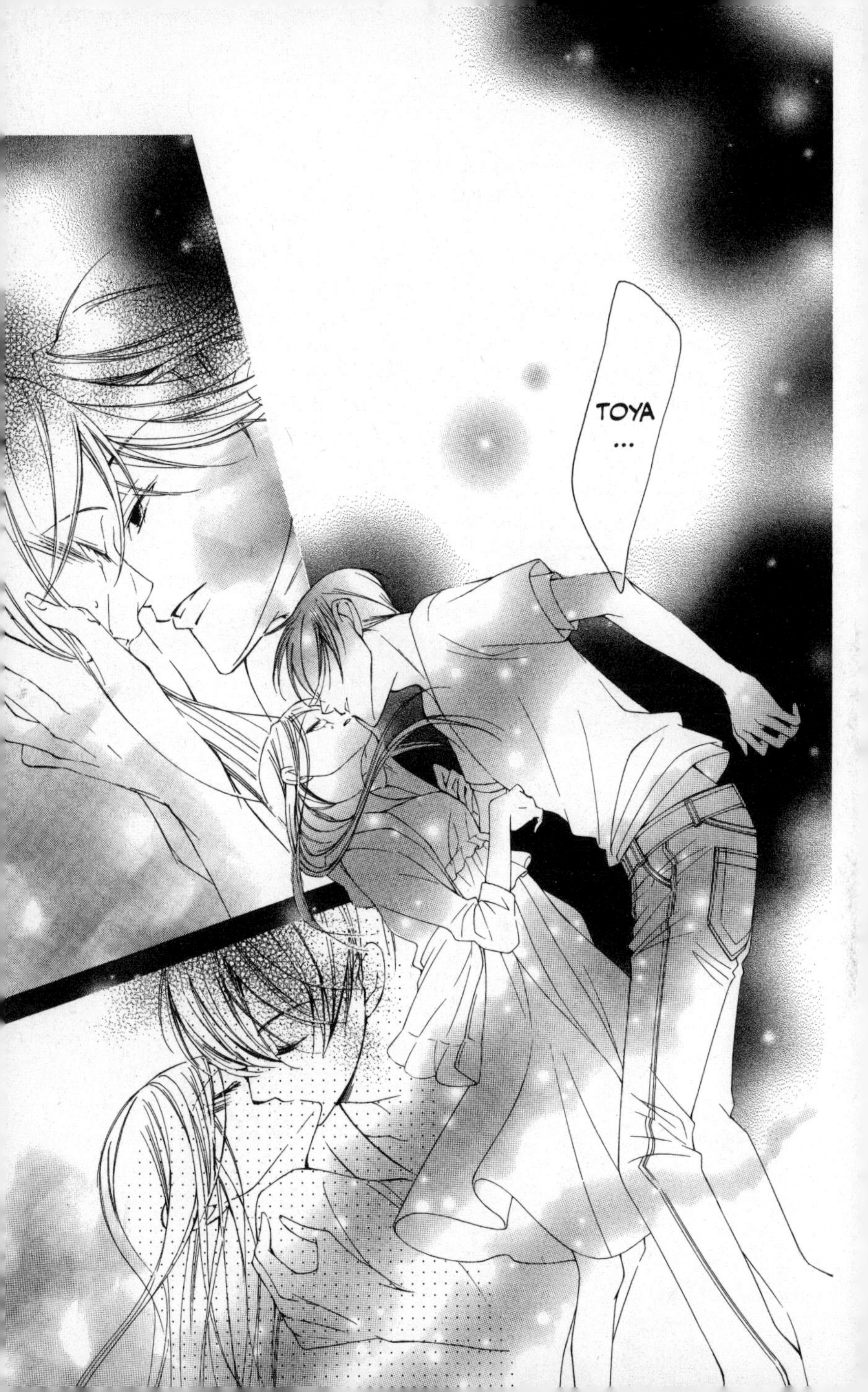
TOYA
...

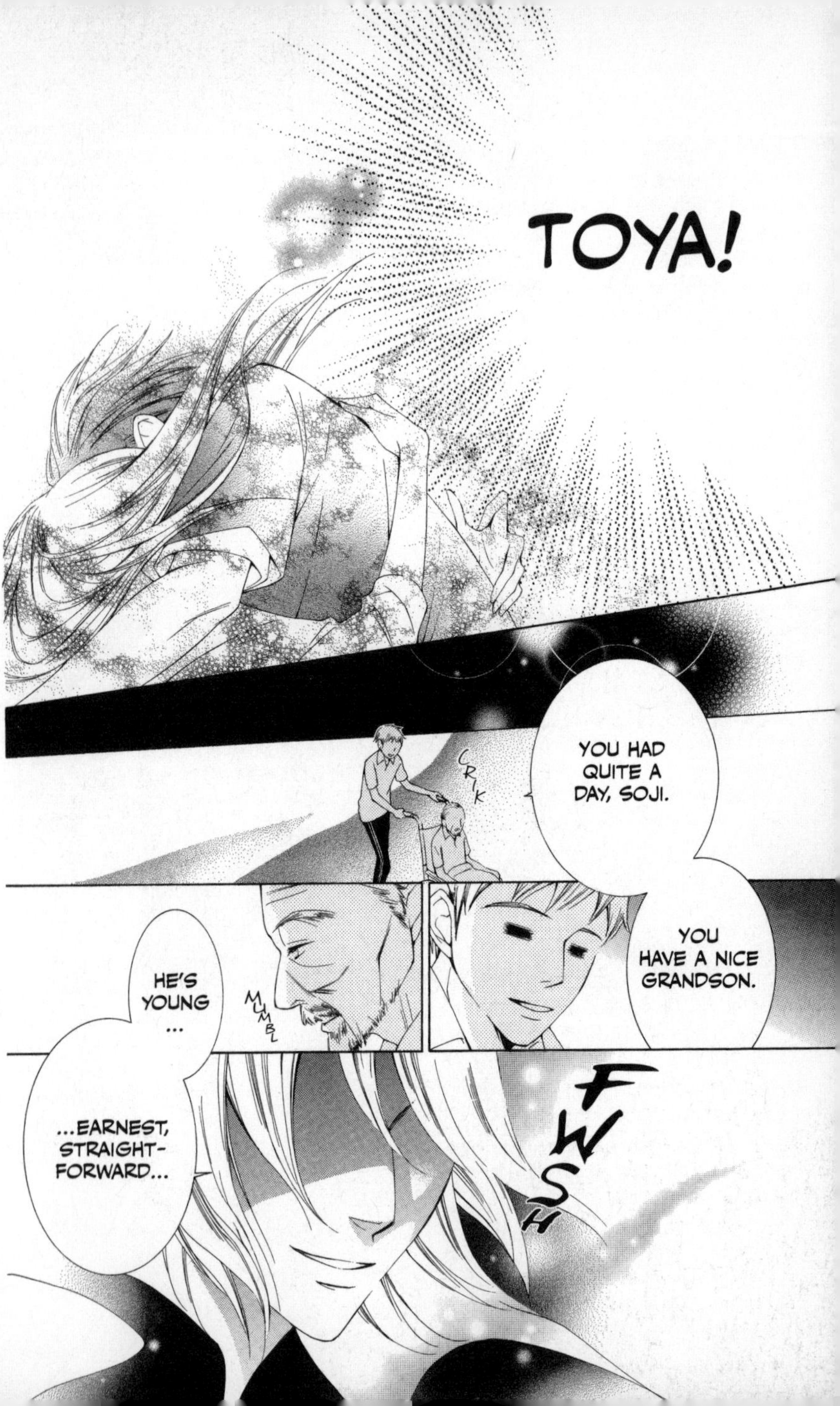
TOYA!
CRIK
YOU HAD QUITE A DAY, SOJI.
YOU HAVE A NICE GRANDSON.
HE'S YOUNG...
MUMBL
FWSH
...EARNEST, STRAIGHT-FORWARD...

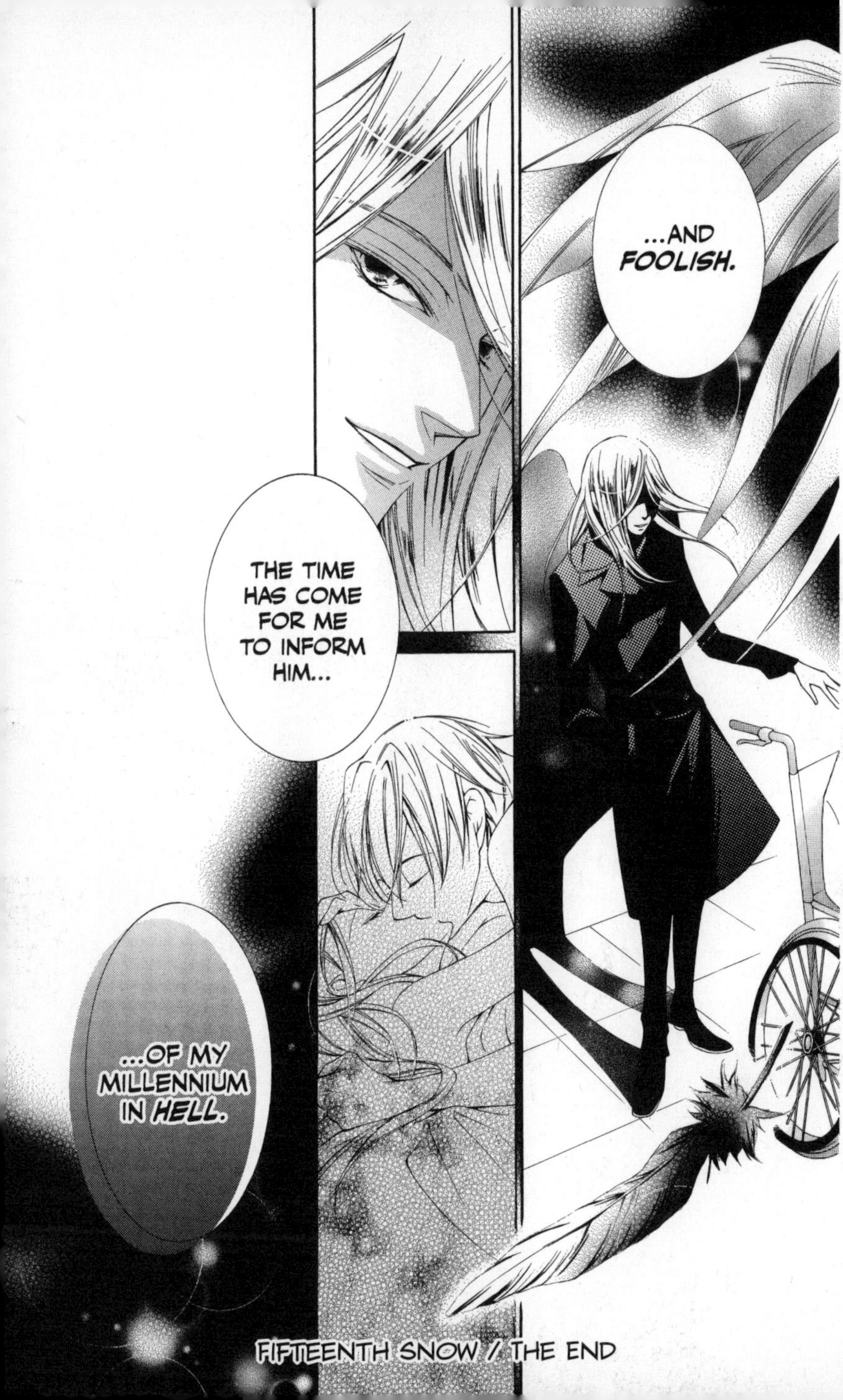
...AND FOOLISH.
THE TIME HAS COME FOR ME TO INFORM HIM...
...OF MY MILLENNIUM IN HELL.
FIFTEENTH SNOW / THE END

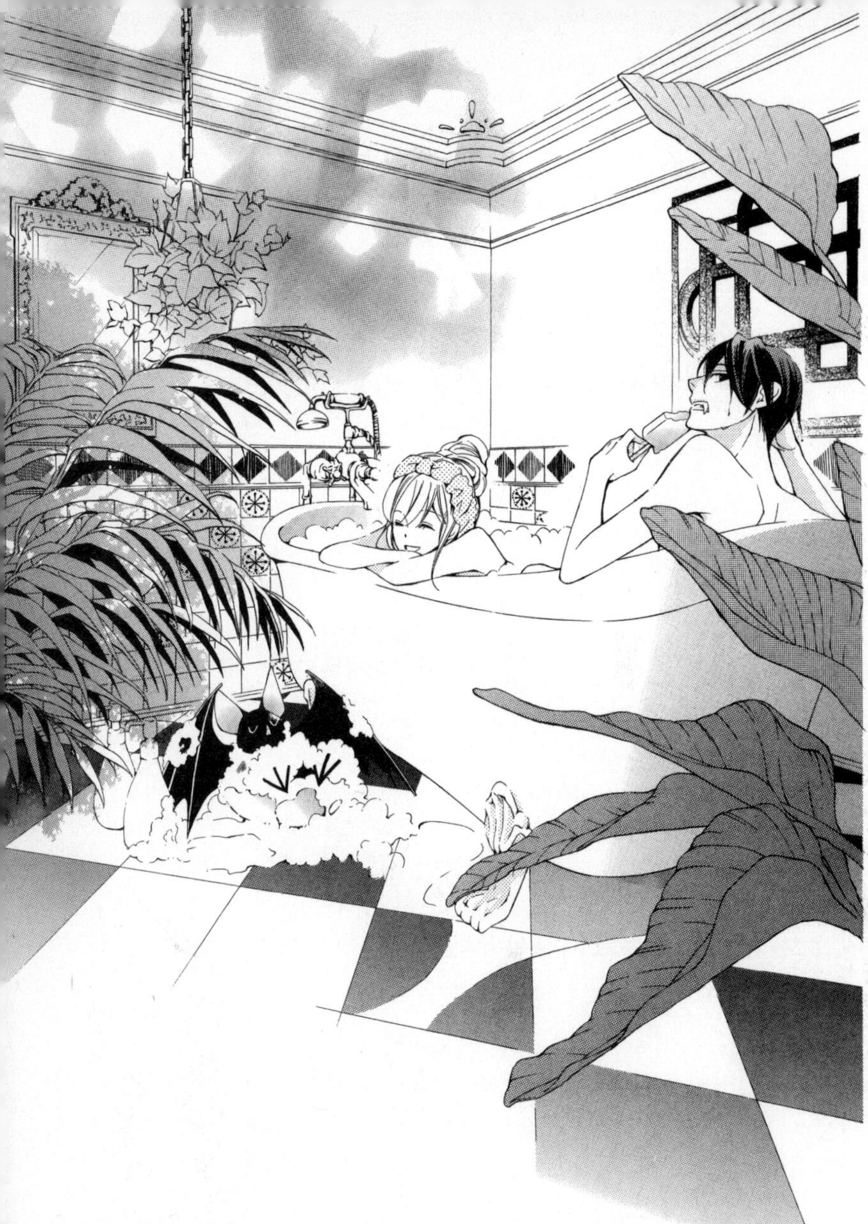

SIXTEENTH SNOW

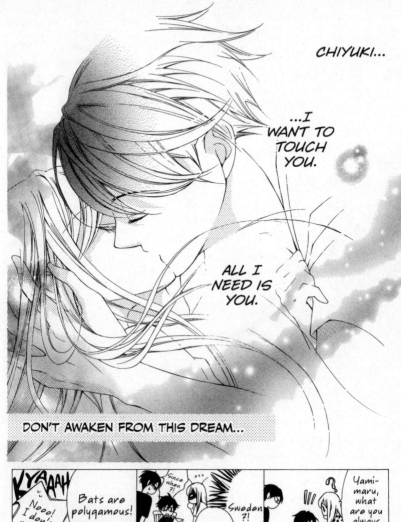

CHIYUKI...
...I WANT TO TOUCH YOU.
ALL I NEED IS YOU.
DON'T AWAKEN FROM THIS DREAM...

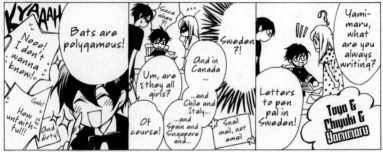

Toya & Chiyuki & Yamimaru
Yami-maru, what are you always writing?
Letters to pen pal in Sweden!
Since when ?!
Sweden ?!
And in Canada ...
Um, are they all girls?
...and Chile and Italy...
...and Spain and Singapore and...
Of course!
Snail mail, not email
KYAAAH
Bats are polygamous!
Nooo! I don't wanna know!
Gah! How unfaith-ful!!
And dirty!

How many wives does he have?!

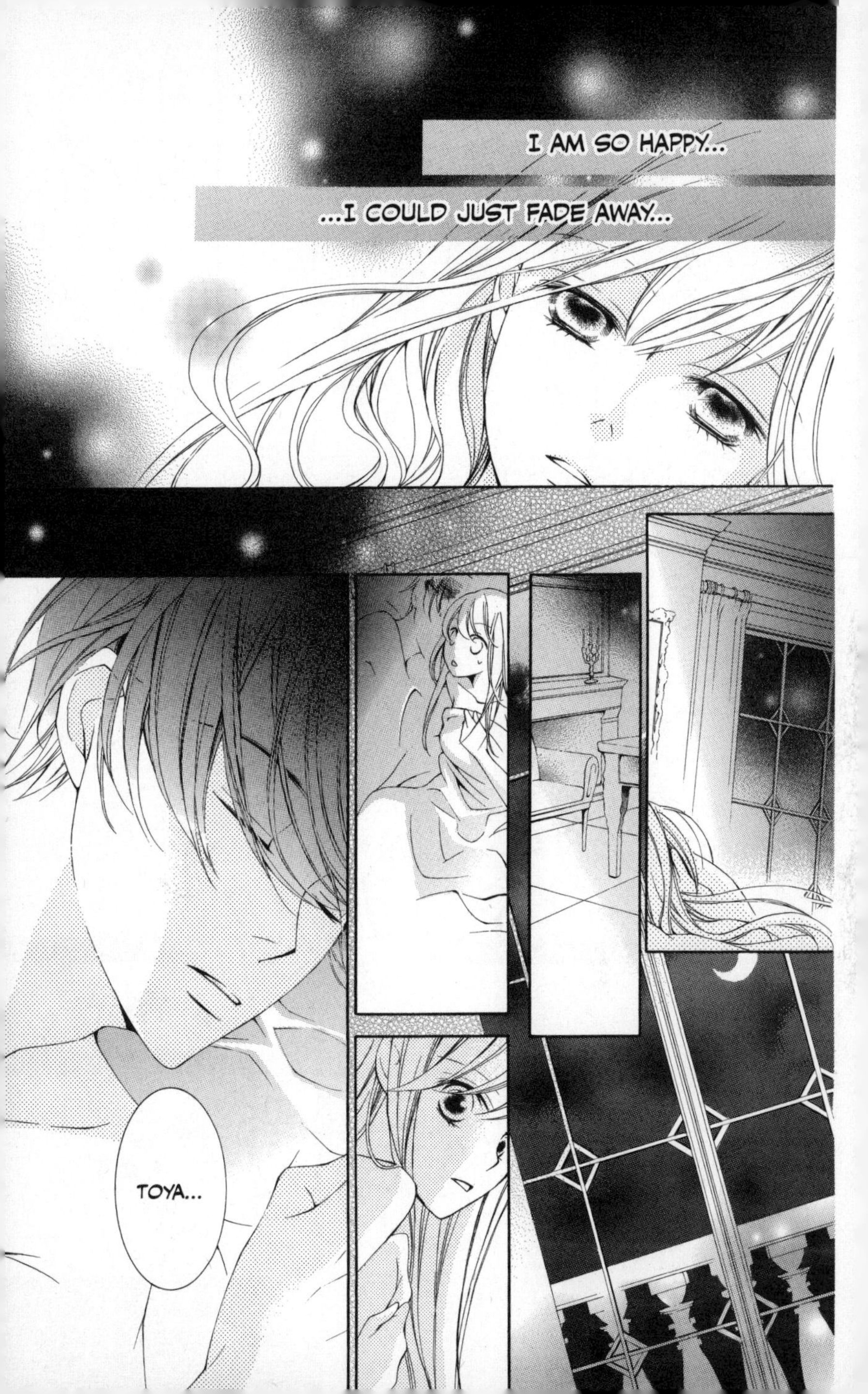
I AM SO HAPPY...
...I COULD JUST FADE AWAY...
TOYA...

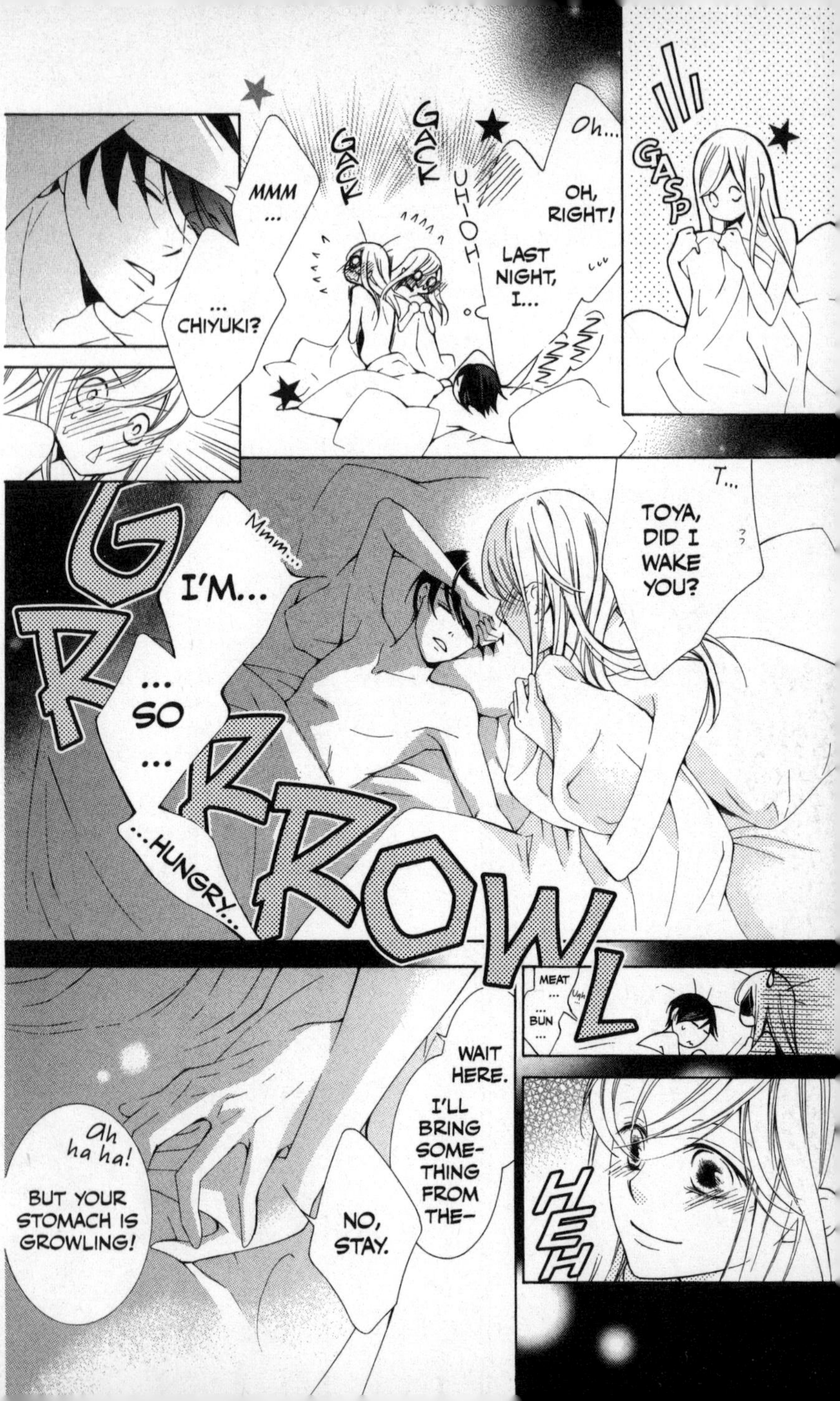
GASP
Oh...
OH, RIGHT!
LAST NIGHT, I...
UHIOH
GACK
GACK
ZZZZ
MMM ...
... CHIYUKI?
T...
TOYA, DID I WAKE YOU?
Mmm...
I'M...
... SO ...
...HUNGRY...
GRRROWL
MEAT ... ... BUN ...
Ugh
HEH
WAIT HERE.
I'LL BRING SOME-THING FROM THE–
NO, STAY.
ah ha ha!
BUT YOUR STOMACH IS GROWLING!

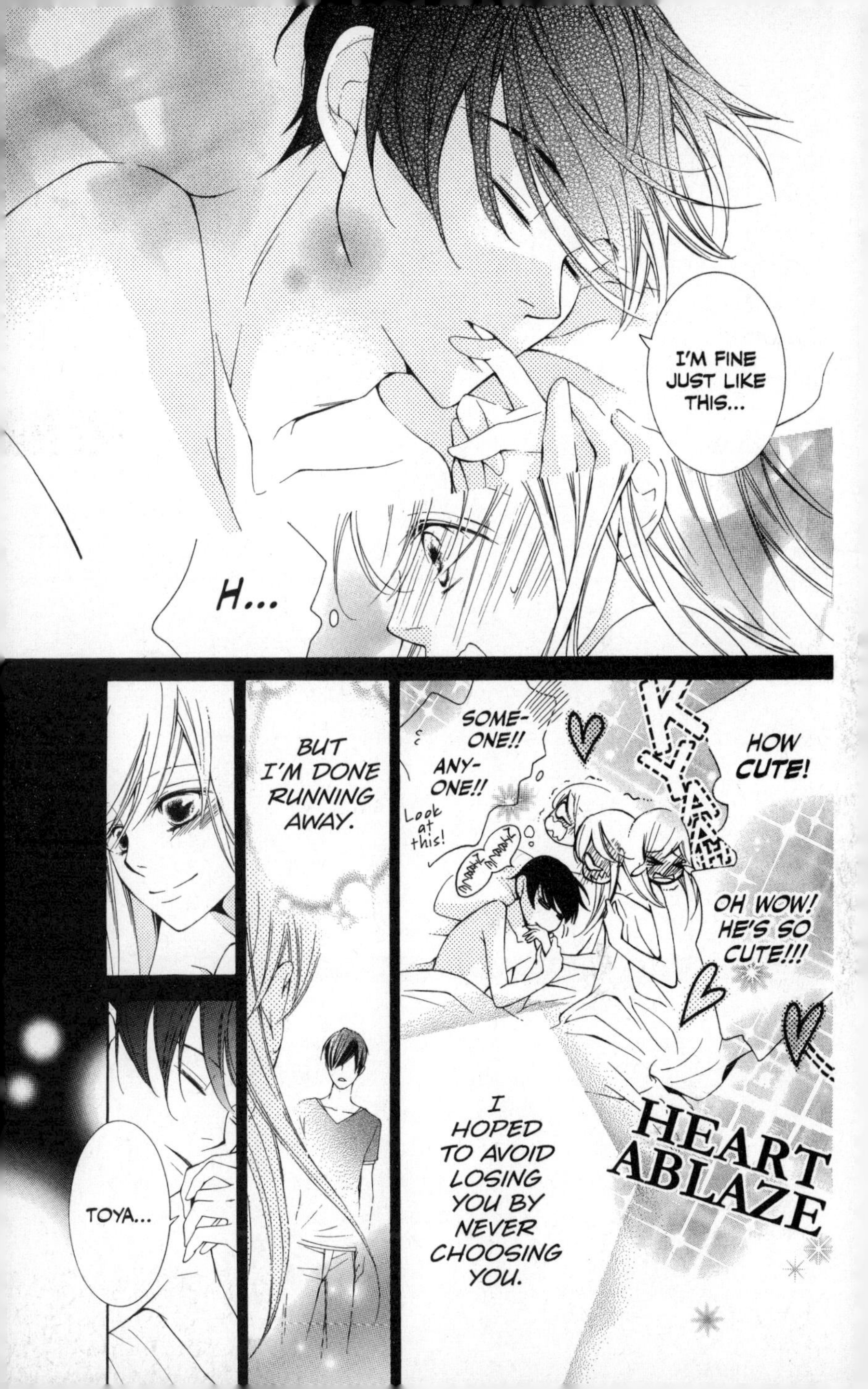
I'M FINE JUST LIKE THIS...
H...
HOW CUTE!
SOME-ONE!!
ANY-ONE!!
Look at this!
OH WOW! HE'S SO CUTE!!!
HEART ABLAZE
I HOPED TO AVOID LOSING YOU BY NEVER CHOOSING YOU.
BUT I'M DONE RUNNING AWAY.
TOYA...

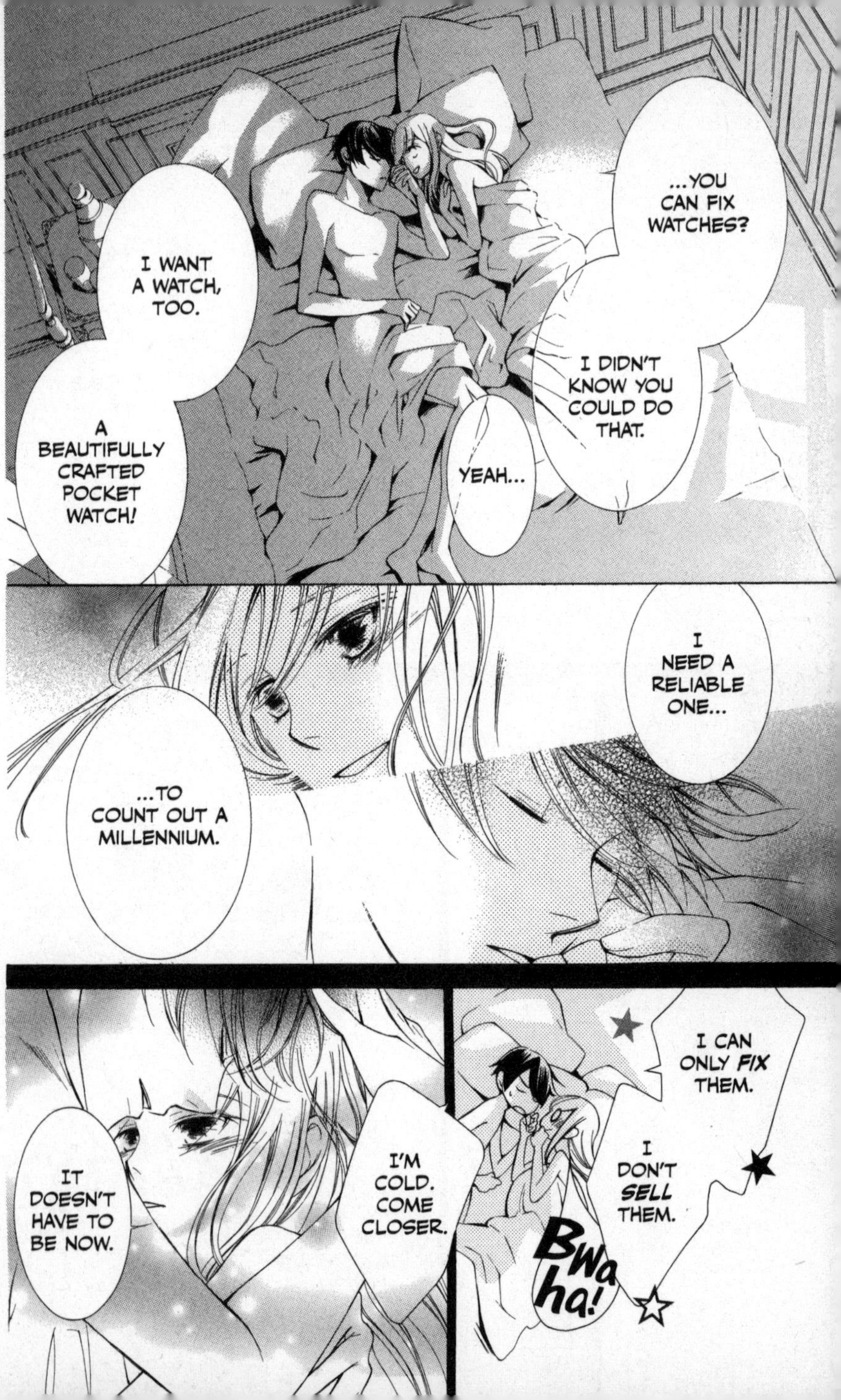
...YOU CAN FIX WATCHES?
I DIDN'T KNOW YOU COULD DO THAT.
YEAH...
I WANT A WATCH, TOO.
A BEAUTIFULLY CRAFTED POCKET WATCH!
I NEED A RELIABLE ONE...
...TO COUNT OUT A MILLENNIUM.
I CAN ONLY *FIX* THEM.
I DON'T *SELL* THEM.
BWaha!
I'M COLD. COME CLOSER.
IT DOESN'T HAVE TO BE NOW.

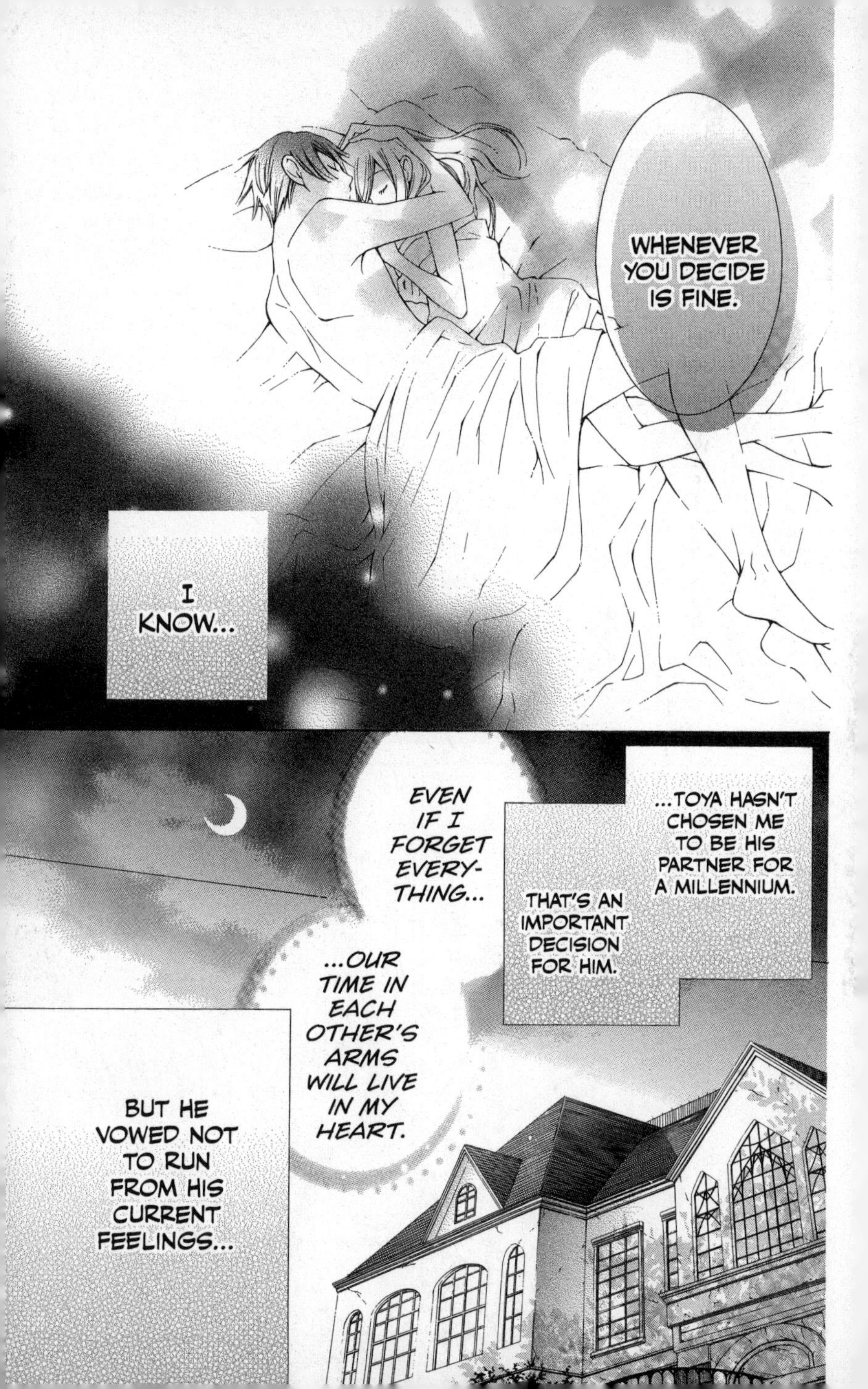
WHENEVER YOU DECIDE IS FINE.
I KNOW...
...TOYA HASN'T CHOSEN ME TO BE HIS PARTNER FOR A MILLENNIUM.
THAT'S AN IMPORTANT DECISION FOR HIM.
EVEN IF I FORGET EVERYTHING...
...OUR TIME IN EACH OTHER'S ARMS WILL LIVE IN MY HEART.
BUT HE VOWED NOT TO RUN FROM HIS CURRENT FEELINGS...

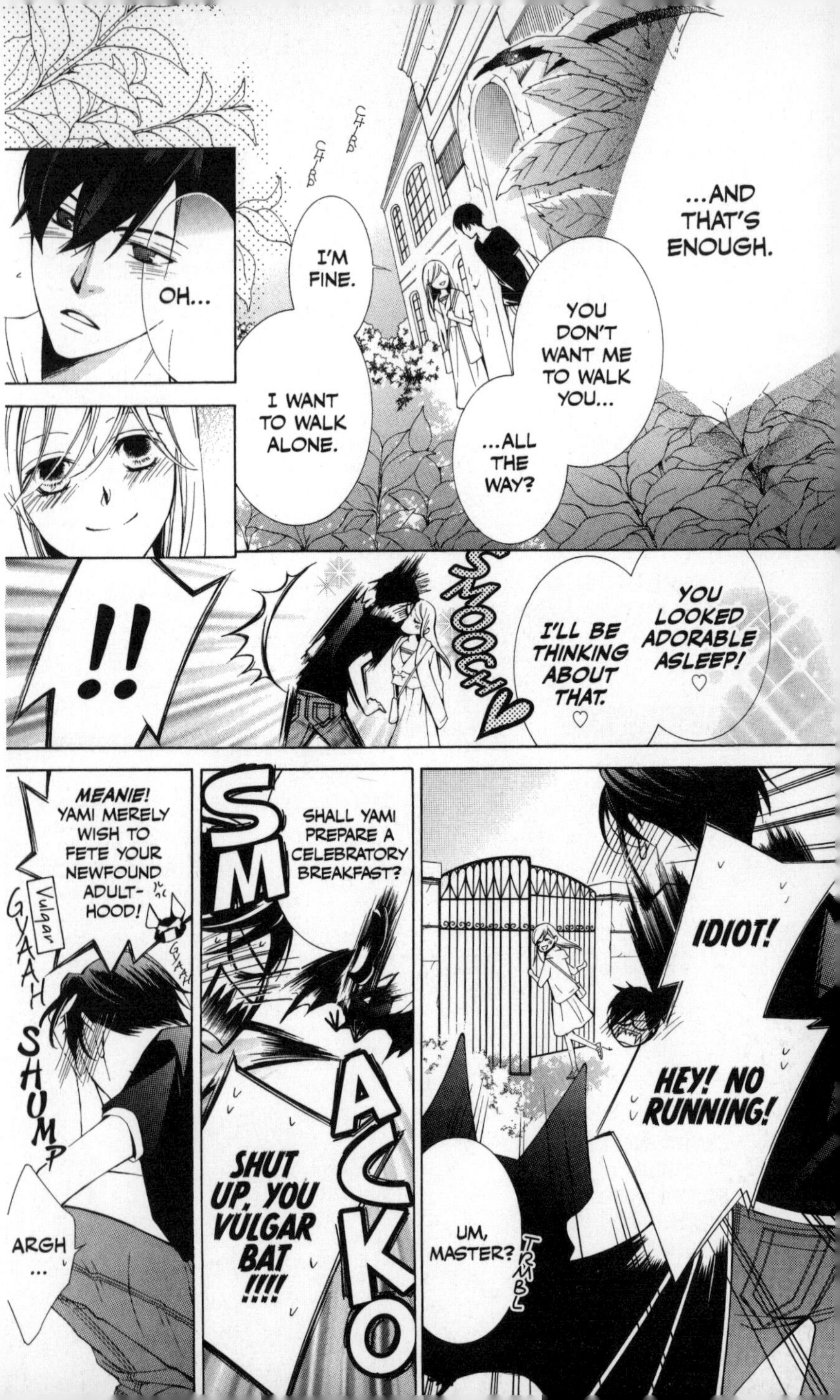
...AND THAT'S ENOUGH.
YOU DON'T WANT ME TO WALK YOU...
...ALL THE WAY?
I'M FINE.
I WANT TO WALK ALONE.
CHIRP
CHIRP
OH...
YOU LOOKED ADORABLE ASLEEP! ♡
I'LL BE THINKING ABOUT THAT. ♡
SMOOCH♥
!!
IDIOT!
HEY! NO RUNNING!
UM, MASTER?
TRMBL
SHALL YAMI PREPARE A CELEBRATORY BREAKFAST?
SMACKO
SHUT UP, YOU VULGAR BAT!!!!
MEANIE! YAMI MERELY WISH TO FETE YOUR NEWFOUND ADULT-HOOD!
Vulgar
GYAAH
SHUMP
ARGH...

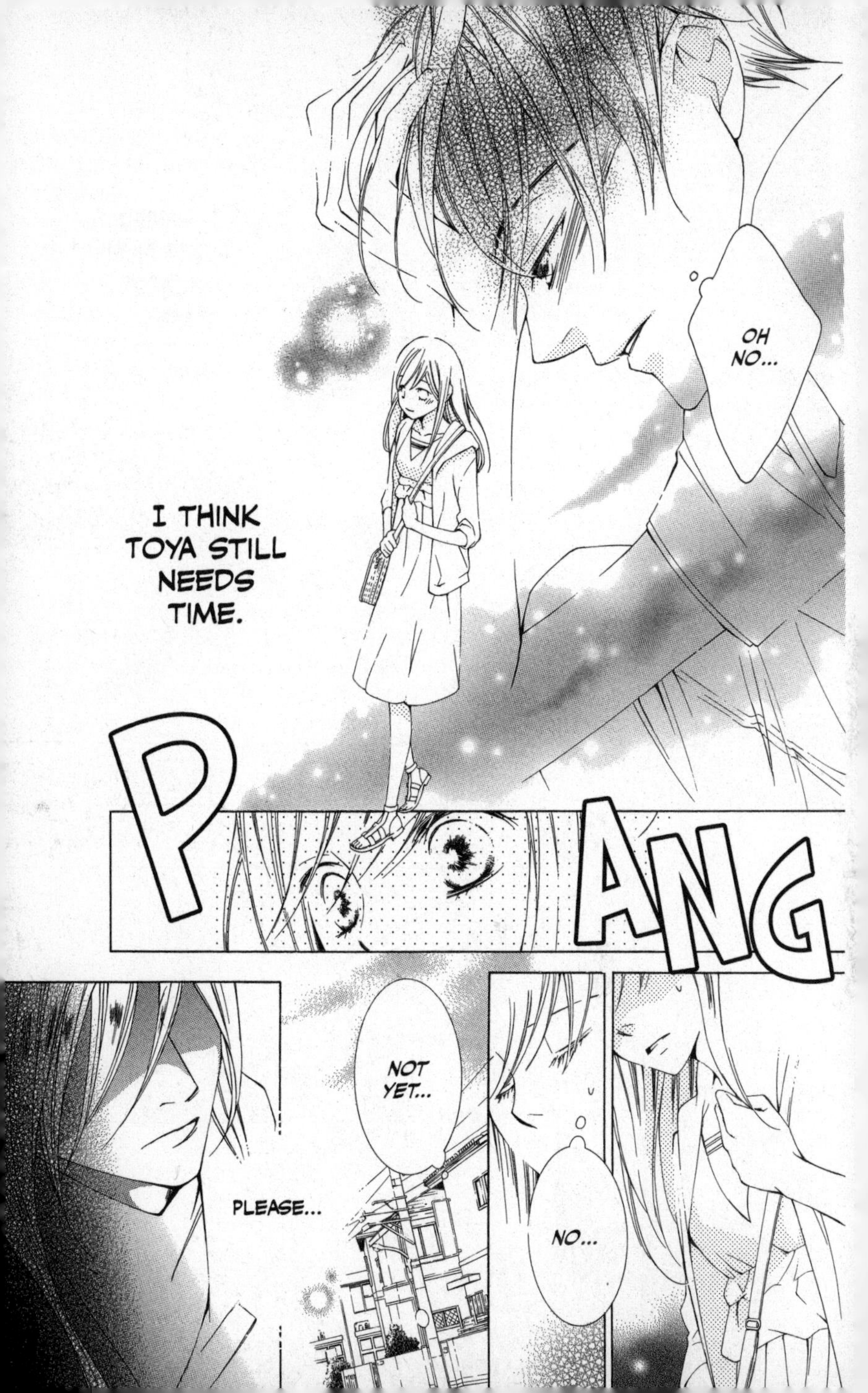
OH NO...
I THINK TOYA STILL NEEDS TIME.
PANG
NO...
NOT YET...
PLEASE...

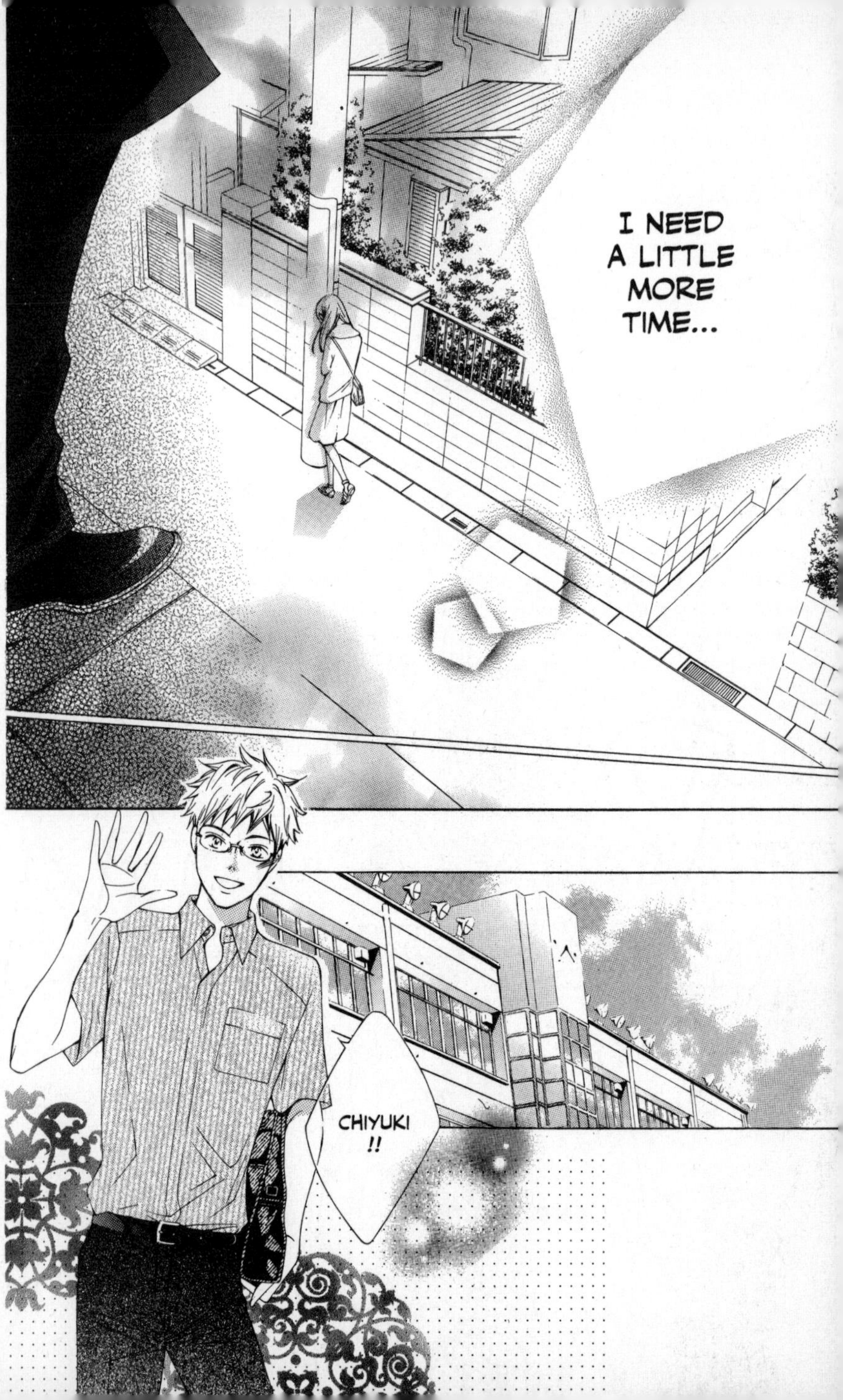
I NEED A LITTLE MORE TIME...
CHIYUKI !!

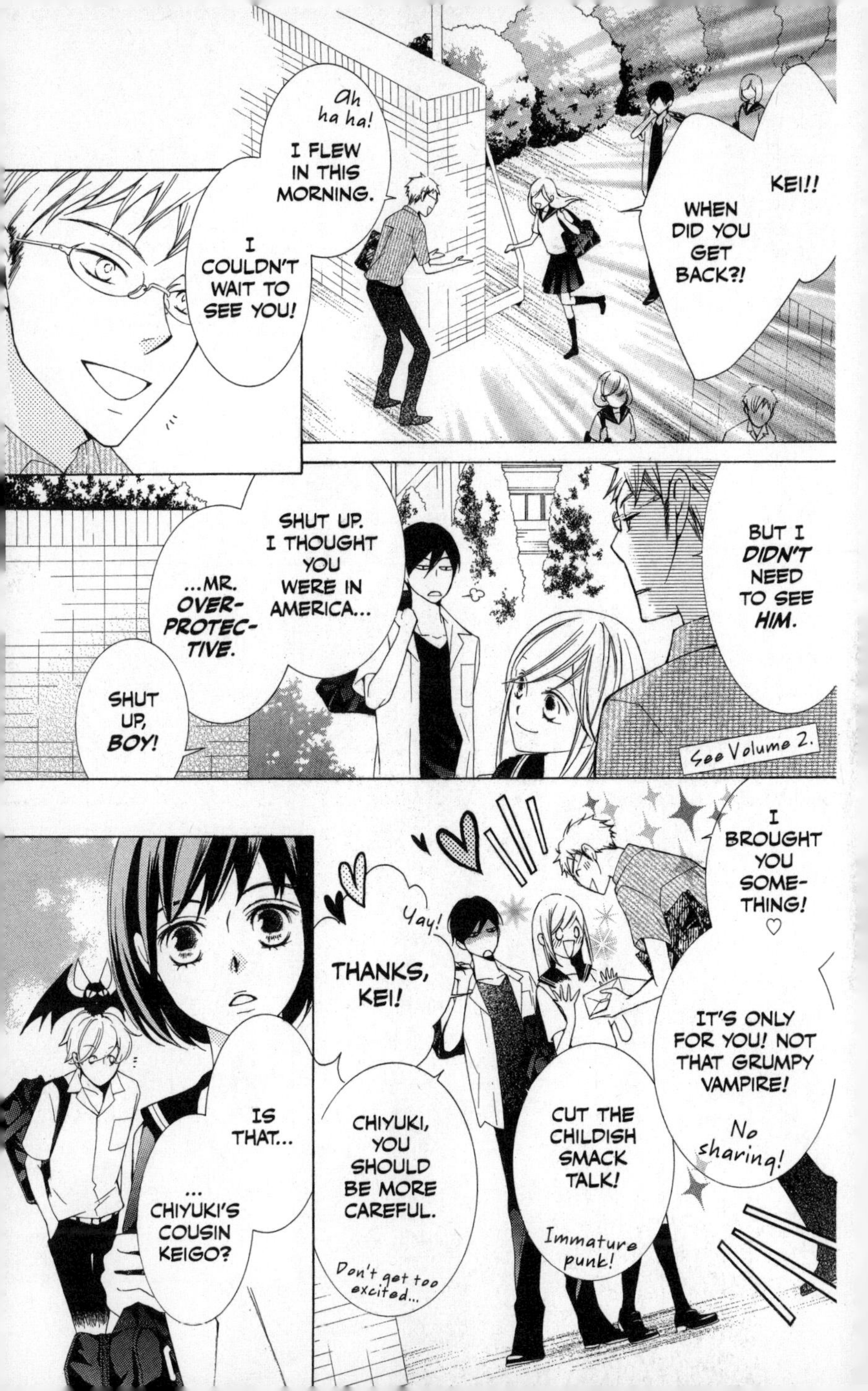
KEI!!
WHEN DID YOU GET BACK?!
ah ha ha!
I FLEW IN THIS MORNING.
I COULDN'T WAIT TO SEE YOU!
BUT I DIDN'T NEED TO SEE HIM.
See Volume 2.
SHUT UP. I THOUGHT YOU WERE IN AMERICA...
...MR. OVER-PROTEC-TIVE.
SHUT UP, BOY!
I BROUGHT YOU SOME-THING! ♡
Yay!
THANKS, KEI!
IT'S ONLY FOR YOU! NOT THAT GRUMPY VAMPIRE!
No sharing!
CUT THE CHILDISH SMACK TALK!
Immature punk!
CHIYUKI, YOU SHOULD BE MORE CAREFUL.
Don't get too excited...
IS THAT...
...CHIYUKI'S COUSIN KEIGO?

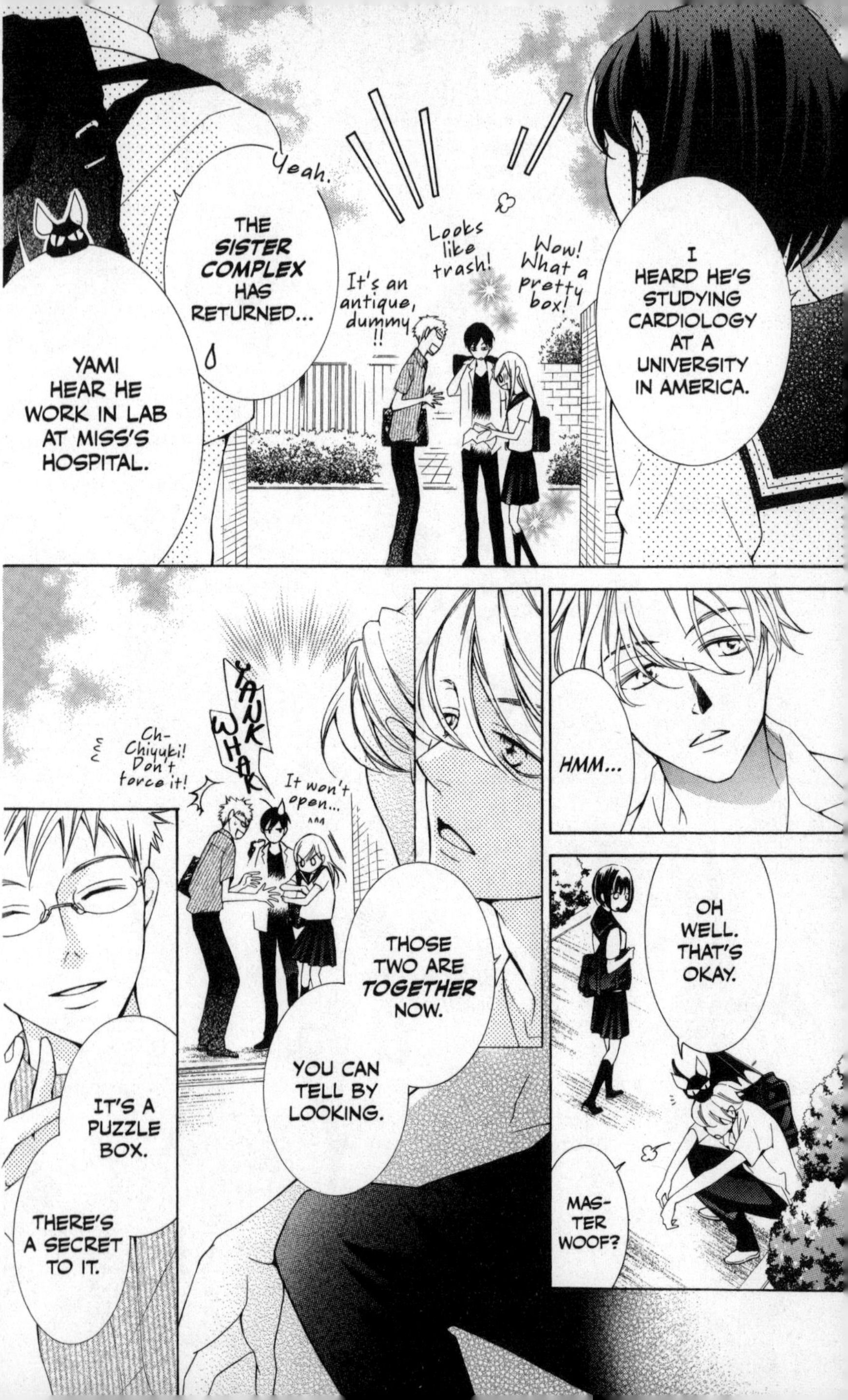
I HEARD HE'S STUDYING CARDIOLOGY AT A UNIVERSITY IN AMERICA.
Wow! What a pretty box!
Looks like trash!
It's an antique, dummy!!
Yeah.
THE SISTER COMPLEX HAS RETURNED...
YAMI HEAR HE WORK IN LAB AT MISS'S HOSPITAL.
HMM...
OH WELL. THAT'S OKAY.
MAS-TER WOOF?
THOSE TWO ARE TOGETHER NOW.
YOU CAN TELL BY LOOKING.
YANK
WHAK
Ch-Chiyuki! Don't force it!
It won't open...
IT'S A PUZZLE BOX.
THERE'S A SECRET TO IT.

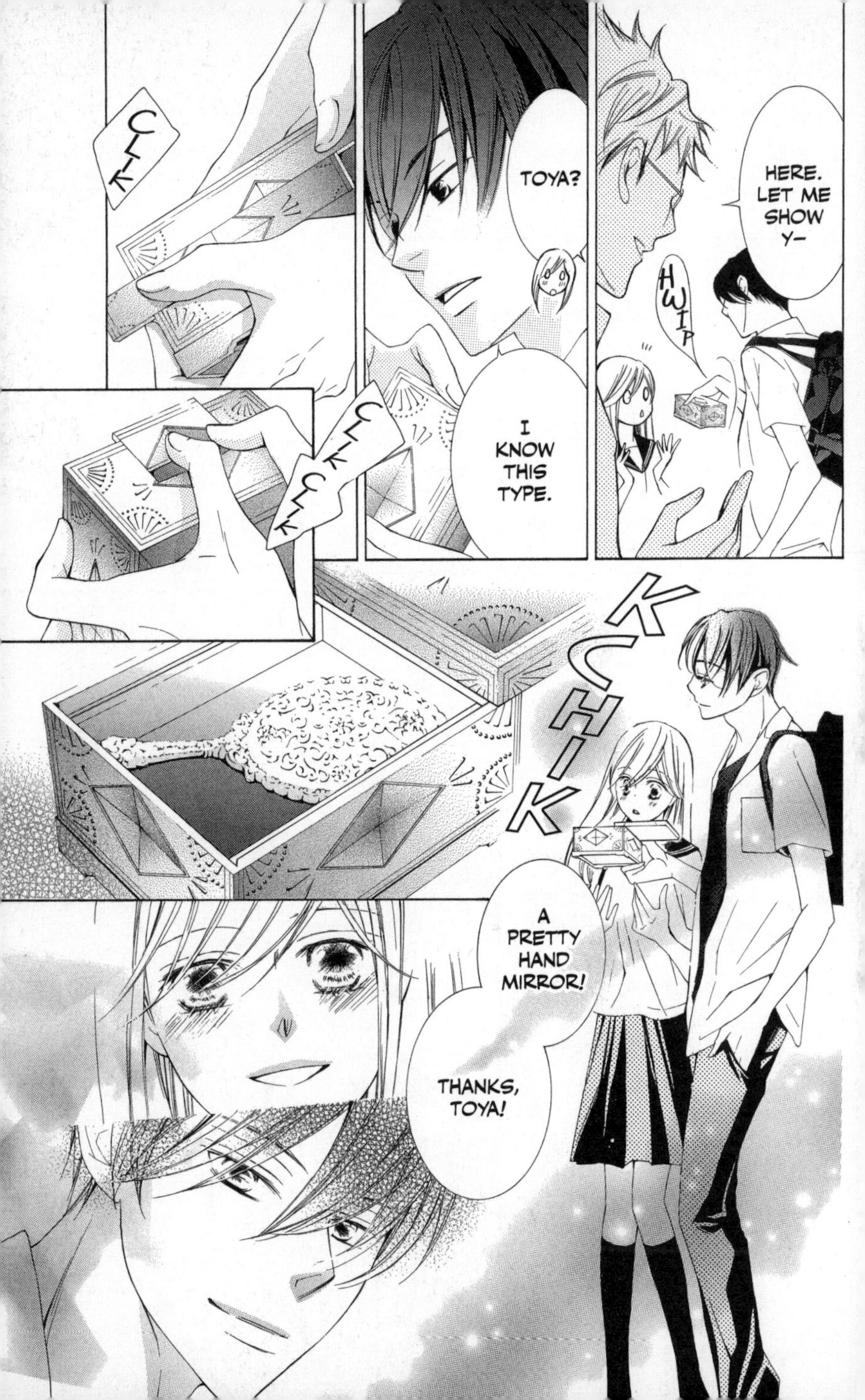
HERE. LET ME SHOW Y—
HWIP
TOYA?
I KNOW THIS TYPE.
CLIK
CLIK CLIK
KCHIK
A PRETTY HAND MIRROR!
THANKS, TOYA!

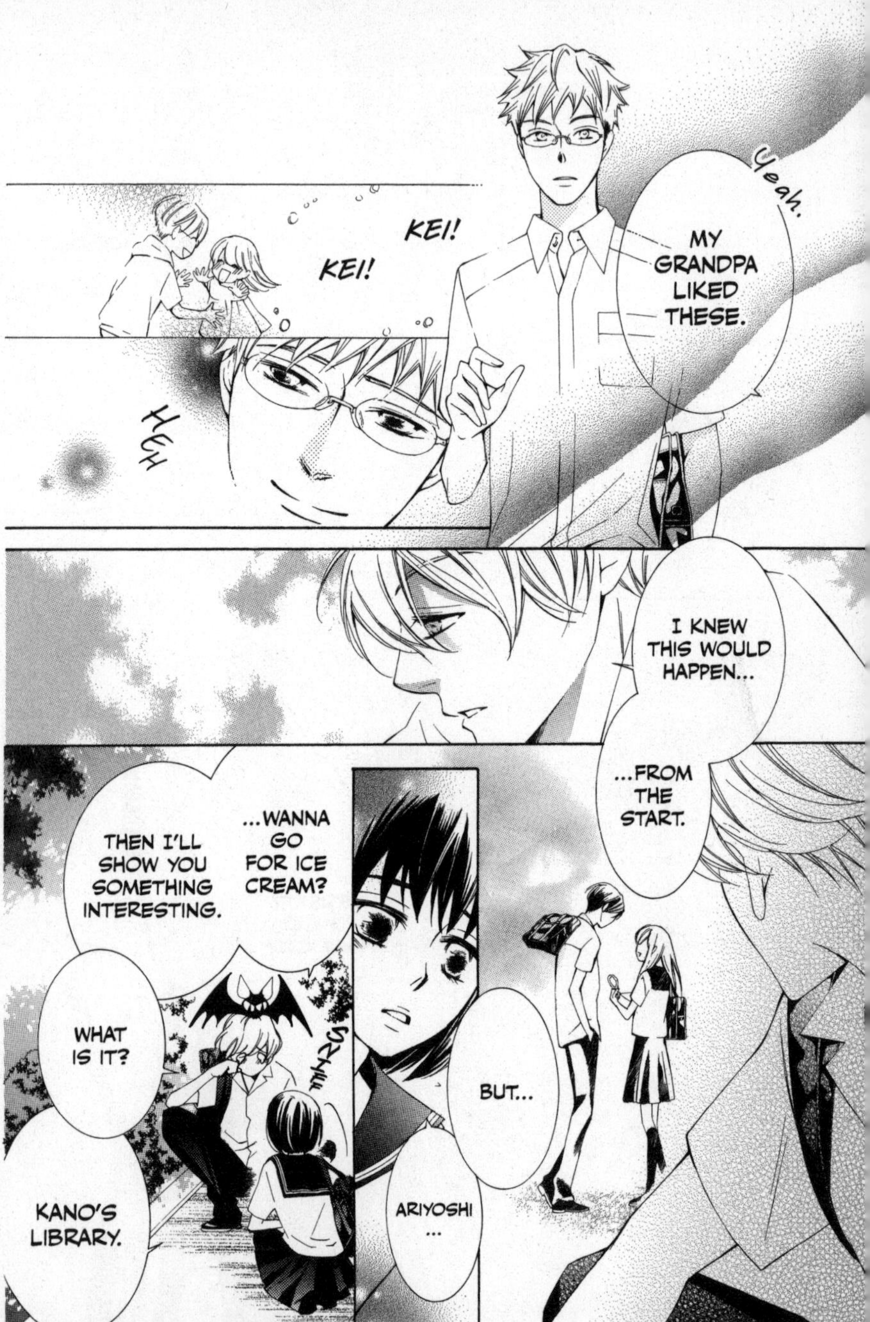
Yeah.
MY GRANDPA LIKED THESE.
KEI!
KEI!
HEH
I KNEW THIS WOULD HAPPEN...
...FROM THE START.
BUT...
ARIYOSHI ...
...WANNA GO FOR ICE CREAM?
THEN I'LL SHOW YOU SOMETHING INTERESTING.
SNIFF
WHAT IS IT?
KANO'S LIBRARY.

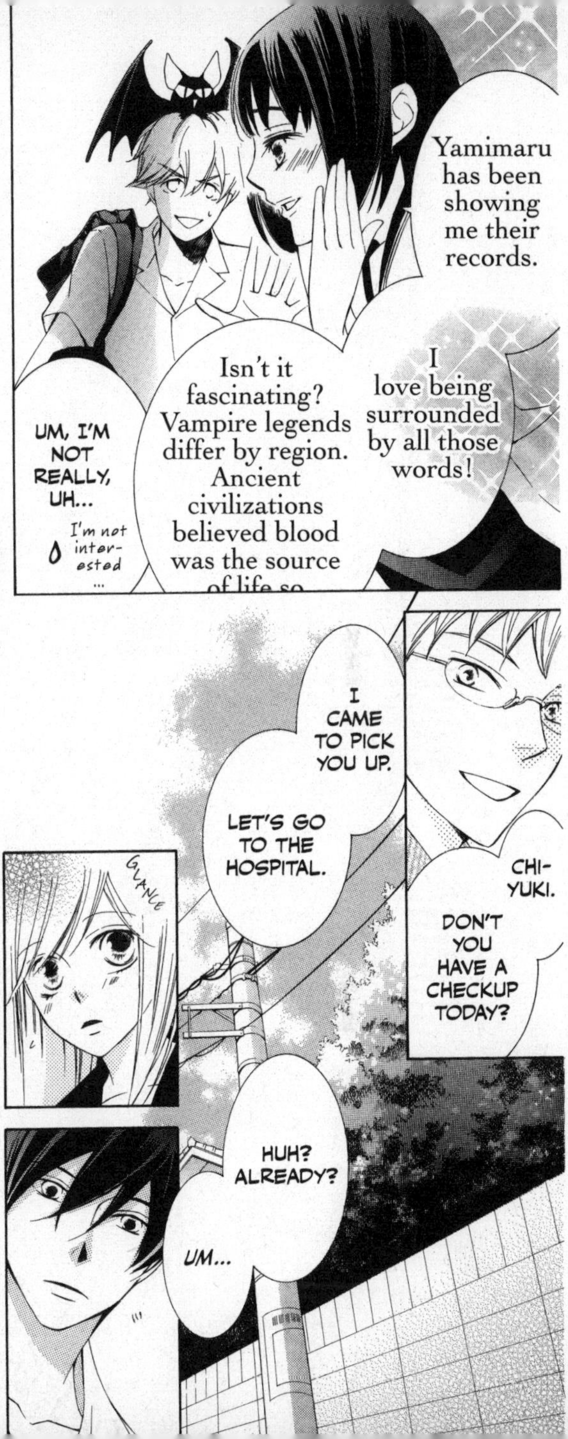
Yamimaru has been showing me their records.
I love being surrounded by all those words!
Isn't it fascinating? Vampire legends differ by region. Ancient civilizations believed blood was the source
UM, I'M NOT REALLY, UH...
I'm not interested...
I CAME TO PICK YOU UP.
CHI-YUKI.
DON'T YOU HAVE A CHECKUP TODAY?
LET'S GO TO THE HOSPITAL.
GLANCE
HUH? ALREADY?
UM...

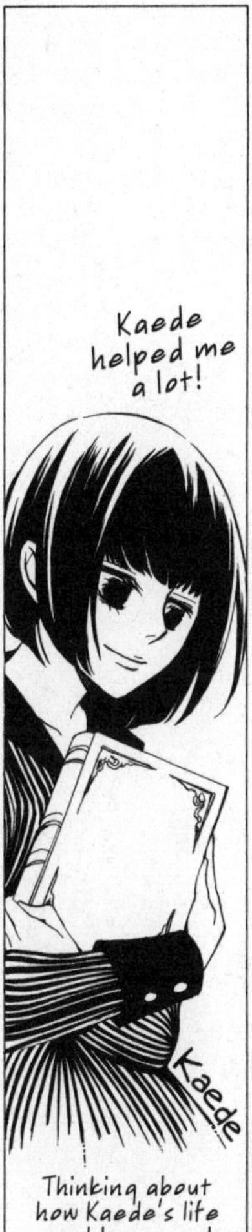
Kaede helped me a lot!
Kaede
Thinking about how Kaede's life would proceed after meeting Chiyuki and the others was a little sad.
She seems to get along well with Satsuki, but that will end sadly, too.

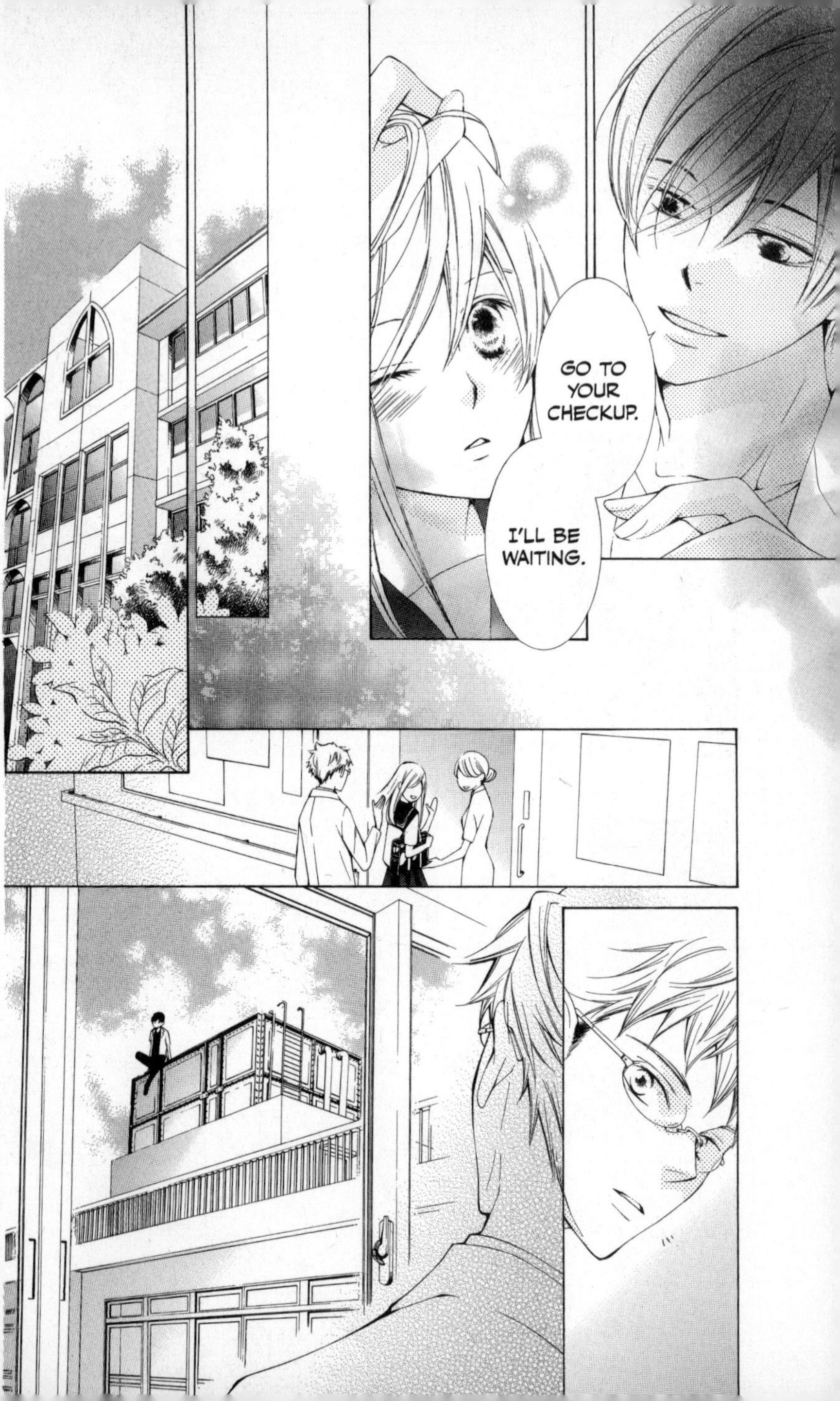
GO TO YOUR CHECKUP.
I'LL BE WAITING.

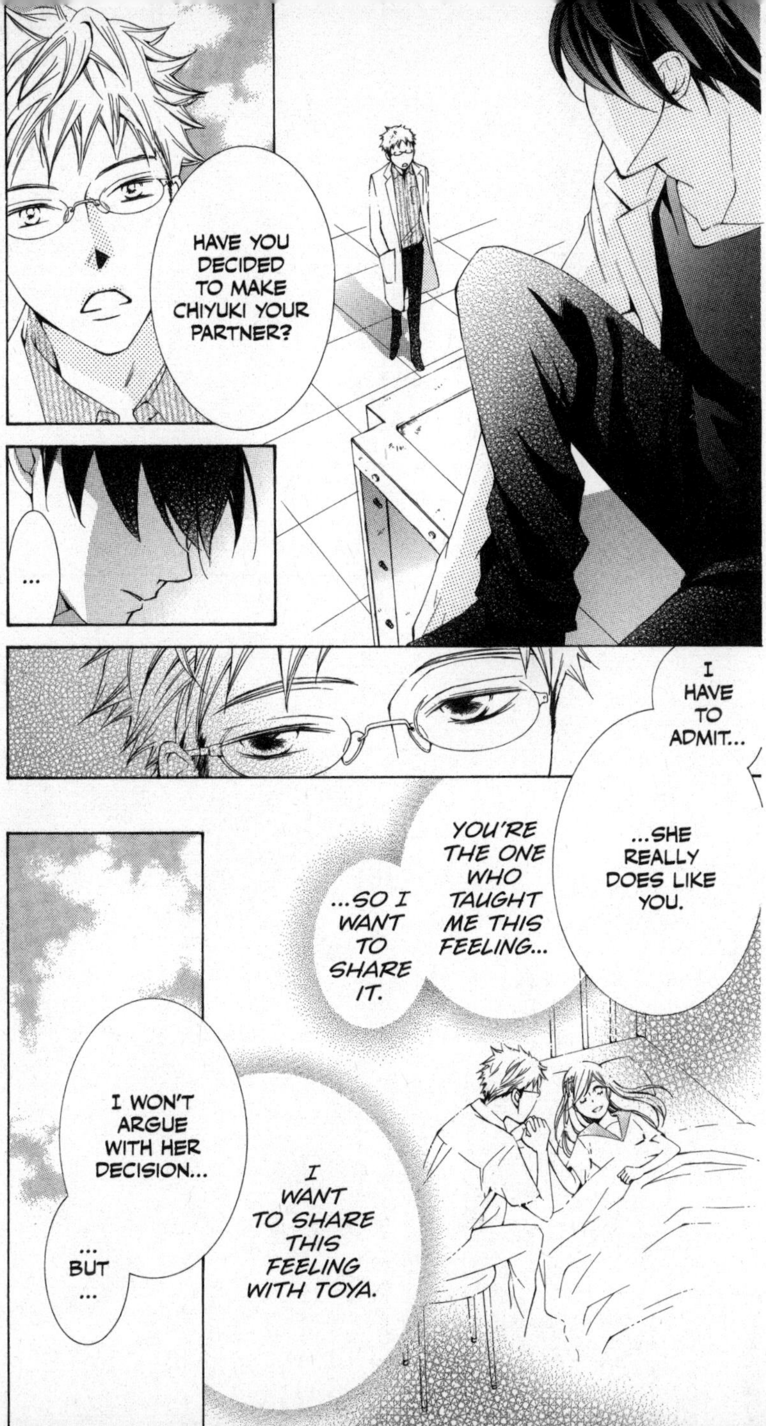
HAVE YOU DECIDED TO MAKE CHIYUKI YOUR PARTNER?
...
I HAVE TO ADMIT...
...SHE REALLY DOES LIKE YOU.
YOU'RE THE ONE WHO TAUGHT ME THIS FEELING...
...SO I WANT TO SHARE IT.
I WON'T ARGUE WITH HER DECISION...
...BUT...
I WANT TO SHARE THIS FEELING WITH TOYA.

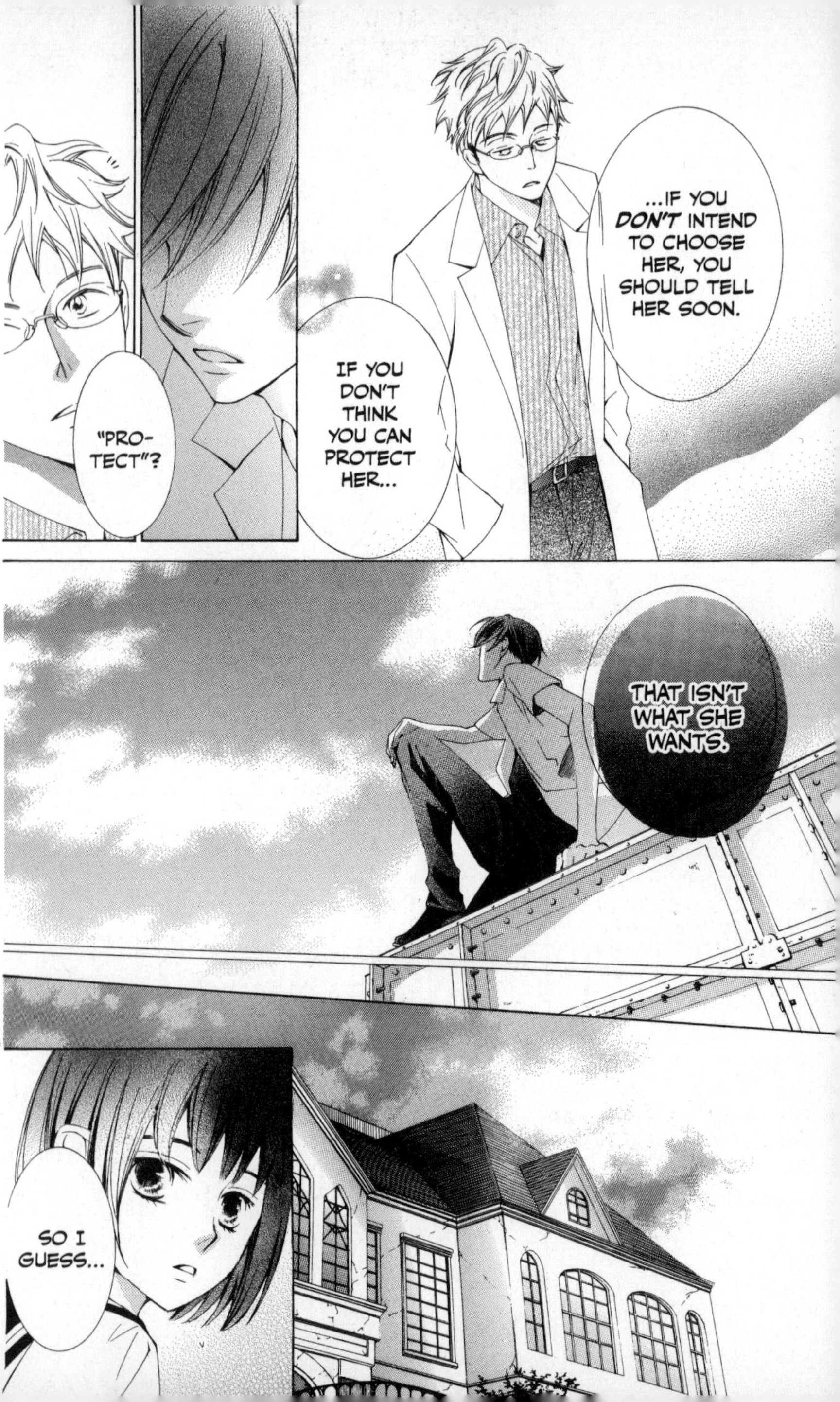
...IF YOU *DON'T* INTEND TO CHOOSE HER, YOU SHOULD TELL HER SOON.
IF YOU DON'T THINK YOU CAN PROTECT HER...
"PRO-TECT"?
THAT ISN'T WHAT SHE WANTS.
SO I GUESS...

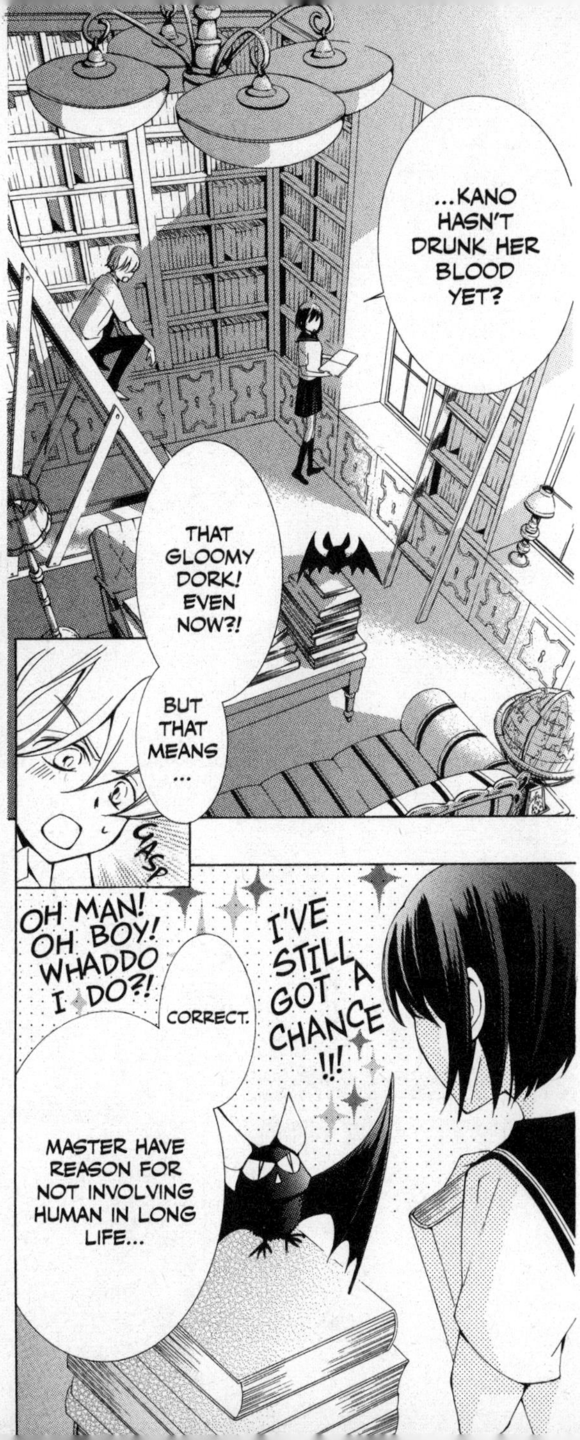
...KANO HASN'T DRUNK HER BLOOD YET?
THAT GLOOMY DORK! EVEN NOW?!
BUT THAT MEANS...
GASP
I'VE STILL GOT A CHANCE!!!
OH MAN! OH BOY! WHADDO I DO?!
CORRECT.
MASTER HAVE REASON FOR NOT INVOLVING HUMAN IN LONG LIFE...

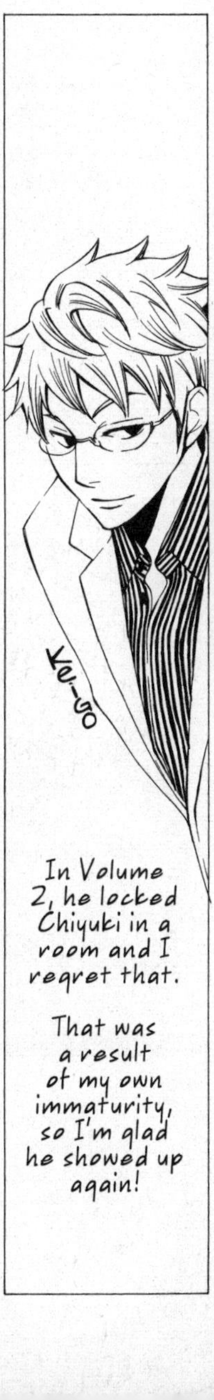
KEIGO

In Volume 2, he locked Chiyuki in a room and I regret that.

That was a result of my own immaturity, so I'm glad he showed up again!

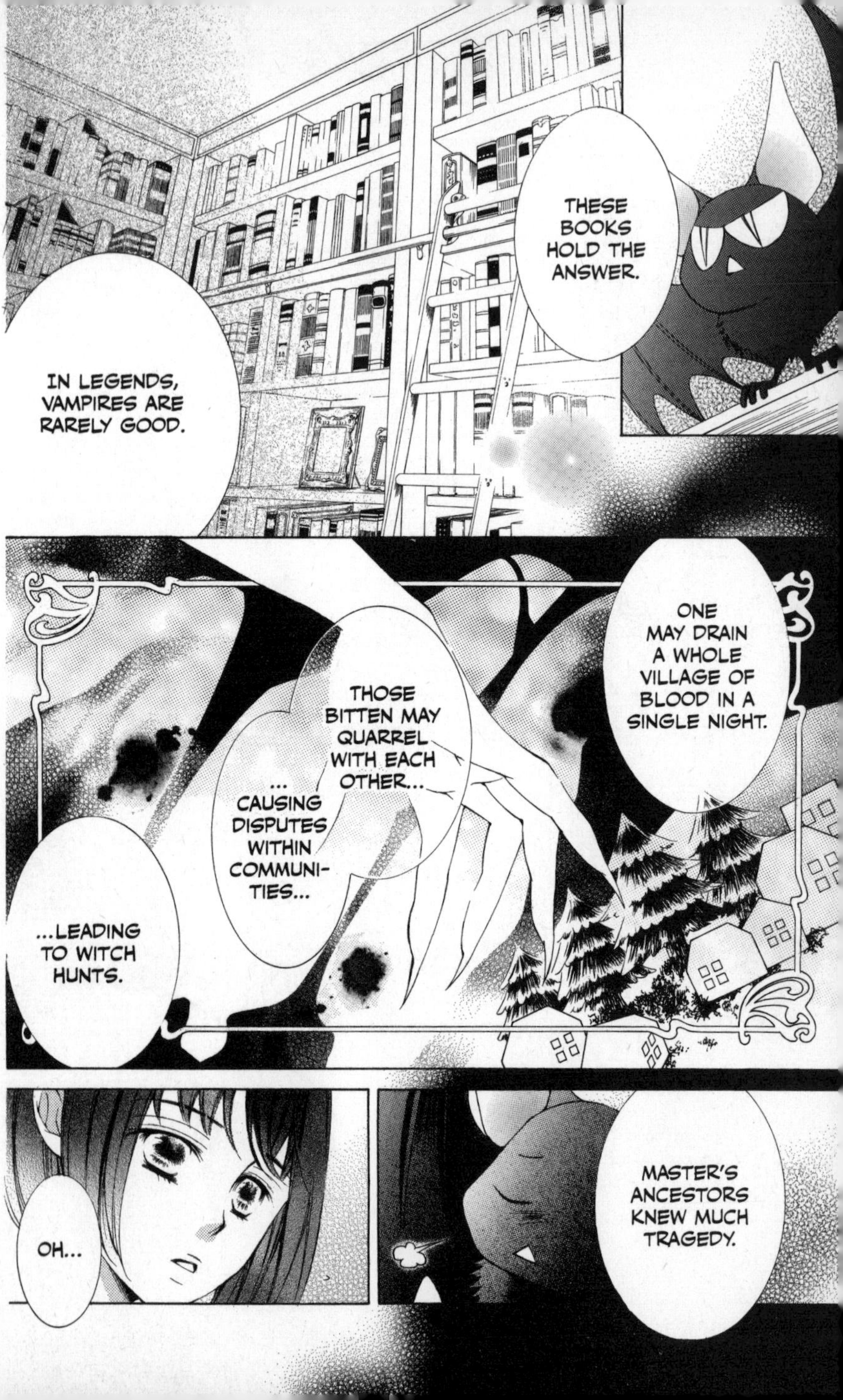
THESE BOOKS HOLD THE ANSWER.
IN LEGENDS, VAMPIRES ARE RARELY GOOD.
ONE MAY DRAIN A WHOLE VILLAGE OF BLOOD IN A SINGLE NIGHT.
THOSE BITTEN MAY QUARREL WITH EACH OTHER...
...CAUSING DISPUTES WITHIN COMMUNITIES...
...LEADING TO WITCH HUNTS.
MASTER'S ANCESTORS KNEW MUCH TRAGEDY.
OH...

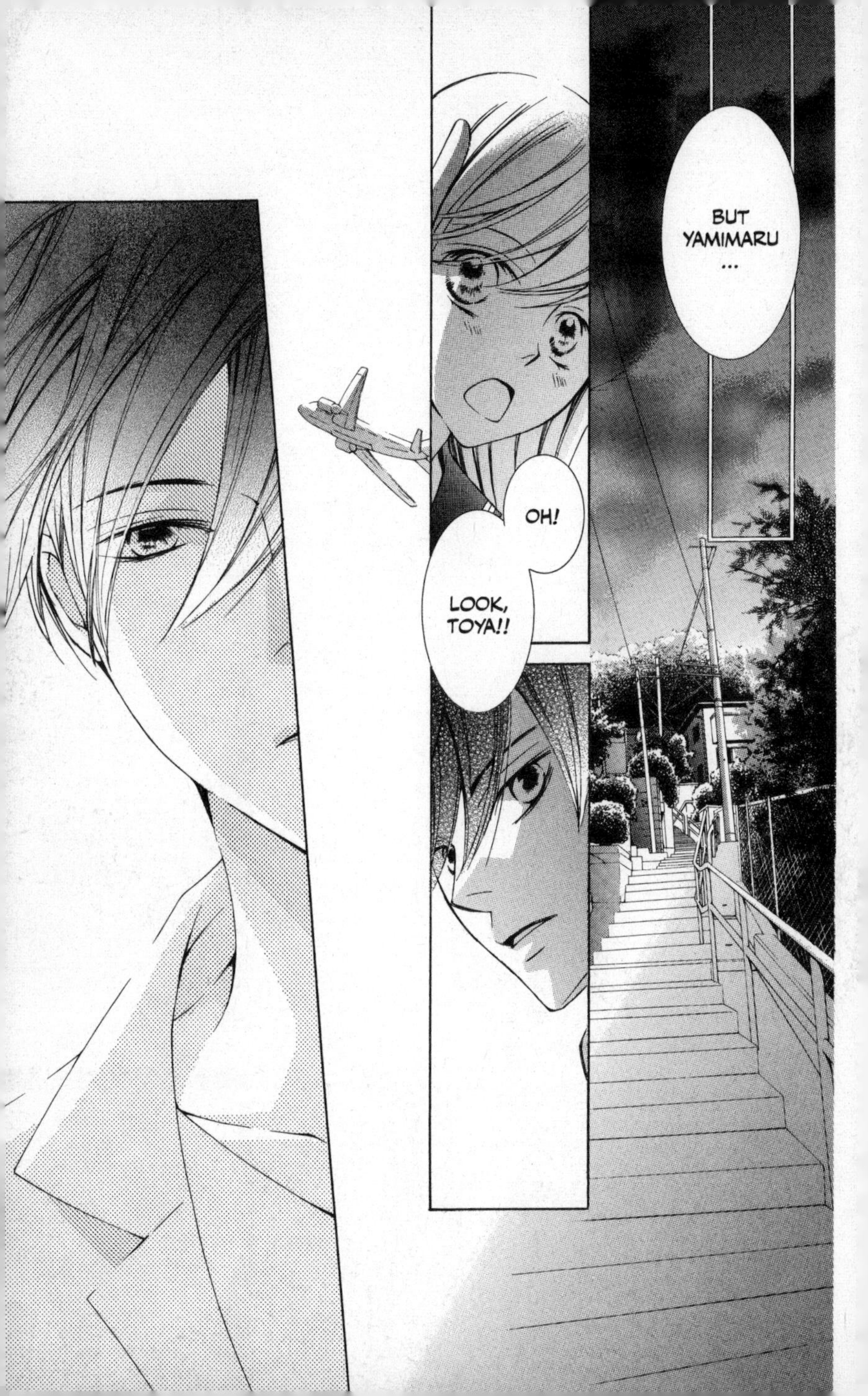
BUT YAMIMARU ...
OH!
LOOK, TOYA!!

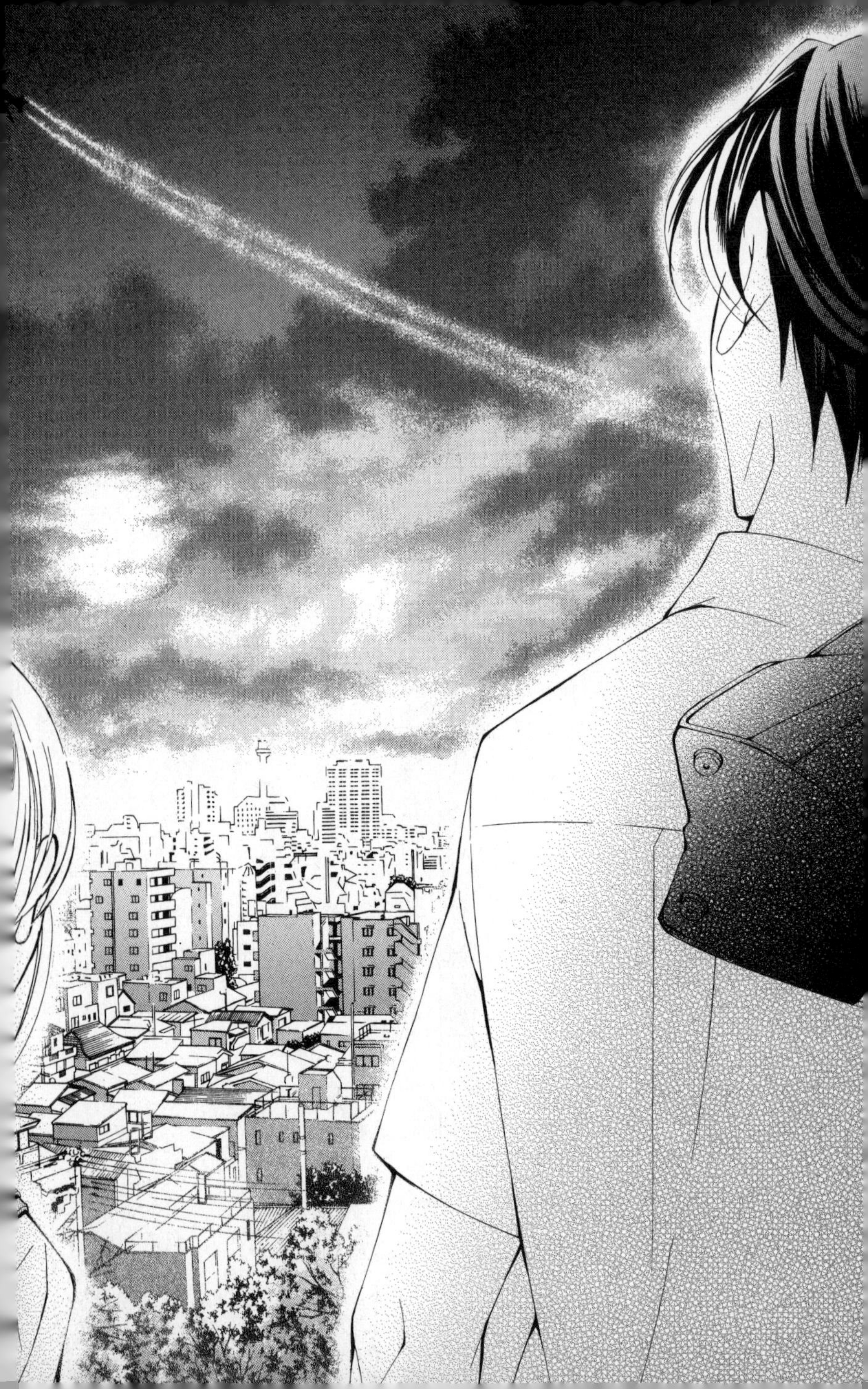

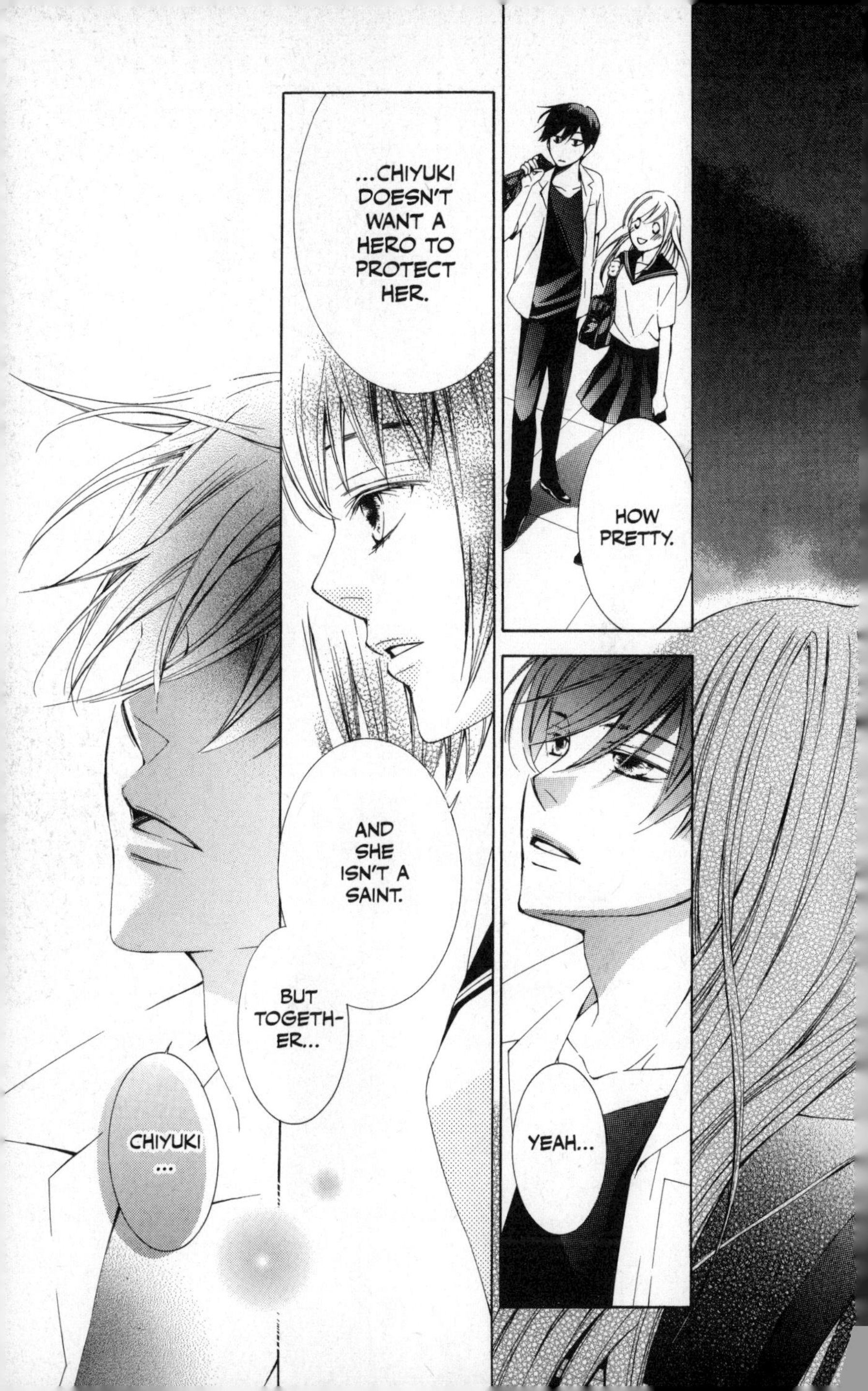
HOW PRETTY.
YEAH...
...CHIYUKI DOESN'T WANT A HERO TO PROTECT HER.
AND SHE ISN'T A SAINT.
BUT TOGETH-ER...
CHIYUKI ...

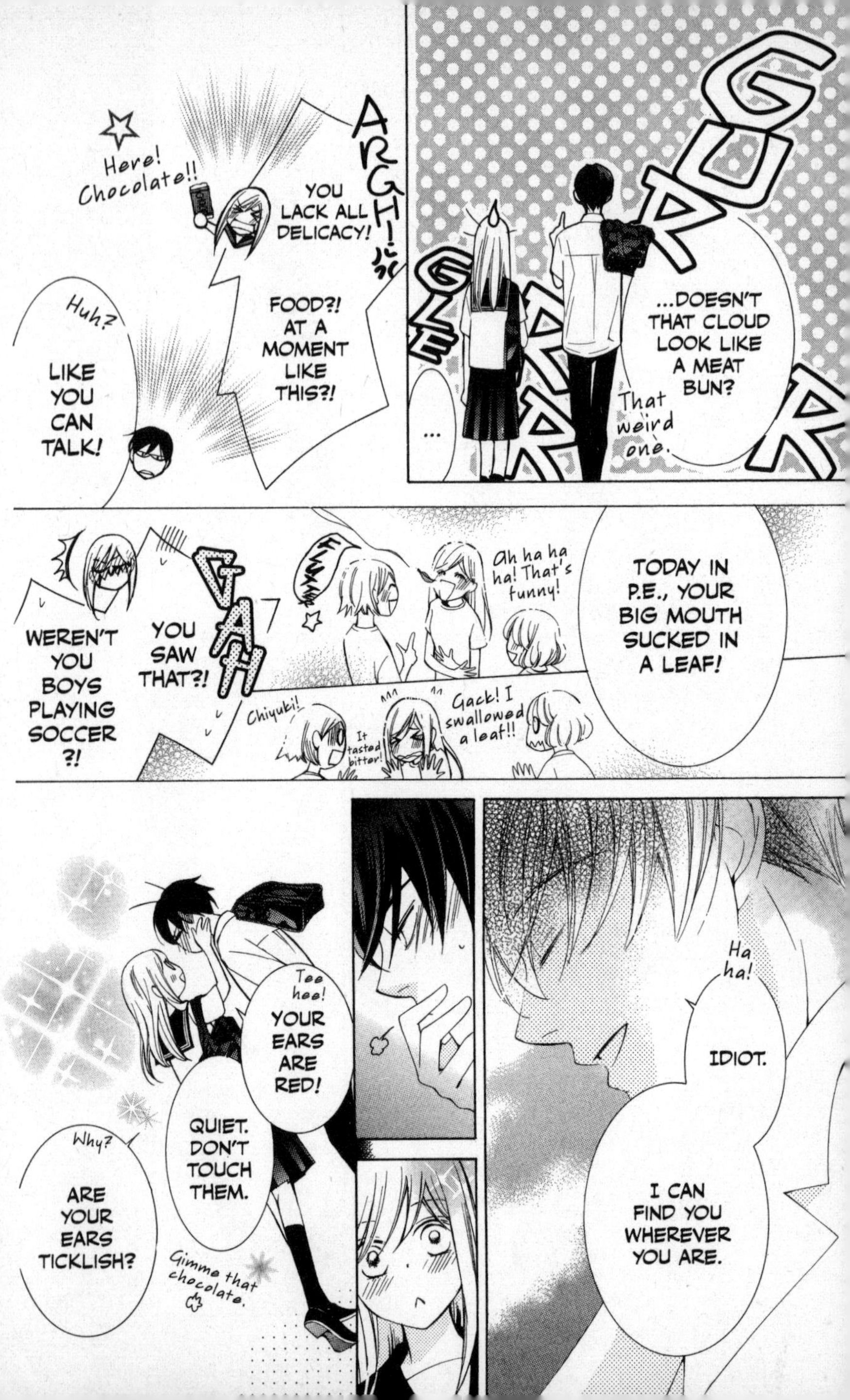
...DOESN'T THAT CLOUD LOOK LIKE A MEAT BUN?
That weird one.
...
ARGH!
YOU LACK ALL DELICACY!
Here! Chocolate!!
FOOD?! AT A MOMENT LIKE THIS?!
Huh?
LIKE YOU CAN TALK!
TODAY IN P.E., YOUR BIG MOUTH SUCKED IN A LEAF!
Ah ha ha! That's funny!
Gack! I swallowed a leaf!!
It tasted bitter!
Chiyuki!
GAH
YOU SAW THAT?!
WEREN'T YOU BOYS PLAYING SOCCER?!
Ha ha!
IDIOT.
I CAN FIND YOU WHEREVER YOU ARE.
Tee hee!
YOUR EARS ARE RED!
QUIET. DON'T TOUCH THEM.
Why?
ARE YOUR EARS TICKLISH?
Gimme that chocolate.

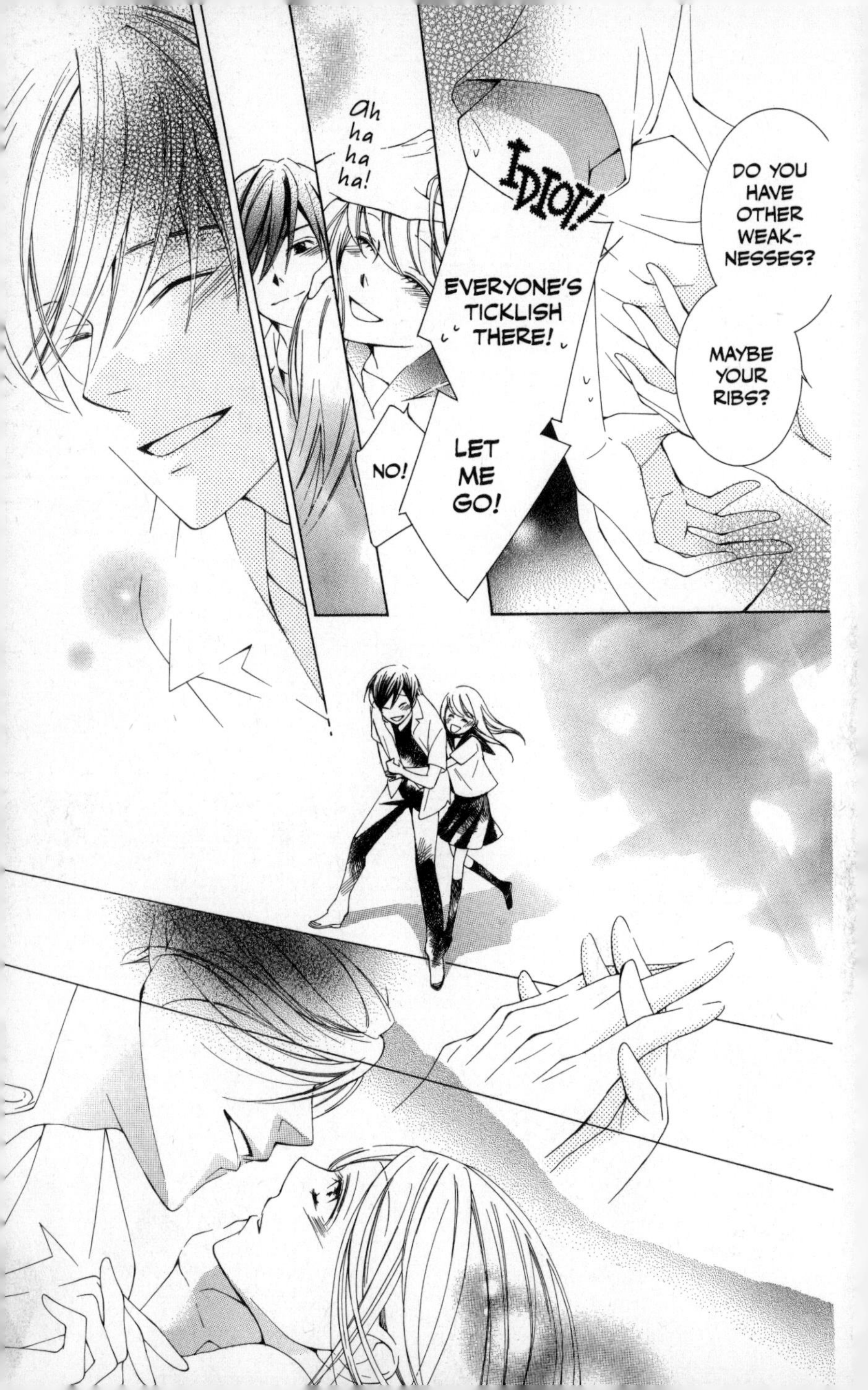
DO YOU HAVE OTHER WEAK-NESSES?
MAYBE YOUR RIBS?
IDIOT!
EVERYONE'S TICKLISH THERE!
LET ME GO!
Ah ha ha ha!
NO!

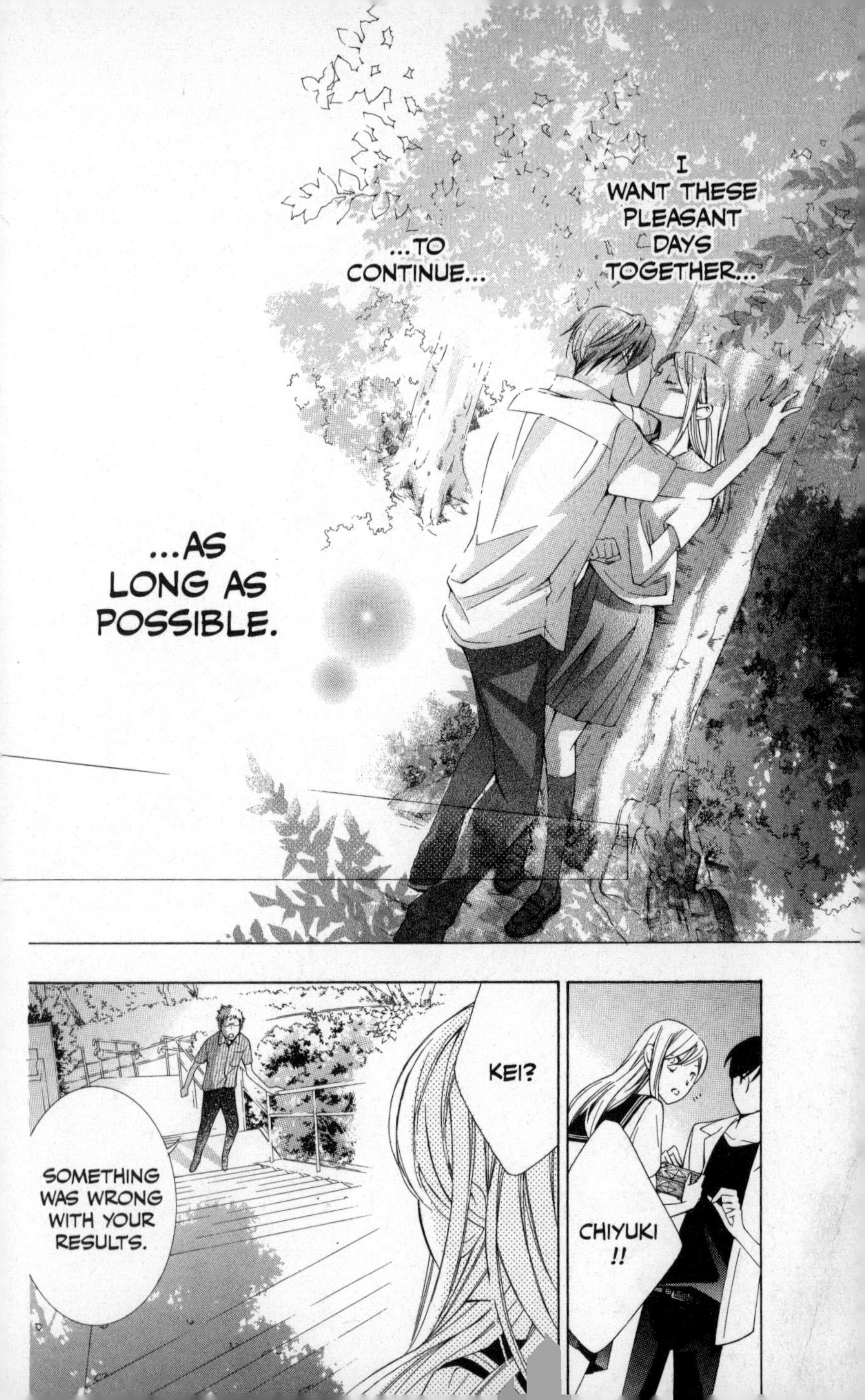
I WANT THESE PLEASANT DAYS TOGETHER...
...TO CONTINUE...
...AS LONG AS POSSIBLE.
CHIYUKI !!
KEI?
SOMETHING WAS WRONG WITH YOUR RESULTS.

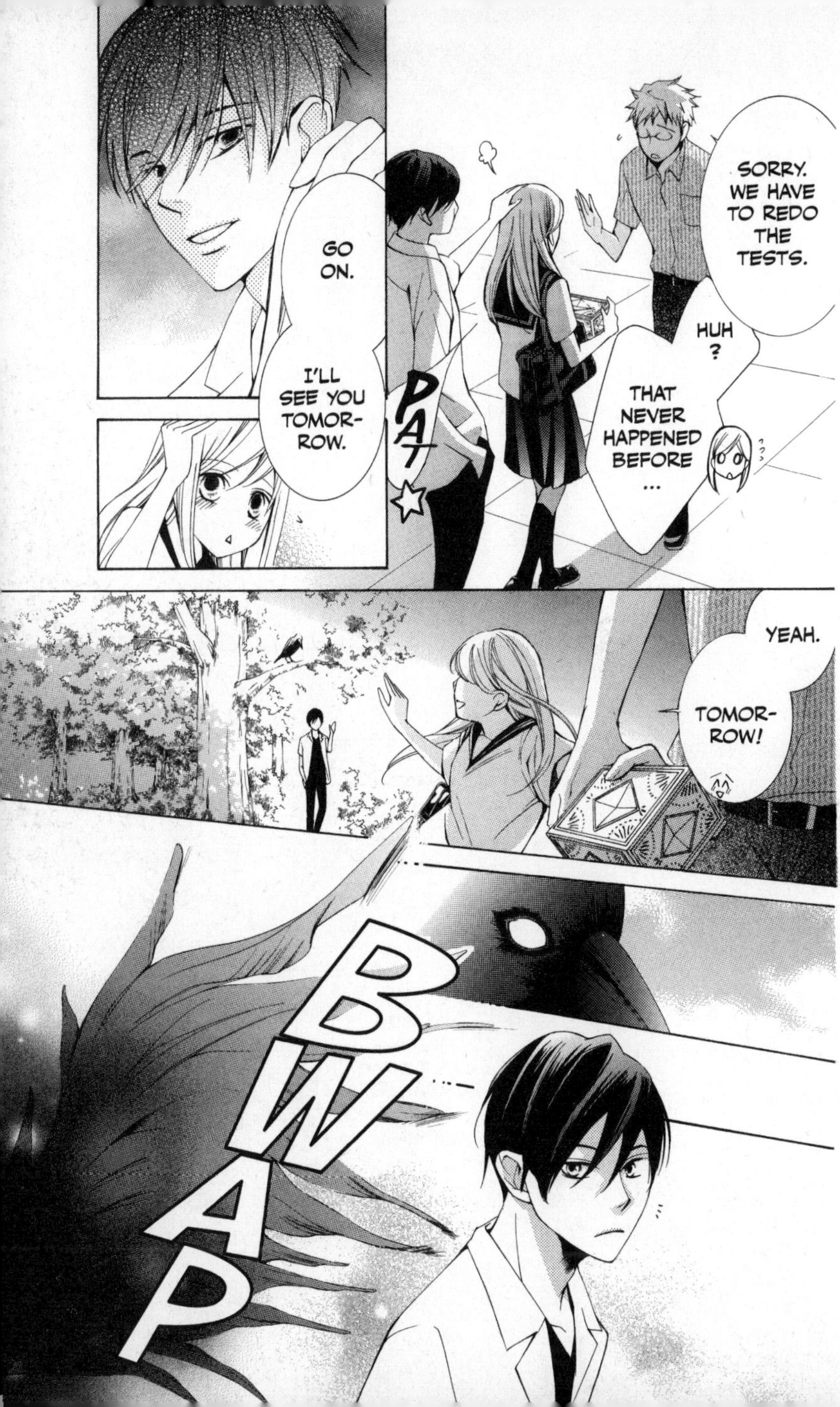
SORRY. WE HAVE TO REDO THE TESTS.
HUH?
THAT NEVER HAPPENED BEFORE ...
PAT
GO ON.
I'LL SEE YOU TOMOR-ROW.
YEAH.
TOMOR-ROW!
BWAP

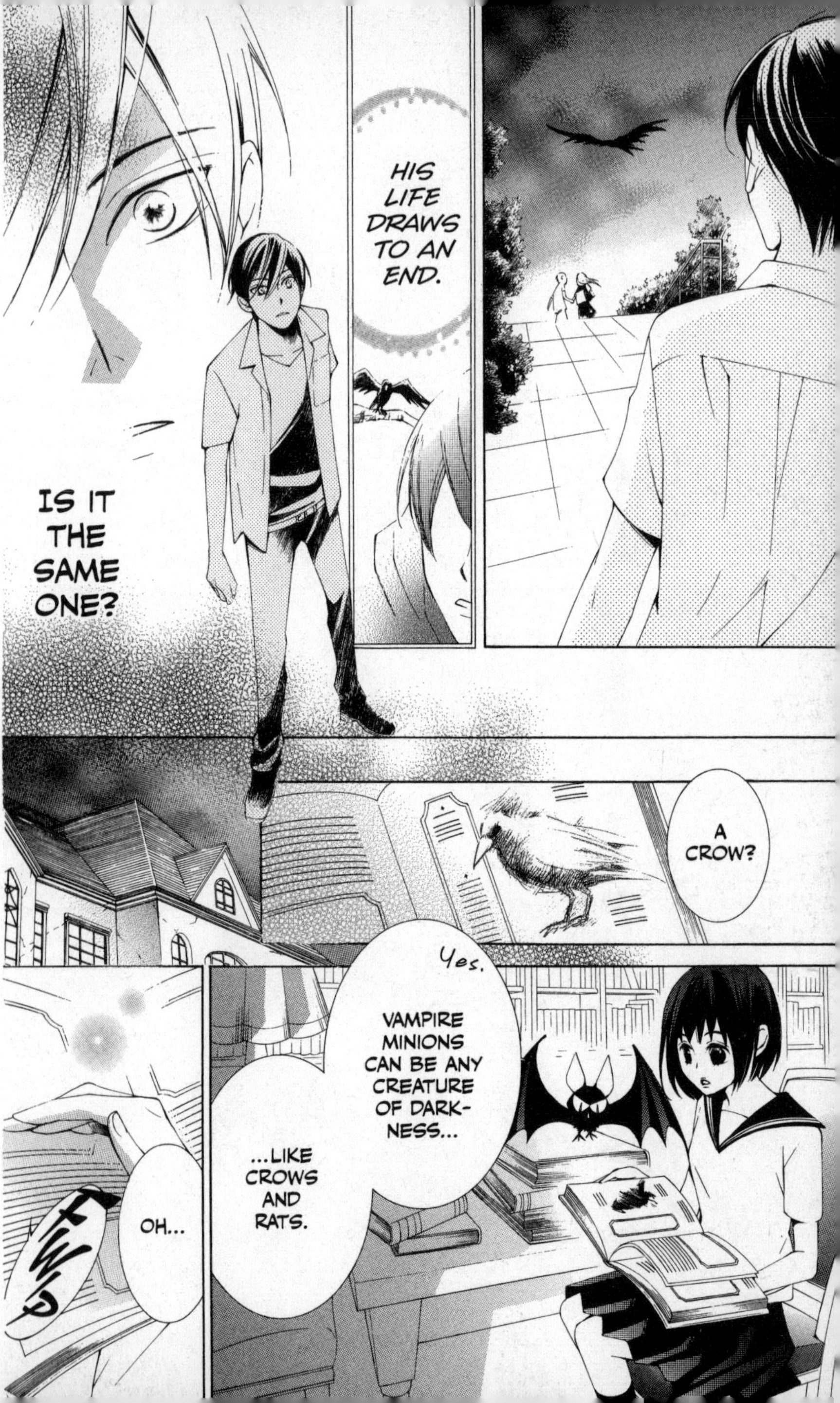
HIS LIFE DRAWS TO AN END.
IS IT THE SAME ONE?
A CROW?
Yes.
VAMPIRE MINIONS CAN BE ANY CREATURE OF DARKNESS...
...LIKE CROWS AND RATS.
OH...
FWIP

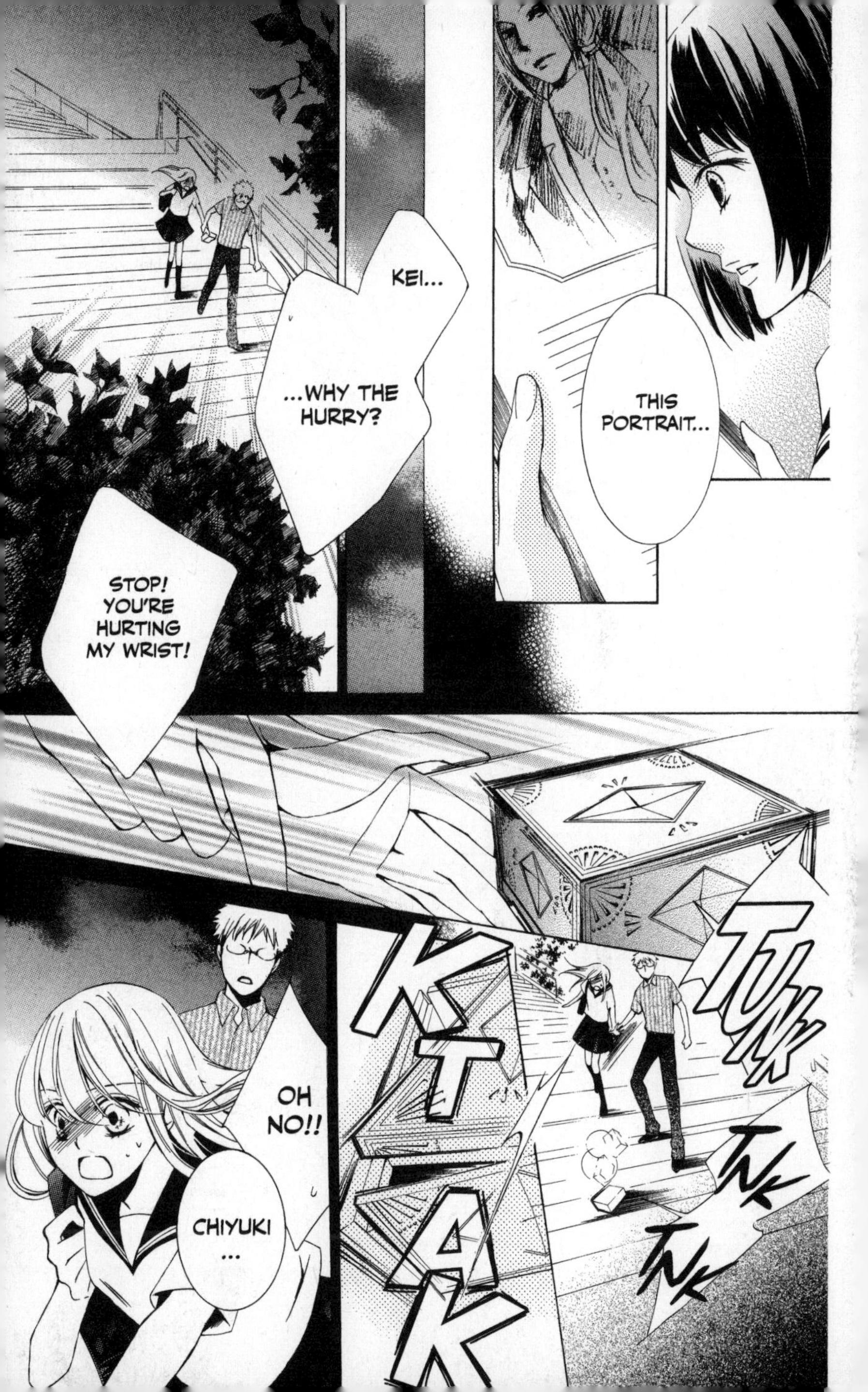
THIS PORTRAIT...
KEI...
...WHY THE HURRY?
STOP! YOU'RE HURTING MY WRIST!
TUNK
TNK
TNK
KTAK
OH NO!!
CHIYUKI ...

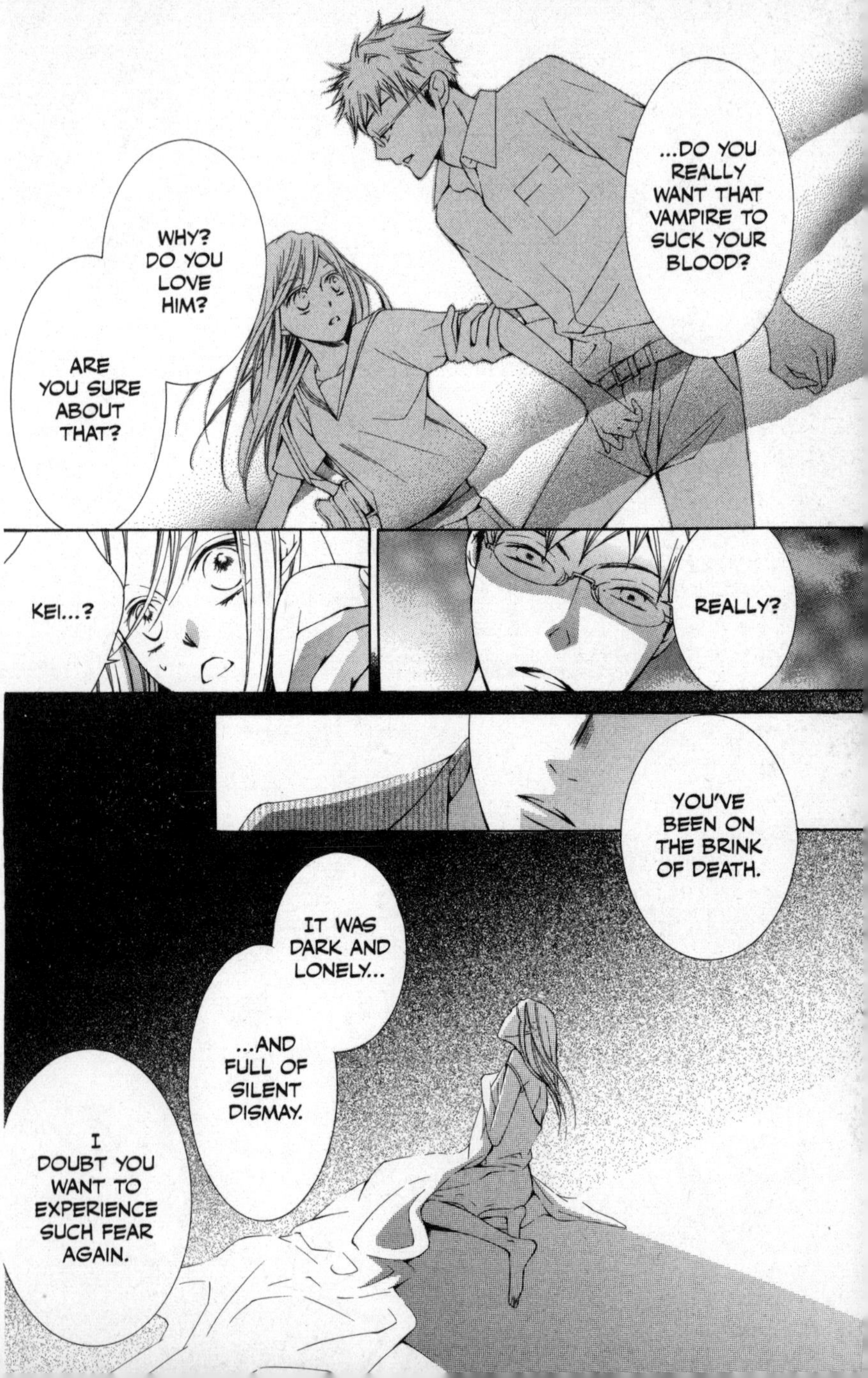
...DO YOU REALLY WANT THAT VAMPIRE TO SUCK YOUR BLOOD?
WHY? DO YOU LOVE HIM?
ARE YOU SURE ABOUT THAT?
REALLY?
KEI...?
YOU'VE BEEN ON THE BRINK OF DEATH.
IT WAS DARK AND LONELY...
...AND FULL OF SILENT DISMAY.
I DOUBT YOU WANT TO EXPERIENCE SUCH FEAR AGAIN.

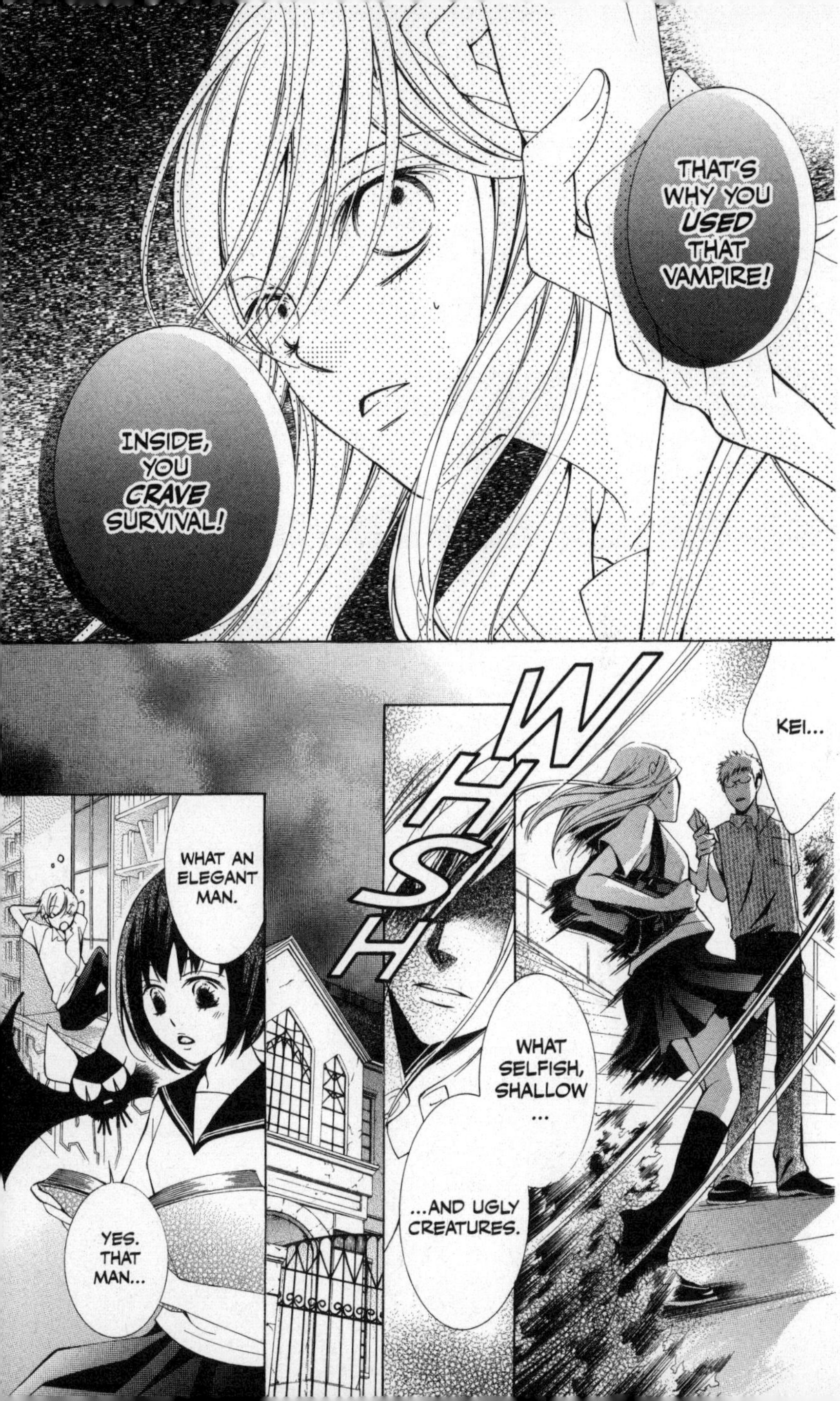
THAT'S WHY YOU USED THAT VAMPIRE!
INSIDE, YOU CRAVE SURVIVAL!
KEI...
WHSH
WHAT SELFISH, SHALLOW ...
...AND UGLY CREATURES.
WHAT AN ELEGANT MAN.
YES. THAT MAN...

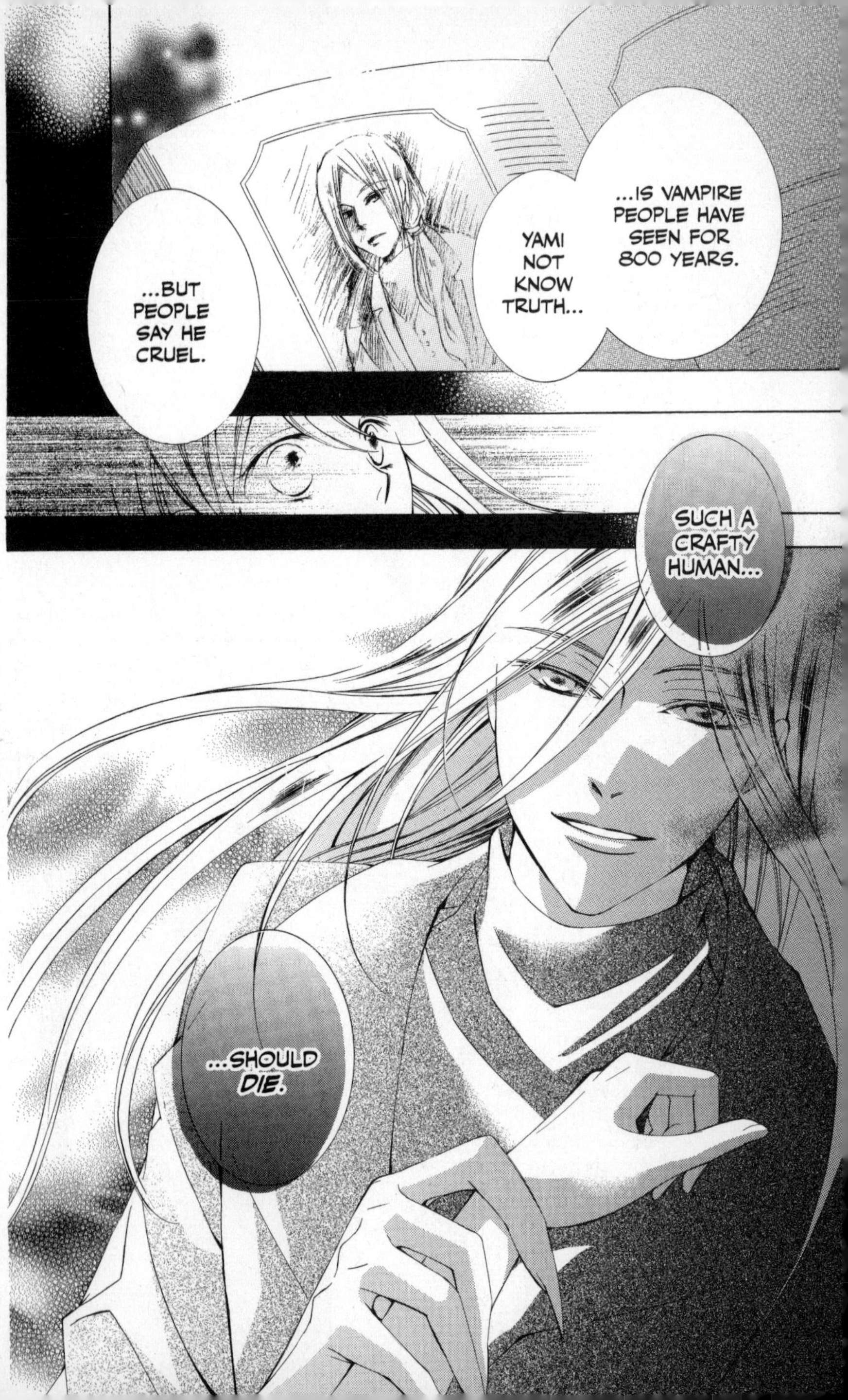
...IS VAMPIRE PEOPLE HAVE SEEN FOR 800 YEARS.
YAMI NOT KNOW TRUTH...
...BUT PEOPLE SAY HE CRUEL.
SUCH A CRAFTY HUMAN...
...SHOULD DIE.

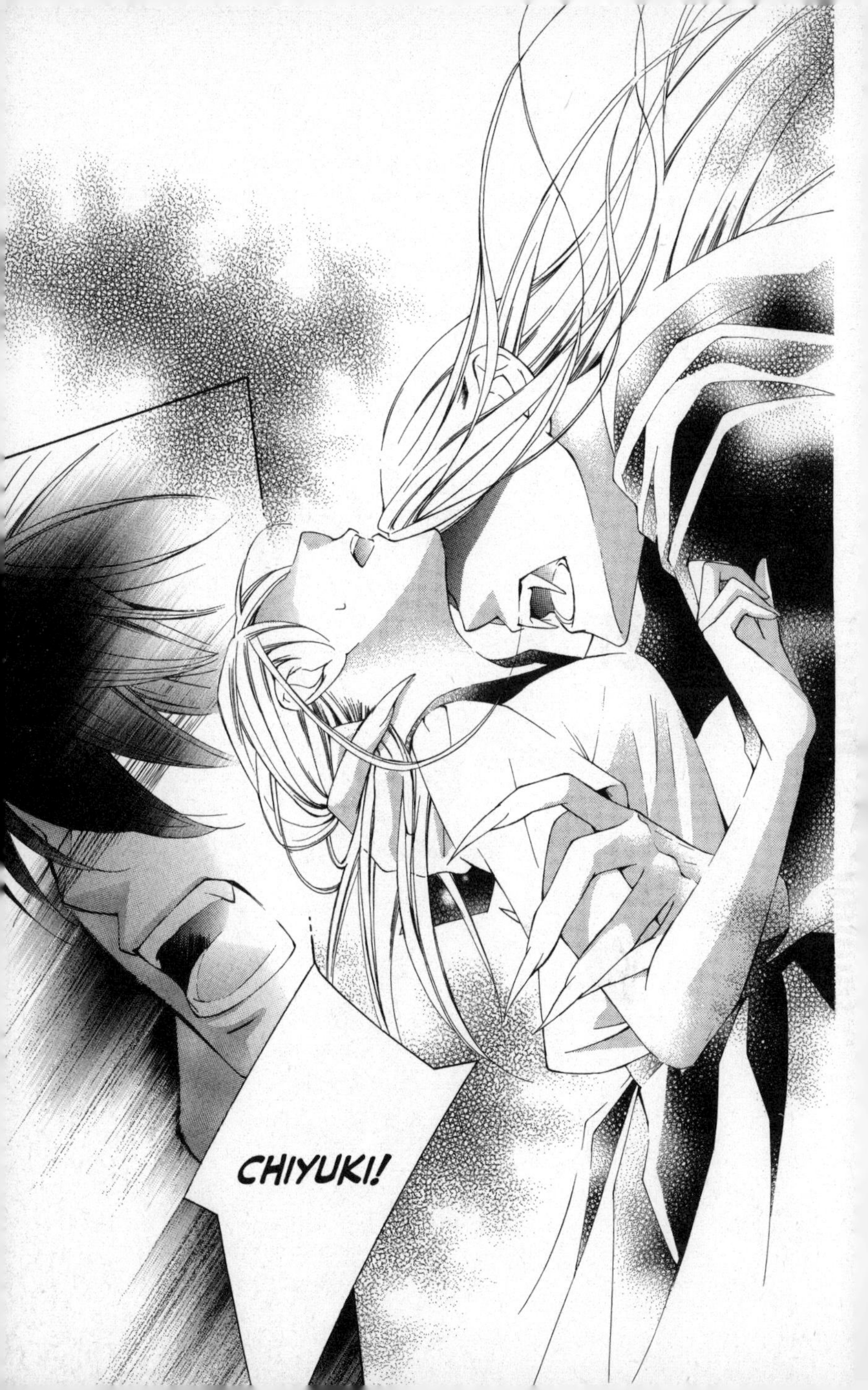
CHIYUKI!

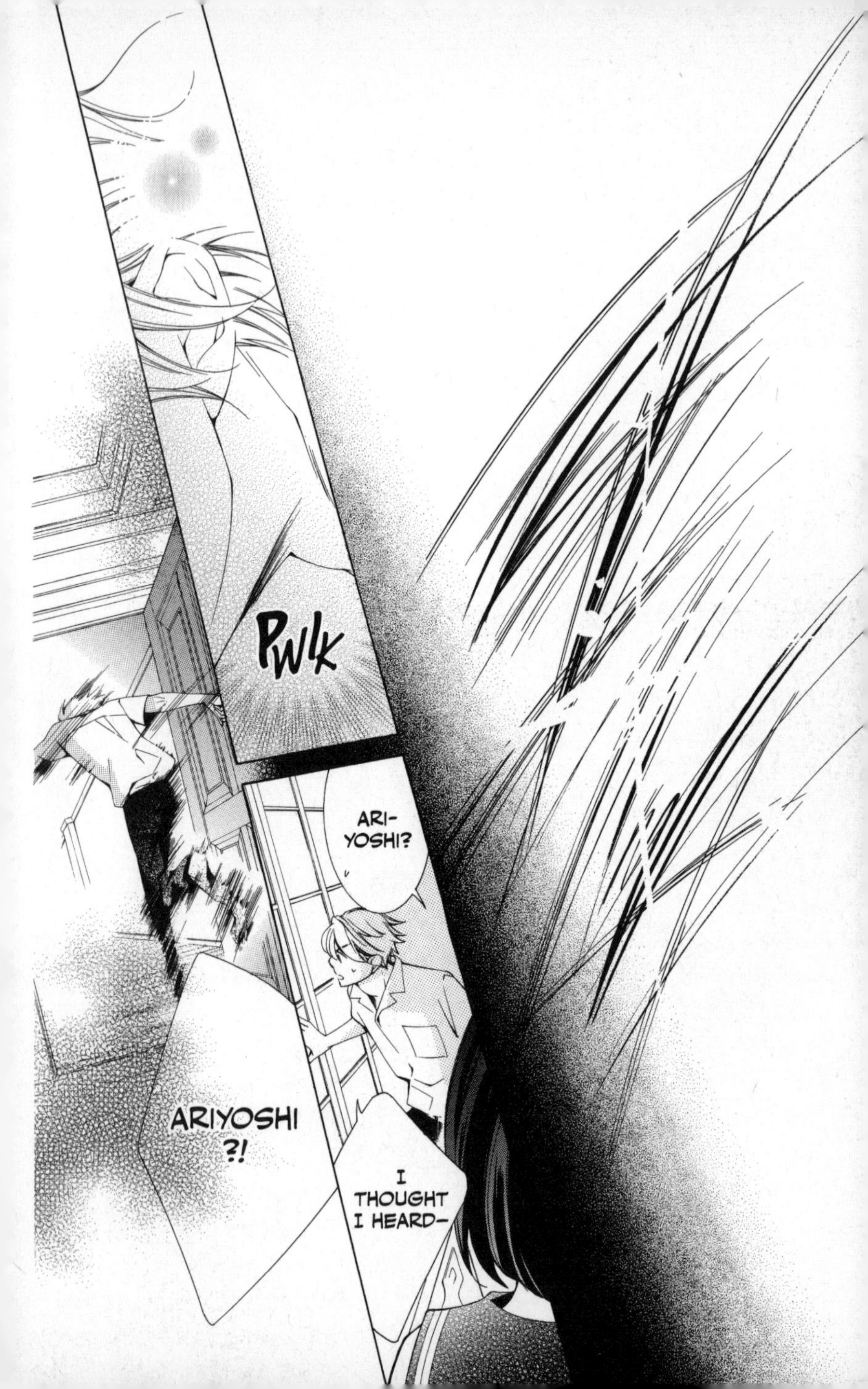
PWLK
ARI-YOSHI?
I THOUGHT I HEARD–
ARIYOSHI ?!

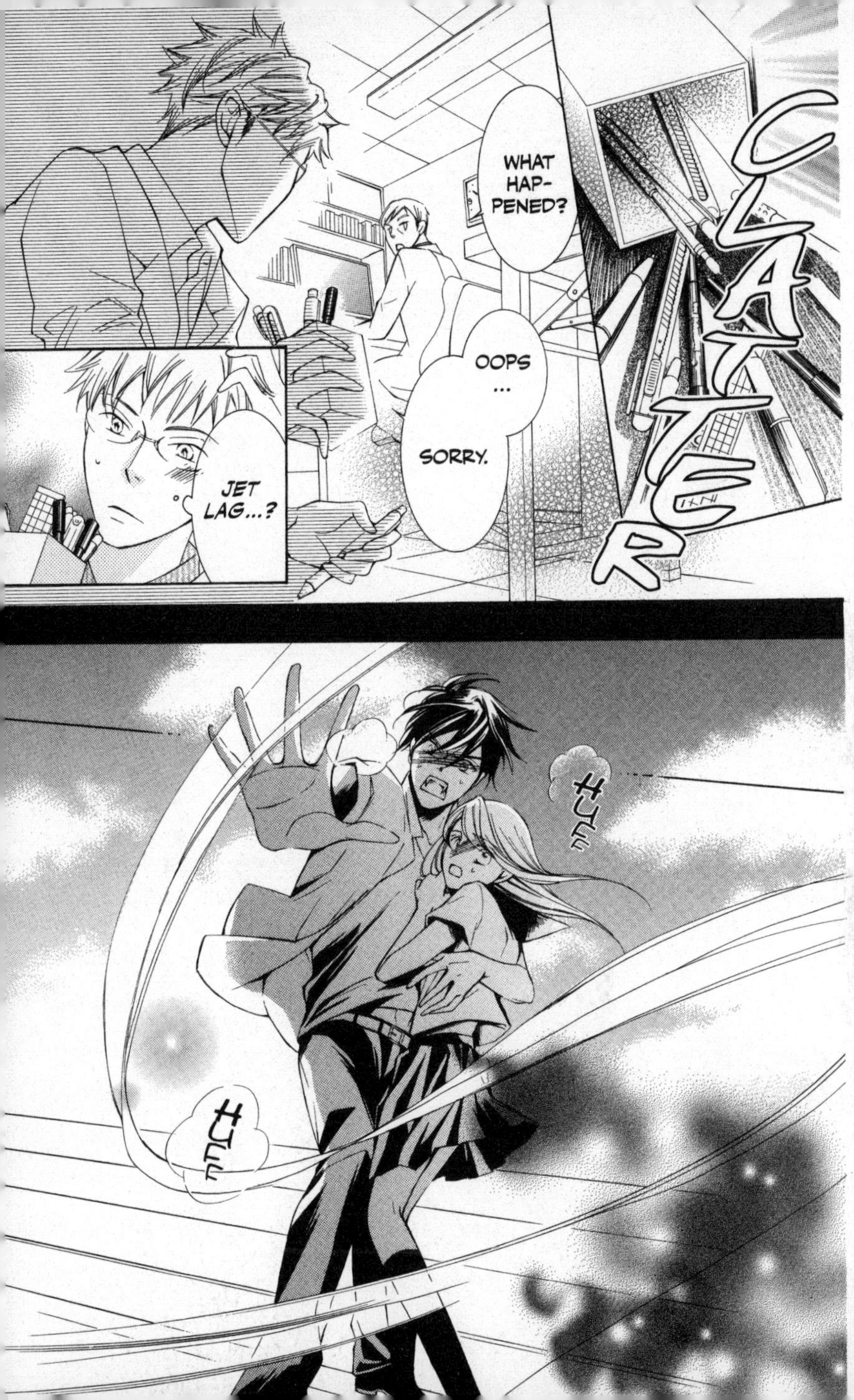
CLATTER
WHAT HAPPENED?
OOPS ...
SORRY.
JET LAG...?
HUFF
HUFF

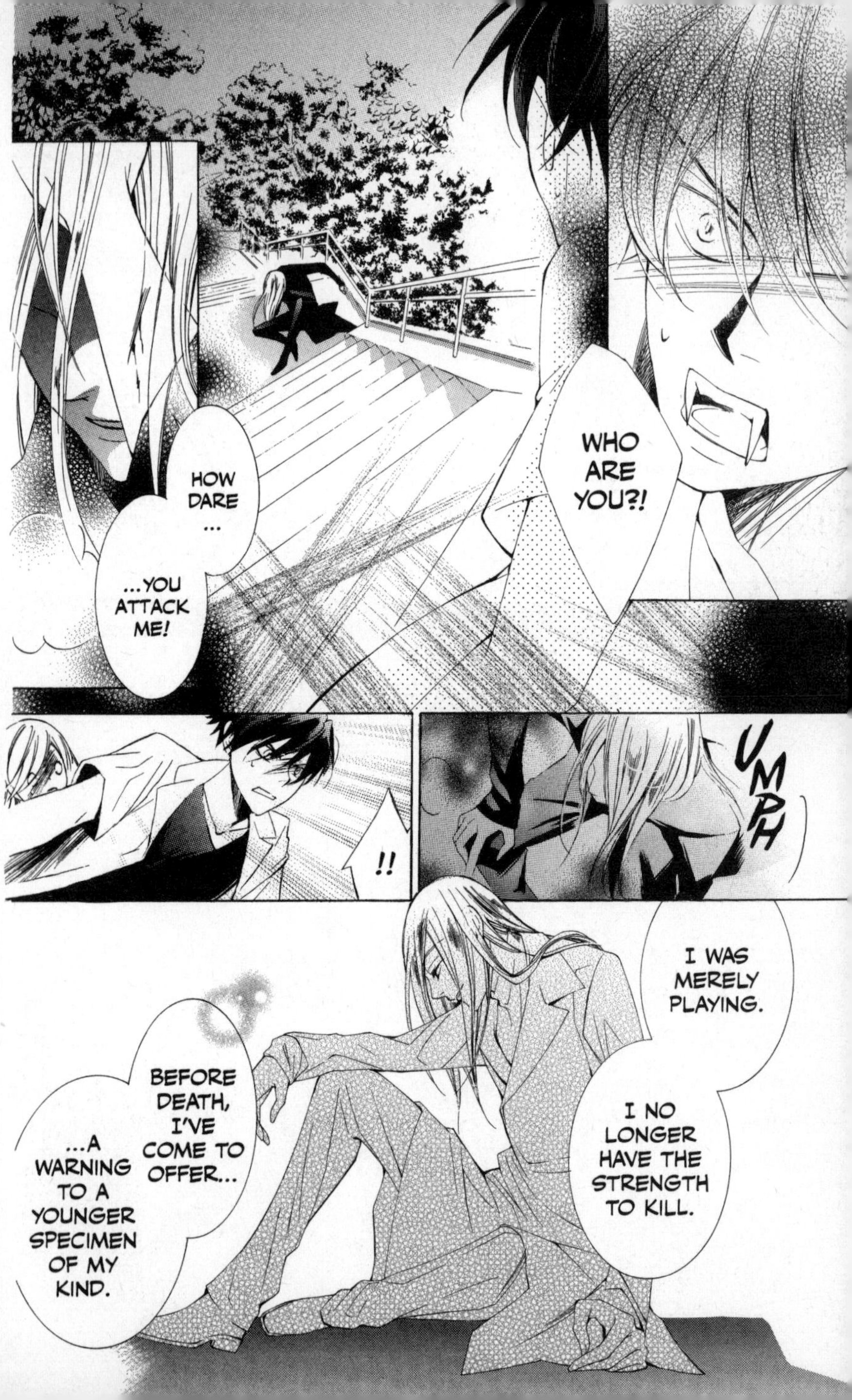
WHO ARE YOU?!
HOW DARE...
...YOU ATTACK ME!
UMPH
!!
I WAS MERELY PLAYING.
I NO LONGER HAVE THE STRENGTH TO KILL.
BEFORE DEATH, I'VE COME TO OFFER...
...A WARNING TO A YOUNGER SPECIMEN OF MY KIND.

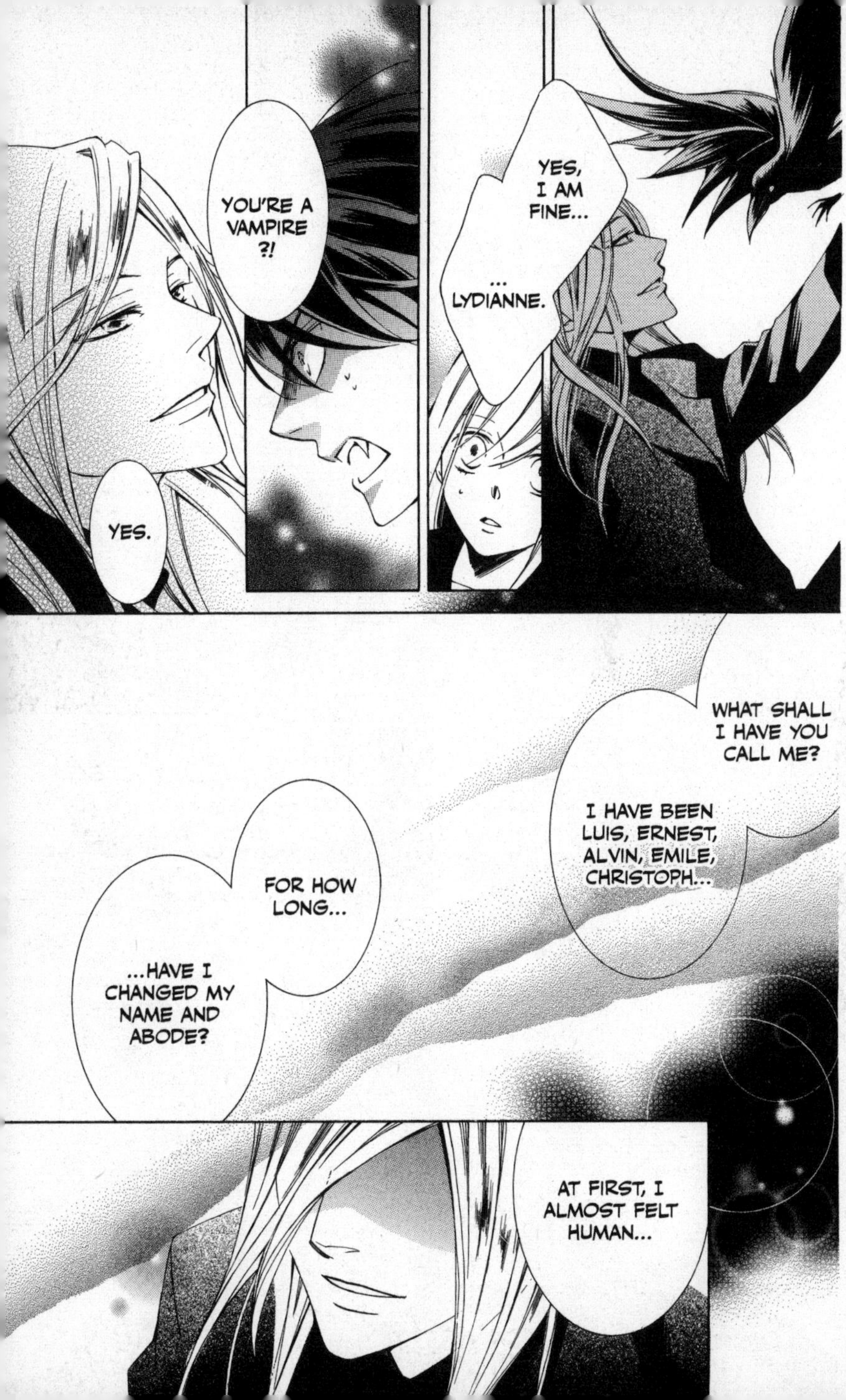
YES, I AM FINE...
...LYDIANNE.
YOU'RE A VAMPIRE?!
YES.
WHAT SHALL I HAVE YOU CALL ME?
I HAVE BEEN LUIS, ERNEST, ALVIN, EMILE, CHRISTOPH...
FOR HOW LONG...
...HAVE I CHANGED MY NAME AND ABODE?
AT FIRST, I ALMOST FELT HUMAN...

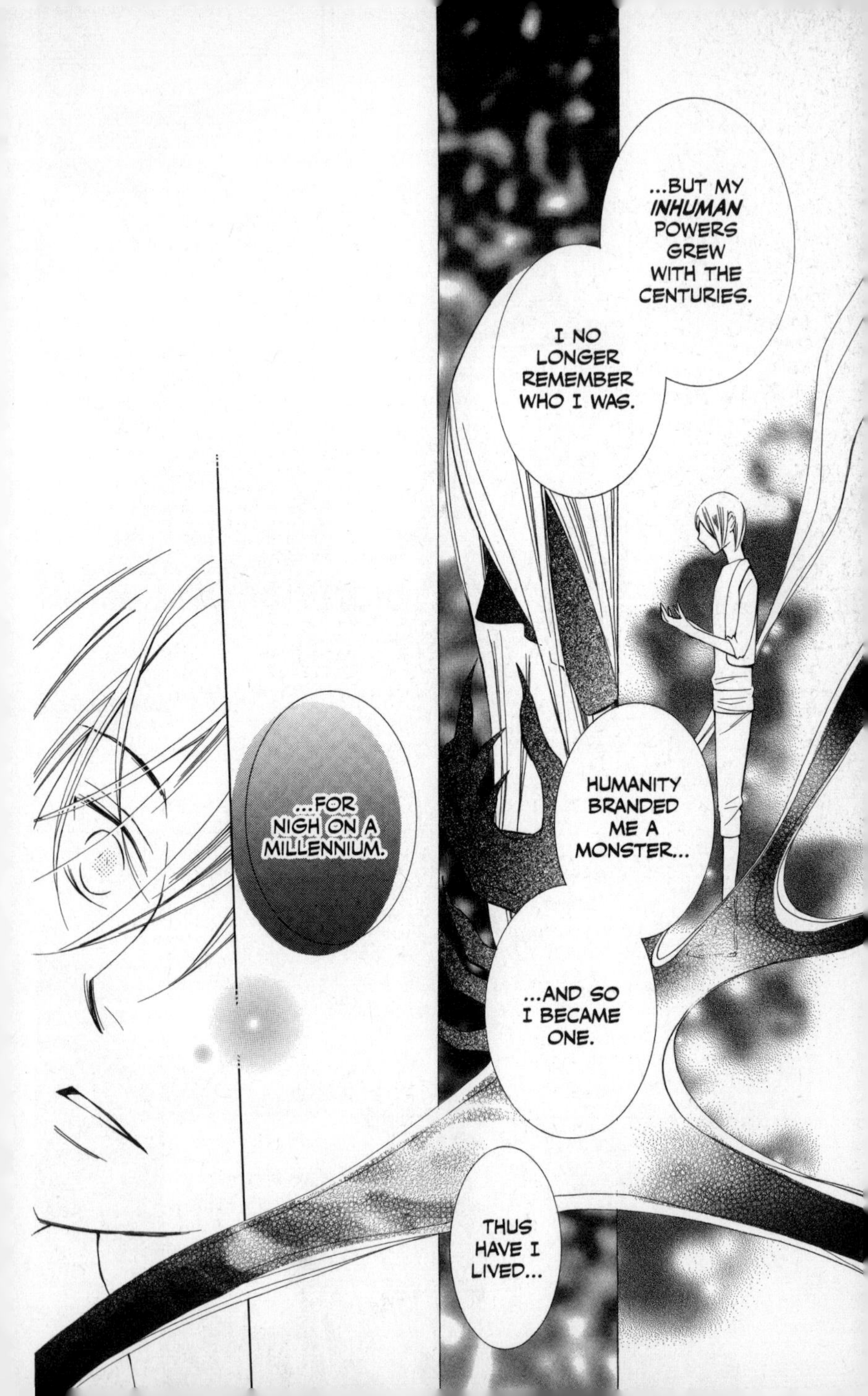
...BUT MY *INHUMAN* POWERS GREW WITH THE CENTURIES.
I NO LONGER REMEMBER WHO I WAS.
HUMANITY BRANDED ME A MONSTER...
...AND SO I BECAME ONE.
THUS HAVE I LIVED...
...FOR NIGH ON A MILLENNIUM.

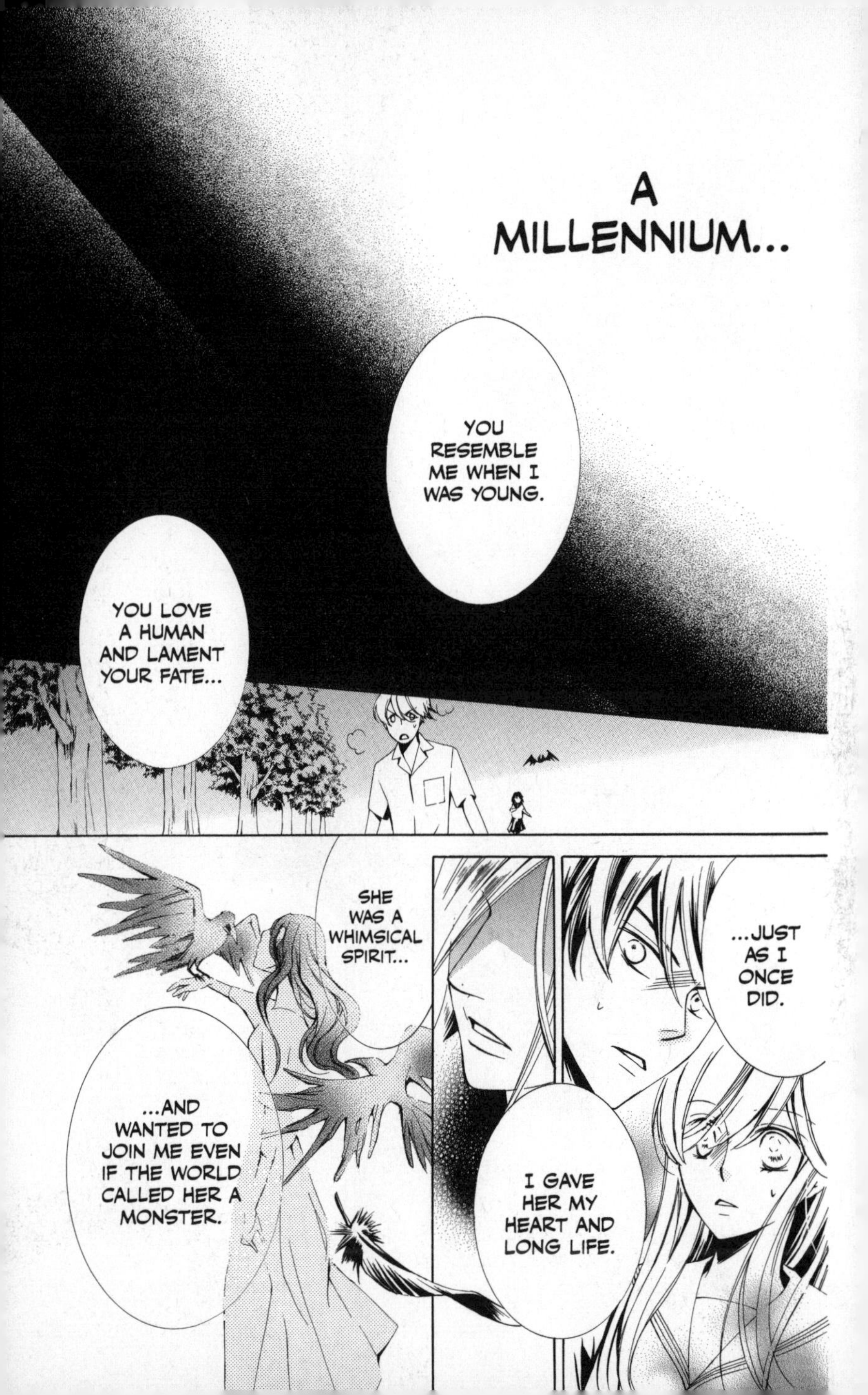
A MILLENNIUM...
YOU RESEMBLE ME WHEN I WAS YOUNG.
YOU LOVE A HUMAN AND LAMENT YOUR FATE...
...JUST AS I ONCE DID.
I GAVE HER MY HEART AND LONG LIFE.
SHE WAS A WHIMSICAL SPIRIT...
...AND WANTED TO JOIN ME EVEN IF THE WORLD CALLED HER A MONSTER.

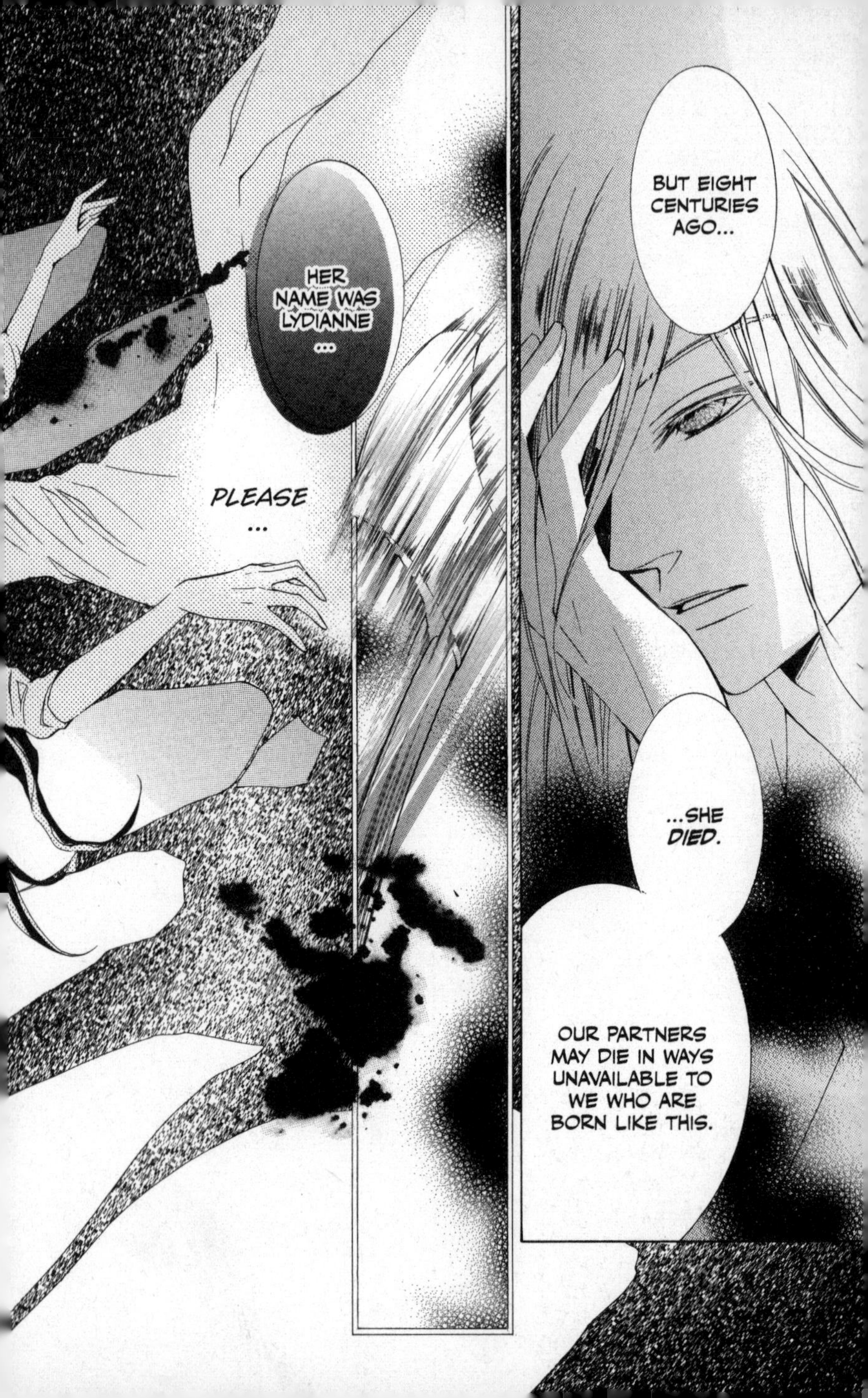
BUT EIGHT CENTURIES AGO...
...SHE *DIED*.
OUR PARTNERS MAY DIE IN WAYS UNAVAILABLE TO WE WHO ARE BORN LIKE THIS.
HER NAME WAS LYDIANNE...
PLEASE...

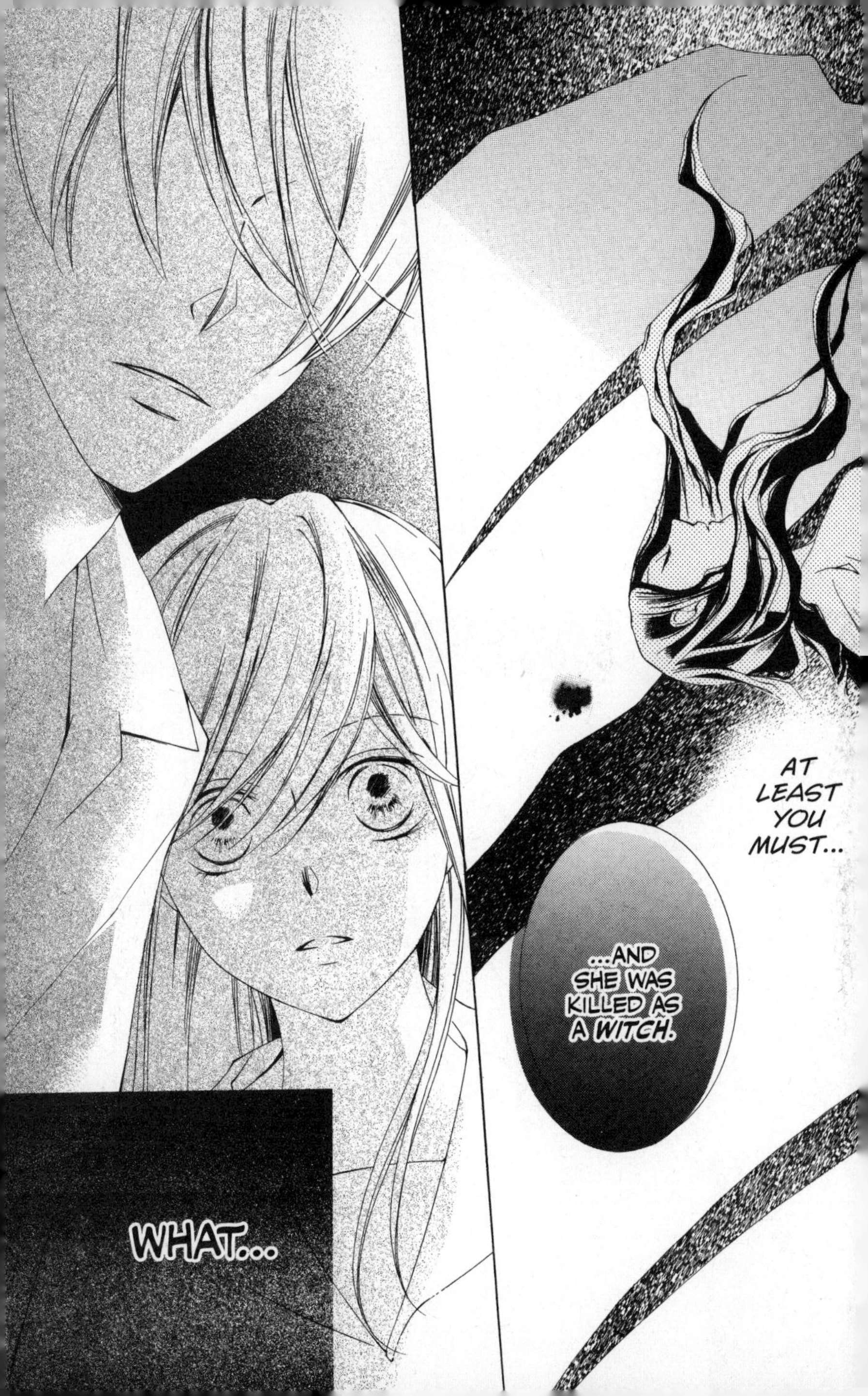
AT LEAST YOU MUST...
...AND SHE WAS KILLED AS A *WITCH.*
WHAT...

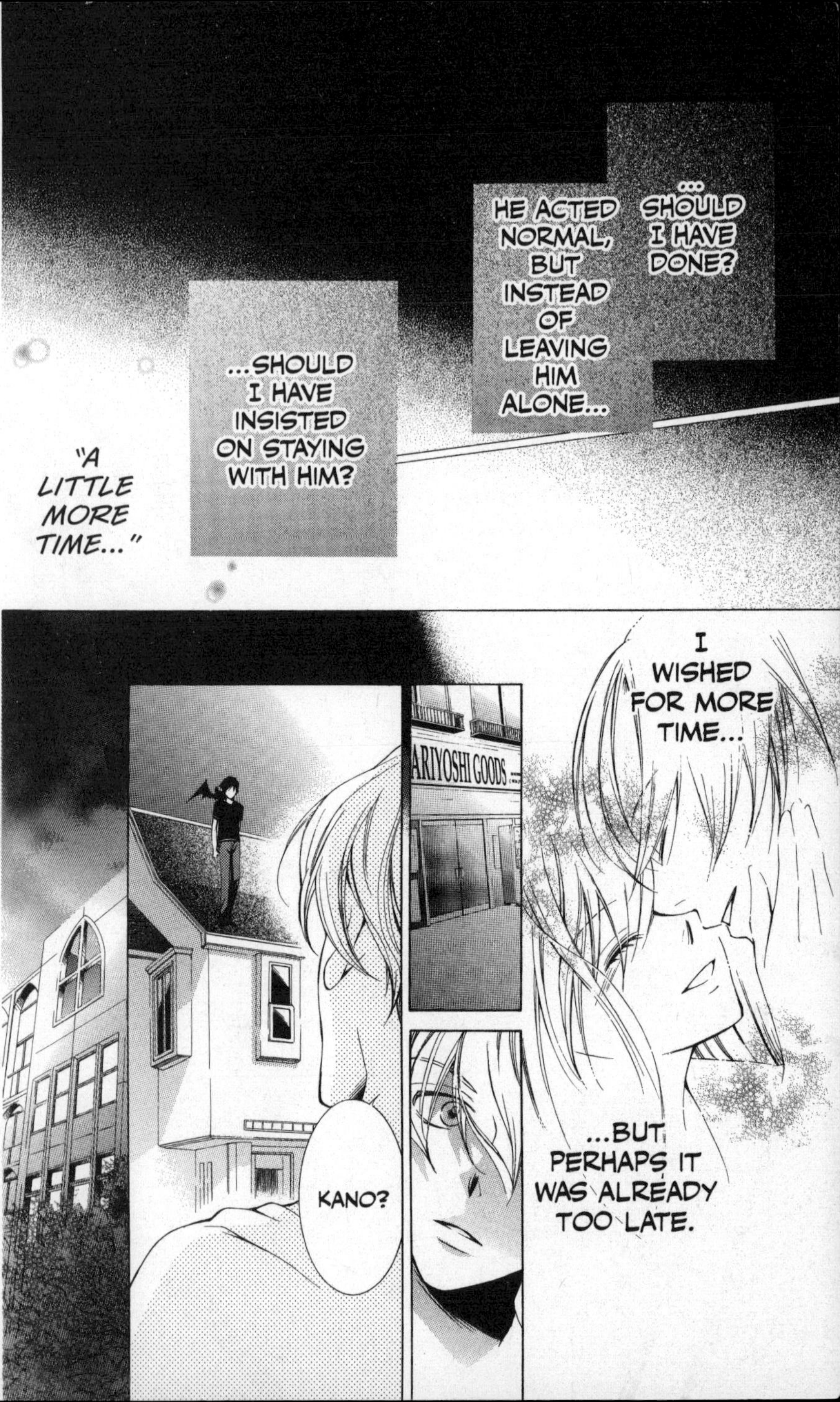
... SHOULD I HAVE DONE?
HE ACTED NORMAL, BUT INSTEAD OF LEAVING HIM ALONE...
...SHOULD I HAVE INSISTED ON STAYING WITH HIM?
"A LITTLE MORE TIME..."
I WISHED FOR MORE TIME...
ARIYOSHI GOODS
...BUT PERHAPS IT WAS ALREADY TOO LATE.
KANO?

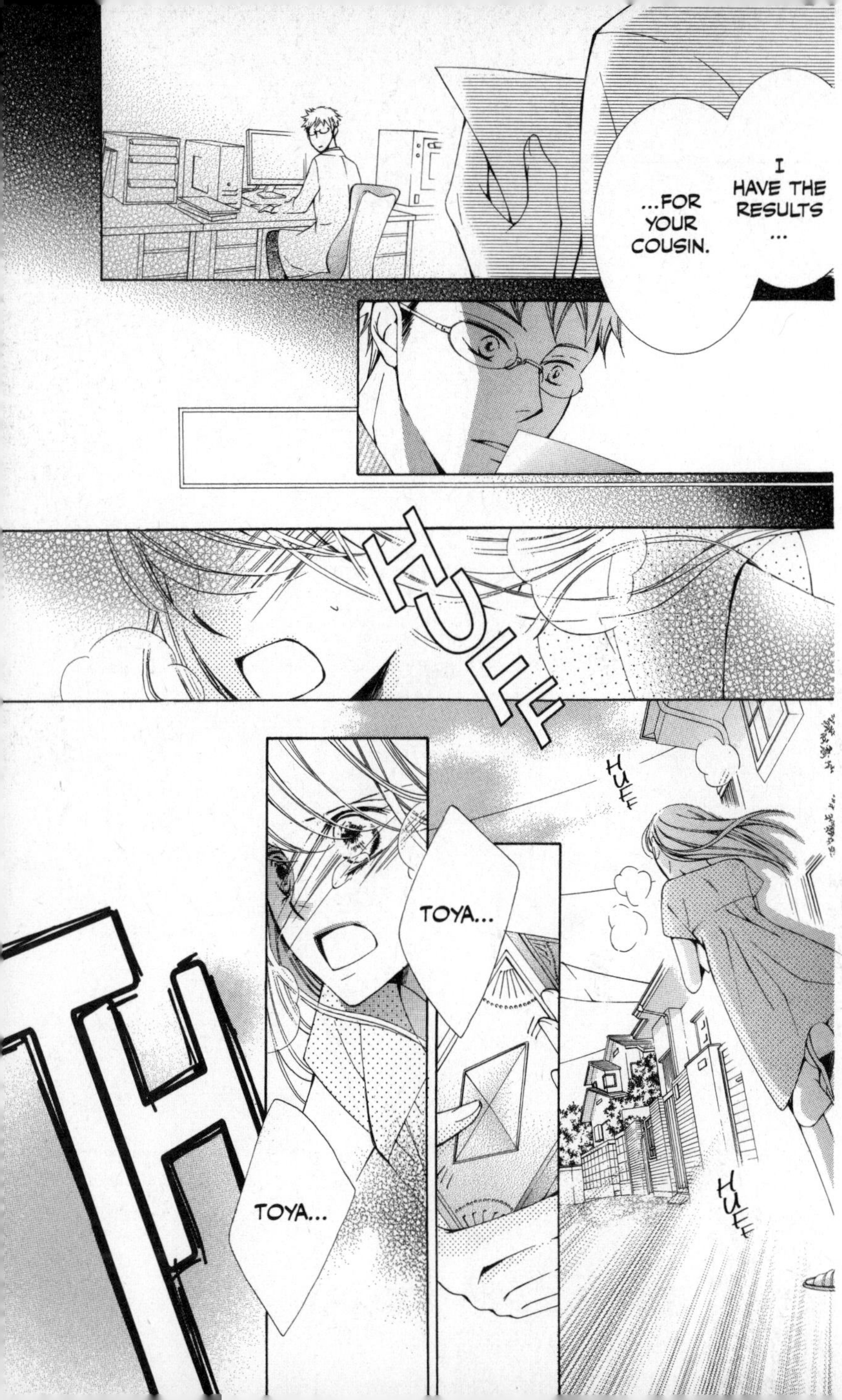
I HAVE THE RESULTS...
...FOR YOUR COUSIN.
HUFF
HUFF
HUFF
TOYA...
TOYA...
TH

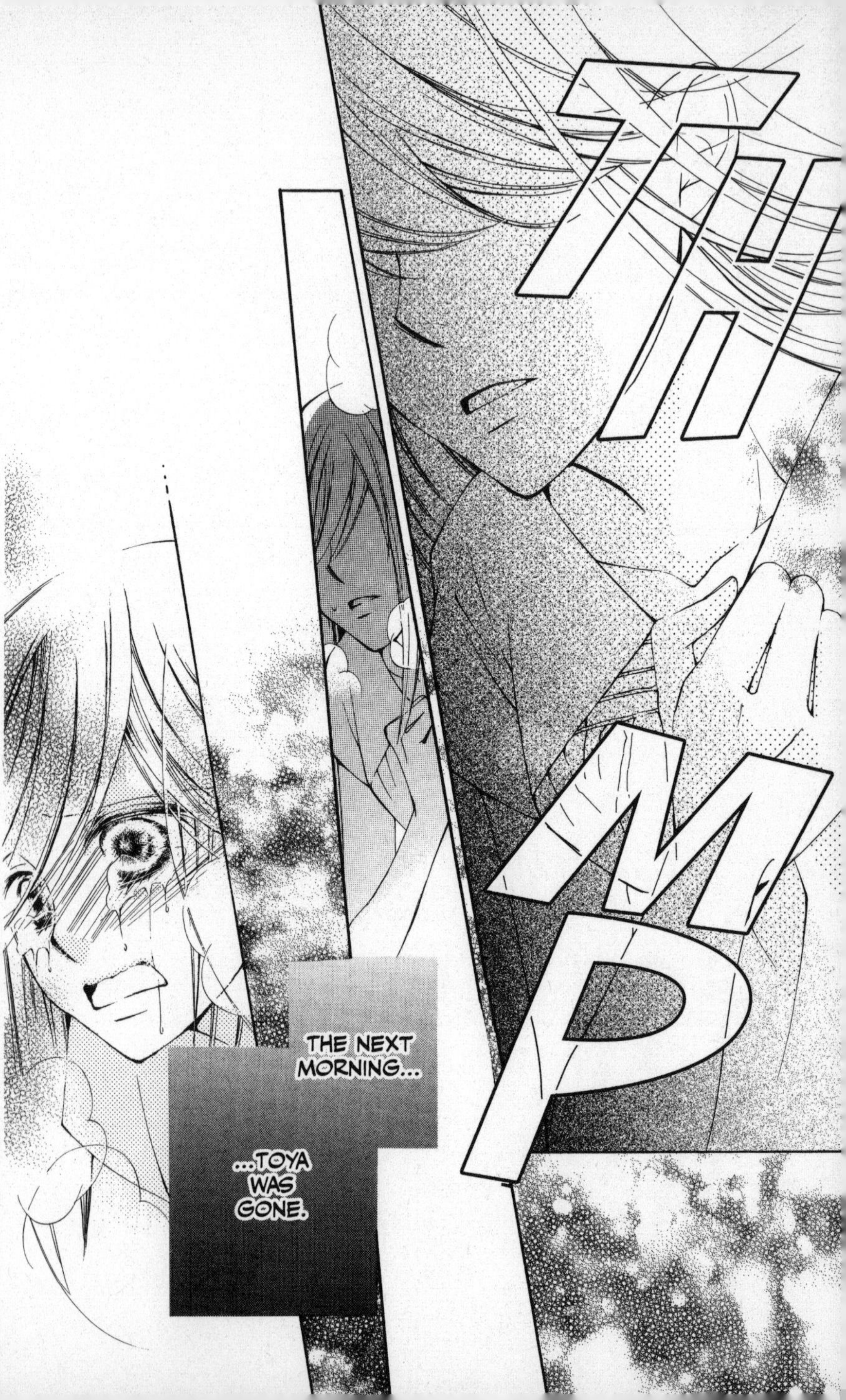
THUMP
THE NEXT MORNING...
...TOYA WAS GONE.

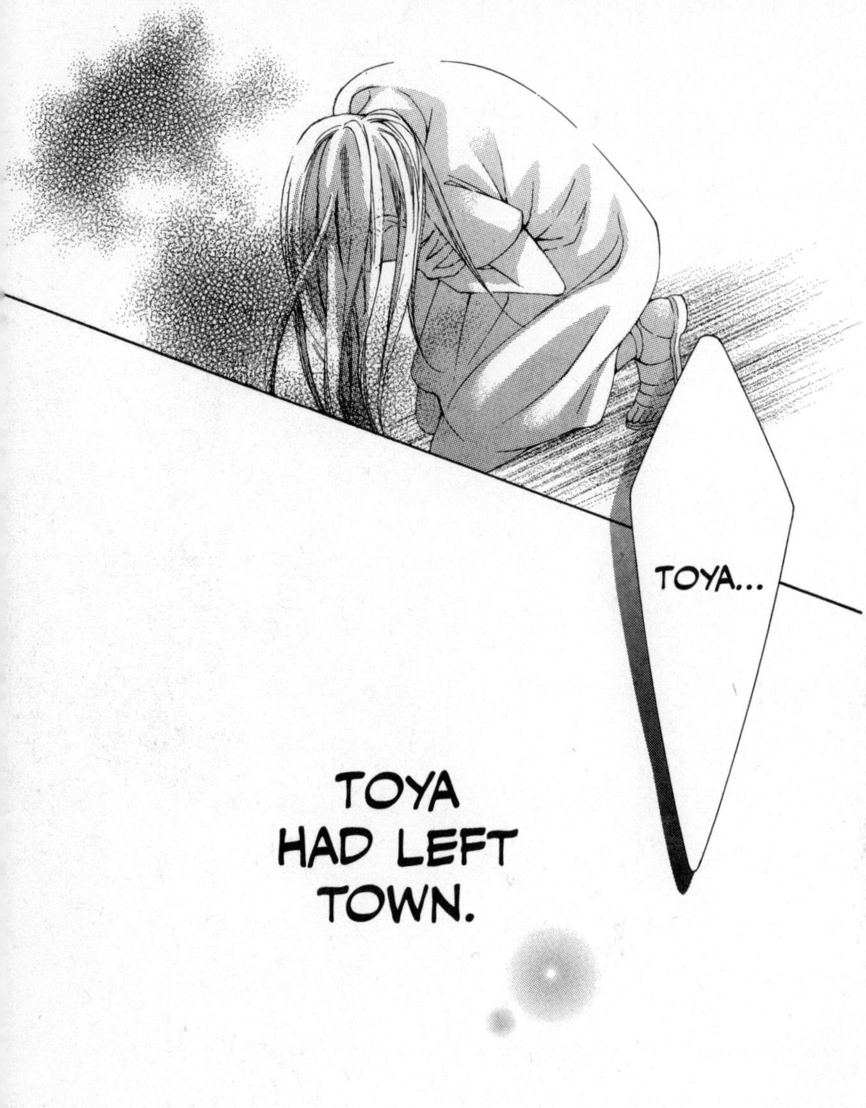
TOYA...
TOYA HAD LEFT TOWN.

SIXTEENTH SNOW / THE END

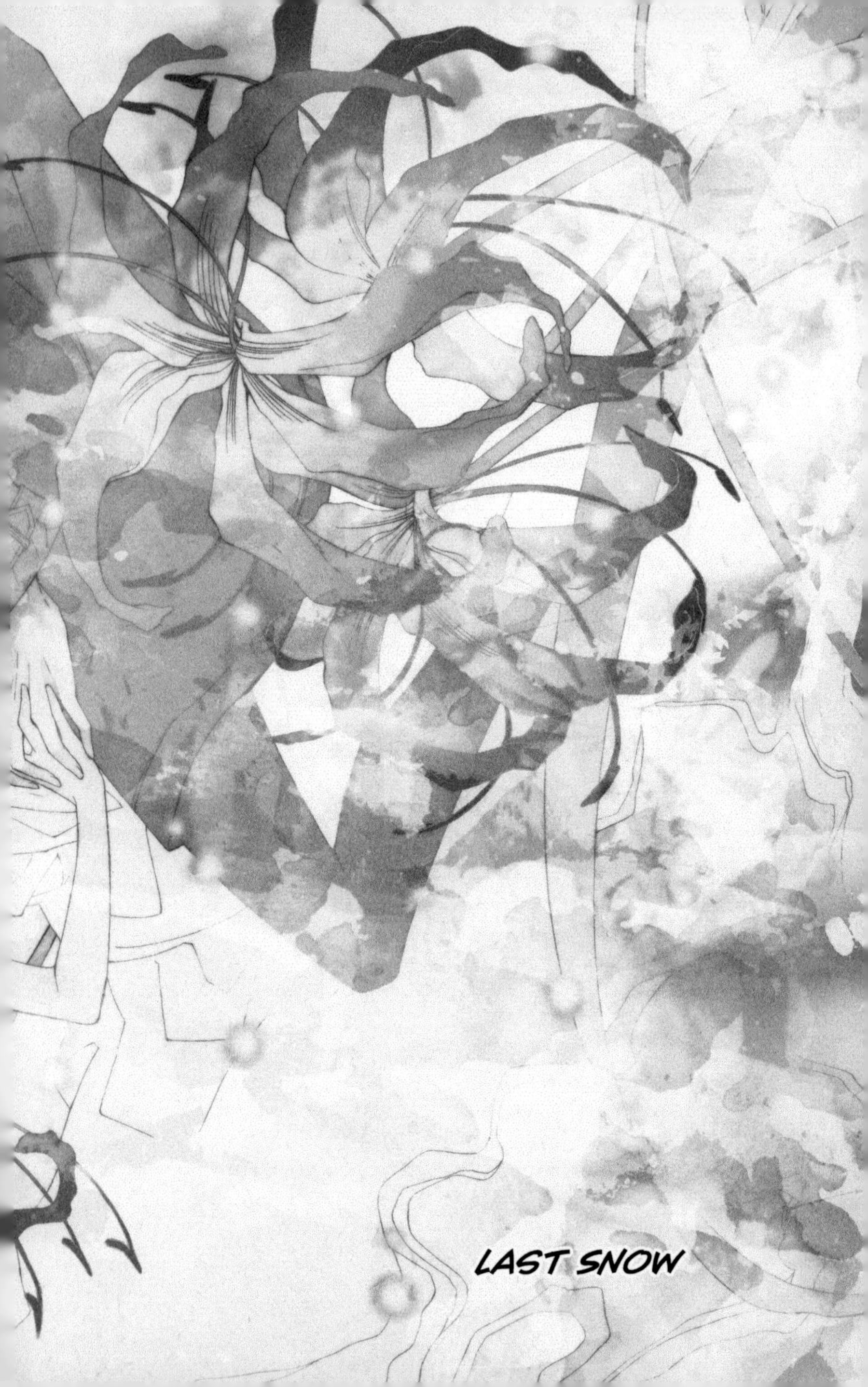
LAST SNOW

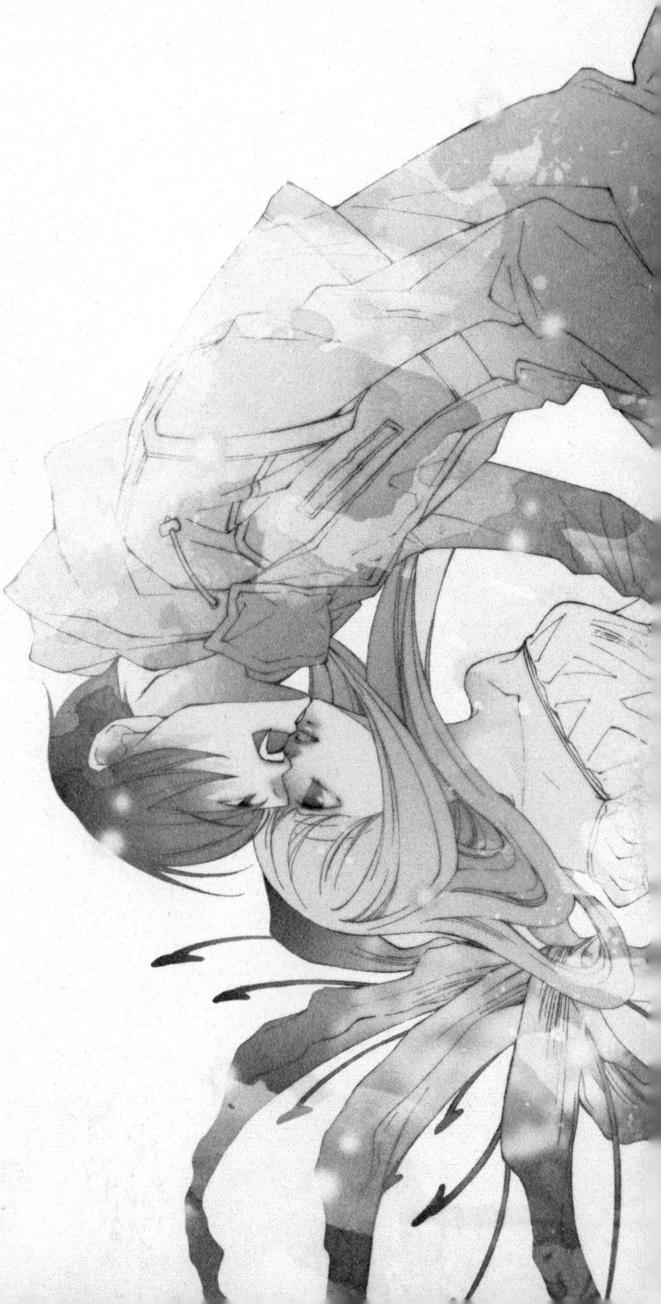

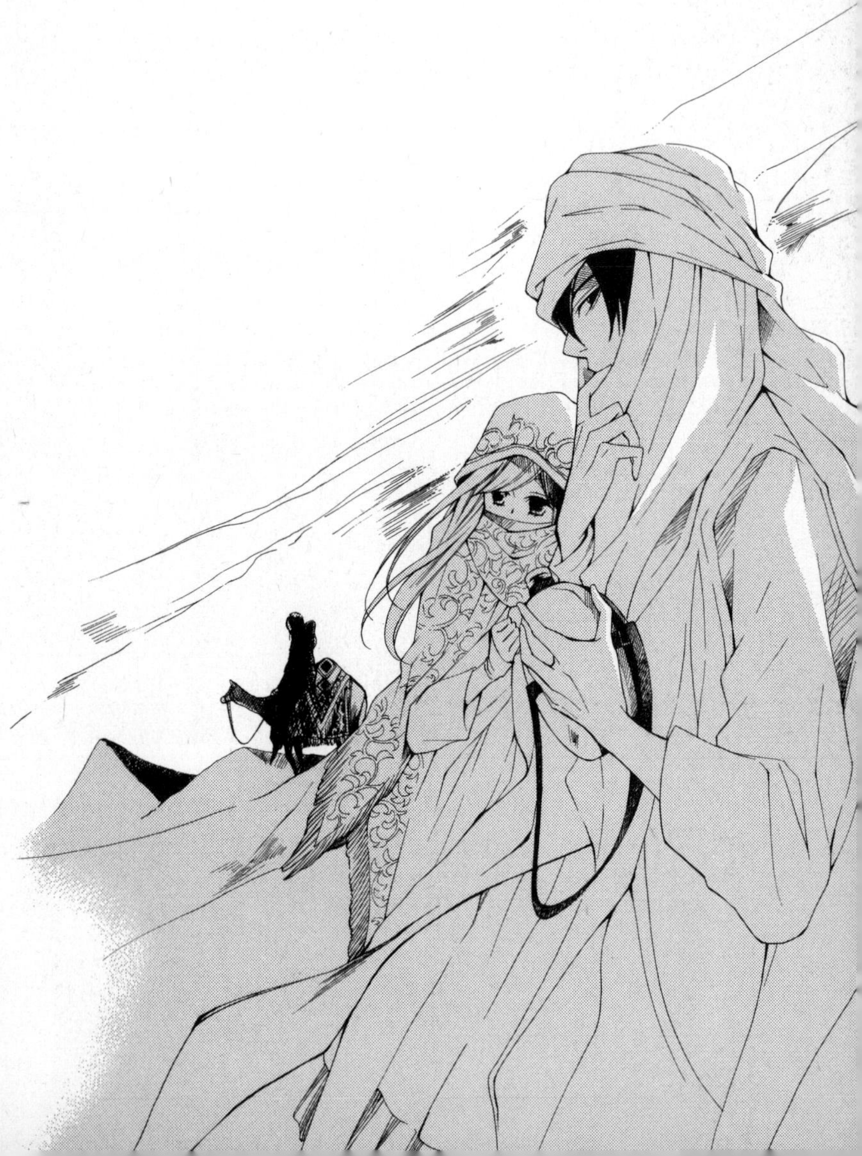

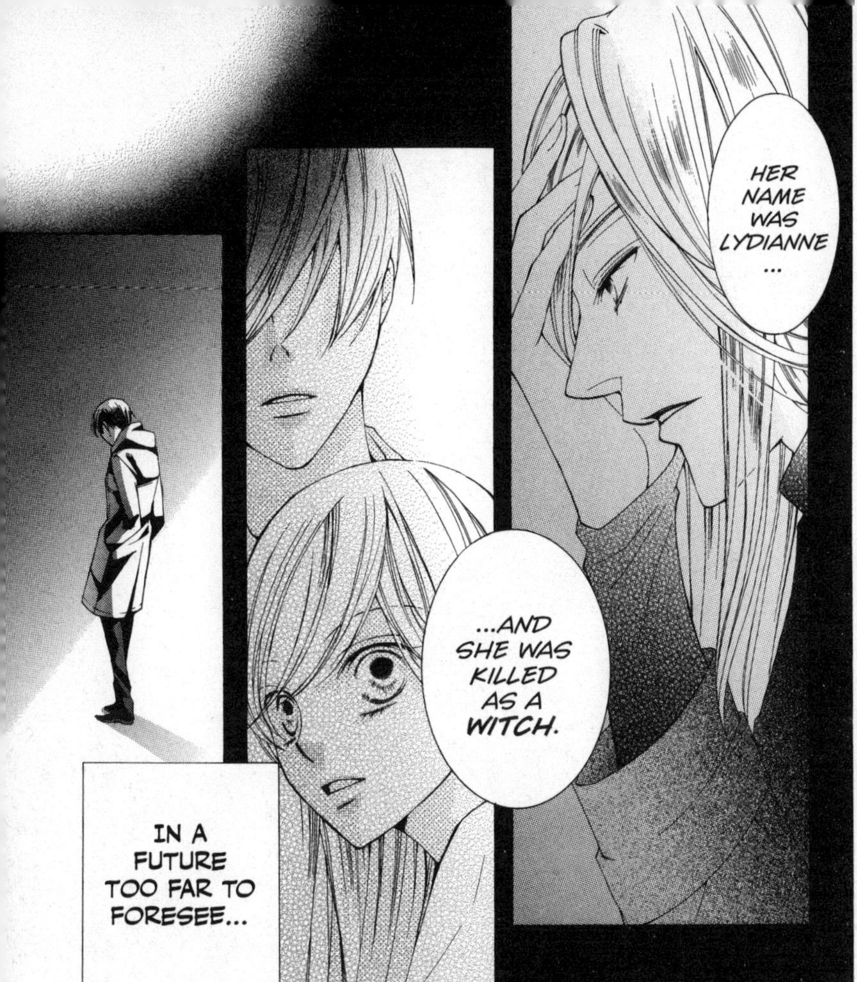
HER NAME WAS LYDIANNE...
...AND SHE WAS KILLED AS A WITCH.
IN A FUTURE TOO FAR TO FORESEE...

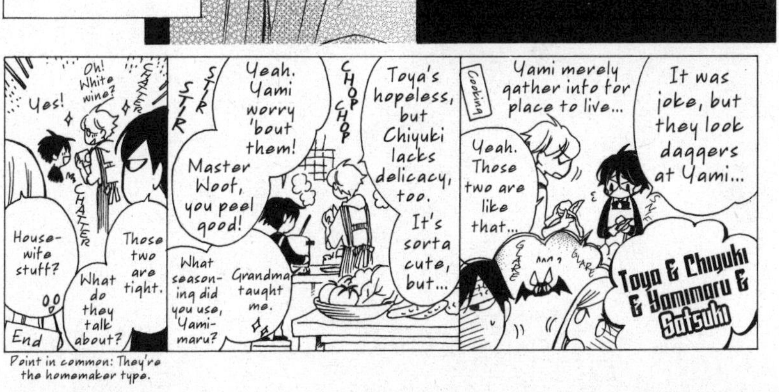
Toya & Chiyuki & Yamimaru & Satsuki
It was joke, but they look daggers at Yami...
Yami merely gather info for place to live...
Cooking
Yeah. Those two are like that...
Toya's hopeless, but Chiyuki lacks delicacy, too.
CHOP CHOP
Yeah. Yami worry 'bout them!
STIR STIR
Master Woof, you peel good!
It's sorta cute, but...
What seasoning did you use, Yamimaru?
Grandma taught me.
CHATTER
Oh! White wine?
Yes!
CHATTER
Those two are tight.
House-wife stuff?
What do they talk about?
End
Point in common: They're the homemaker type.

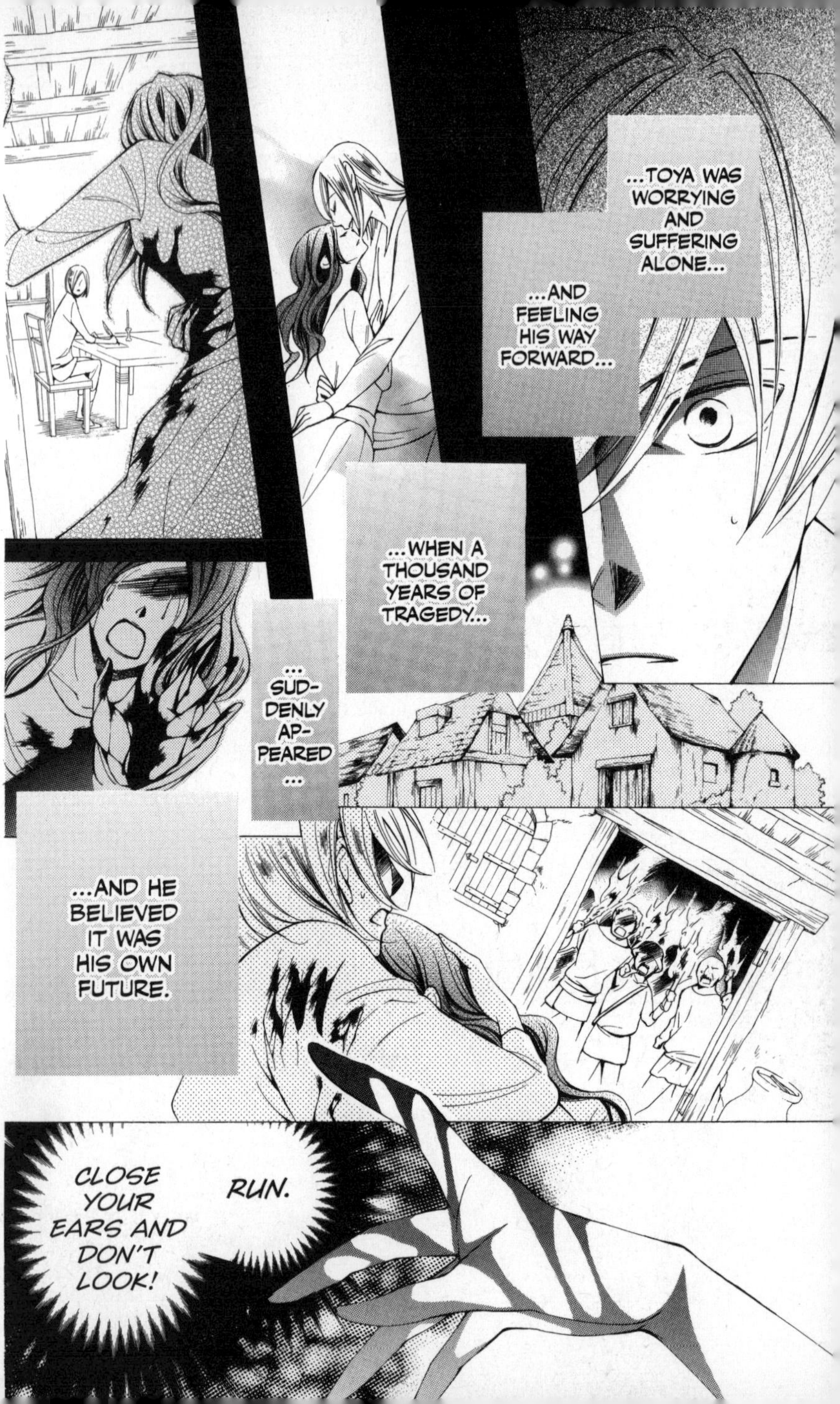
...TOYA WAS WORRYING AND SUFFERING ALONE...
...AND FEELING HIS WAY FORWARD...
...WHEN A THOUSAND YEARS OF TRAGEDY...
...SUD-DENLY AP-PEARED...
...AND HE BELIEVED IT WAS HIS OWN FUTURE.
RUN.
CLOSE YOUR EARS AND DON'T LOOK!

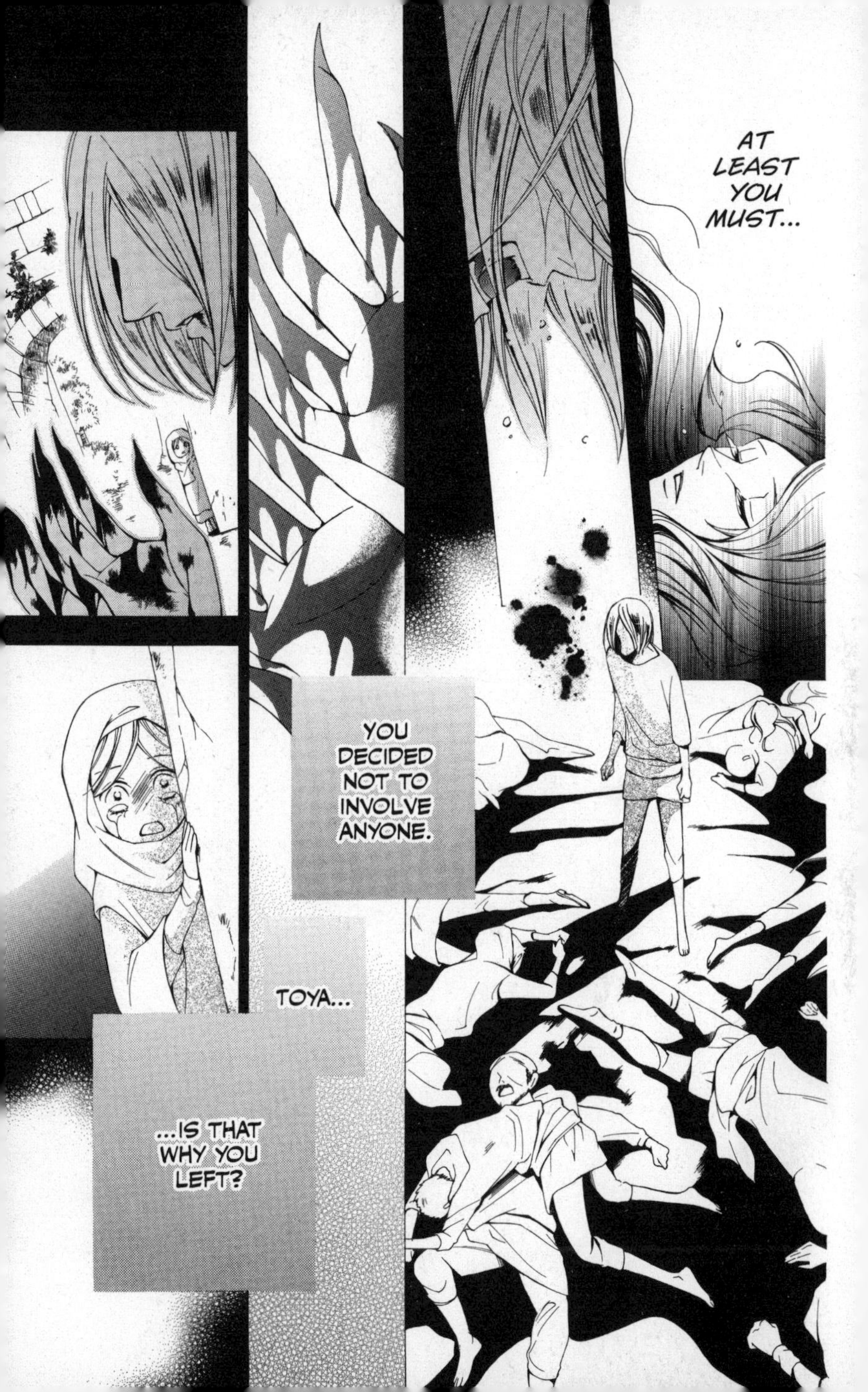
AT LEAST YOU MUST...
YOU DECIDED NOT TO INVOLVE ANYONE.
TOYA...
...IS THAT WHY YOU LEFT?

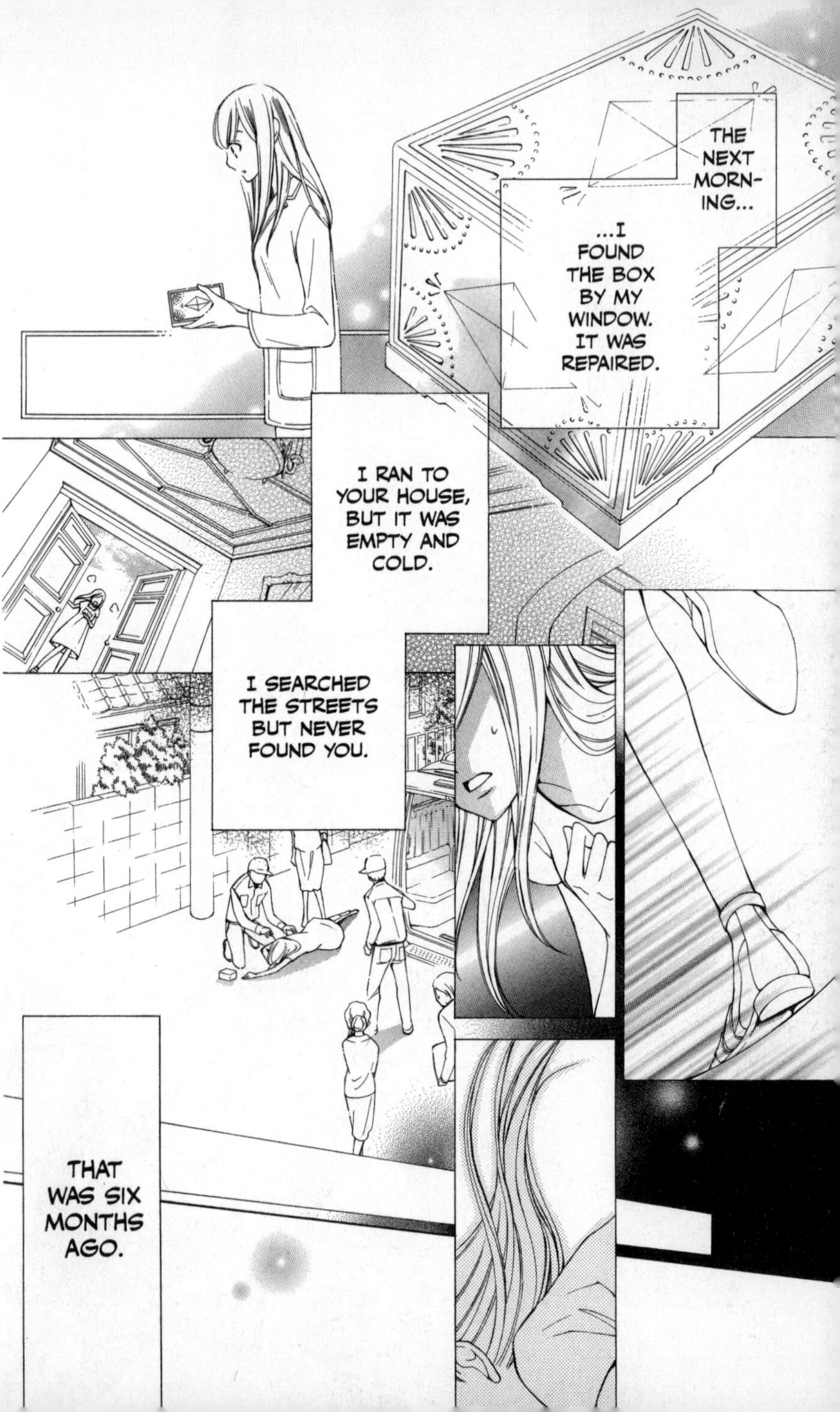
THE NEXT MORNING...
...I FOUND THE BOX BY MY WINDOW. IT WAS REPAIRED.
I RAN TO YOUR HOUSE, BUT IT WAS EMPTY AND COLD.
I SEARCHED THE STREETS BUT NEVER FOUND YOU.
THAT WAS SIX MONTHS AGO.

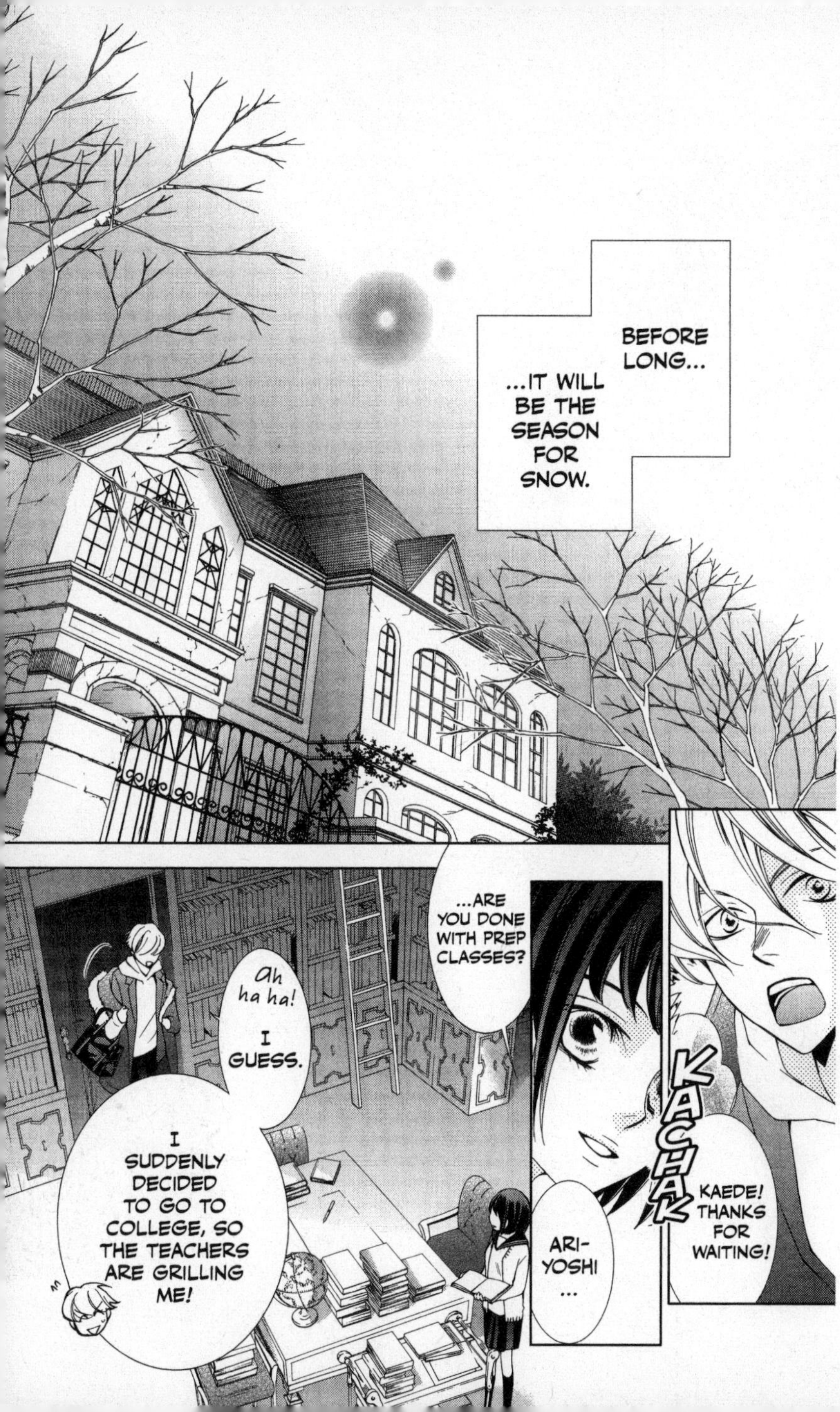
BEFORE LONG...
...IT WILL BE THE SEASON FOR SNOW.
KACHAK
KAEDE! THANKS FOR WAITING!
ARI-YOSHI ...
...ARE YOU DONE WITH PREP CLASSES?
ah ha ha! I GUESS.
I SUDDENLY DECIDED TO GO TO COLLEGE, SO THE TEACHERS ARE GRILLING ME!

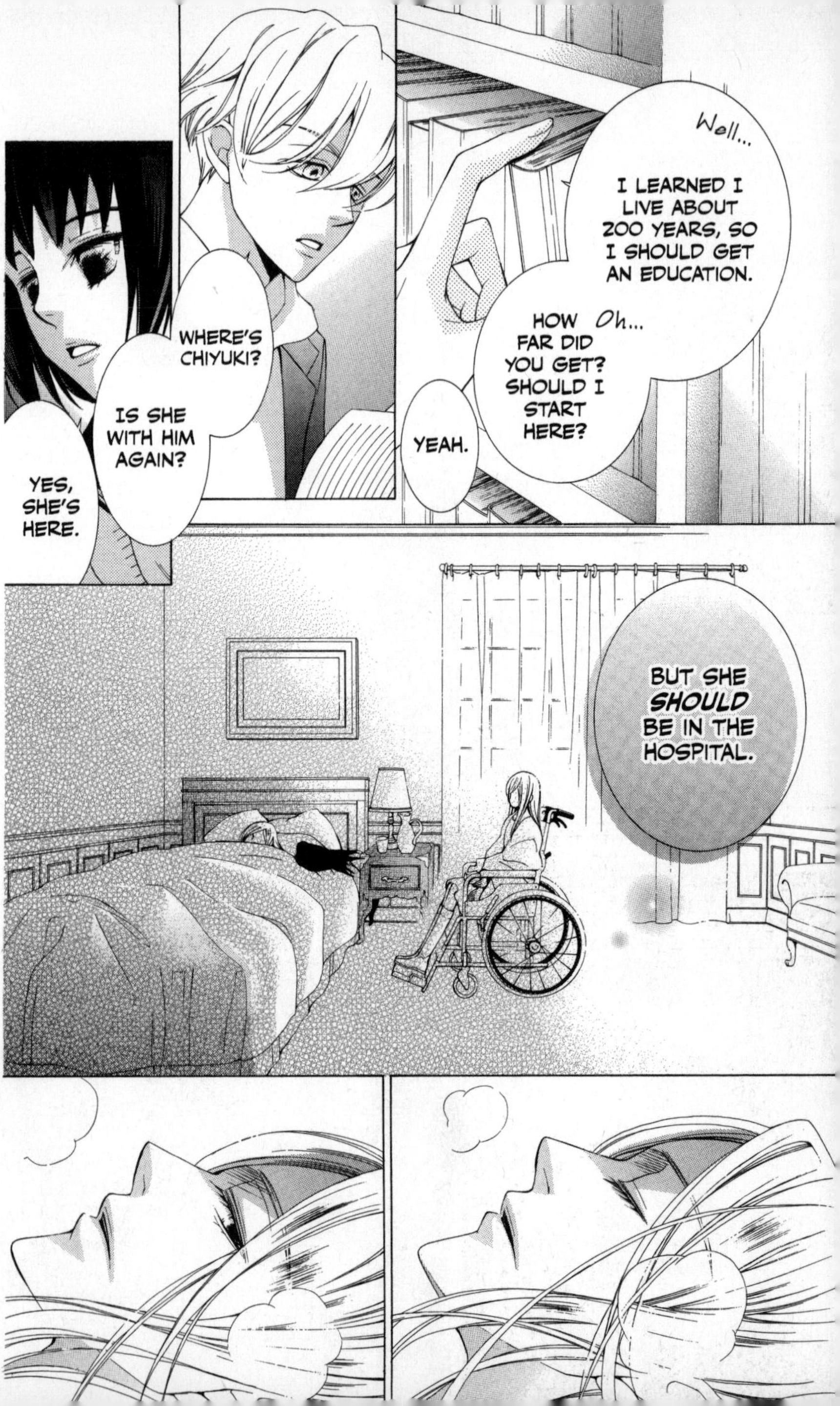
Well...
I LEARNED I LIVE ABOUT 200 YEARS, SO I SHOULD GET AN EDUCATION.
Oh...
HOW FAR DID YOU GET? SHOULD I START HERE?
YEAH.
WHERE'S CHIYUKI?
IS SHE WITH HIM AGAIN?
YES, SHE'S HERE.
BUT SHE SHOULD BE IN THE HOSPITAL.

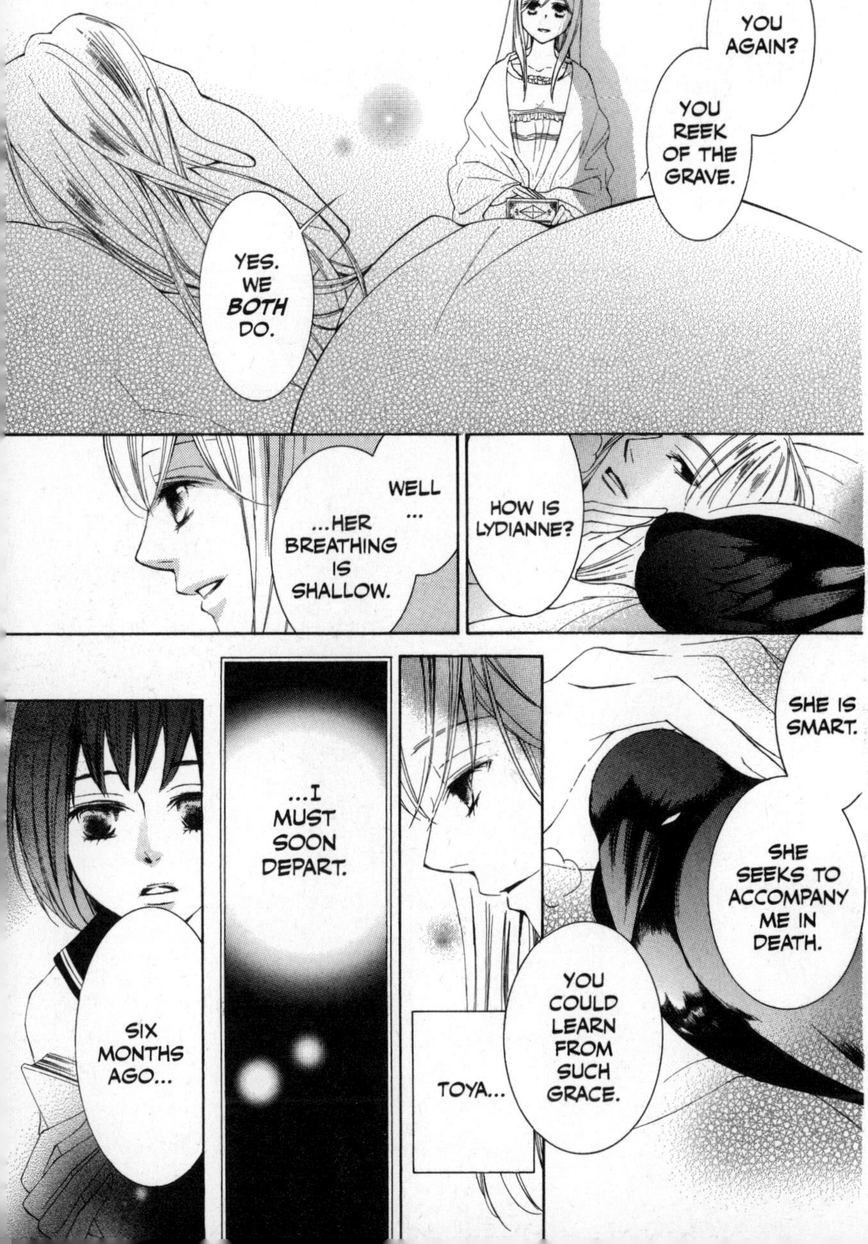
YOU AGAIN?
YOU REEK OF THE GRAVE.
YES. WE *BOTH* DO.
HOW IS LYDIANNE?
WELL ...
...HER BREATHING IS SHALLOW.
SHE IS SMART.
SHE SEEKS TO ACCOMPANY ME IN DEATH.
YOU COULD LEARN FROM SUCH GRACE.
TOYA...
...I MUST SOON DEPART.
SIX MONTHS AGO...

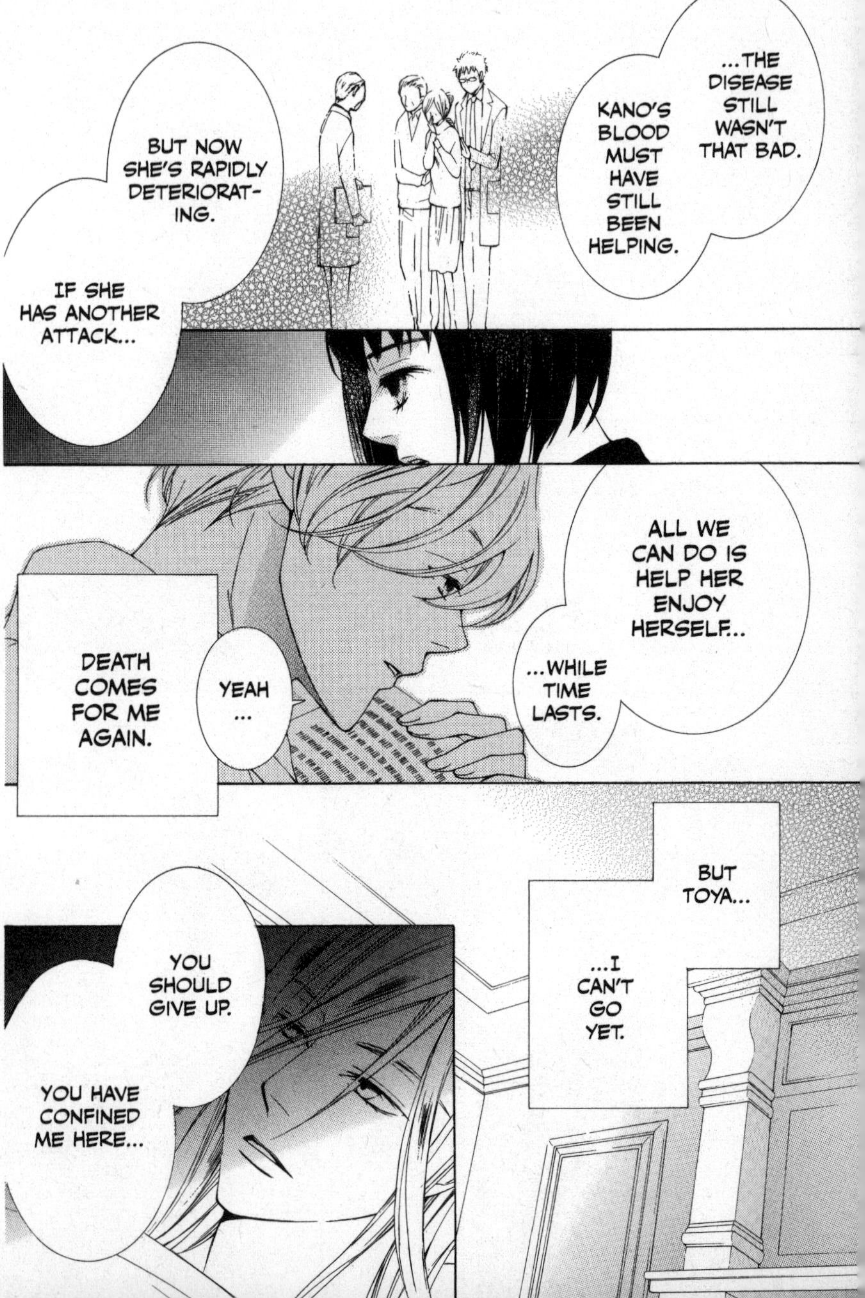
...THE DISEASE STILL WASN'T THAT BAD.
KANO'S BLOOD MUST HAVE STILL BEEN HELPING.
BUT NOW SHE'S RAPIDLY DETERIORAT-ING.
IF SHE HAS ANOTHER ATTACK...
ALL WE CAN DO IS HELP HER ENJOY HERSELF...
...WHILE TIME LASTS.
YEAH...
DEATH COMES FOR ME AGAIN.
BUT TOYA...
...I CAN'T GO YET.
YOU SHOULD GIVE UP.
YOU HAVE CONFINED ME HERE...

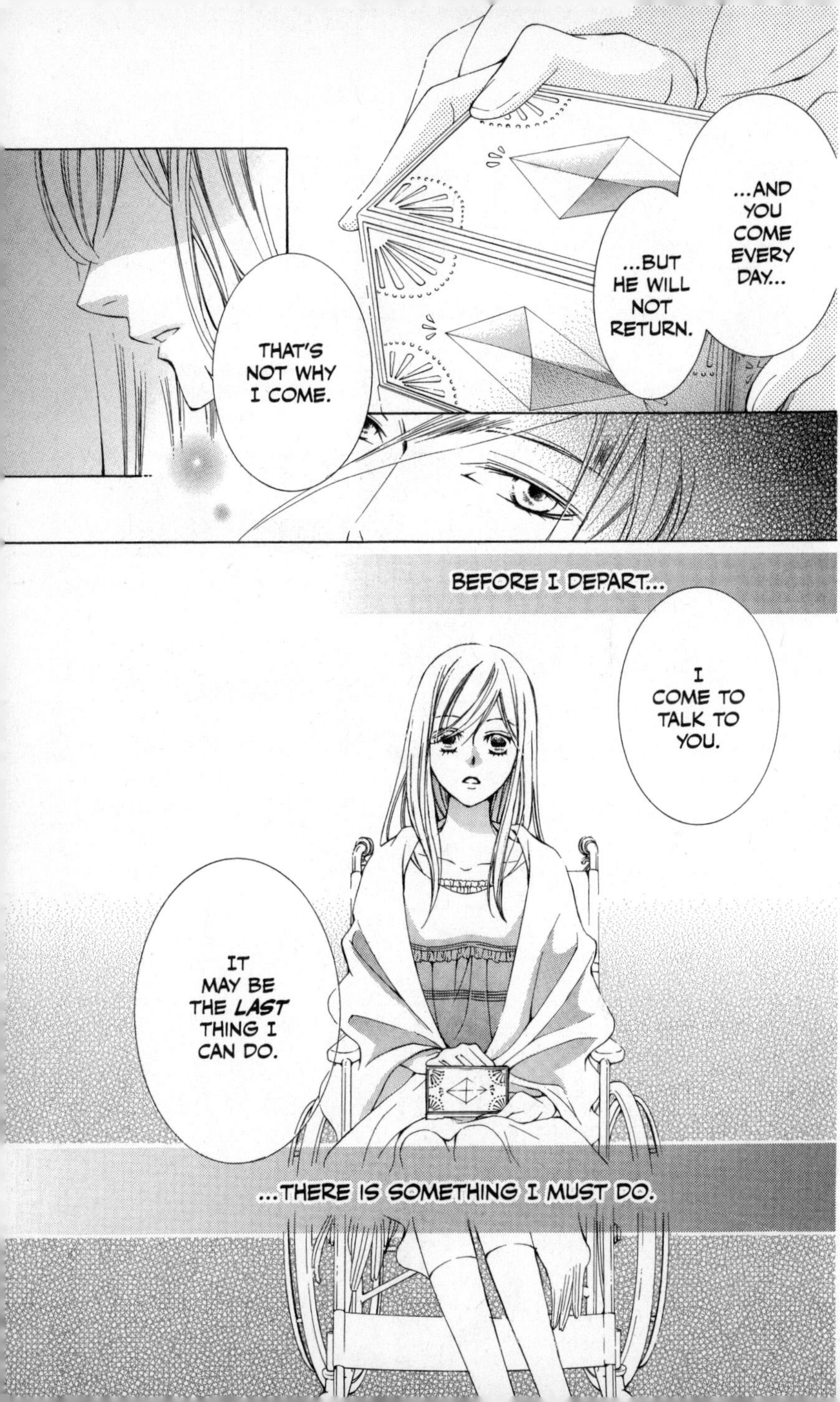
...AND YOU COME EVERY DAY...
...BUT HE WILL NOT RETURN.
THAT'S NOT WHY I COME.
BEFORE I DEPART...
I COME TO TALK TO YOU.
IT MAY BE THE *LAST* THING I CAN DO.
...THERE IS SOMETHING I MUST DO.

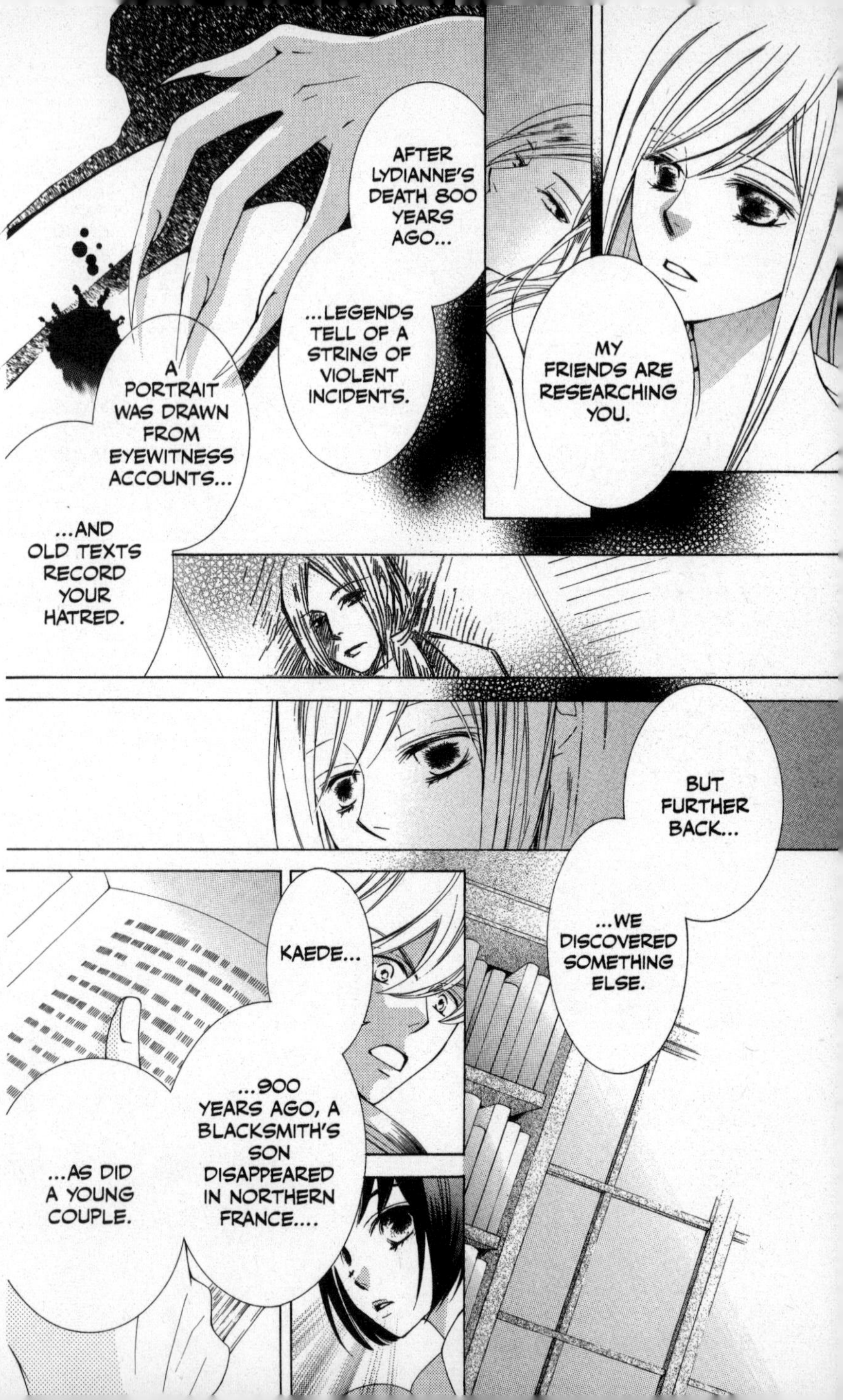
MY FRIENDS ARE RESEARCHING YOU.
AFTER LYDIANNE'S DEATH 800 YEARS AGO...
...LEGENDS TELL OF A STRING OF VIOLENT INCIDENTS.
A PORTRAIT WAS DRAWN FROM EYEWITNESS ACCOUNTS...
...AND OLD TEXTS RECORD YOUR HATRED.
BUT FURTHER BACK...
...WE DISCOVERED SOMETHING ELSE.
KAEDE...
...900 YEARS AGO, A BLACKSMITH'S SON DISAPPEARED IN NORTHERN FRANCE....
...AS DID A YOUNG COUPLE.

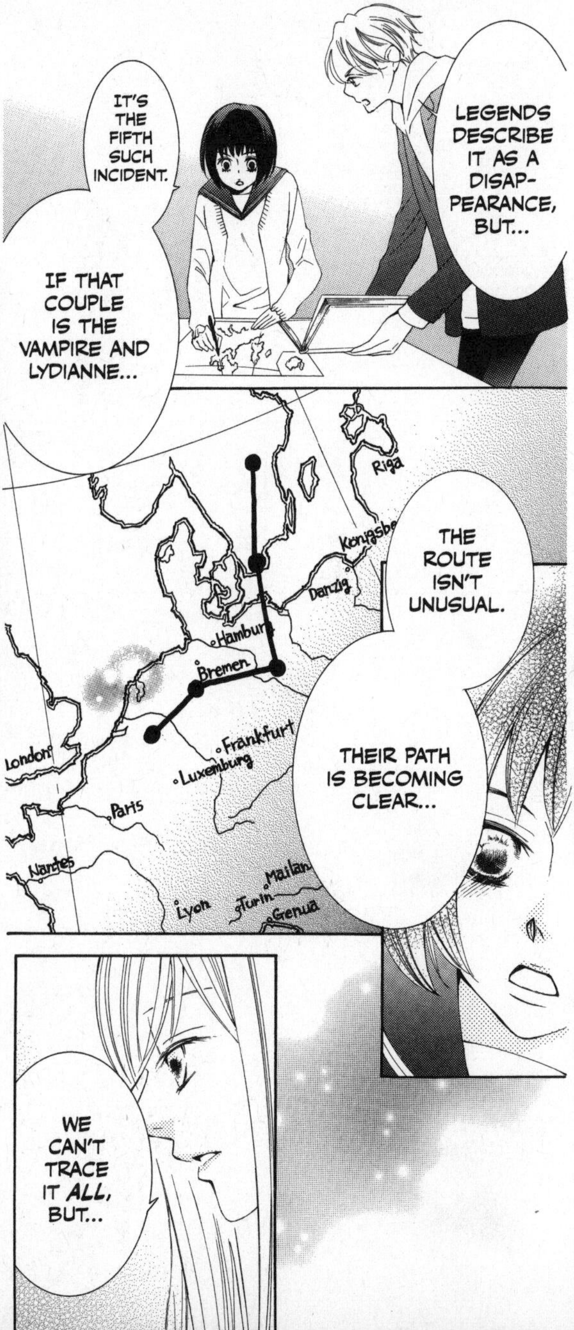
LEGENDS DESCRIBE IT AS A DISAP-PEARANCE, BUT...
IT'S THE FIFTH SUCH INCIDENT.
IF THAT COUPLE IS THE VAMPIRE AND LYDIANNE...
Riga
Königsbe
Danzig
Hamburg
Bremen
Frankfurt
London
Luxemburg
Paris
Nantes
Lyon
Turin
Mailan
Genua
THE ROUTE ISN'T UNUSUAL.
THEIR PATH IS BECOMING CLEAR...
WE CAN'T TRACE IT *ALL*, BUT...

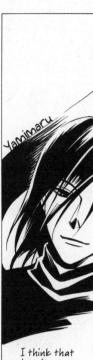

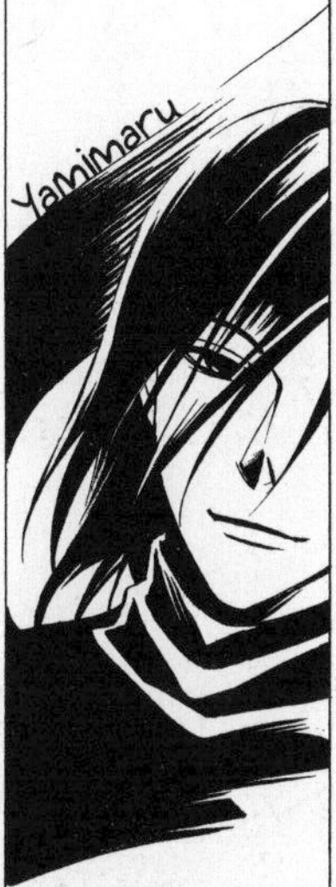
Yamimaru

I think that when it comes to Yamimaru as a human, the adult version is closer to his true self. But the smaller one is easier to draw. (The adult one is super hard to draw...) Ugh.

He talks funny because he was born in a foreign country and the person who taught him Japanese wasn't very good.

Is that explanation good enough?

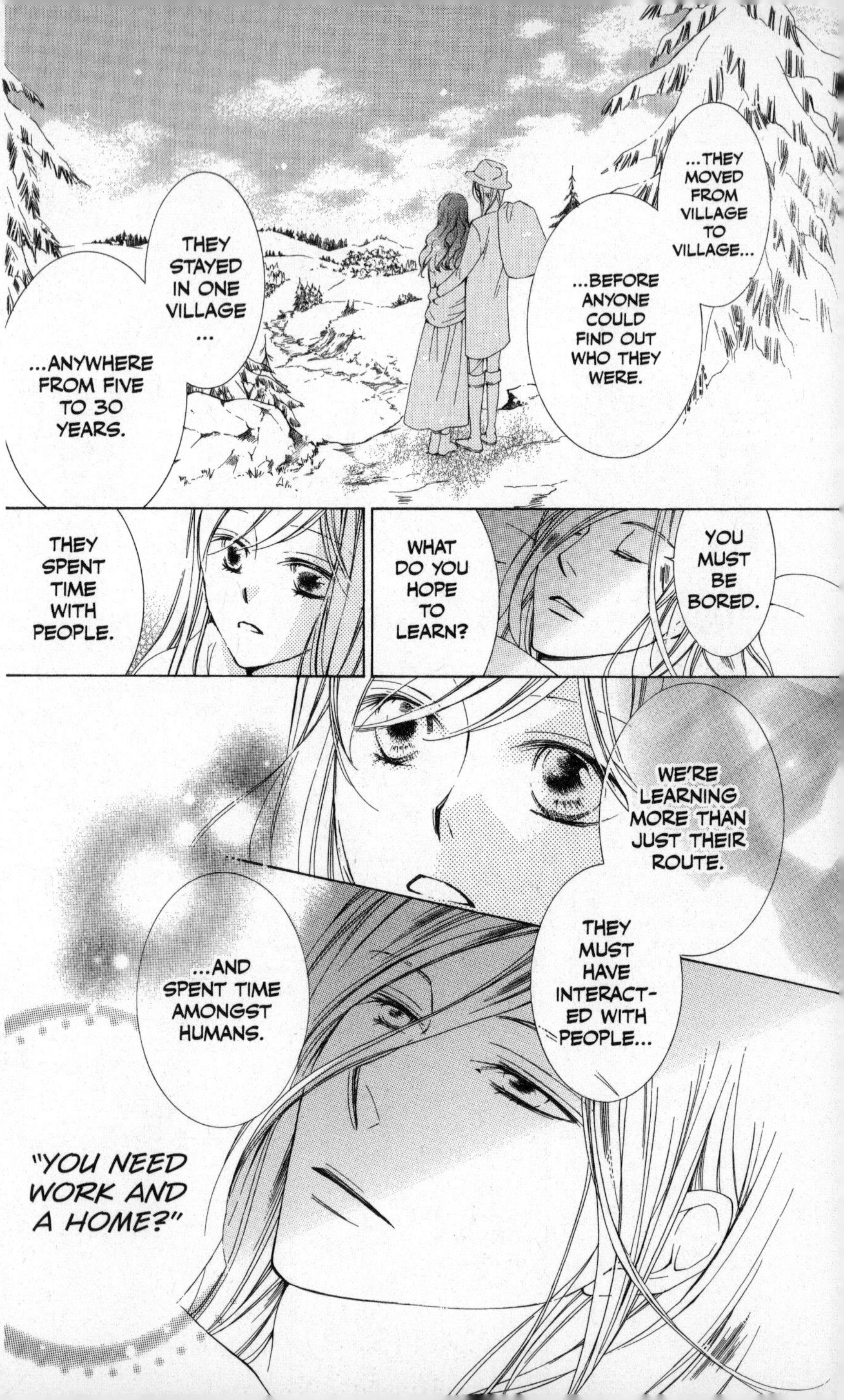
...THEY MOVED FROM VILLAGE TO VILLAGE...
...BEFORE ANYONE COULD FIND OUT WHO THEY WERE.
THEY STAYED IN ONE VILLAGE ...
...ANYWHERE FROM FIVE TO 30 YEARS.
YOU MUST BE BORED.
WHAT DO YOU HOPE TO LEARN?
THEY SPENT TIME WITH PEOPLE.
WE'RE LEARNING MORE THAN JUST THEIR ROUTE.
THEY MUST HAVE INTERACTED WITH PEOPLE...
...AND SPENT TIME AMONGST HUMANS.
"YOU NEED WORK AND A HOME?"

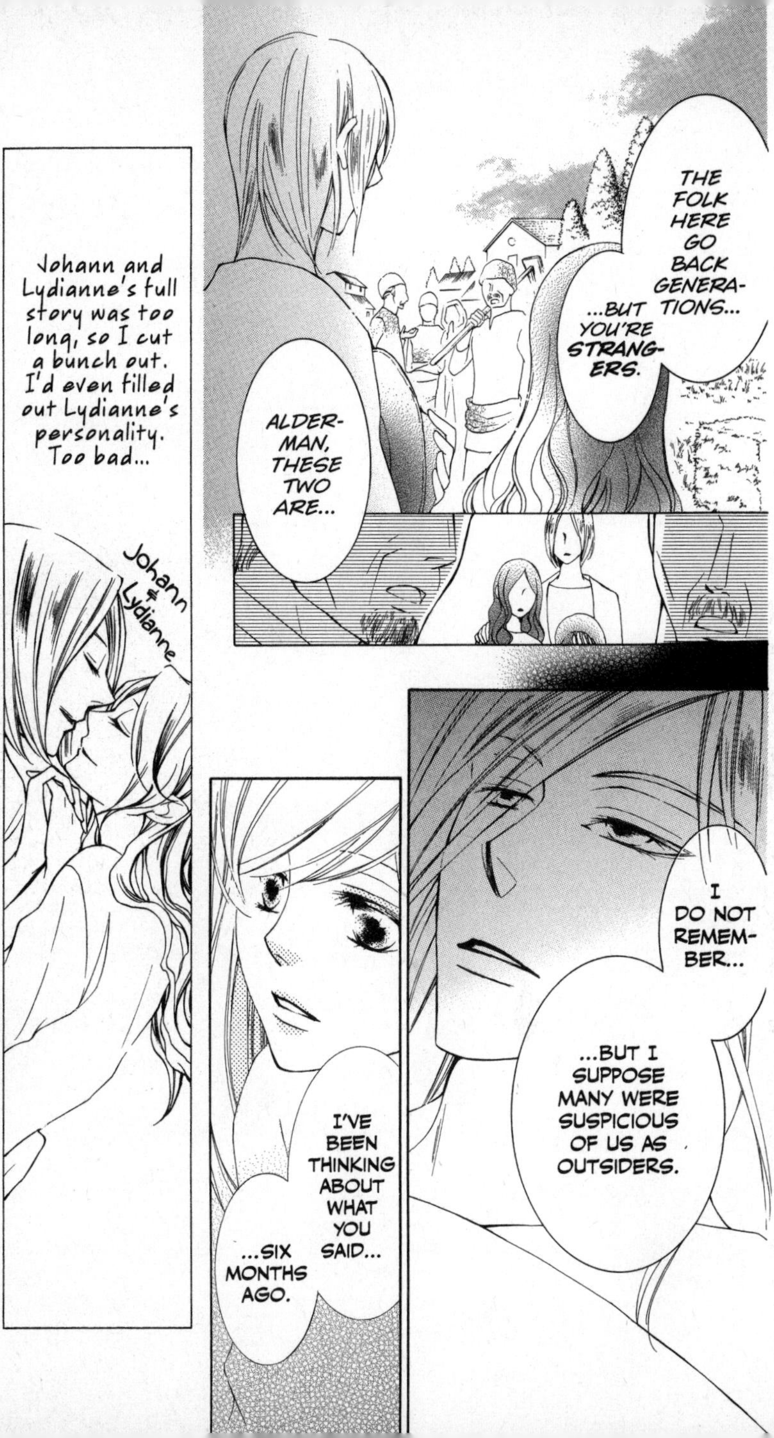
THE FOLK HERE GO BACK GENERATIONS...
...BUT YOU'RE STRANGERS.
ALDERMAN, THESE TWO ARE...
I DO NOT REMEMBER...
...BUT I SUPPOSE MANY WERE SUSPICIOUS OF US AS OUTSIDERS.
I'VE BEEN THINKING ABOUT WHAT YOU SAID...
...SIX MONTHS AGO.
Johann and Lydianne's full story was too long, so I cut a bunch out. I'd even filled out Lydianne's personality. Too bad...
Johann & Lydianne

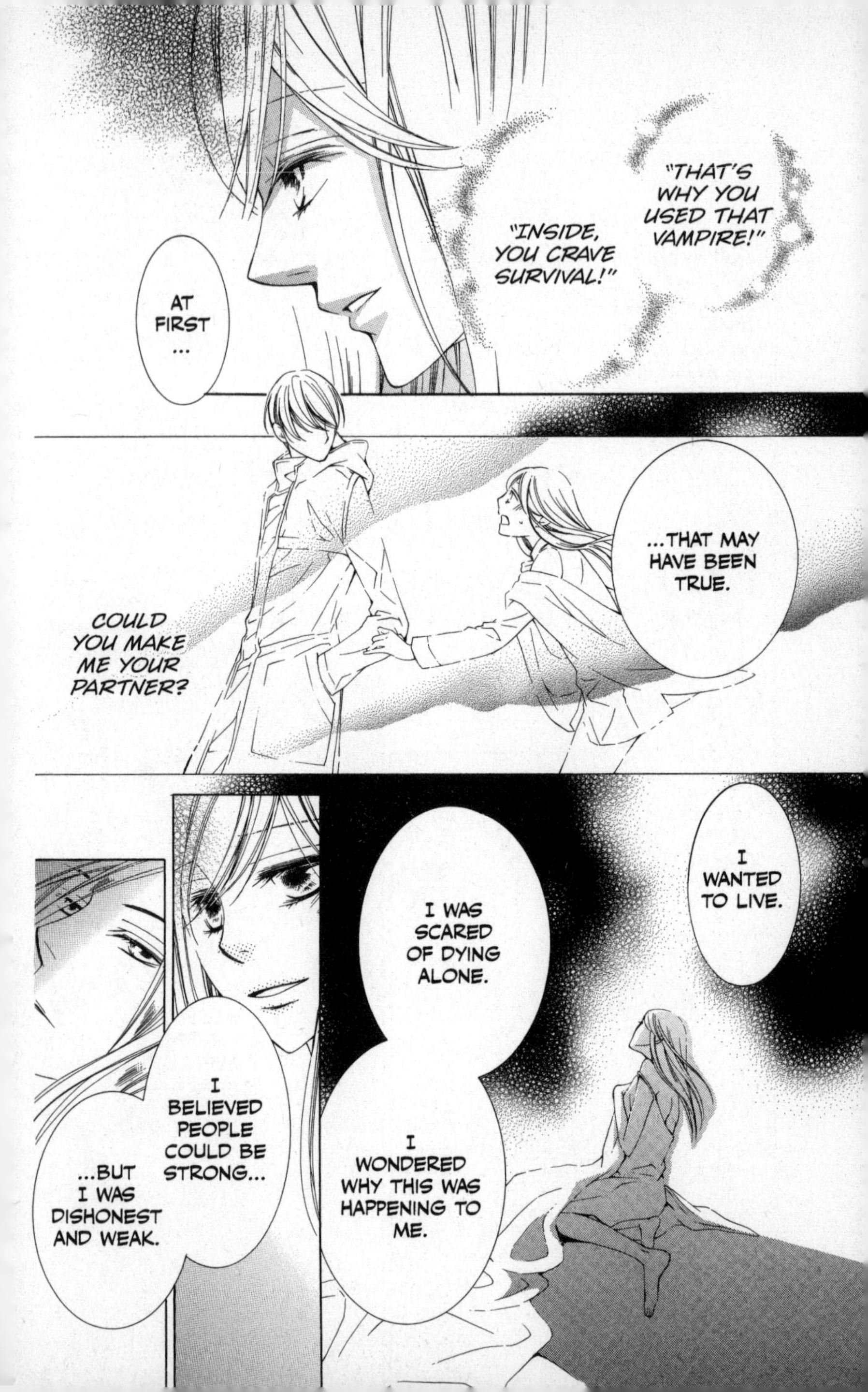
"THAT'S WHY YOU USED THAT VAMPIRE!"
"INSIDE, YOU CRAVE SURVIVAL!"
AT FIRST ...
...THAT MAY HAVE BEEN TRUE.
COULD YOU MAKE ME YOUR PARTNER?
I WANTED TO LIVE.
I WAS SCARED OF DYING ALONE.
I WONDERED WHY THIS WAS HAPPENING TO ME.
I BELIEVED PEOPLE COULD BE STRONG...
...BUT I WAS DISHONEST AND WEAK.

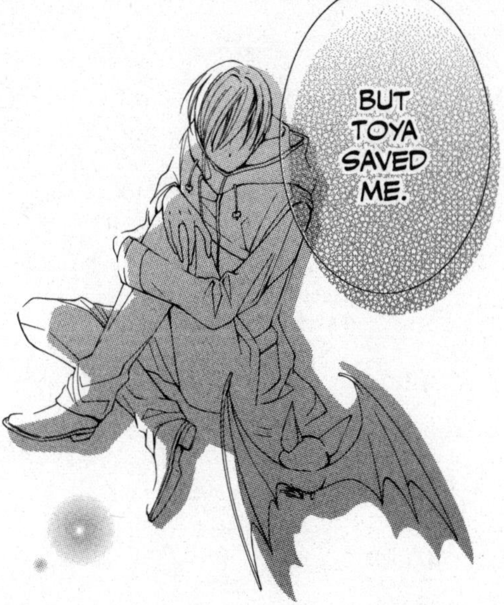
BUT TOYA SAVED ME.

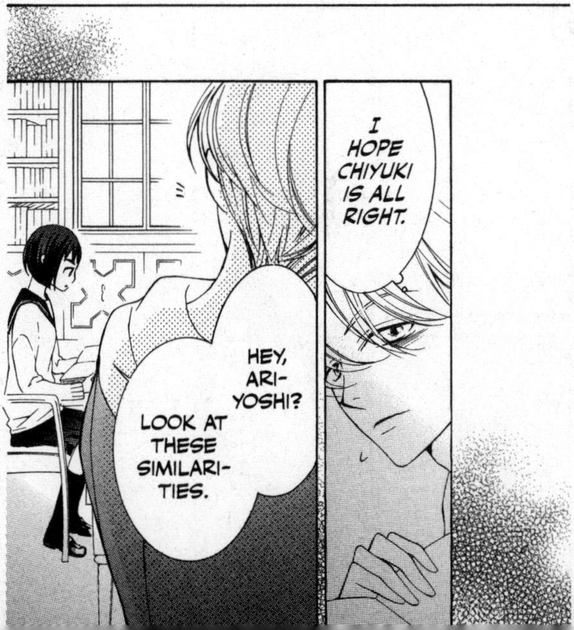
I HOPE CHIYUKI IS ALL RIGHT.
HEY, ARI-YOSHI?
LOOK AT THESE SIMILARI-TIES.

A few words

✿ This is the end! My theme for the interstitial pages was the characters someday, somewhere.

✿ I wasn't sure if it was really a good idea to continue this series after ten years, and once I got started, it was difficult and I couldn't do as much as I wanted. But it was a miracle to have this opportunity, so I'm truly grateful!

✿ Heartfelt thanks to all who helped publish this book!

And above all, thanks to the readers who stuck with it!!

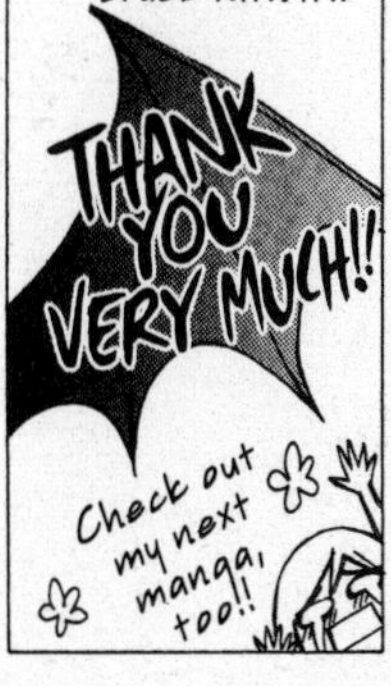
THANK YOU VERY MUCH!!

✿ Check out my next manga, too!! ✿

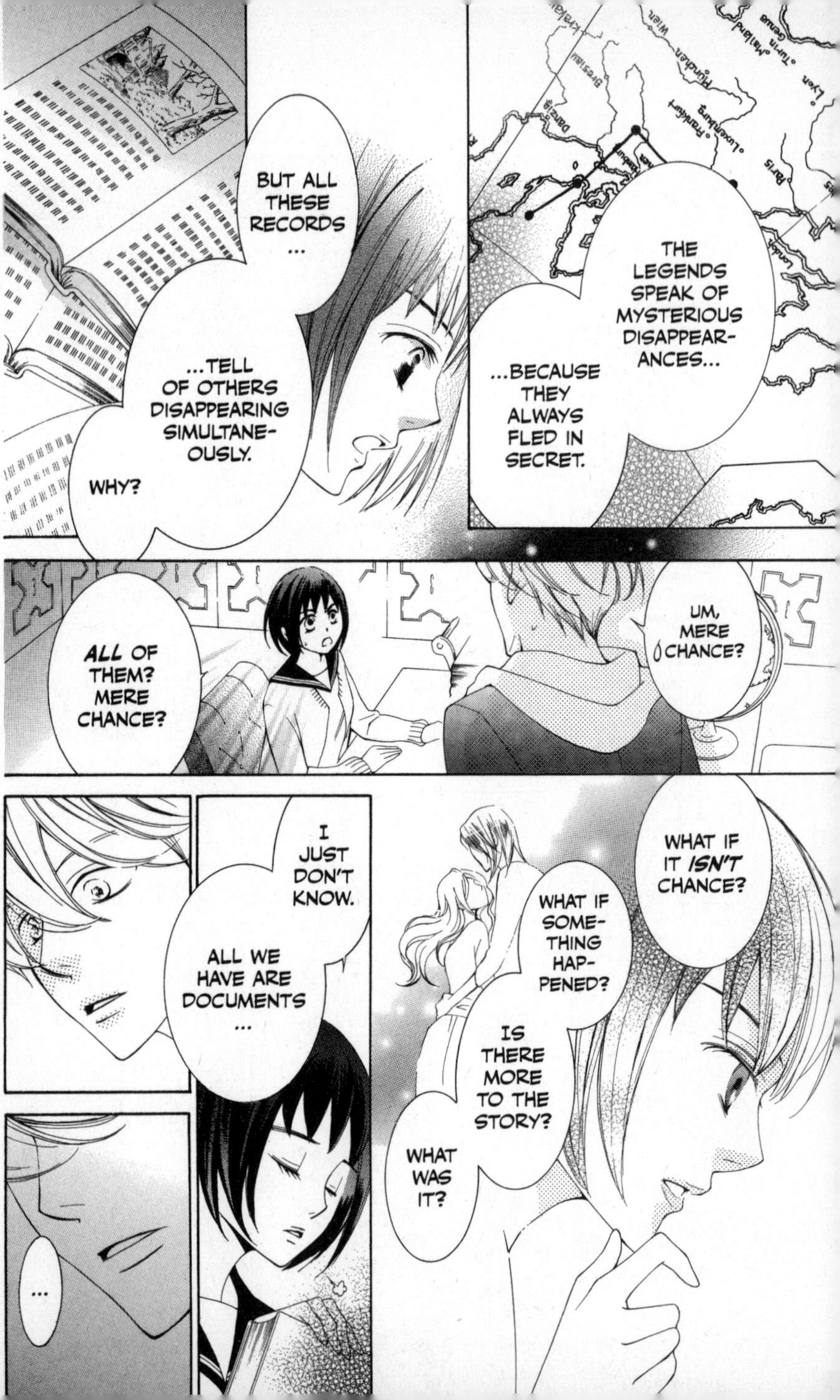
THE LEGENDS SPEAK OF MYSTERIOUS DISAPPEARANCES...
...BECAUSE THEY ALWAYS FLED IN SECRET.
BUT ALL THESE RECORDS ...
...TELL OF OTHERS DISAPPEARING SIMULTANEOUSLY.
WHY?
UM, MERE CHANCE?
ALL OF THEM? MERE CHANCE?
WHAT IF IT *ISN'T* CHANCE?
WHAT IF SOMETHING HAPPENED?
IS THERE MORE TO THE STORY?
WHAT WAS IT?
I JUST DON'T KNOW.
ALL WE HAVE ARE DOCUMENTS ...
...

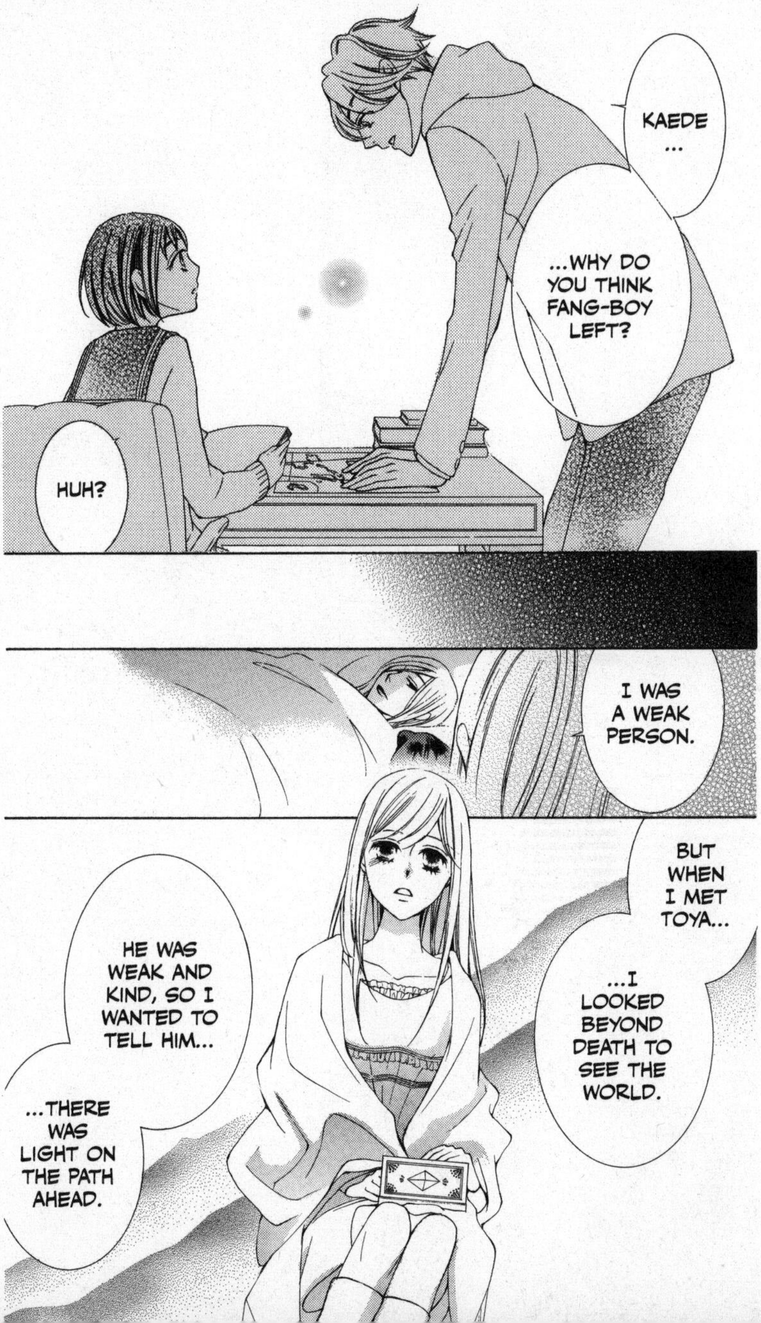
KAEDE ...
...WHY DO YOU THINK FANG-BOY LEFT?
HUH?
I WAS A WEAK PERSON.
BUT WHEN I MET TOYA...
...I LOOKED BEYOND DEATH TO SEE THE WORLD.
HE WAS WEAK AND KIND, SO I WANTED TO TELL HIM...
...THERE WAS LIGHT ON THE PATH AHEAD.

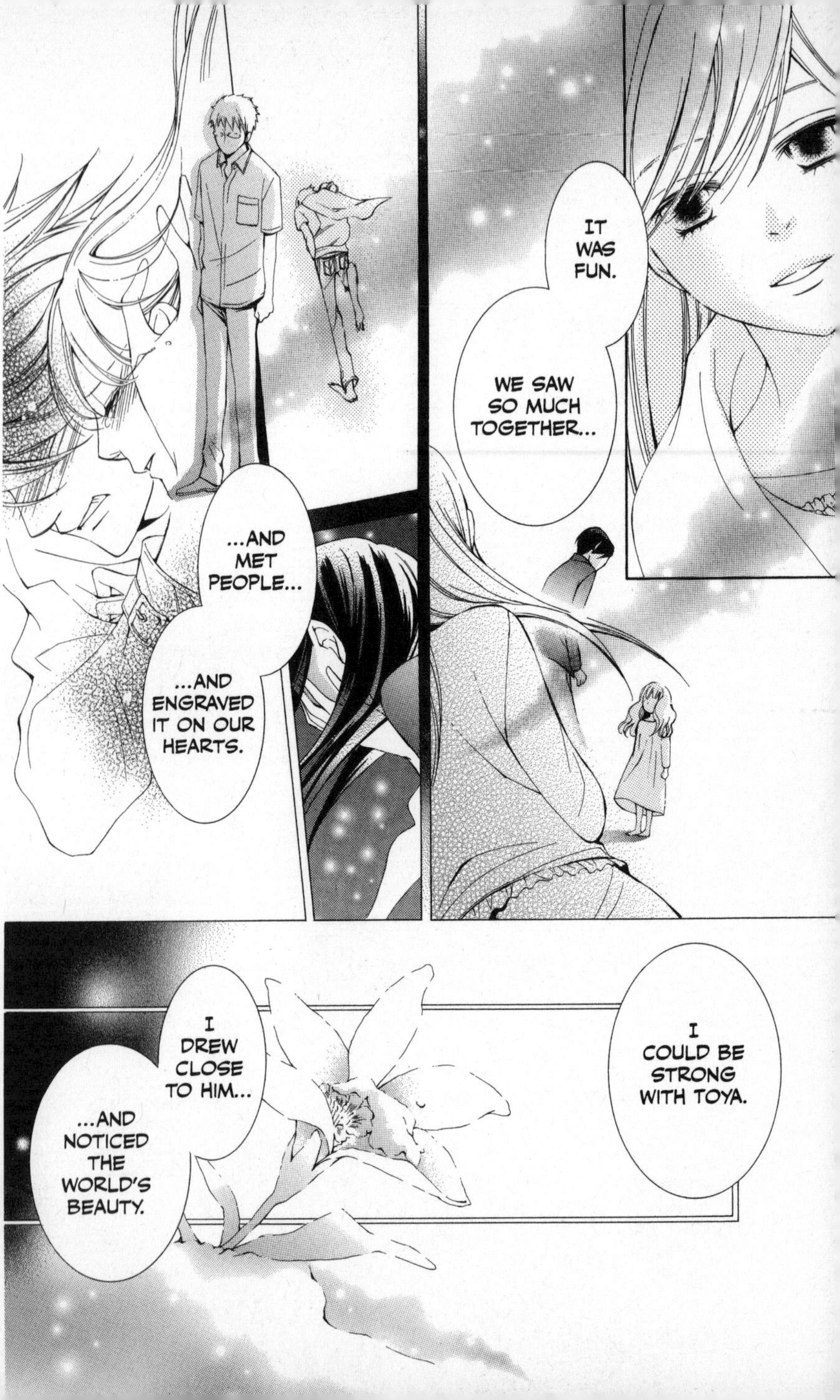
IT WAS FUN.
WE SAW SO MUCH TOGETHER...
...AND MET PEOPLE...
...AND ENGRAVED IT ON OUR HEARTS.
I COULD BE STRONG WITH TOYA.
I DREW CLOSE TO HIM...
...AND NOTICED THE WORLD'S BEAUTY.

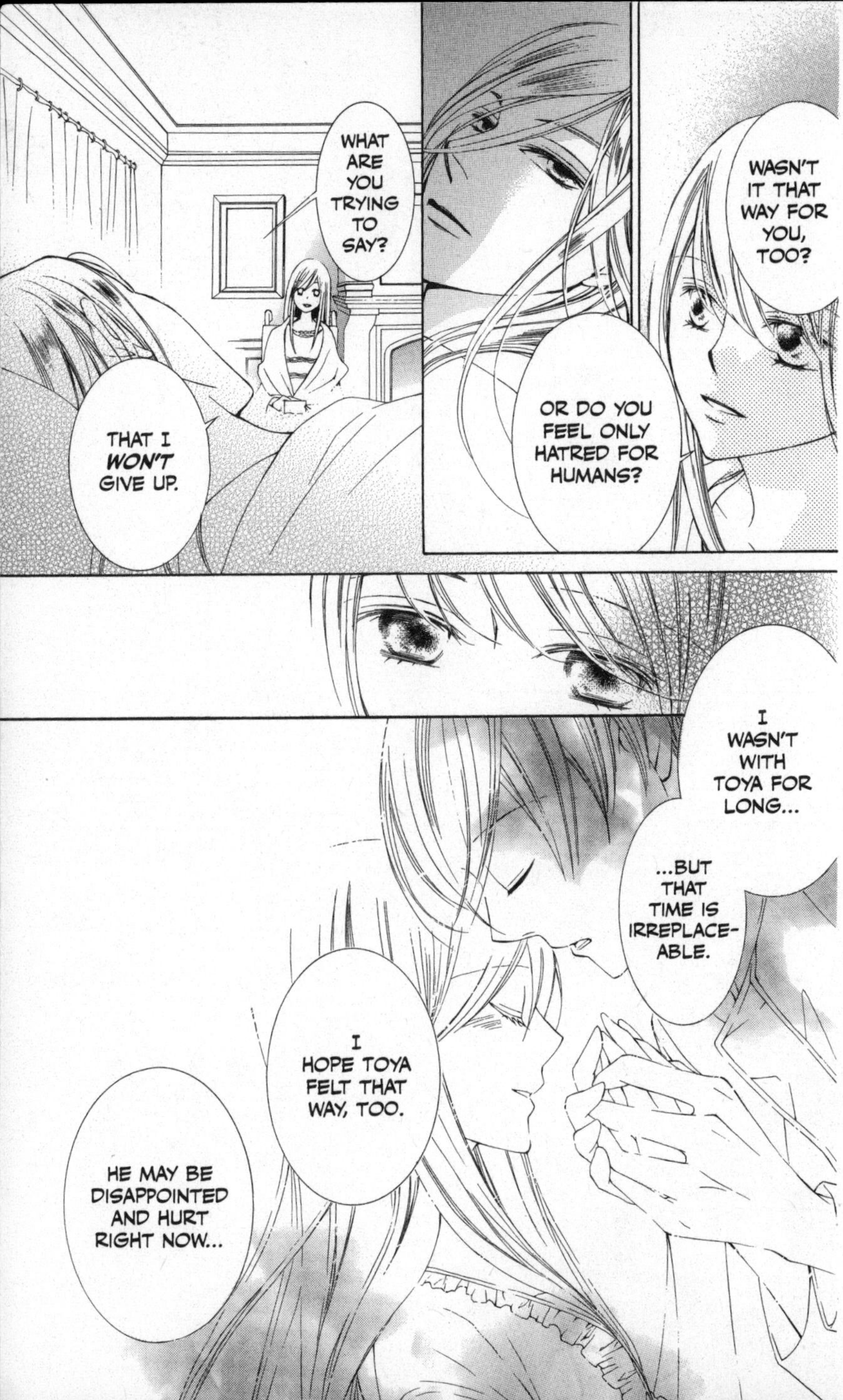
WASN'T IT THAT WAY FOR YOU, TOO?
OR DO YOU FEEL ONLY HATRED FOR HUMANS?
WHAT ARE YOU TRYING TO SAY?
THAT I *WON'T* GIVE UP.
I WASN'T WITH TOYA FOR LONG...
...BUT THAT TIME IS IRREPLACEABLE.
I HOPE TOYA FELT THAT WAY, TOO.
HE MAY BE DISAPPOINTED AND HURT RIGHT NOW...

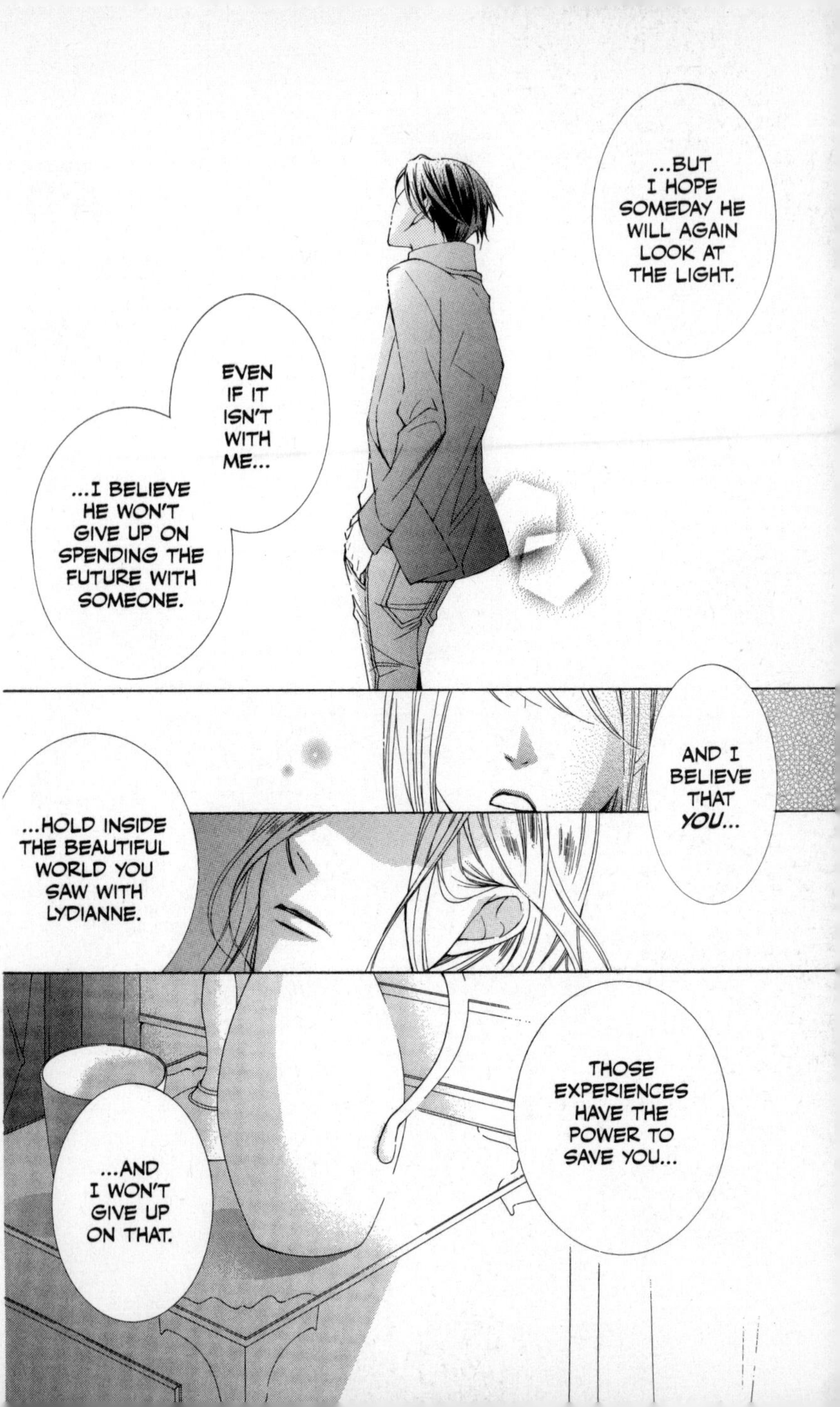
...BUT I HOPE SOMEDAY HE WILL AGAIN LOOK AT THE LIGHT.
EVEN IF IT ISN'T WITH ME...
...I BELIEVE HE WON'T GIVE UP ON SPENDING THE FUTURE WITH SOMEONE.
AND I BELIEVE THAT *YOU*...
...HOLD INSIDE THE BEAUTIFUL WORLD YOU SAW WITH LYDIANNE.
THOSE EXPERIENCES HAVE THE POWER TO SAVE YOU...
...AND I WON'T GIVE UP ON THAT.

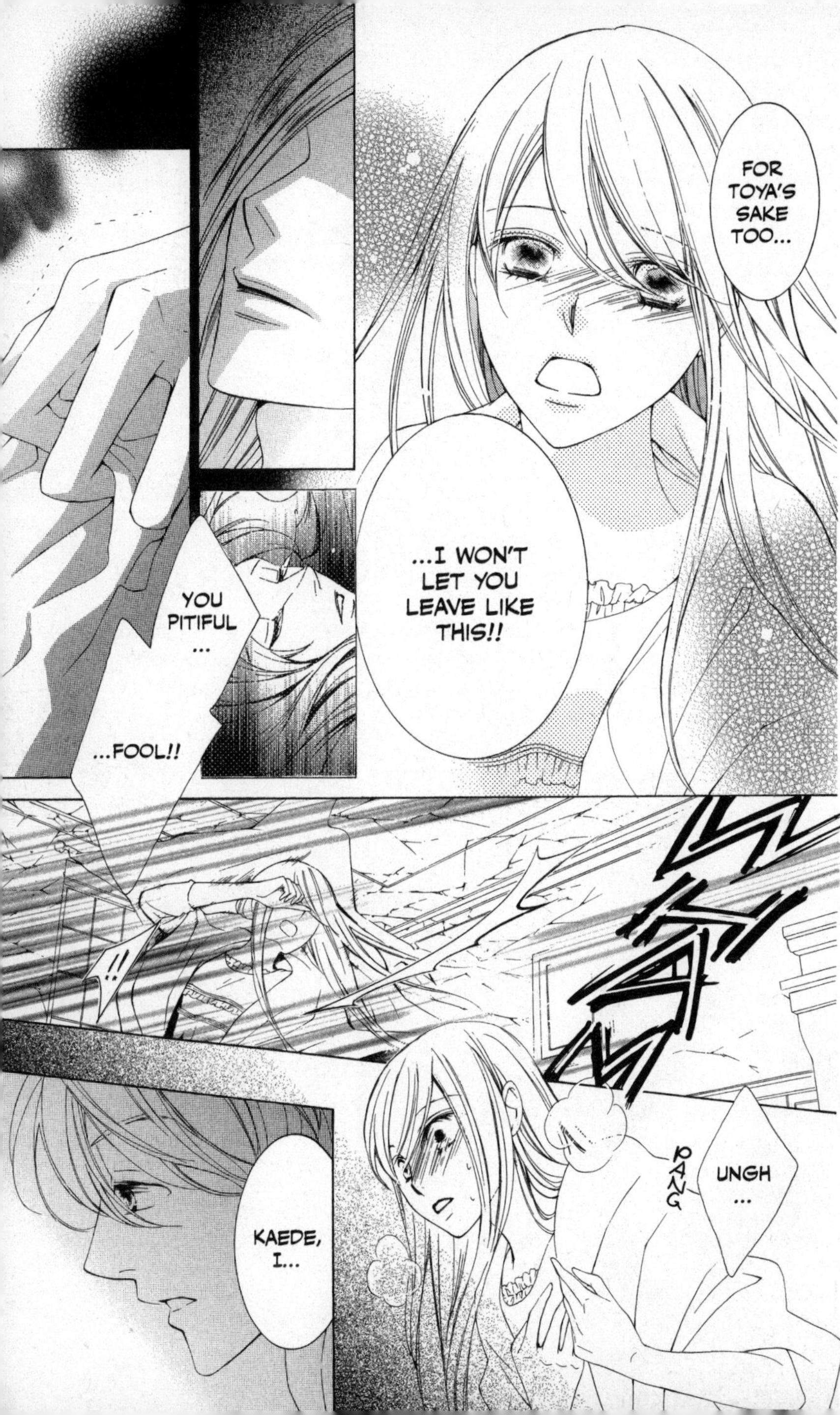
FOR TOYA'S SAKE TOO...
...I WON'T LET YOU LEAVE LIKE THIS!!
YOU PITIFUL ...
...FOOL!!
!!
RANG
UNGH ...
KAEDE, I...

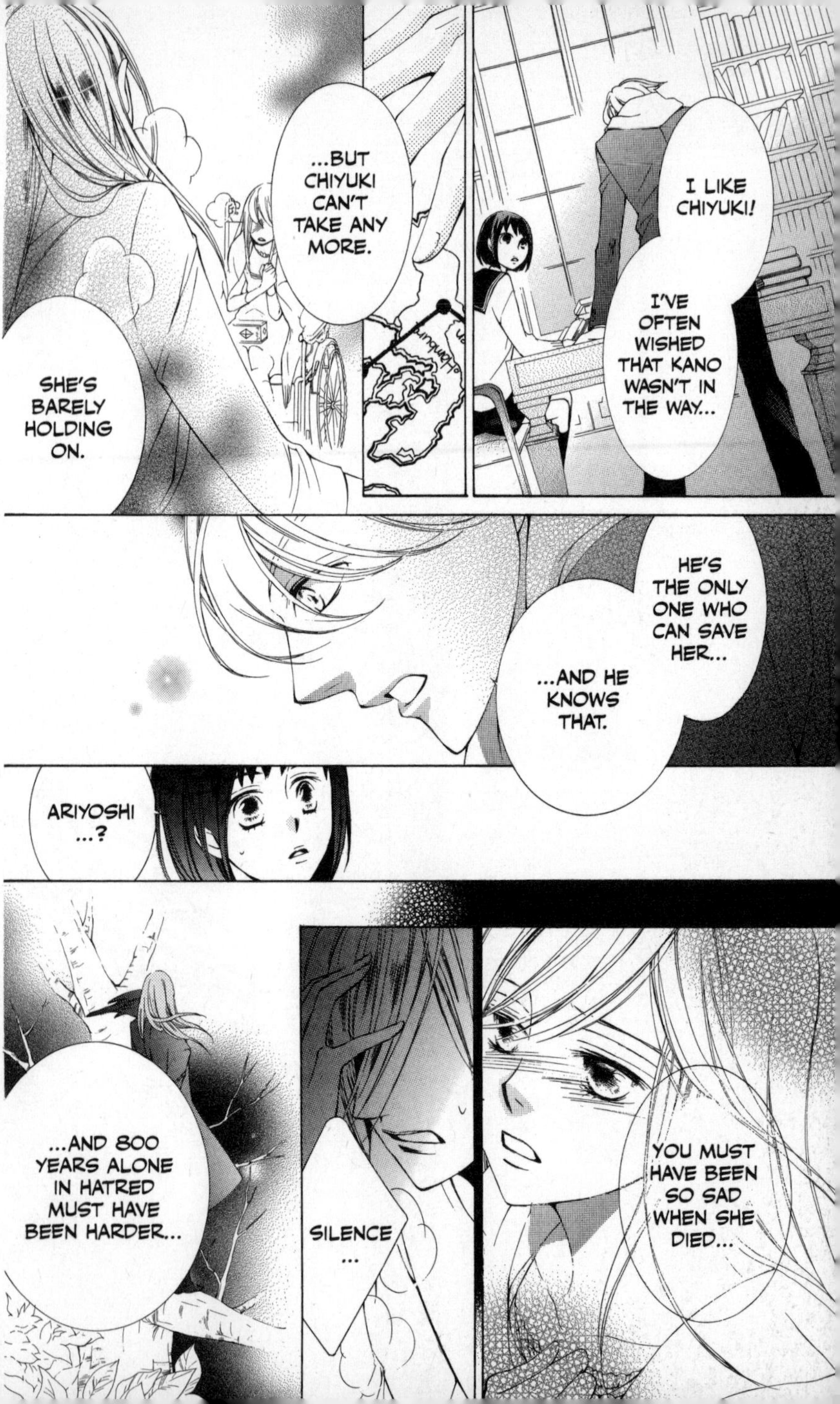
I LIKE CHIYUKI!
I'VE OFTEN WISHED THAT KANO WASN'T IN THE WAY...
...BUT CHIYUKI CAN'T TAKE ANY MORE.
SHE'S BARELY HOLDING ON.
HE'S THE ONLY ONE WHO CAN SAVE HER...
...AND HE KNOWS THAT.
ARIYOSHI ...?
YOU MUST HAVE BEEN SO SAD WHEN SHE DIED...
SILENCE ...
...AND 800 YEARS ALONE IN HATRED MUST HAVE BEEN HARDER...

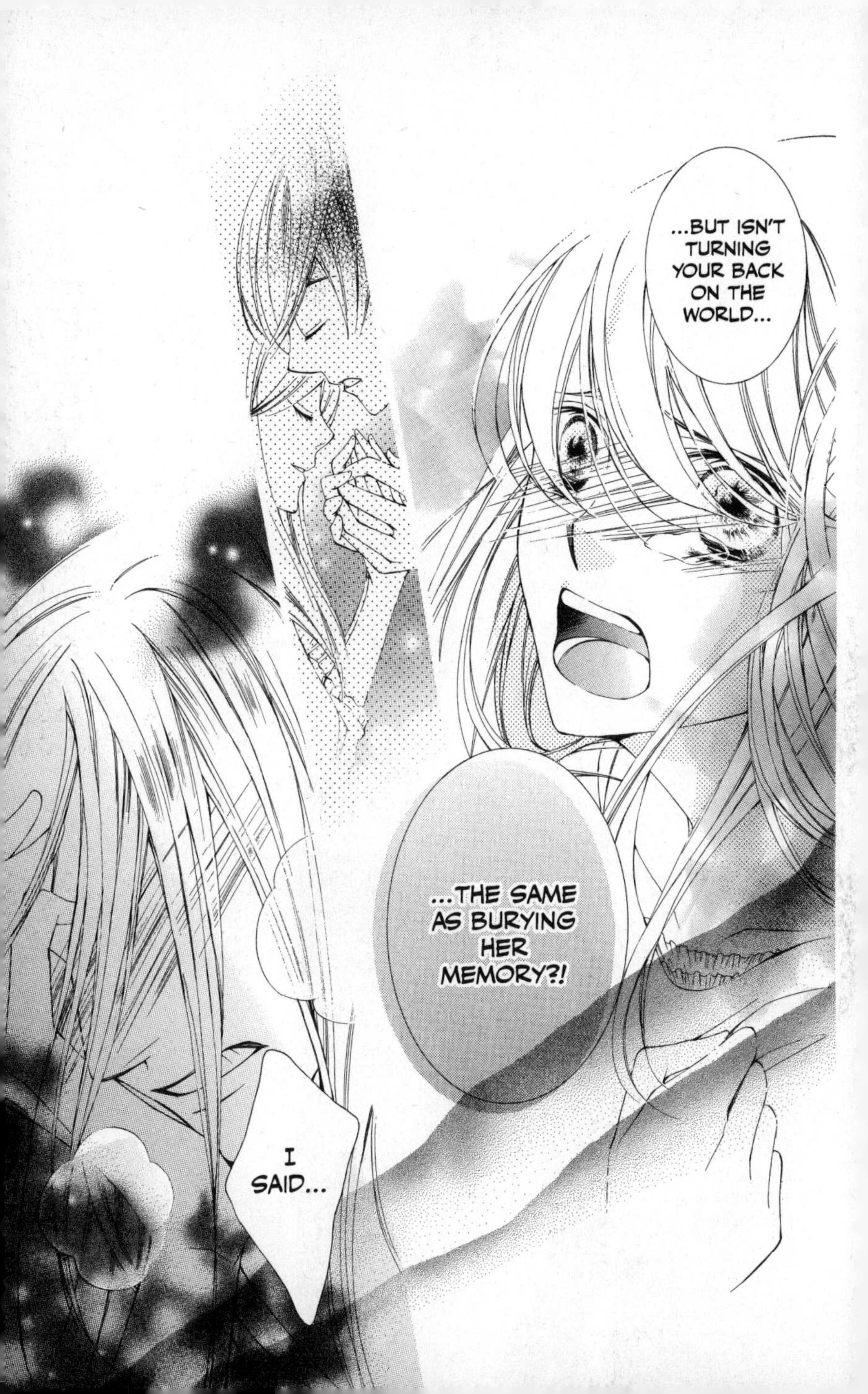
...BUT ISN'T TURNING YOUR BACK ON THE WORLD...
...THE SAME AS BURYING HER MEMORY?!
I SAID...

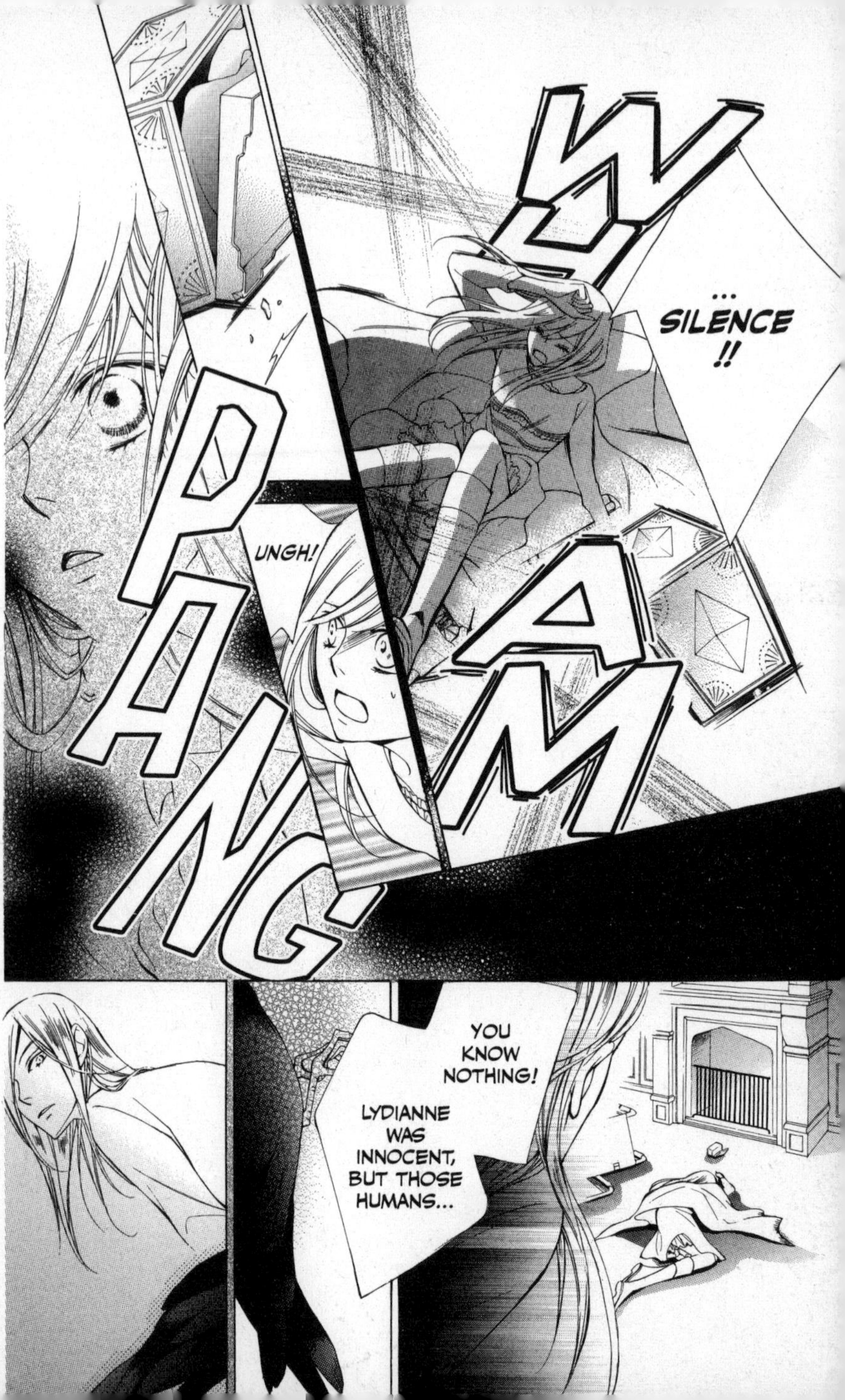
WHAM
... SILENCE !!
UNGH!
PANG!
YOU KNOW NOTHING!
LYDIANNE WAS INNOCENT, BUT THOSE HUMANS...

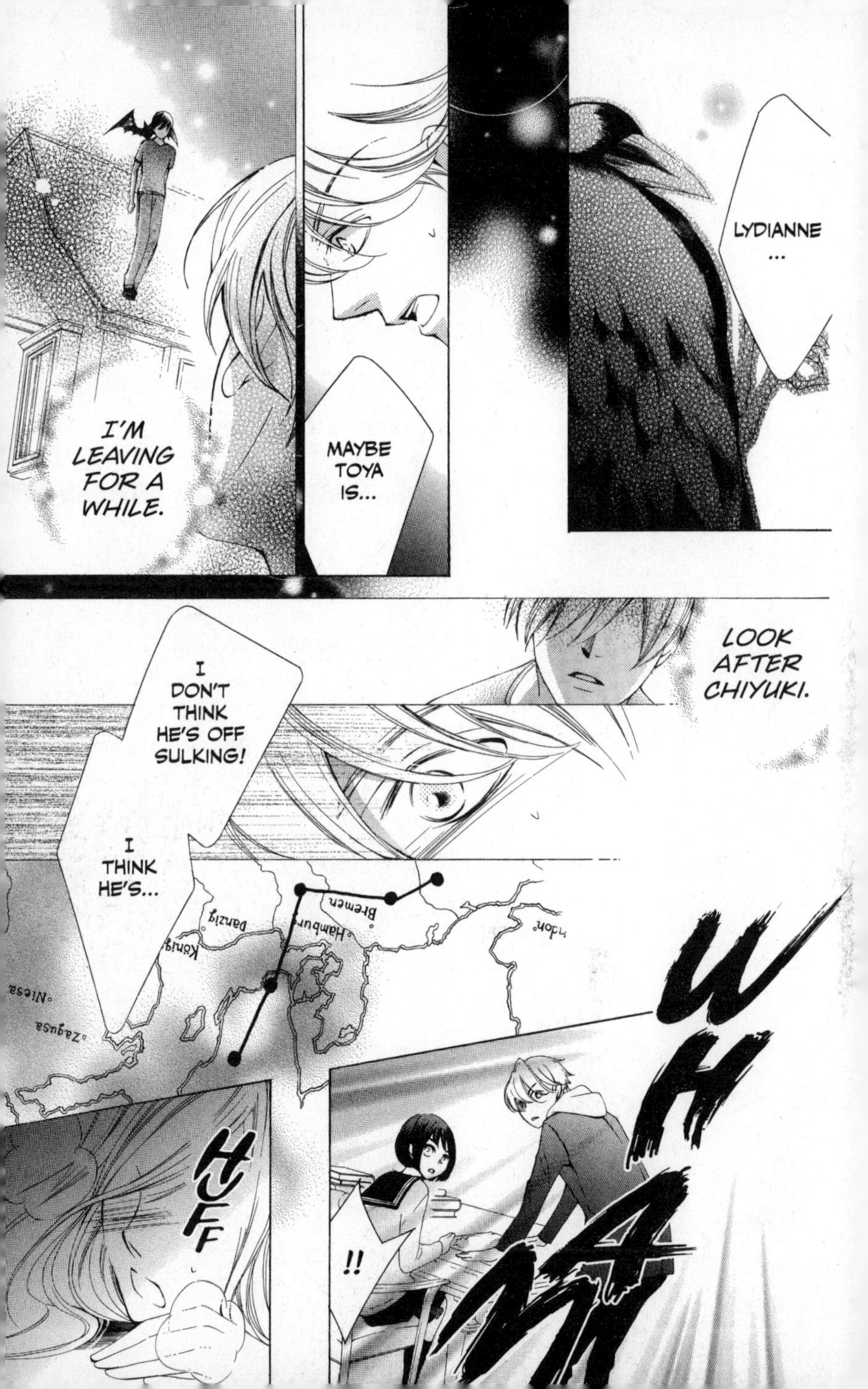
LYDIANNE ...
MAYBE TOYA IS...
I'M LEAVING FOR A WHILE.
LOOK AFTER CHIYUKI.
I DON'T THINK HE'S OFF SULKING!
I THINK HE'S...
Bremen
Hamburg
Danzig
Zagusa
Niesa
WHAM
!!
HUFF

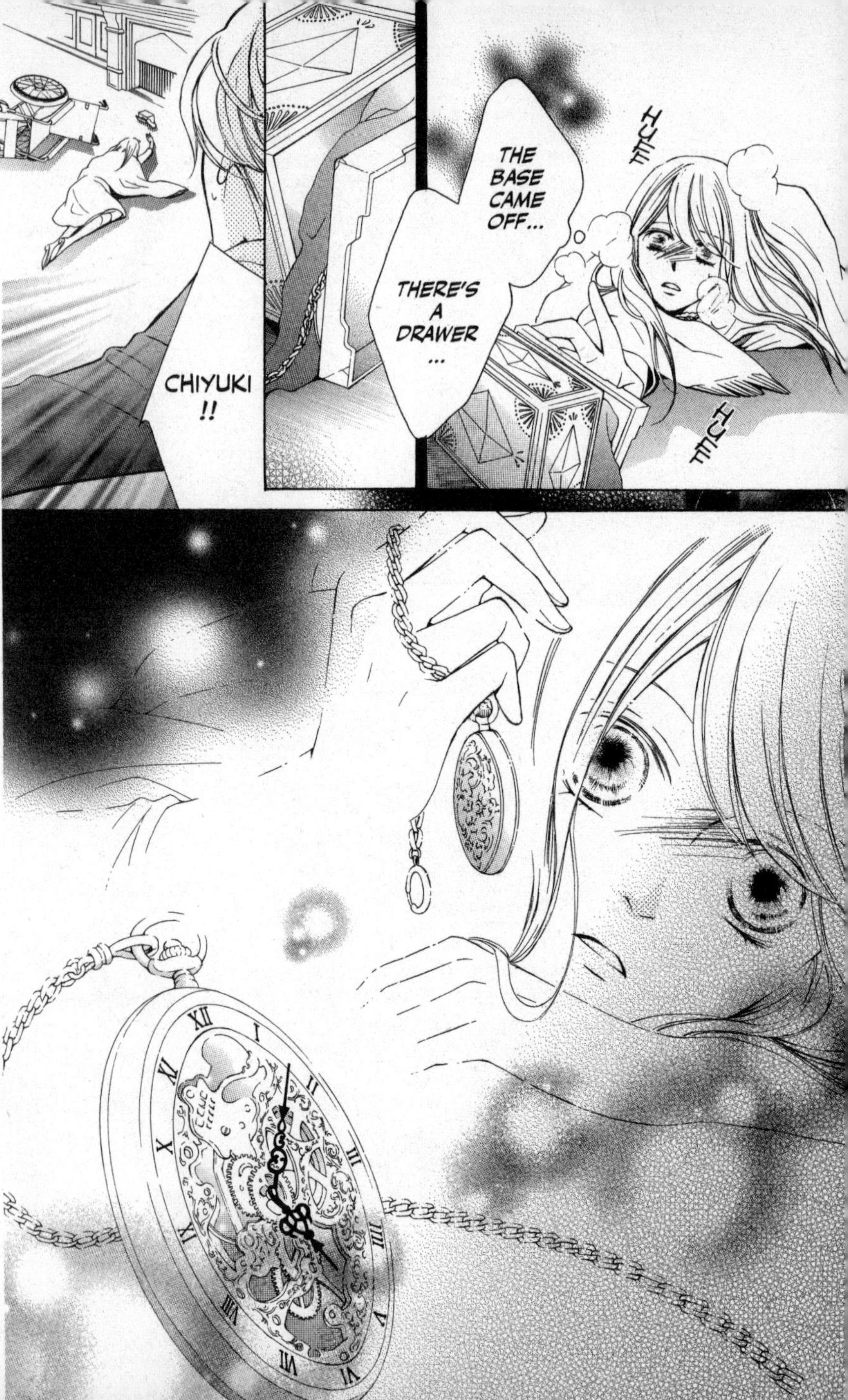
HUFF
THE BASE CAME OFF...
THERE'S A DRAWER ...
HUFF
CHIYUKI !!

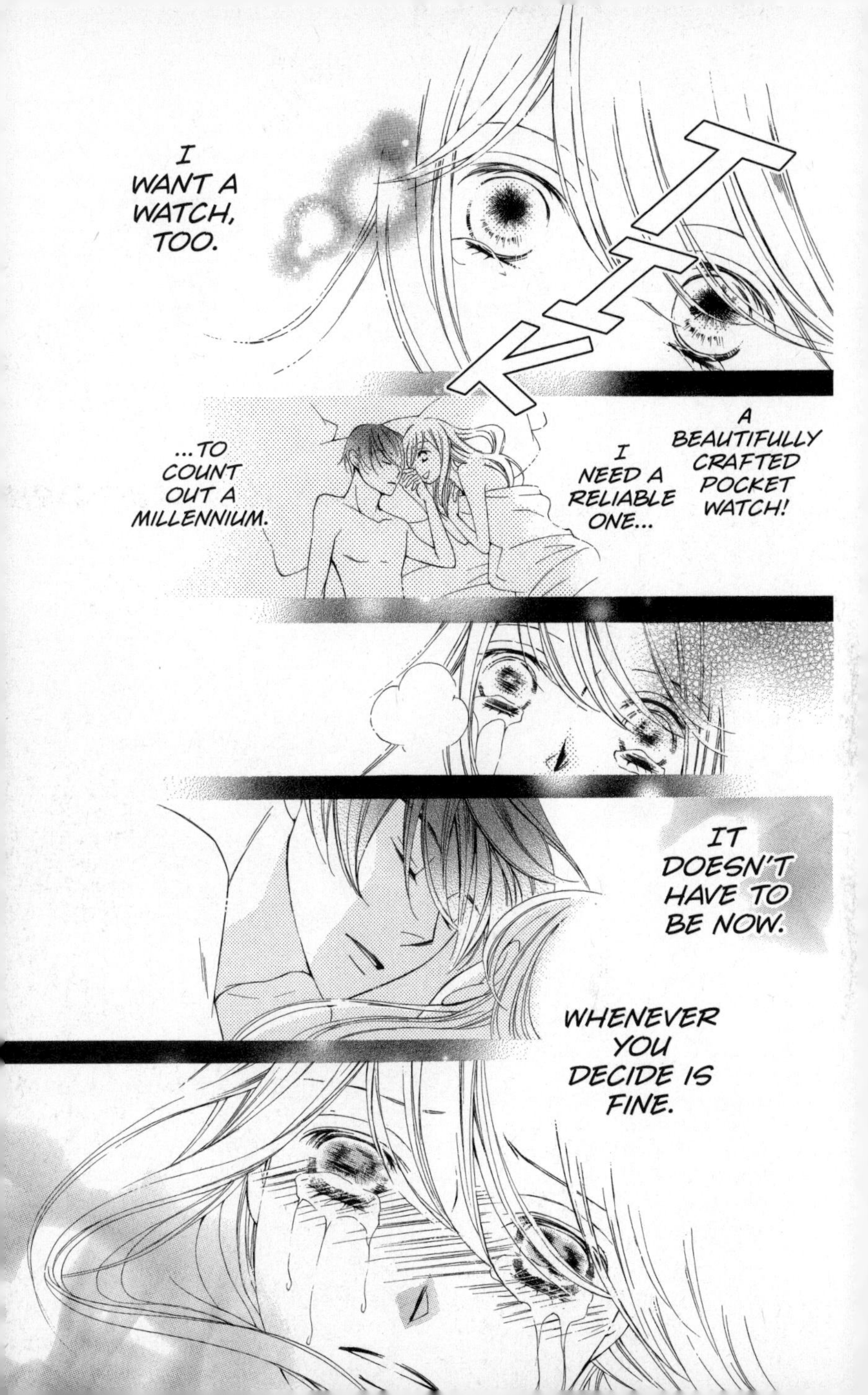
I WANT A WATCH, TOO.
A BEAUTIFULLY CRAFTED POCKET WATCH!
I NEED A RELIABLE ONE...
...TO COUNT OUT A MILLENNIUM.
IT DOESN'T HAVE TO BE NOW.
WHENEVER YOU DECIDE IS FINE.

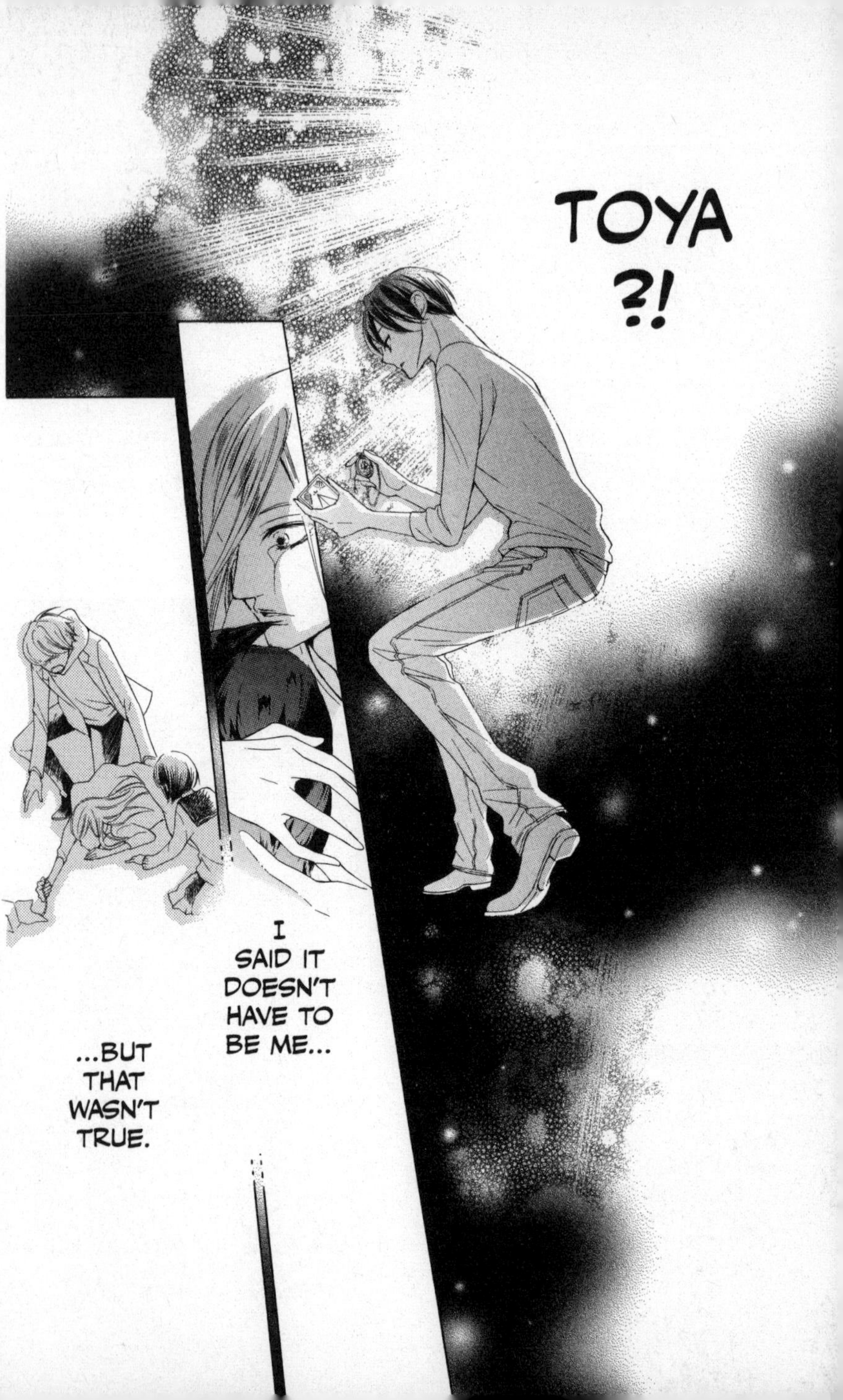
TOYA ?!
I SAID IT DOESN'T HAVE TO BE ME...
...BUT THAT WASN'T TRUE.

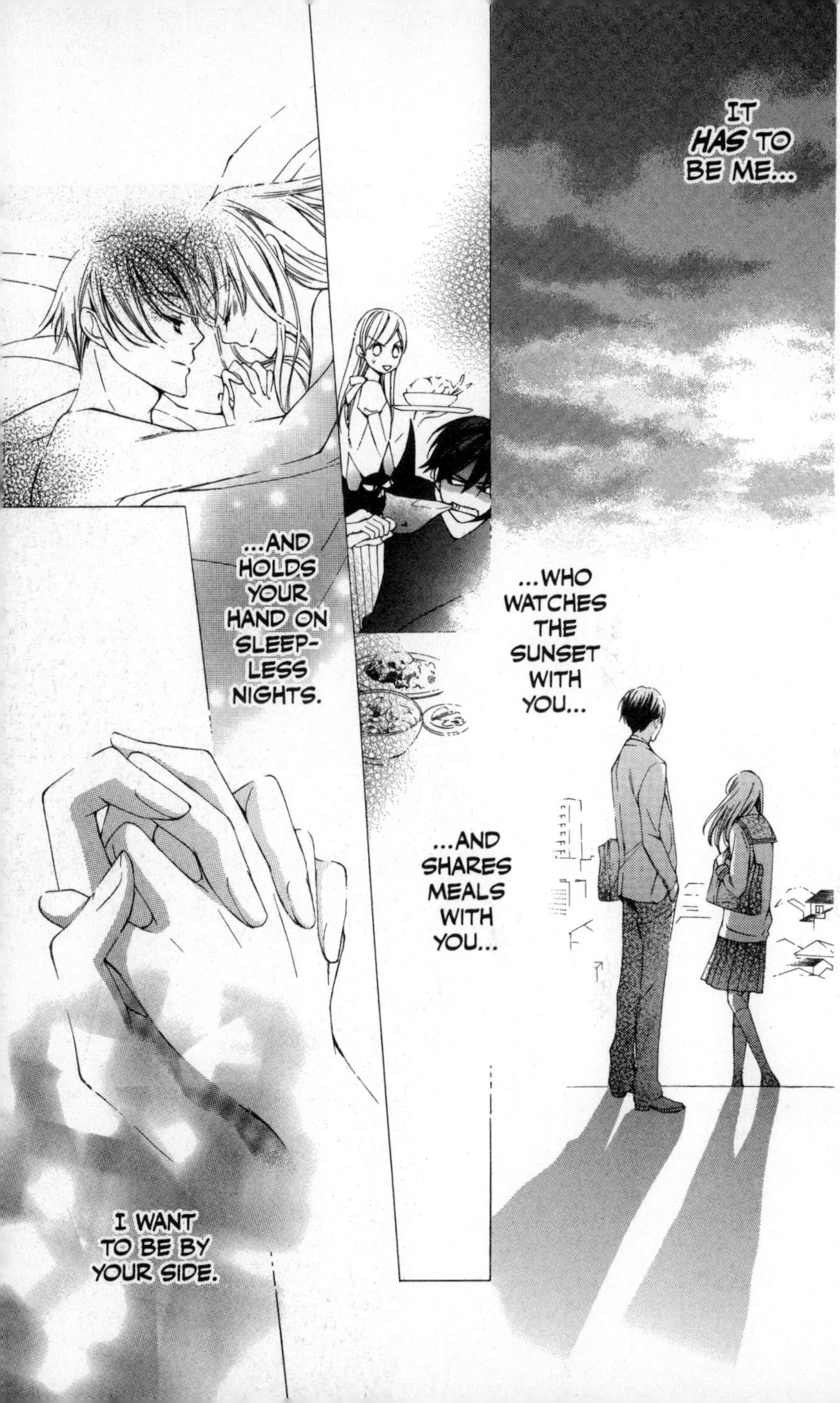
IT HAS TO BE ME...
...WHO WATCHES THE SUNSET WITH YOU...
...AND SHARES MEALS WITH YOU...
...AND HOLDS YOUR HAND ON SLEEP-LESS NIGHTS.
I WANT TO BE BY YOUR SIDE.

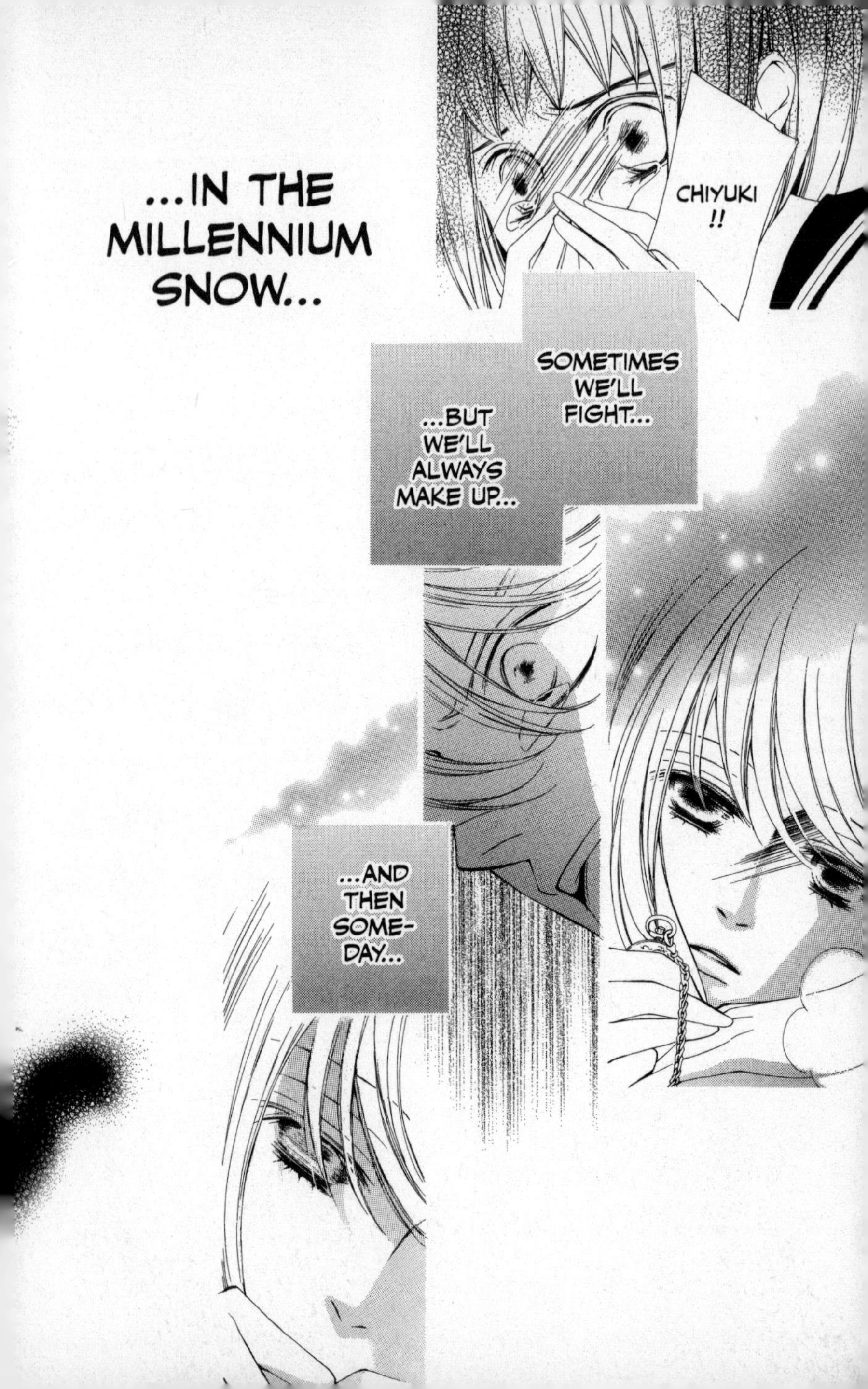
...IN THE MILLENNIUM SNOW...
CHIYUKI !!
SOMETIMES WE'LL FIGHT...
...BUT WE'LL ALWAYS MAKE UP...
...AND THEN SOME-DAY...

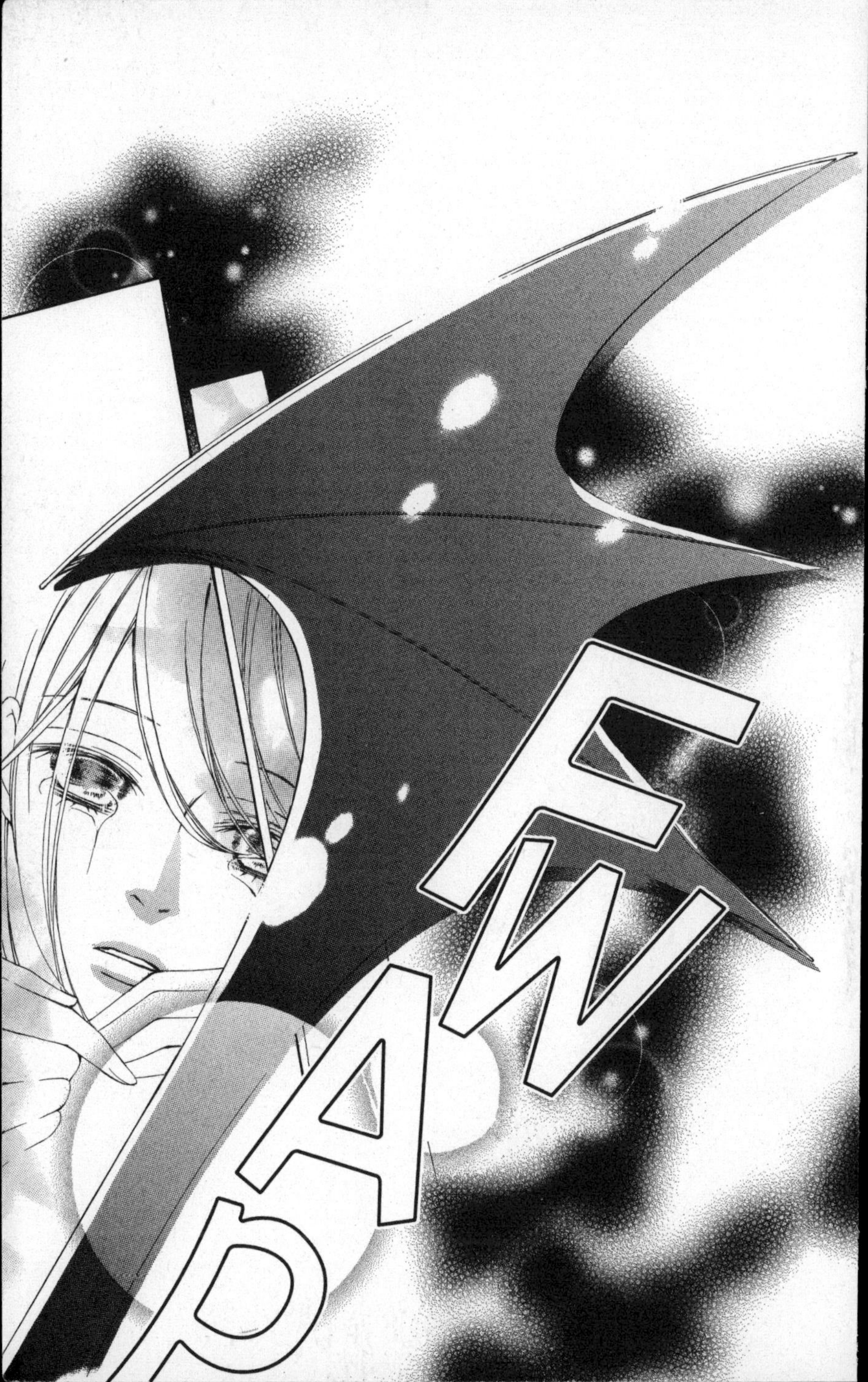
FWAP

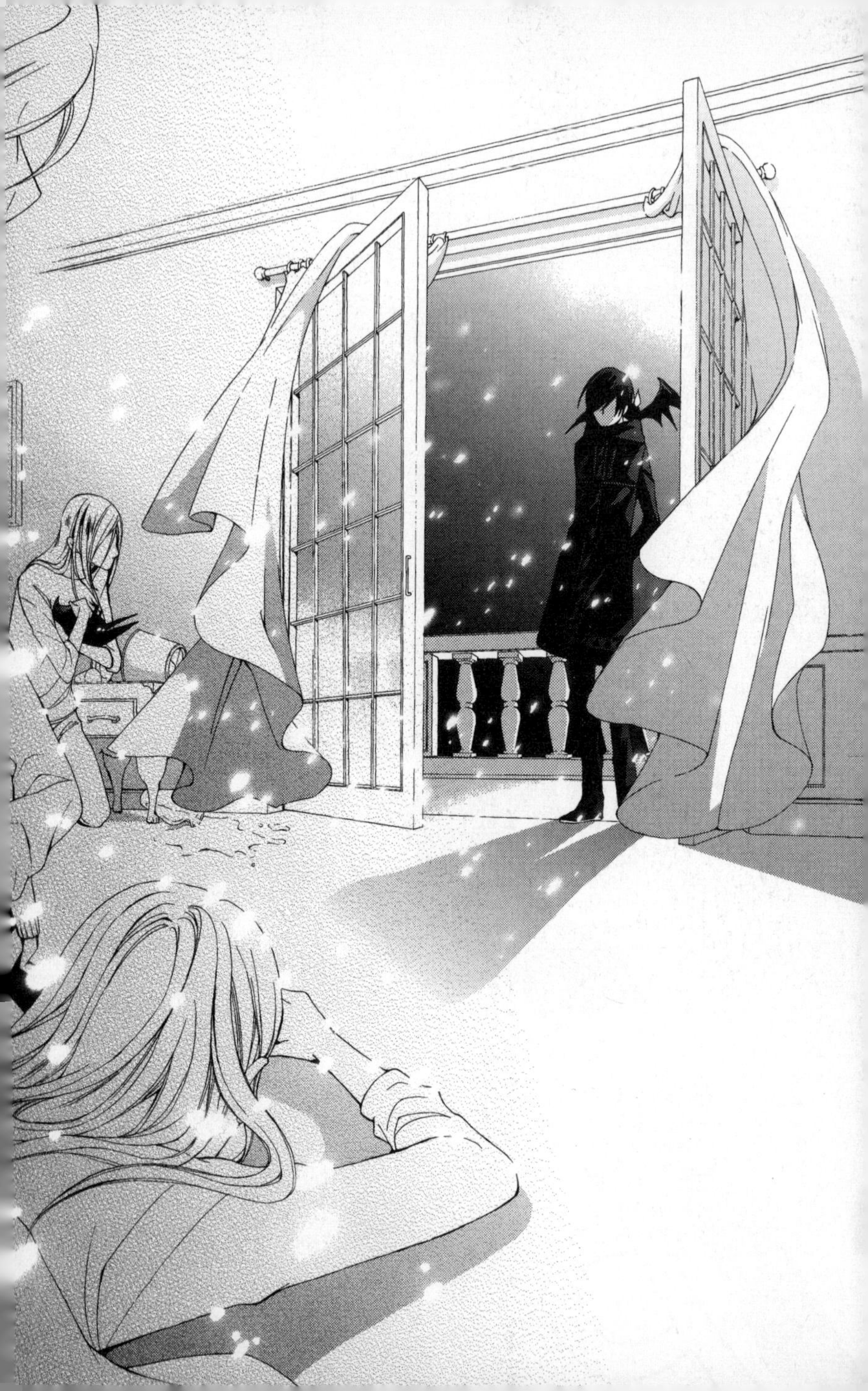

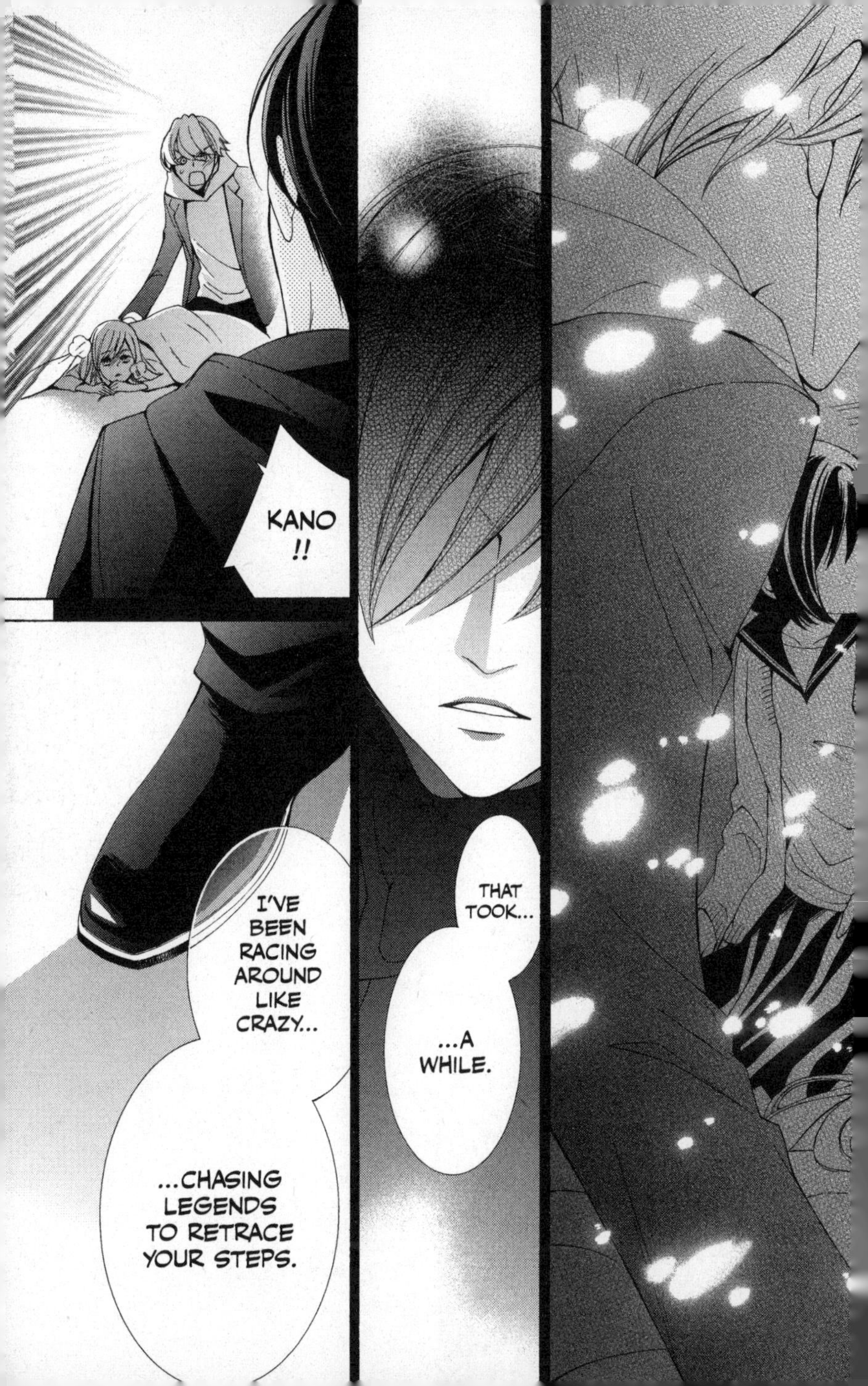
THAT TOOK...
...A WHILE.
KANO !!
I'VE BEEN RACING AROUND LIKE CRAZY...
...CHASING LEGENDS TO RETRACE YOUR STEPS.

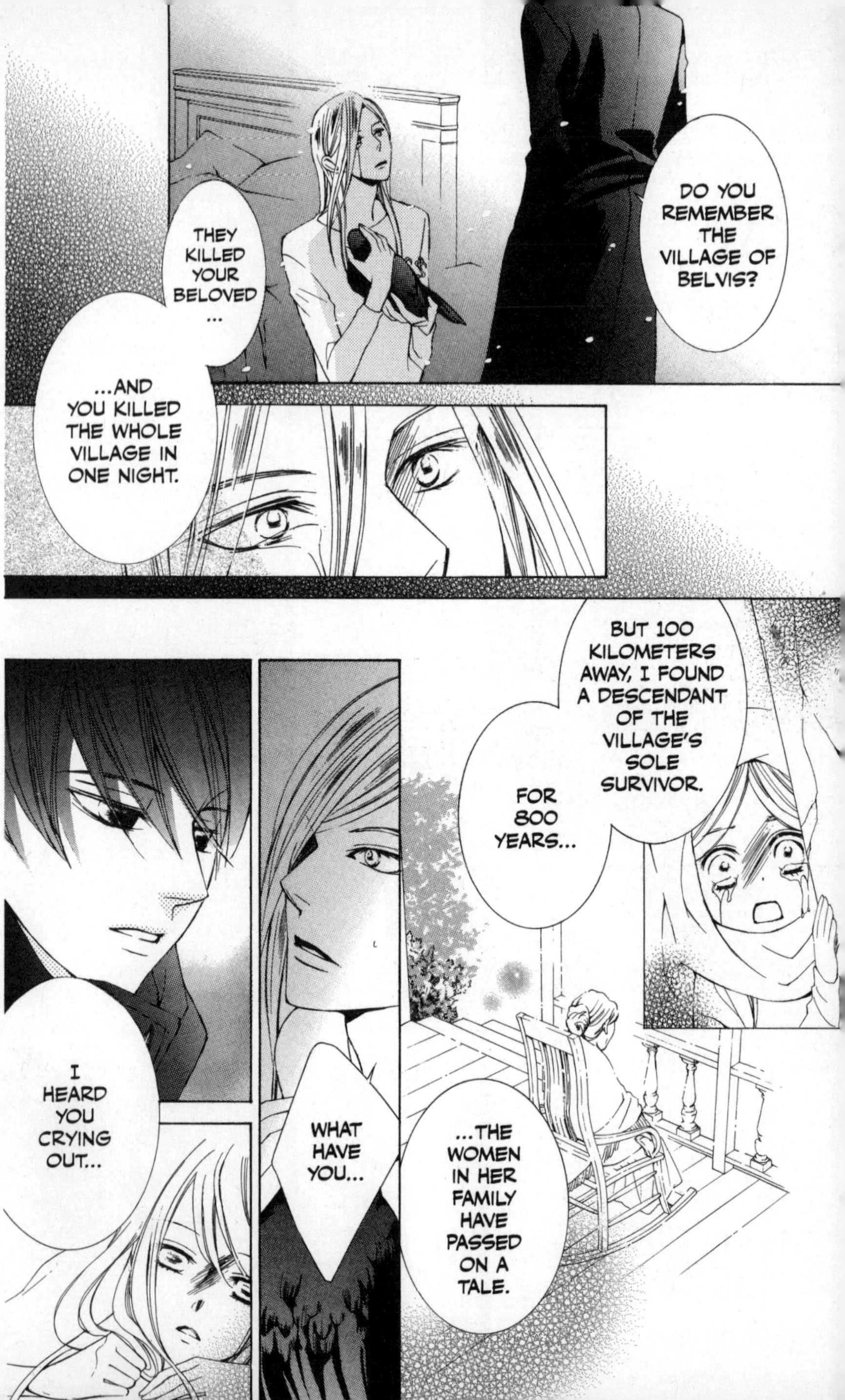
DO YOU REMEMBER THE VILLAGE OF BELVIS?
THEY KILLED YOUR BELOVED ...
...AND YOU KILLED THE WHOLE VILLAGE IN ONE NIGHT.
BUT 100 KILOMETERS AWAY, I FOUND A DESCENDANT OF THE VILLAGE'S SOLE SURVIVOR.
FOR 800 YEARS...
...THE WOMEN IN HER FAMILY HAVE PASSED ON A TALE.
WHAT HAVE YOU...
I HEARD YOU CRYING OUT...

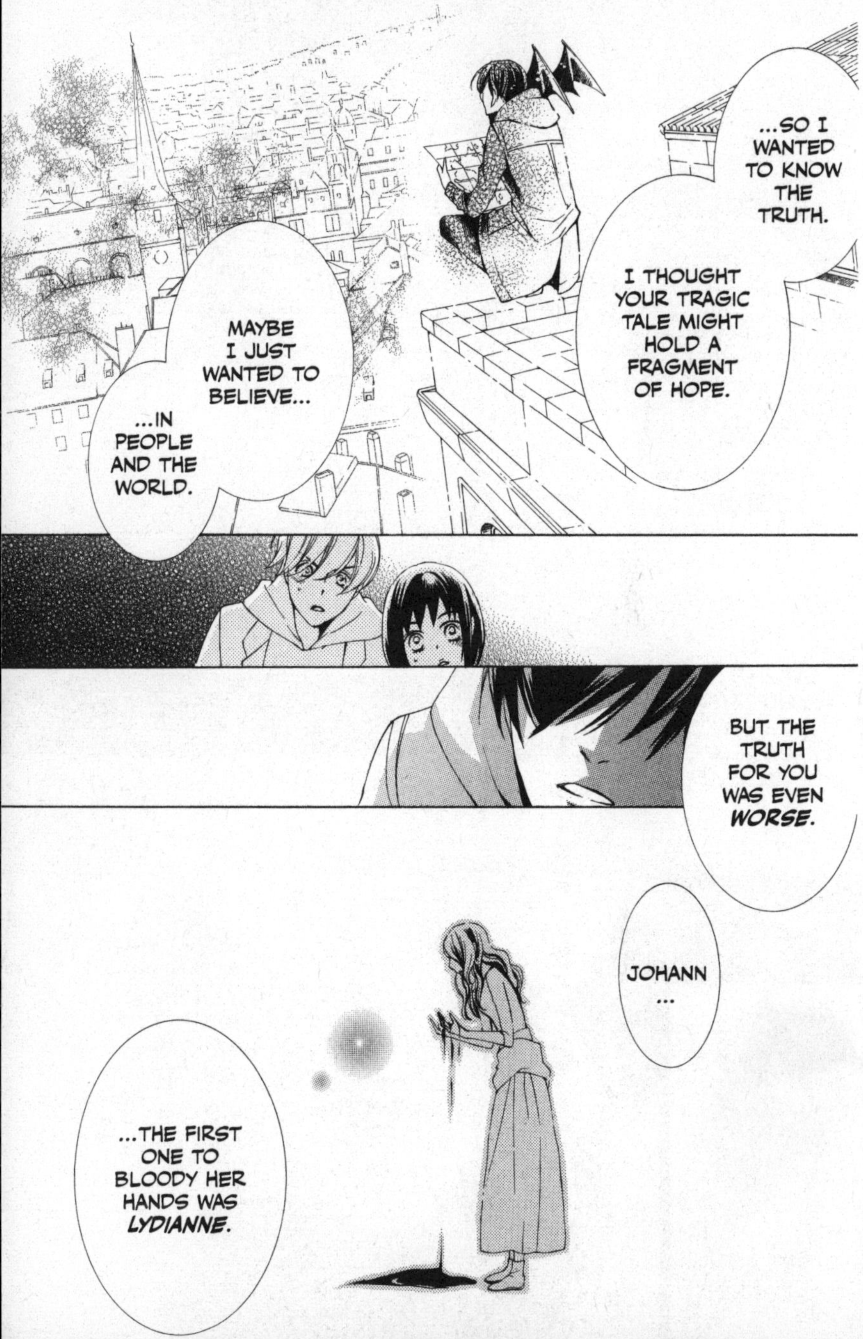
...SO I WANTED TO KNOW THE TRUTH.
I THOUGHT YOUR TRAGIC TALE MIGHT HOLD A FRAGMENT OF HOPE.
MAYBE I JUST WANTED TO BELIEVE...
...IN PEOPLE AND THE WORLD.
BUT THE TRUTH FOR YOU WAS EVEN *WORSE*.
JOHANN ...
...THE FIRST ONE TO BLOODY HER HANDS WAS *LYDIANNE*.

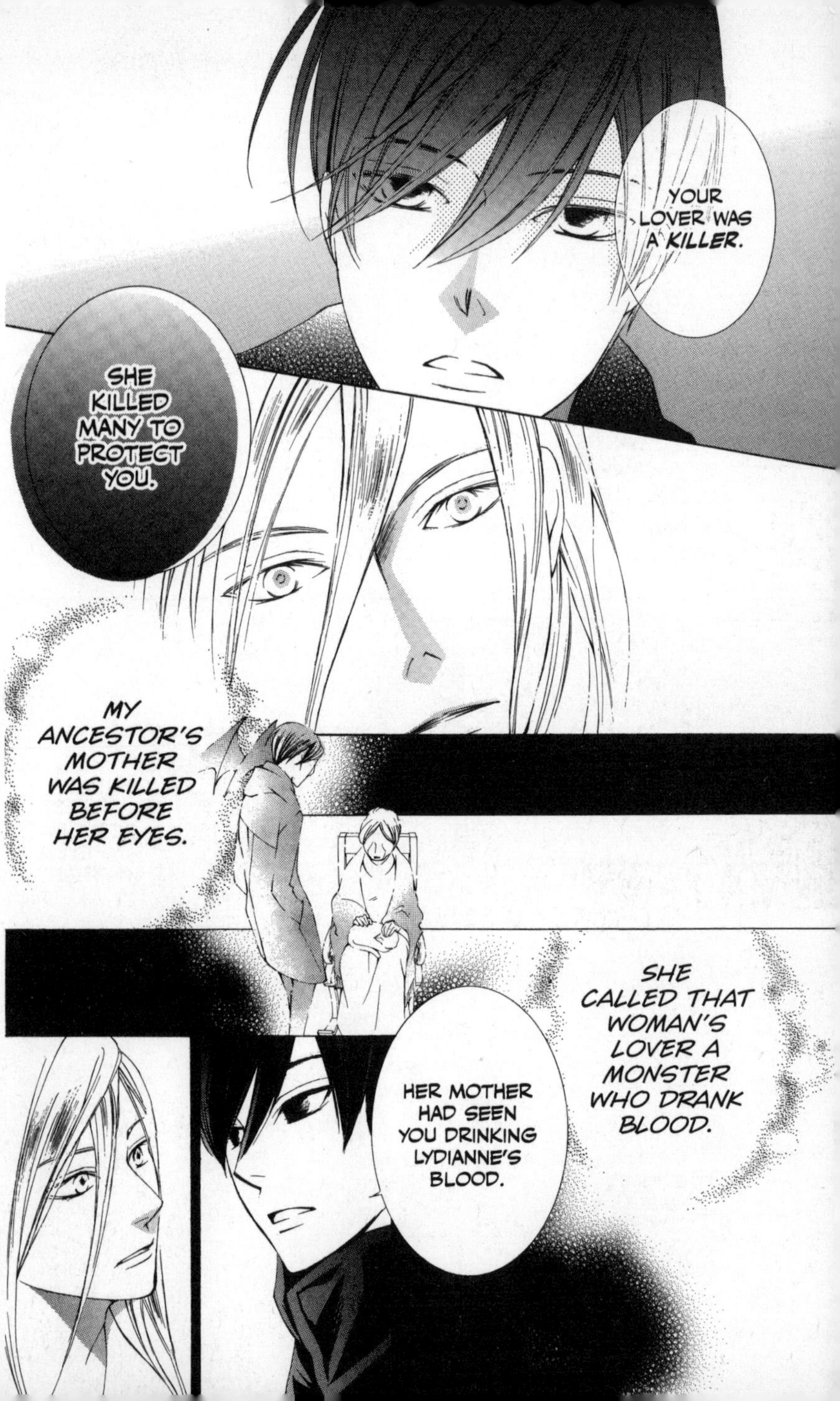
YOUR LOVER WAS A KILLER.
SHE KILLED MANY TO PROTECT YOU.
MY ANCESTOR'S MOTHER WAS KILLED BEFORE HER EYES.
SHE CALLED THAT WOMAN'S LOVER A MONSTER WHO DRANK BLOOD.
HER MOTHER HAD SEEN YOU DRINKING LYDIANNE'S BLOOD.

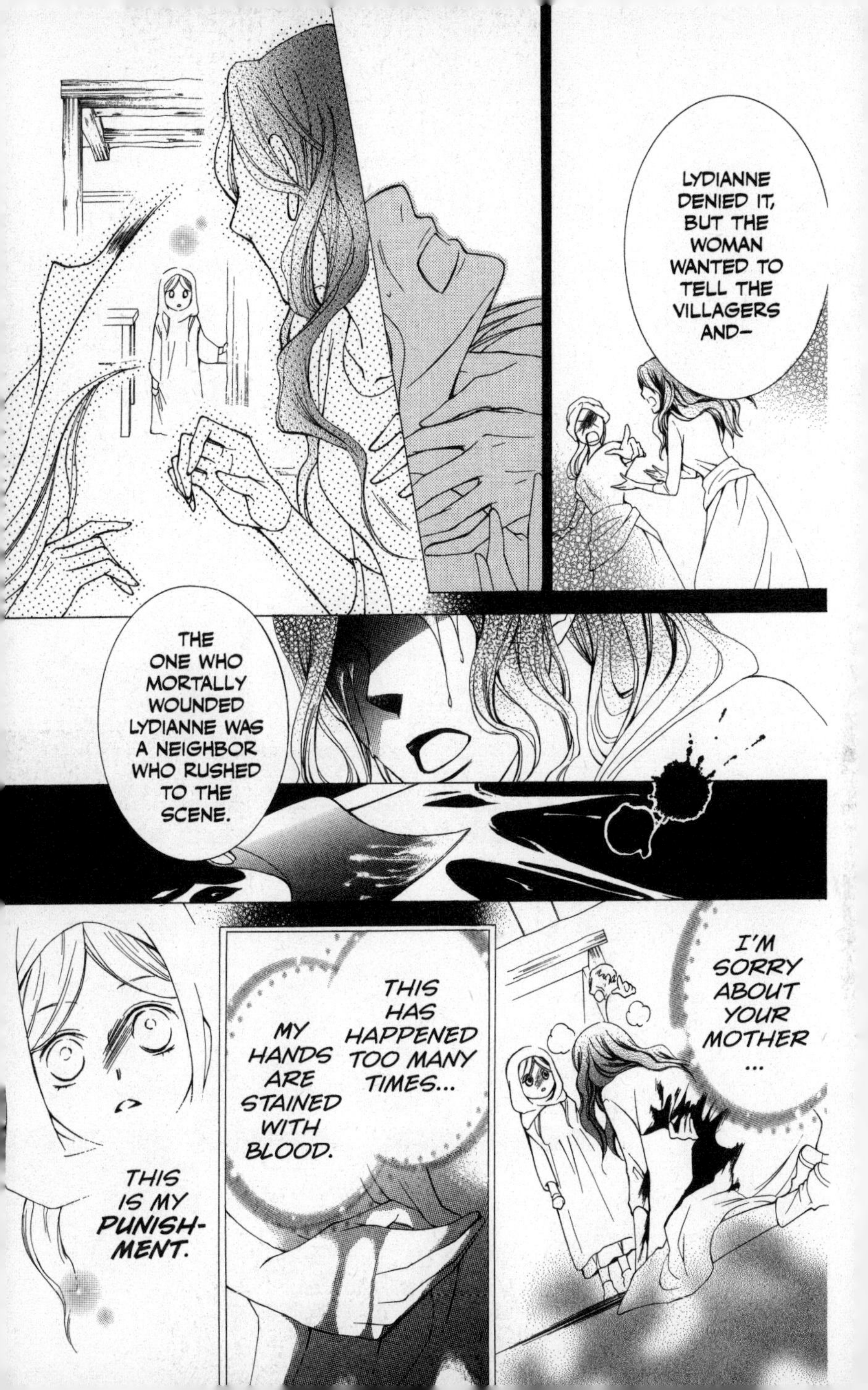
LYDIANNE DENIED IT, BUT THE WOMAN WANTED TO TELL THE VILLAGERS AND-
THE ONE WHO MORTALLY WOUNDED LYDIANNE WAS A NEIGHBOR WHO RUSHED TO THE SCENE.
I'M SORRY ABOUT YOUR MOTHER ...
THIS HAS HAPPENED TOO MANY TIMES...
MY HANDS ARE STAINED WITH BLOOD.
THIS IS MY PUNISHMENT.

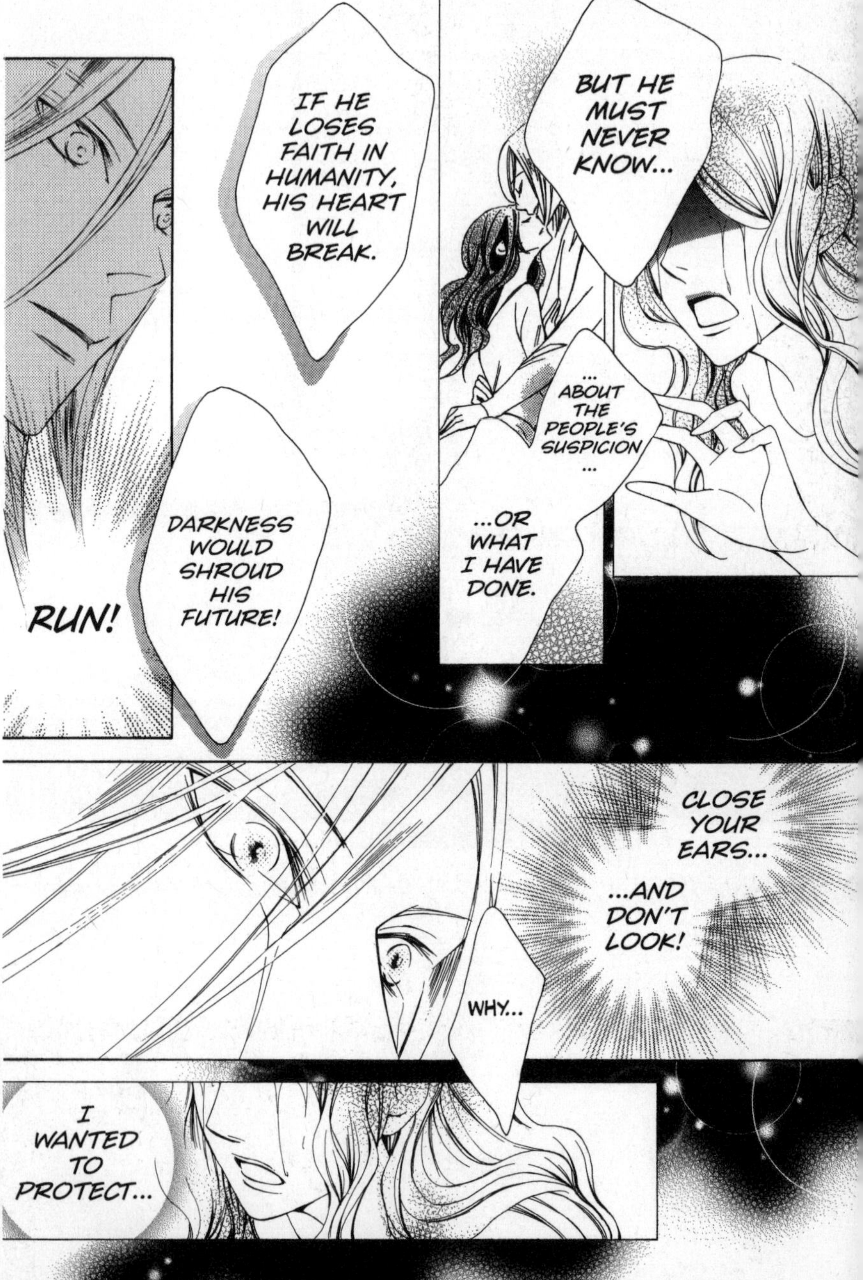
BUT HE MUST NEVER KNOW...
...ABOUT THE PEOPLE'S SUSPICION...
...OR WHAT I HAVE DONE.
IF HE LOSES FAITH IN HUMANITY, HIS HEART WILL BREAK.
DARKNESS WOULD SHROUD HIS FUTURE!
RUN!
CLOSE YOUR EARS...
...AND DON'T LOOK!
WHY...
I WANTED TO PROTECT...

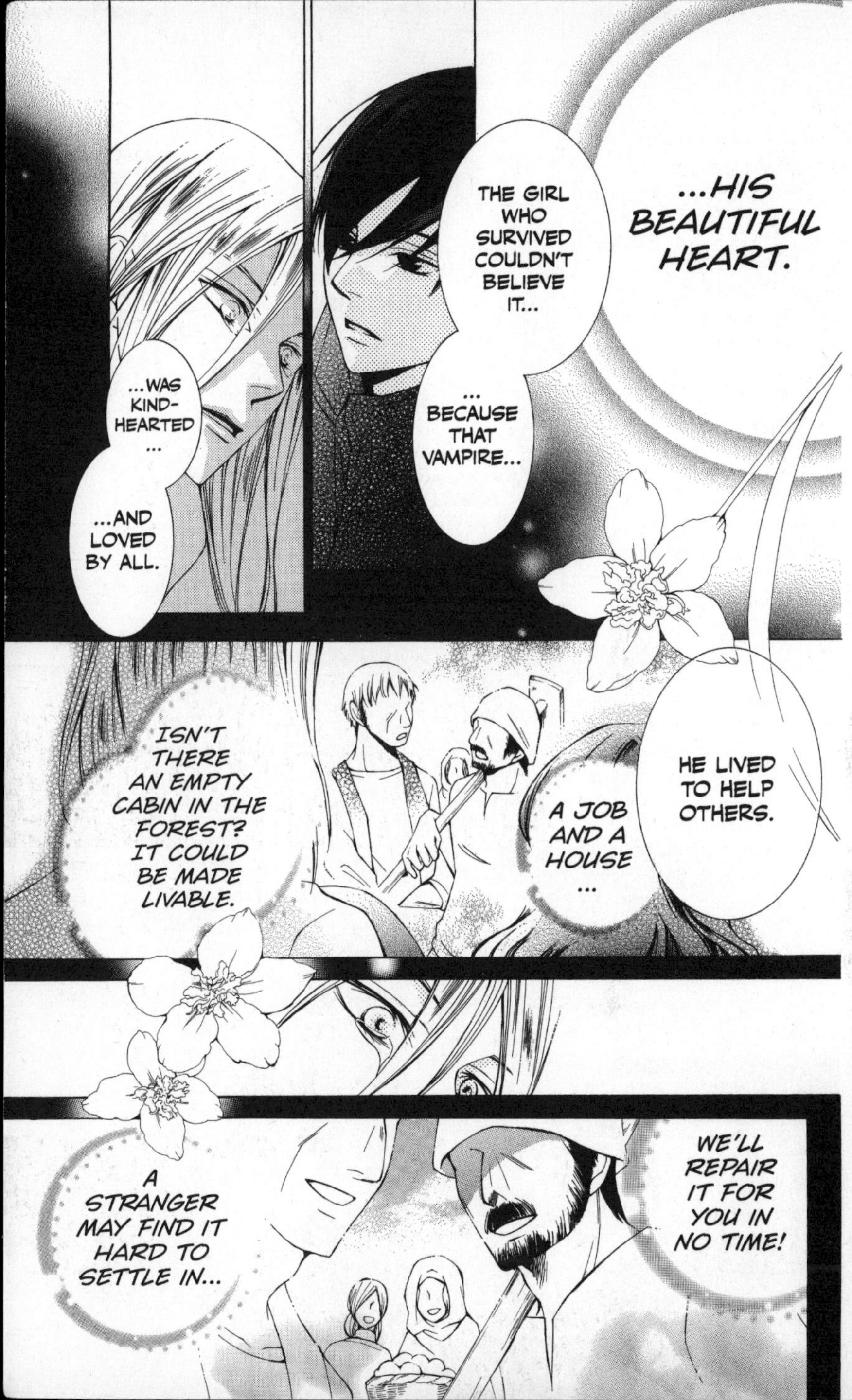
...HIS BEAUTIFUL HEART.
THE GIRL WHO SURVIVED COULDN'T BELIEVE IT...
...BECAUSE THAT VAMPIRE...
...WAS KIND-HEARTED...
...AND LOVED BY ALL.
HE LIVED TO HELP OTHERS.
A JOB AND A HOUSE...
ISN'T THERE AN EMPTY CABIN IN THE FOREST? IT COULD BE MADE LIVABLE.
WE'LL REPAIR IT FOR YOU IN NO TIME!
A STRANGER MAY FIND IT HARD TO SETTLE IN...

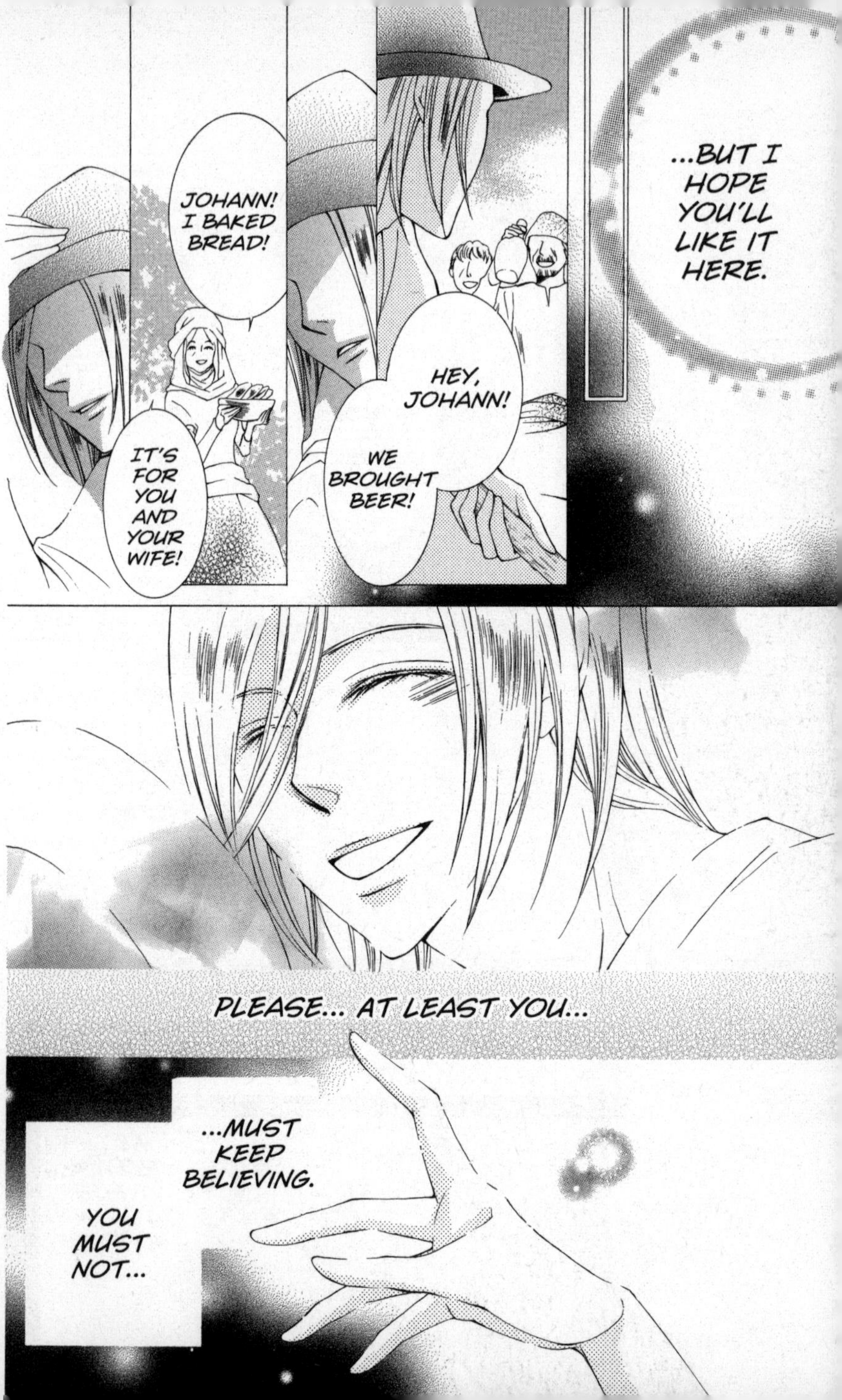
...BUT I HOPE YOU'LL LIKE IT HERE.
HEY, JOHANN!
WE BROUGHT BEER!
JOHANN! I BAKED BREAD!
IT'S FOR YOU AND YOUR WIFE!
PLEASE... AT LEAST YOU...
...MUST KEEP BELIEVING.
YOU MUST NOT...

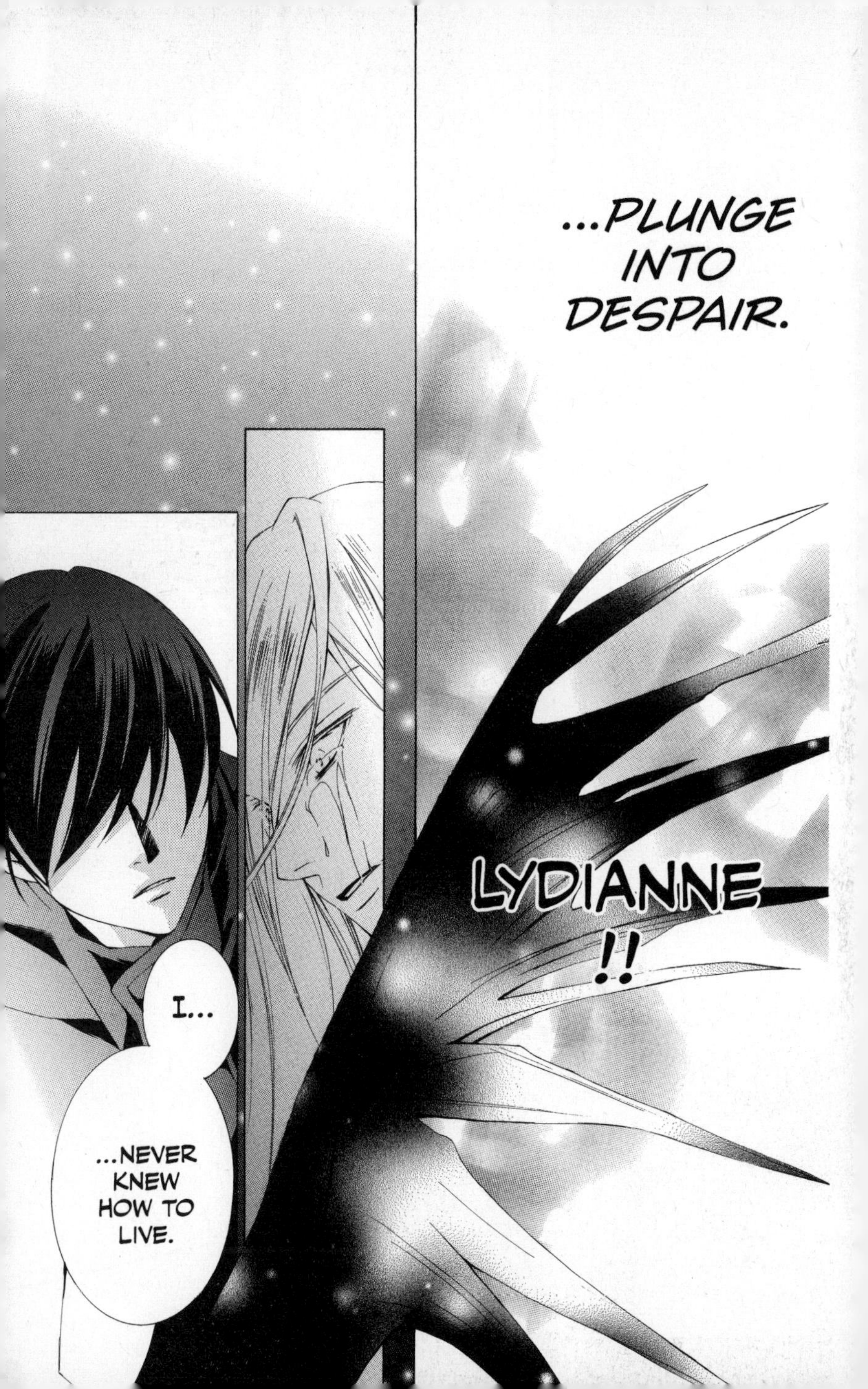
...PLUNGE INTO DESPAIR.
LYDIANNE !!
I...
...NEVER KNEW HOW TO LIVE.

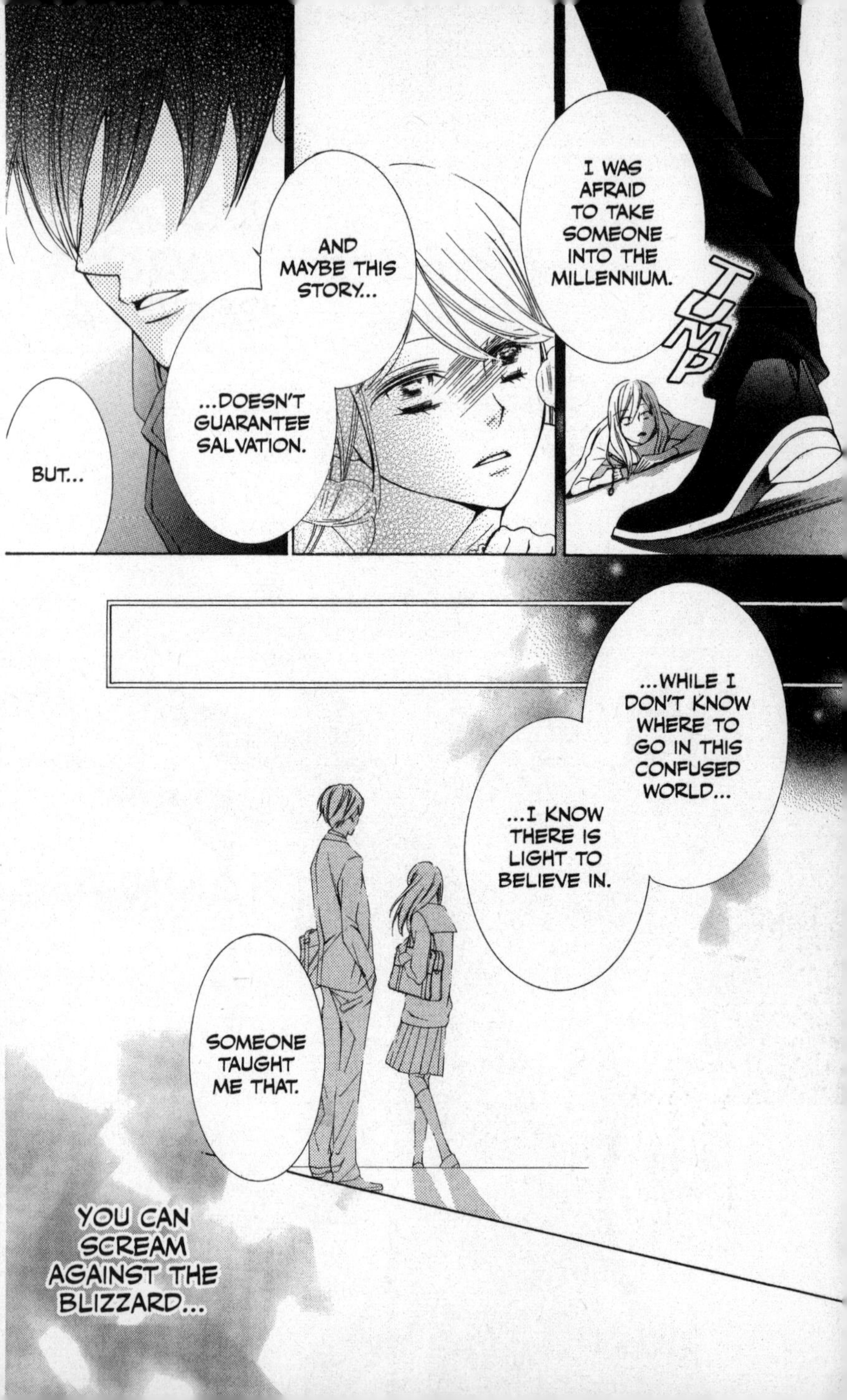
I WAS AFRAID TO TAKE SOMEONE INTO THE MILLENNIUM.
TUMP
AND MAYBE THIS STORY...
...DOESN'T GUARANTEE SALVATION.
BUT...
...WHILE I DON'T KNOW WHERE TO GO IN THIS CONFUSED WORLD...
...I KNOW THERE IS LIGHT TO BELIEVE IN.
SOMEONE TAUGHT ME THAT.
YOU CAN SCREAM AGAINST THE BLIZZARD...

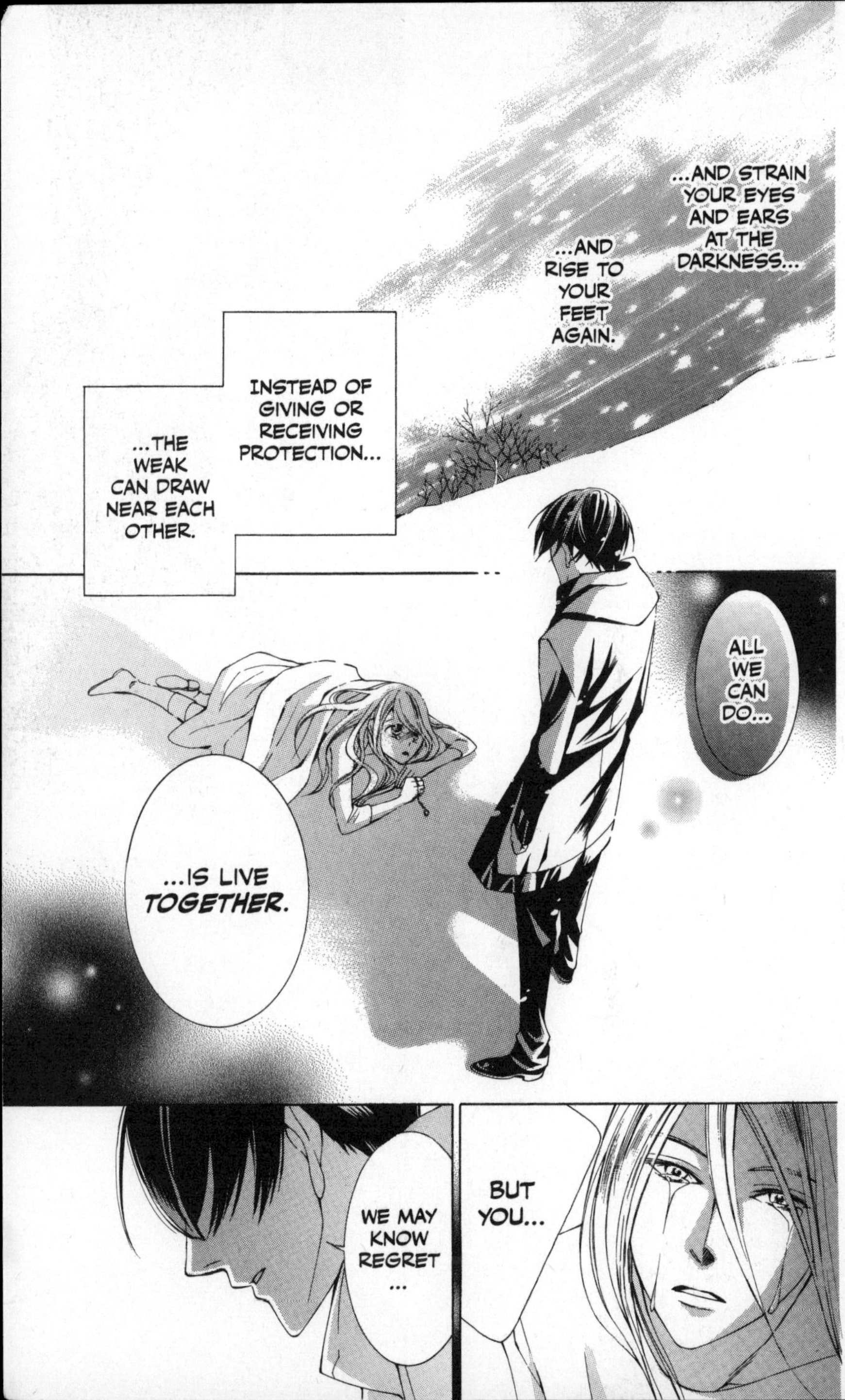
...AND STRAIN YOUR EYES AND EARS AT THE DARKNESS...
...AND RISE TO YOUR FEET AGAIN.
INSTEAD OF GIVING OR RECEIVING PROTECTION...
...THE WEAK CAN DRAW NEAR EACH OTHER.
ALL WE CAN DO...
...IS LIVE *TOGETHER*.
BUT YOU...
WE MAY KNOW REGRET ...

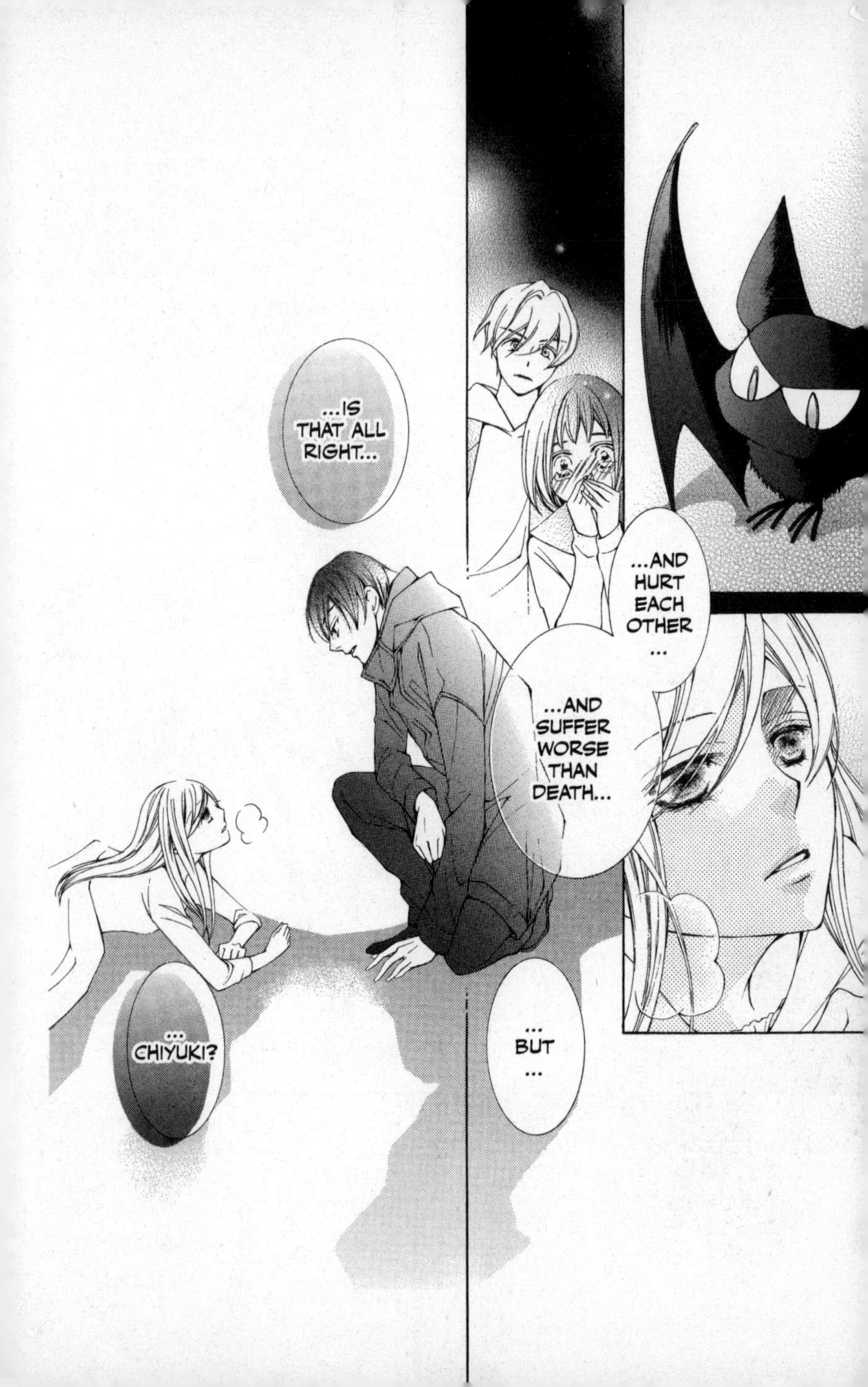
...AND HURT EACH OTHER ...
...AND SUFFER WORSE THAN DEATH...
... BUT ...
...IS THAT ALL RIGHT...
... CHIYUKI?

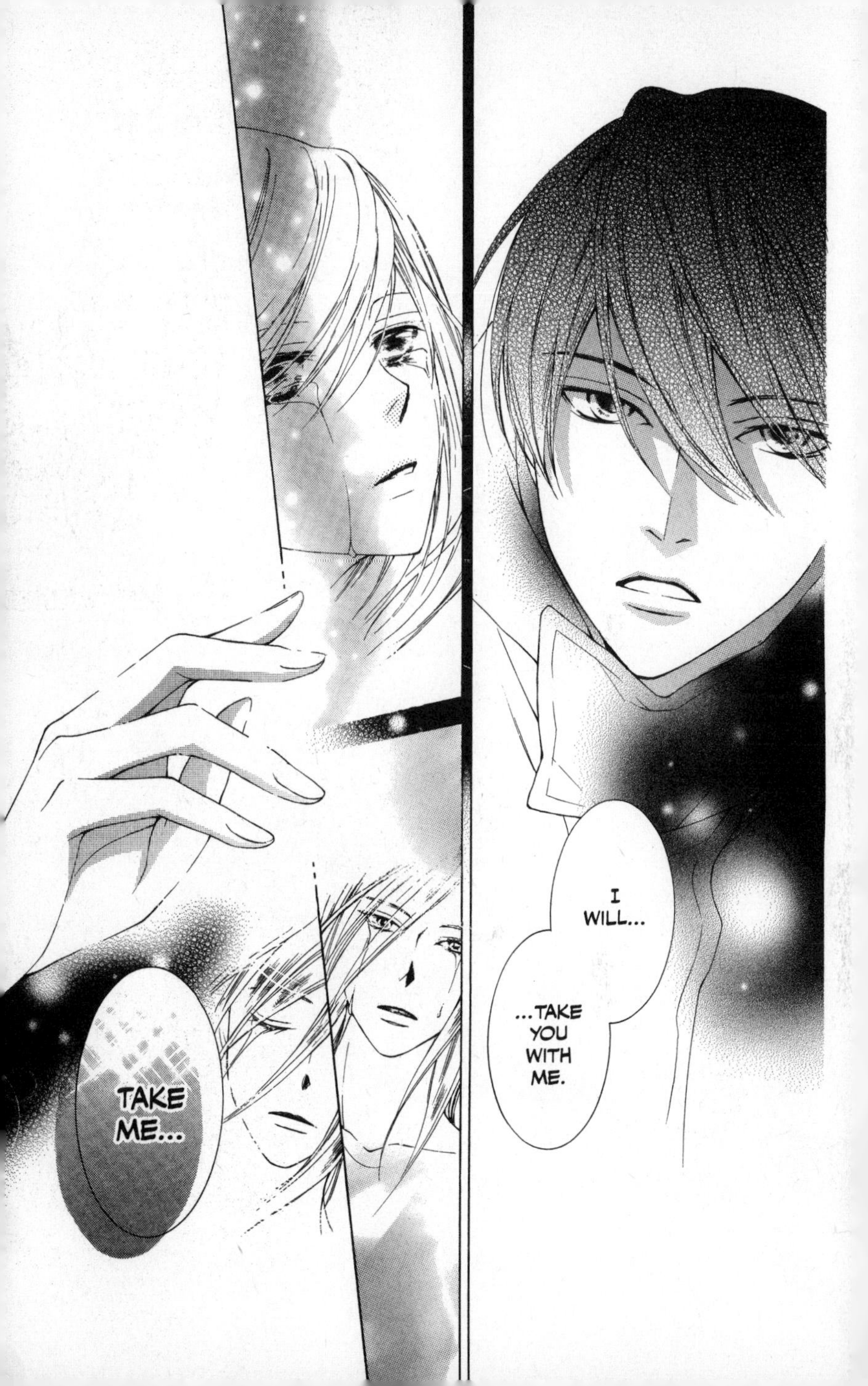
I WILL...
...TAKE YOU WITH ME.
TAKE ME...

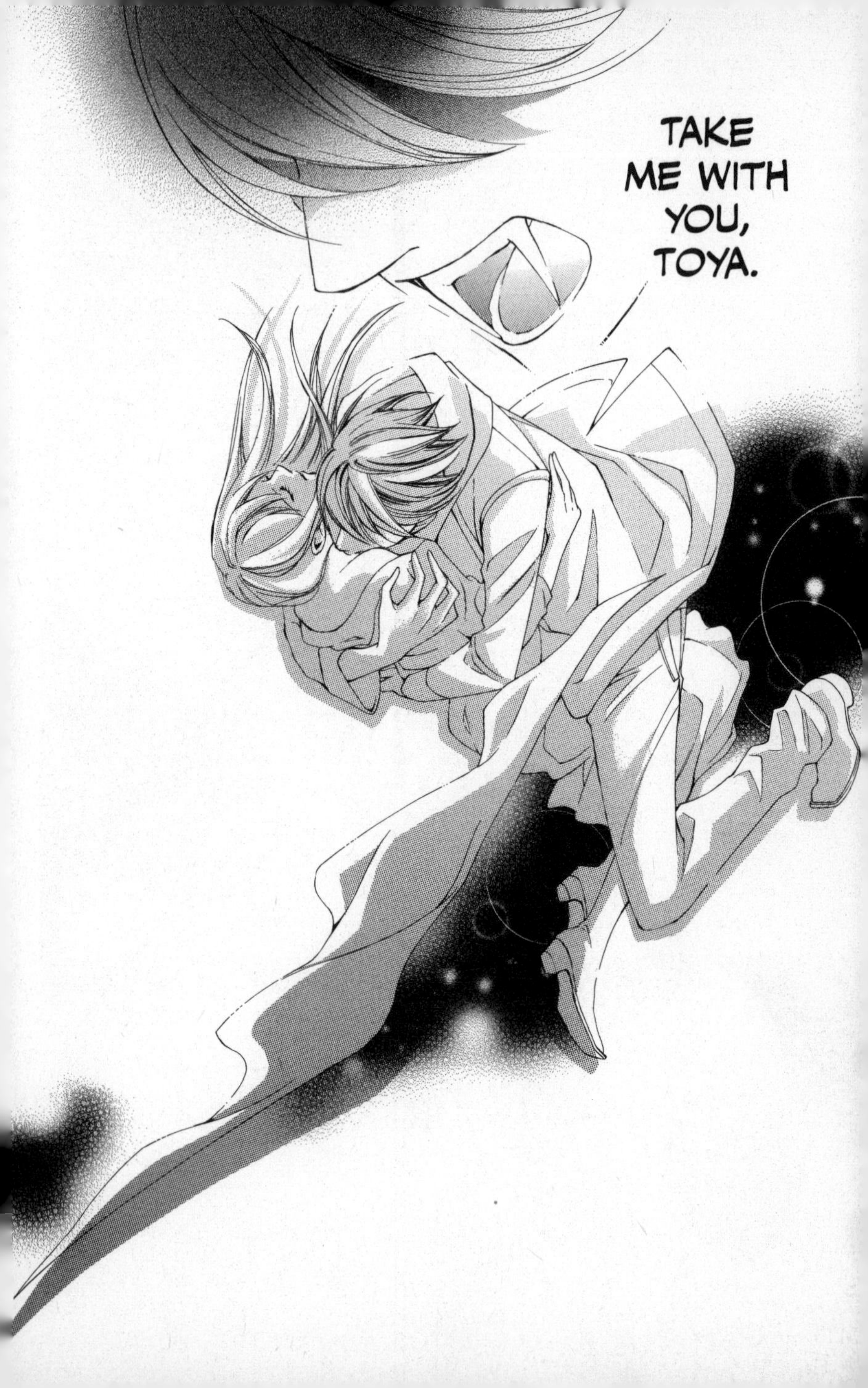
TAKE ME WITH YOU, TOYA.

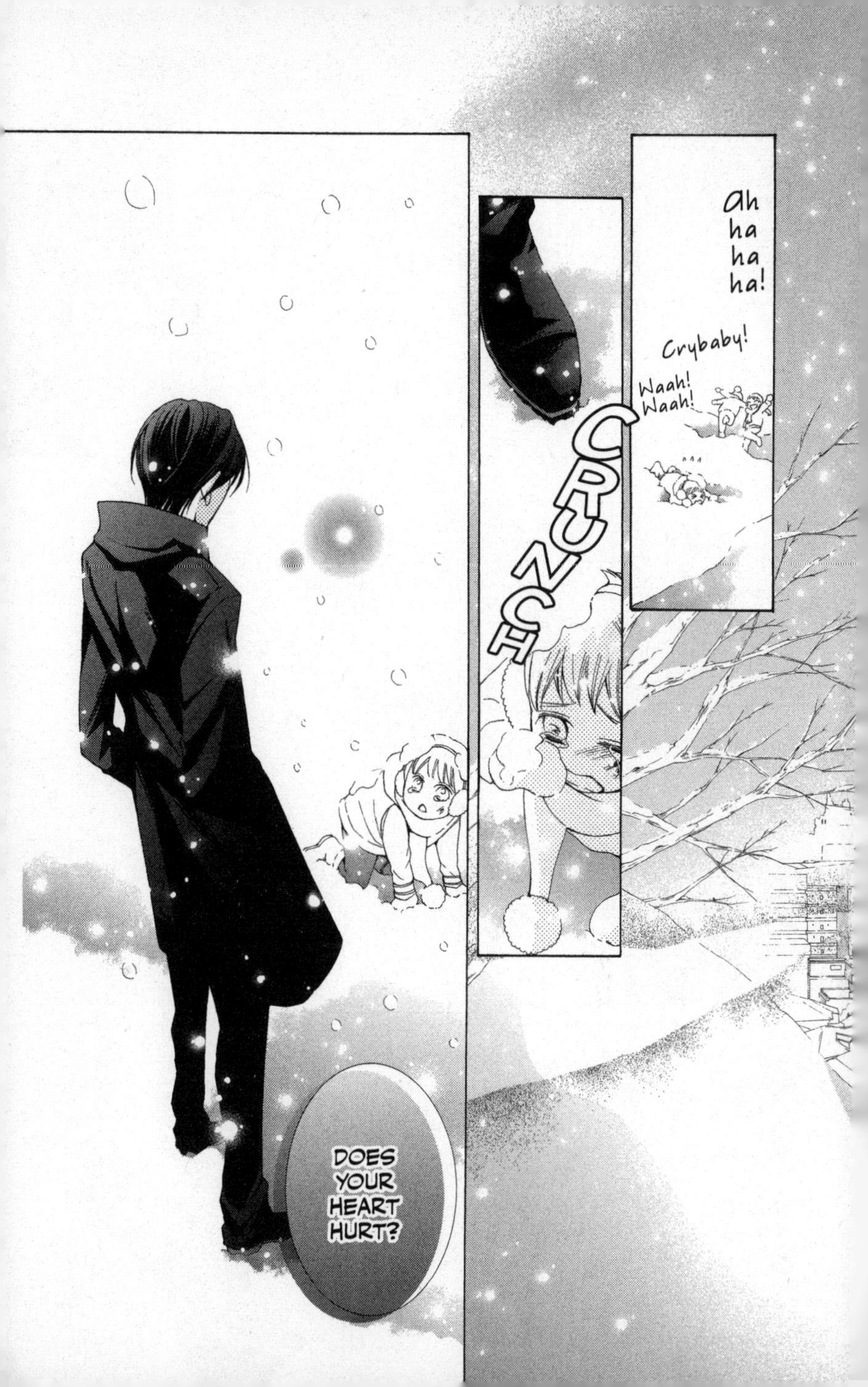
Ah ha ha ha!
Crybaby!
Waah! Waah!
CRUNCH
DOES YOUR HEART HURT?

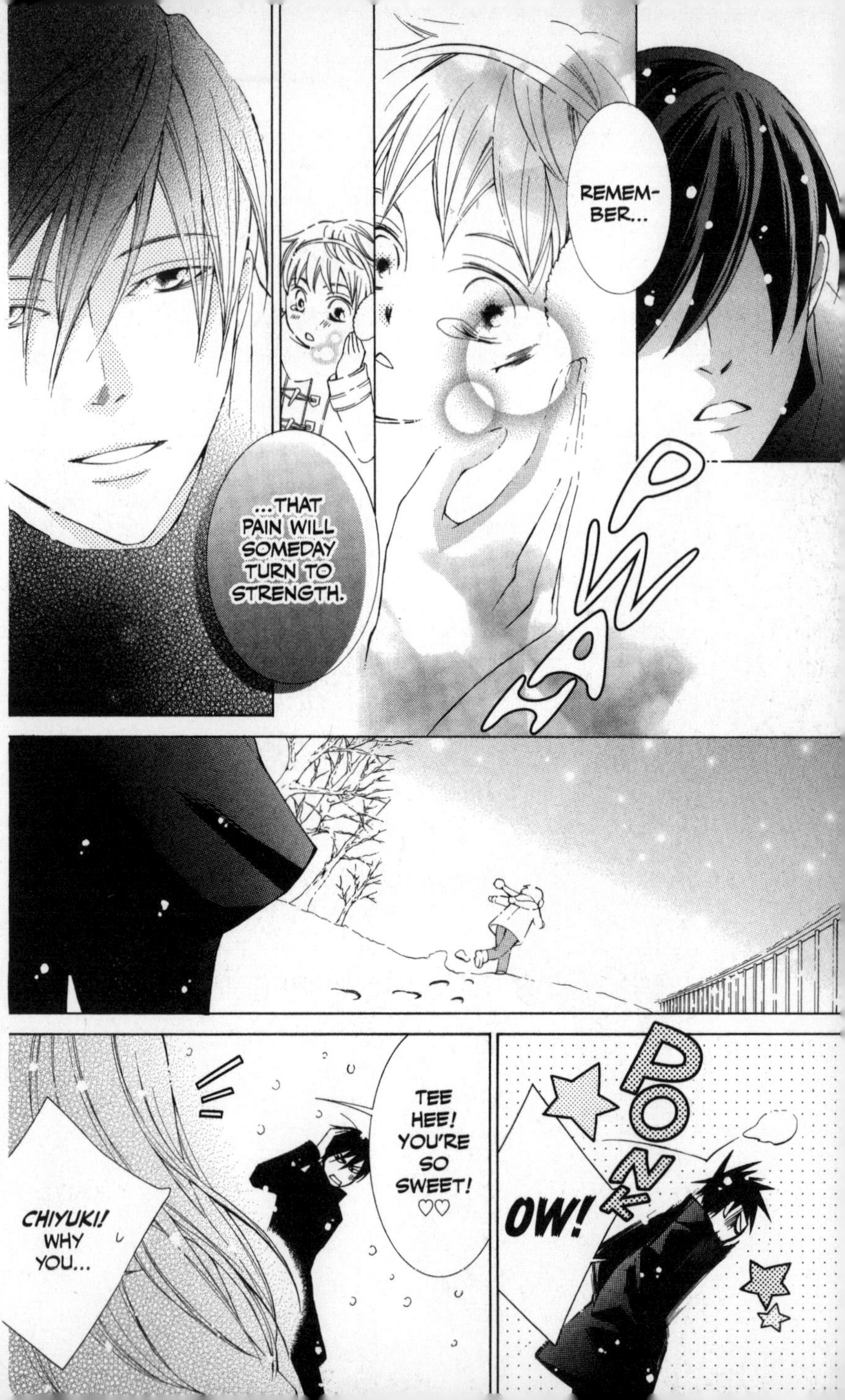
REMEMBER...
...THAT PAIN WILL SOMEDAY TURN TO STRENGTH.
PONK
OW!
TEE HEE! YOU'RE SO SWEET! ♡♡
CHIYUKI! WHY YOU...

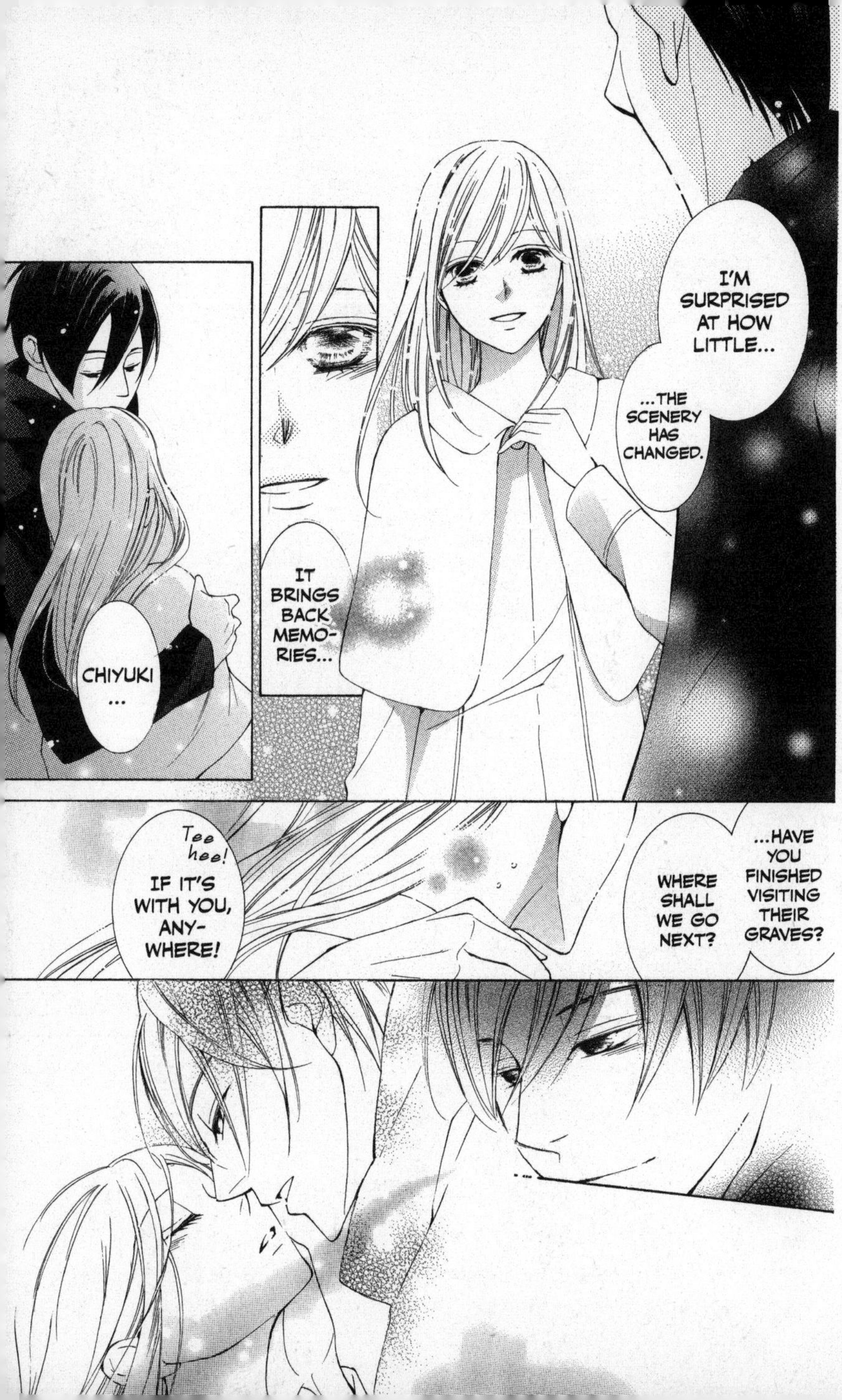
I'M SURPRISED AT HOW LITTLE...
...THE SCENERY HAS CHANGED.
IT BRINGS BACK MEMO-RIES...
CHIYUKI ...
...HAVE YOU FINISHED VISITING THEIR GRAVES?
WHERE SHALL WE GO NEXT?
Tee hee!
IF IT'S WITH YOU, ANY-WHERE!

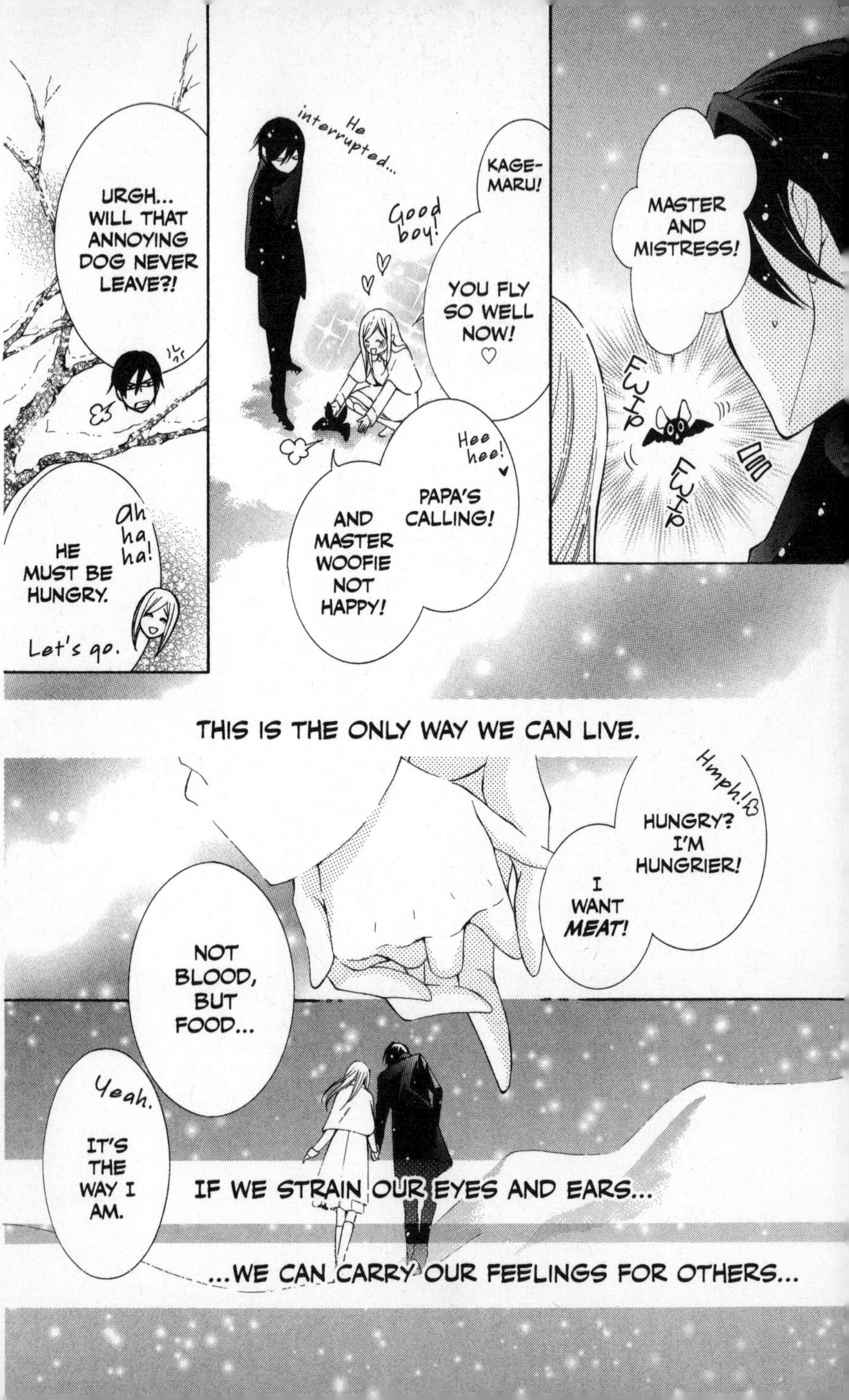
MASTER AND MISTRESS!
FWIP
FWIP
KAGE-MARU!
YOU FLY SO WELL NOW! ♡
Good boy!
He interrupted...
PAPA'S CALLING!
Hee hee!
AND MASTER WOOFIE NOT HAPPY!
URGH... WILL THAT ANNOYING DOG NEVER LEAVE?!
HE MUST BE HUNGRY.
Ah ha ha!
Let's go.
THIS IS THE ONLY WAY WE CAN LIVE.
Hmph!
HUNGRY? I'M HUNGRIER!
I WANT *MEAT*!
NOT BLOOD, BUT FOOD...
Yeah.
IT'S THE WAY I AM.
IF WE STRAIN OUR EYES AND EARS...
...WE CAN CARRY OUR FEELINGS FOR OTHERS...

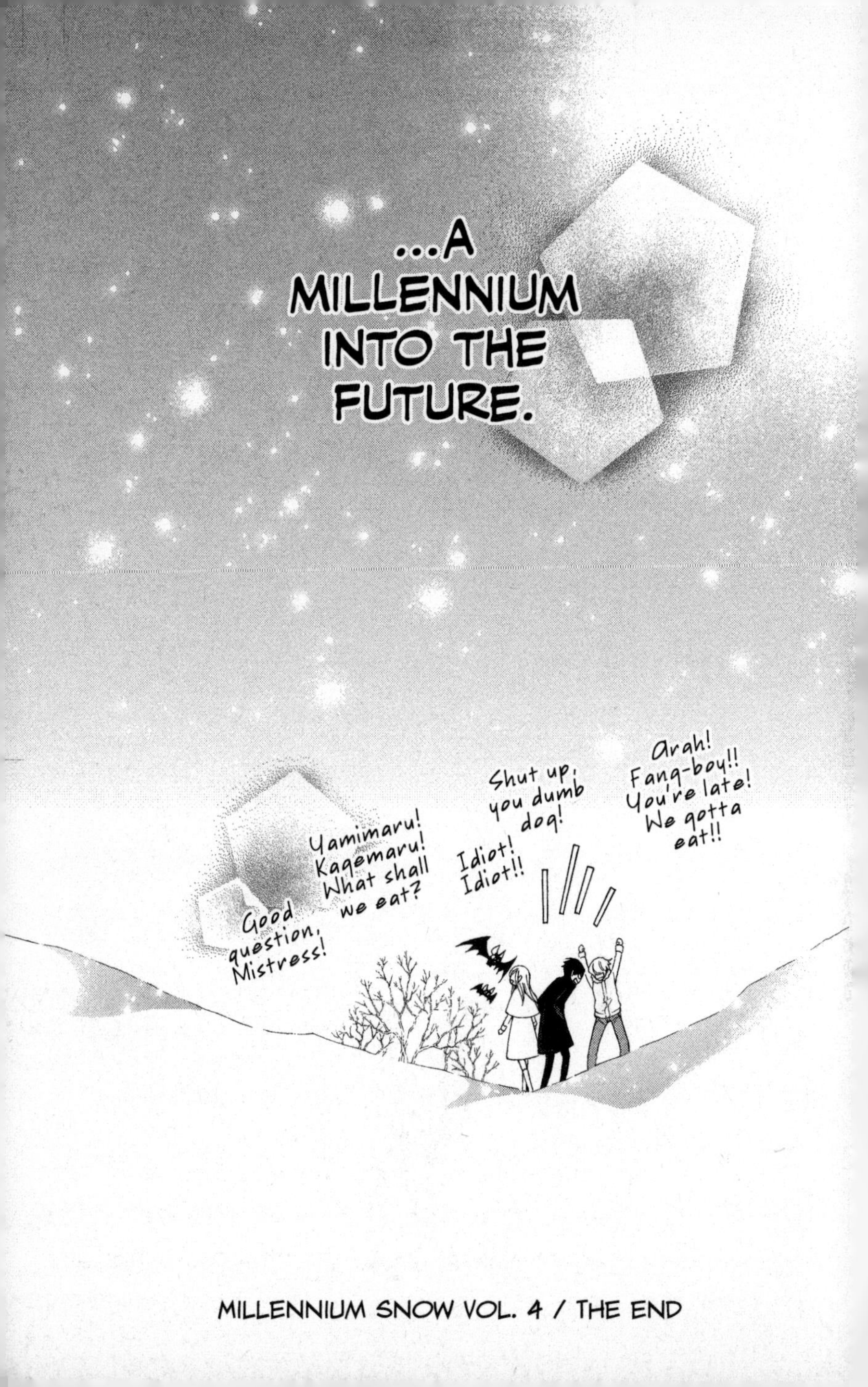
...A MILLENNIUM INTO THE FUTURE.
Arah! Fang-boy!! You're late! We gotta eat!!
Shut up, you dumb dog!
Idiot! Idiot!!
Yamimaru! Kagemaru! What shall we eat?
Good question, Mistress!
MILLENNIUM SNOW VOL. 4 / THE END

Glossary

Page 8, panel 2: Haru, Aki
Haru means "spring", *Aki* means "fall" and Toya's name includes the kanji for "winter."

Page 23, panel 1: 200 yen
About $2 U.S.

Page 51, panel 3: 2,950 yen, 50 yen
¥2,950 is about $29 U.S. and ¥50 is about $.50 U.S.

Bisco Hatori made her manga debut with *Isshun Bkan no Romance* (A Moment of Romance) in *LaLa DX* magazine. The comedy *Ouran High School Host Club* is her breakout hit. When she's stuck thinking up characters' names, she gets inspired by loud, upbeat music (her radio is set to NACK5 FM). She enjoys reading all kinds of manga, but she's especially fond of the sci-fi drama *Please Save My Earth* and *Slam Dunk*, a basketball classic...

MILLENNIUM SNOW
VOL. 4
Shojo Beat Edition

STORY & ART BY
BISCO HATORI

Translation & English Adaptation/John Werry
Touch-up Art & Lettering/Annaliese Christman
Design/Izumi Evers
Editor/Pancha Diaz

Sennen no Yuki by Bisco Hatori © Bisco Hatori 2014
All rights reserved.
First published in Japan in 2014 by HAKUSENSHA, Inc., Tokyo.
English language translation rights arranged with HAKUSENSHA, Inc., Tokyo.

Printed in the U.S.A.

Published by VIZ Media, LLC
P.O. Box 77010
San Francisco, CA 94107

10 9 8 7 6 5 4 3 2 1
First printing, December 2014

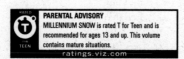

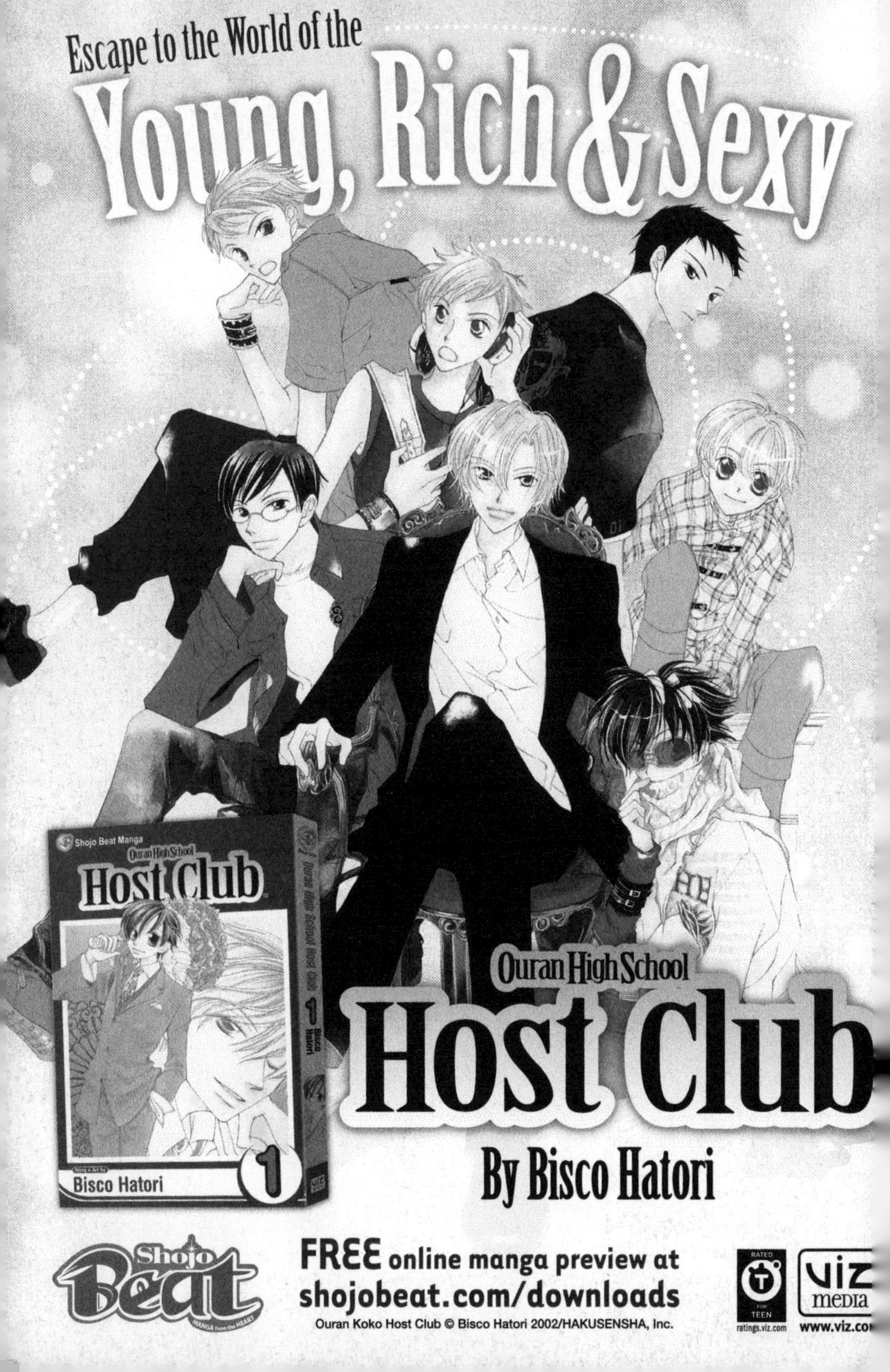
Escape to the World of the
Young, Rich & Sexy
Shojo Beat Manga
Ouran High School
Host Club
Ouran High School Host Club
1
Bisco Hatori
Story & Art by
Bisco Hatori
Ouran High School
Host Club
By Bisco Hatori
Shojo Beat
MANGA from the HEART
FREE online manga preview at
shojobeat.com/downloads
Ouran Koko Host Club © Bisco Hatori 2002/HAKUSENSHA, Inc.
RATED
T
FOR
TEEN
ratings.viz.com
VIZ media
www.viz.co

SURPRISE!

You may be reading the wrong way!

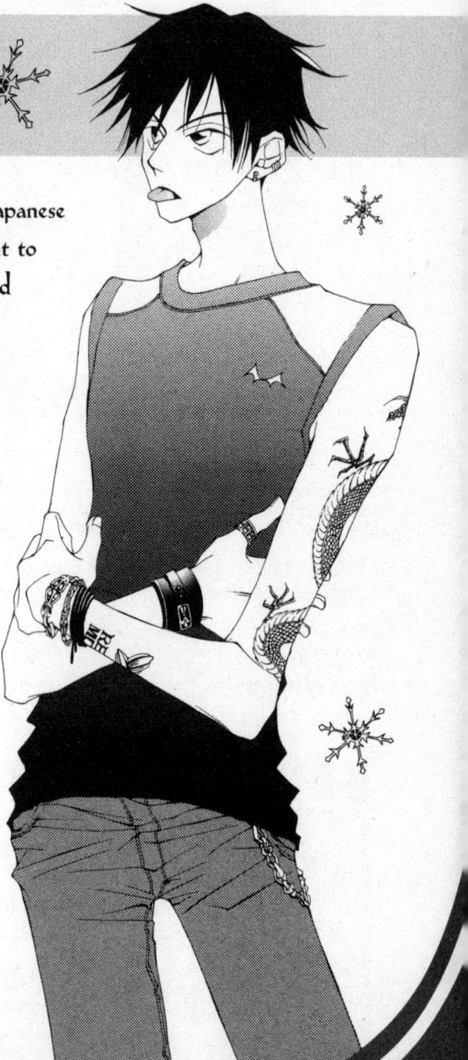

It's true: In keeping with the original Japanese comic format, this book reads from right to left—so action, sound effects, and word balloons are completely reversed. This preserves the orientation of the original artwork—plus, it's fun! Check out the diagram shown here to get the hang of things, and then turn to the other side of the book to get started!

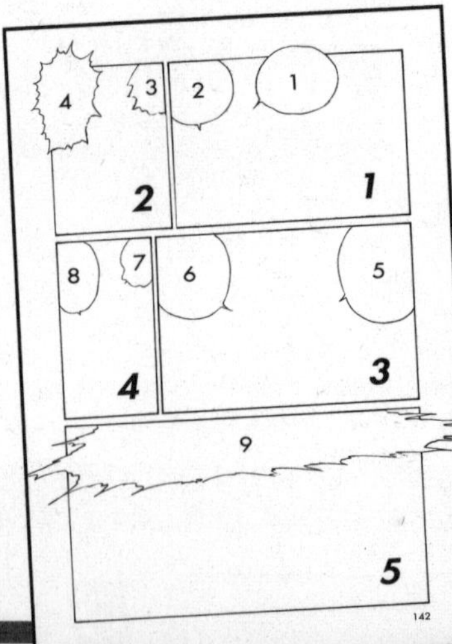

1
2
1
3
4
2
5
6
3
7
8
4
9
5
142